"THE SPIRIT OF '76"

"As the patriots of seventy-six did to
the support of
the Declaration of Independence,
so to the support of
the Constitution and Laws,
let every American pledge his life,
his property, and his sacred honor."

—Abraham Lincoln

THE STAR-SPANGLED BANNER
Written by Francis Scott Key in 1814 and adopted as the United States' national anthem in 1931

Oh, say can you see by the dawn's early light

What so proudly we hailed at the twilight's last gleaming,

Whose broad stripes and bright stars through the perilous fight

O'er the ramparts we watched were so gallantly streaming?

And the rockets' red glare, the bombs bursting in air,

Gave proof through the night that our flag was still there.

Oh, say does that star-spangled banner yet wave

O'er the land of the free and the home of the brave?

THE PLEDGE OF ALLEGIANCE
Written by Francis Bellamy in 1882 and adopted as the United States' national pledge in 1942

I pledge allegiance to the flag

of the United States of America

and to the republic

for which it stands,

one nation under God, indivisible,

with liberty and justice for all.

ADVENTURE TALES OF AMERICA

An Illustrated History of the United States: 1492-1877

Volume 1

ADVENTURE TALES OF AMERICA

An Illustrated History of the United States: 1492-1877

Volume 1

Jody Potts, Ph.D.
Southern Methodist University

ILLUSTRATORS
Foy Lisenby, Ph.D., University of Central Arkansas
Jerry D. Poole, Ph.D., University of Central Arkansas

Signal Media Corporation
Dallas, Texas

AUTHOR

Jody Potts, a native of Texas, received a B.S. degree in education from Baylor University, an M.A. degree in history from Southern Methodist University, and a Ph.D. degree in history from the University of North Texas. She has taught United States history at Southern Methodist University in Dallas since 1972 and served as visiting professor at Alaska Pacific University for three summers.

A specialist in left and right brain learning techniques, Dr. Potts pioneered combining these techniques with the teaching of history and the writing of history textbooks. Since 1984 her graduate courses in SMU's Master of Liberal Arts Program, "History of American Ideas" and "The Lively Mind: Creative and Critical Thinking," have provided an interactive setting for applying and testing the left and right brain learning techniques used in *Adventure Tales of America* and its predecessor, *Adventure Tales of Arkansas,* published in 1986.

In 1984 Dr. Potts founded The Lively Mind, a national consulting firm offering seminars in left and right brain learning techniques for school boards, administrators, faculties, and students. Participating groups have included the University of Texas faculty, the Council for Support and Advancement of Education, Ventures in Education in Alabama, and numerous school districts in California, New York, Texas, and other states.

ILLUSTRATORS

Foy Lisenby, a gifted cartoonist, was professor of history at the University of Central Arkansas from 1962 to 1995, serving for fifteen years as chairman of the UCA History Department. Dr. Lisenby has published a biography of Charles H. Brough and numerous articles on Arkansas history.

Jerry D. Poole served as professor of art at the University of Central Arkansas from 1967 to 1989, chairing the Art Department for seventeen years. He currently is Artist-in-Residence and a consultant for the Center for Academic Excellence at UCA. He also has taught art in elementary and secondary public schools. Dr. Poole is an accomplished silhouette artist and specializes in watercolor painting.

ACKNOWLEDGMENTS

The author is grateful to the following for their valuable critiques of all or parts of *Adventure Tales of America.*

University Reviewers

Jane D. Albritton, Southern Methodist University
Dennis D. Cordell, Southern Methodist University
Michael G. Hall, University of Texas at Austin
Constance B. Hilliard, University of North Texas
Louis L. Jacobs, Southern Methodist University
David J. Weber, Southern Methodist University
Graduate students, "The Lively Mind: Creative and Critical Thinking" course, MLA Program, Southern Methodist University

Public School Reviewers

Susan J. Blanchette, W.T. White High School, DISD, Dallas, Texas
Michael A. Cressey and his Social Studies students, Pearl C. Anderson Learning Center, DISD, Dallas, Texas
Robert A. Edison and his Social Studies students, Pearl C. Anderson Learning Center, DISD, Dallas, Texas
Karen Lee Turner, Lincoln Middle School, Abilene Independent School District, Abilene, Texas
Donna Wenger and her Gifted and Talented students, PACE Program, Plano Independent School District, Plano, Texas

Reviewers of the Abraham Lincoln Section.

This 20-page section of *Adventure Tales of America* is on permanent exhibit at the Lincoln National Boyhood Memorial, Lincoln City, Indiana, courtesy of the National Park Service.

Gerald W. Sanders, Chief of Interpretation, Lincoln Boyhood National Memorial, Lincoln City, Indiana
Thomas Schwartz, Curator of the Lincoln Collection, Illinois State Historical Library, Springfield, Illinois
Gary V. Talley, Chief of Interpretation, Abraham Lincoln Birthplace National Historic Site, Hodgenville, Kentucky

To order *Adventure Tales of America*, call: 1-800 214-2665.

THE FOUNDING FATHERS' MESSAGE FOR STUDENTS

<u>student</u>—a learner; scholar

Thomas Jefferson   **James Madison**   **John Adams**   **Benjamin Franklin**

Knowledge is power. Knowledge is safety. Knowledge is happiness.—Thomas Jefferson

Knowledge will forever govern ignorance; and a people who mean to be their own governors must arm themselves with the power which knowledge gives.—Thomas Jefferson

If a nation expects to be ignorant and free, it expects what never was and never will be.—Thomas Jefferson

The advancement and diffusion of knowledge is the only guardian of true liberty.—James Madison

Whenever the people are well informed, they can be trusted with their own government.—Thomas Jefferson

Liberty cannot be preserved without a general knowledge among the people.—John Adams

The boys of the rising generation are to be the men of the next, and the sole guardians of the principles we deliver over to them.—Thomas Jefferson

Error of opinion may be tolerated where reason is left free to combat it.—Thomas Jefferson

I tolerate with the utmost latitude the right of others to differ from me in opinion.—Thomas Jefferson

Education engrafts a new man on the native stock, and improves what in his nature was vicious and perverse into qualities of virtue and social worth.—Thomas Jefferson

The most effectual means of preventing the perversion of power into tyranny are to illuminate... the minds of the people at large, and more especially to give them knowledge of those facts which history exhibits.... —Thomas Jefferson

The idea of what is true merit should also be often presented to youth, explained and impressed on their minds, as consisting in an inclination joined with an ability to serve mankind, one's country, friends and family; which ability is (with the blessing of God) to be acquired or greatly increased by true learning; and should indeed be the great aim and end of all learning.—Benjamin Franklin

The whole art of government consists in the art of being honest.—Thomas Jefferson

THE PUBLISHER'S WISH FOR STUDENTS

I was thirty years old before I discovered that history is really interesting and fun. In school, my history books and classes dealt only with what happened and when it happened, and the happenings seemed to have little to do with me. I learned the happenings and the dates, and I am glad I did, but the learning wasn't very interesting or much fun.

When I was thirty, a friend recommended an exciting book that I enjoyed reading, until I realized it was a history book. I tried to put it aside, but it was too late—I just had to know how the story came out. I picked up the book again and wondered what kind of history book this could be with real-seeming people, who came from families not unlike mine, who had problems and weaknesses, but who persevered until they achieved what they set out to do. I began to imagine what I would have done if I had lived back in "historic" times. I was hooked on history!

Schools require us to know the happenings and dates for a good reason: these facts are the preparation we need to launch ourselves on the history adventure. Knowing the facts, then, is not the goal of our learning about history; it is the preparation for it.

Adventure Tales of America seeks to tell the real-life, real-people stories of history with excitement and humor, so that you will hardly notice you are also learning the facts. My wish is for you to discover the interest and fun of history now, not when you are thirty!

Philip R. Jonsson

Philip R. Jonsson
Signal Media Publishers
Specialists in Innovative Learning
Dallas, Texas

GETTING THE MOST FROM
ADVENTURE TALES OF AMERICA

Adventure Tales of America is one of the most innovative United States history textbooks available today. Based on the Nobel Prize-winning research of Roger Sperry, it features left and right brain thinking techniques that dramatically improve the learning curve, while making history exciting and enlightening. With this book you will learn faster, remember longer, and score higher on tests—and, most important, enjoy American history.

Adventure Tales of America has raised social studies scores on state tests as much as 18% in Texas (TAAS) and 19% in Arkansas (MPT). You can expect similar success with your test scores.

TO GET THE MOST FROM THIS BOOK, YOU'LL WANT TO FOCUS ON THESE SPECIAL FEATURES AND CLASS ACTIVITY EXAMPLES:

● **LEFT AND RIGHT BRAIN LEARNING STRATEGIES**
In a text/illustration format, *Adventure Tales of America* presents information to both sides of the brain simultaneously through
* **words and analysis for the logical, sequential left brain, and**
* **pictures, humor, emotion, and drama for the creative, global right brain.**
CLASS ACTIVITY: Draw your own pictures of historical events, then write the story. (Drawing is the language of the right brain; words are the language of the left brain.) Notice how much longer you remember pictures than words.

● **COMPREHENSIVE CONTENT IN A NARRATIVE STYLE**
Adventure Tales of America puts the story back in history, making it an exciting adventure tale. From exploration of the New World to the Civil War and Reconstruction, America's story unfolds with high drama—absorbing, entertaining, and memorable.
CLASS ACTIVITY: Dramatize historical events, switching characters occasionally to experience other viewpoints.

● **IN-DEPTH RESEARCH FROM PRIMARY SOURCES**
In *Adventure Tales of America* the historical characters speak in their own words whenever possible, an ideal way to experience primary sources. The Constitutional Convention, for example, is dramatized almost completely from James Madison's notes.
CLASS ACTIVITY: Assume the role of one of the Founding Fathers at a 200-year reunion of the Constitutional Convention. As you renew acquaintances, remind everyone of what you said about various issues.

● **CHARACTER-BUILDING ROLE MODELS**
Heroic Americans such as Benjamin Banneker, Benjamin Franklin, Sequoyah, and Abraham Lincoln helped shape the American character. Biographical sections on these great Americans show their approach to solving problems facing them and their country.
CLASS ACTIVITY: What problems would you like to solve? Consider how these great Americans would approach these problems.

● **IDEAS THAT SHAPED AMERICAN HISTORY AND THE AMERICAN CHARACTER**
Adventure Tales of America is a history of American ideas as well as events, stimulating a deeper understanding of history. The PERSIA acronym, described on pages 60-61, helps you organize the Political, Economic, Religious, Social, Intellectual, and Artistic ideas that explain events and institutions.
CLASS ACTIVITY: Using the PERSIA model, discuss the ideas of various groups involved in American wars and other conflicts.

● **DEMOCRACY AND CAPITALISM**
A metaphor of the Tree of Liberty vividly traces the growth of American democracy and capitalism—from the roots of the Magna Charta and other rights of Englishmen (page 120) through the trunk of colonial charters (pages 39-58), and through the branches of the Declaration of Independence, Articles of Confederation, U.S. Constitution, Bill of Rights, and Reconstruction Amendments. When you come to THE TREE OF LIBERTY (page 254), you'll feel you've climbed it branch by branch!
CLASS ACTIVITY: Imagine you are visiting another country. Explain American democracy and capitalism to your hosts there.

● **MULTICULTURAL EMPHASIS**
A 20-page section on African history, as well as sections on Hispanic influences, the Iroquois Confederacy and the Woman's Rights Movement show the rich diversity of America's cultural heritage.
CLASS ACTIVITY: Discuss the question Hector St. John de Crevecoeur asked in 1782 (page 63): "What then is the American?"

● **CREATIVE AND CRITICAL THINKING SKILLS**
Adventure Tales of America is designed to improve problem-solving and decision-making skills within the context of each chapter.
CLASS ACTIVITY: 1) Discuss how you would have solved the problems facing the writers of the Constitution (pages 148-155).
2) Analyze the causes of the Revolution (pages 116-119) and the Civil War (pages 185-86, 239-243). Decide your positions.

TWO BRAINS ARE BETTER THAN ONE!
Left and Right Brain Thinking Skills

In 1981, Dr. Roger Sperry won the Nobel Prize for discovering that each side (hemisphere) of the brain "thinks" in a different way. Your verbal <u>**left brain hemisphere processes words**</u> and your visual <u>**right brain hemisphere processes pictures**</u>.

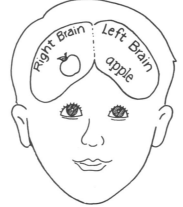

Dr. Sperry's brain research tells us that we can learn much faster and remember longer if information is presented to both sides of the brain at once — to provide **whole brain learning** — as *Adventure Tales of America* does with its **text/cartoon format: words for the left brain** and **pictures for the right brain**. Do you agree? Try this experiment: Look at the frames below and check the one that would help you learn faster and remember longer.

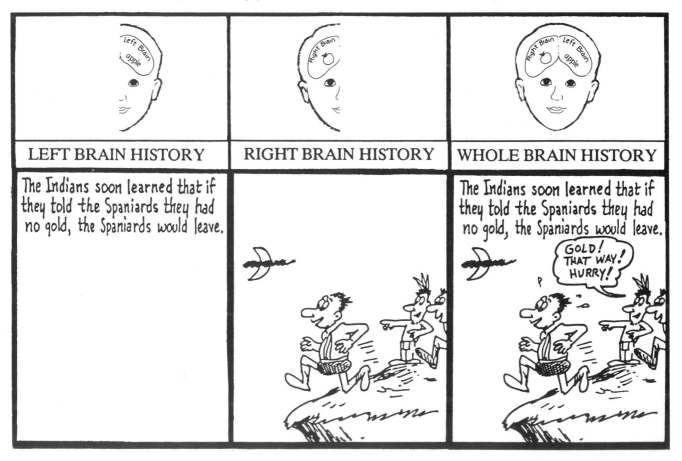

LEFT BRAIN HISTORY	RIGHT BRAIN HISTORY	WHOLE BRAIN HISTORY
The Indians soon learned that if they told the Spaniards they had no gold, the Spaniards would leave.		The Indians soon learned that if they told the Spaniards they had no gold, the Spaniards would leave.

LEFT AND RIGHT BRAIN LEARNING STYLES

All of us use both sides of the brain, but most of us are either left or right brain dominant, which means that we may use left or right brain characteristics more often in the ways that we think, act, and learn. It is important to recognize your brain dominance and value it as your special learning style. The next step is to begin developing the other side, so that you can use your whole brain in thinking, acting, and learning.

BRAIN DOMINANCE TEST

Read each pair of left and right brain characteristics and check the one that seems most like you. A good way to tell is to ask yourself which characteristic helps you learn better. If you strongly identify with both characteristics in a pair, then check both. More checks in the left column indicate left brain dominance. More checks in the right column indicate right brain dominance. Several checks of both characteristics in a pair indicate double dominance: a whole brain thinker.

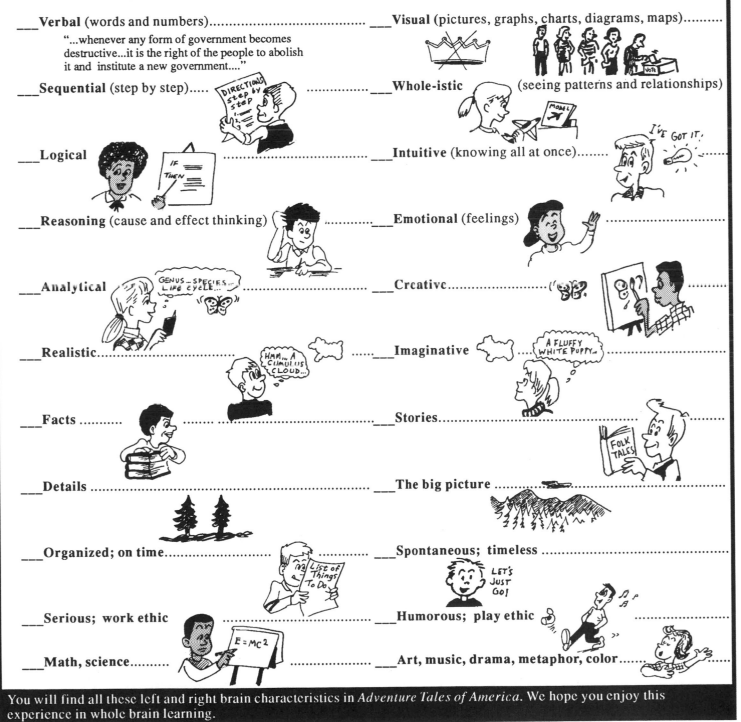

LEFT BRAIN

___ **Verbal** (words and numbers)......................................
    "...whenever any form of government becomes destructive...it is the right of the people to abolish it and institute a new government...."

___ **Sequential** (step by step).....

___ **Logical**

___ **Reasoning** (cause and effect thinking)

___ **Analytical**

___ **Realistic**.....

___ **Facts** ....

___ **Details** ......

___ **Organized; on time**.....

___ **Serious; work ethic**

___ **Math, science**.........

RIGHT BRAIN

___ **Visual** (pictures, graphs, charts, diagrams, maps)..........

___ **Whole-istic** (seeing patterns and relationships)

___ **Intuitive** (knowing all at once)........

___ **Emotional** (feelings)

___ **Creative**.....

___ **Imaginative**

___ **Stories**.....

___ **The big picture** .....

___ **Spontaneous; timeless** .....

___ **Humorous; play ethic**

___ **Art, music, drama, metaphor, color**......

You will find all these left and right brain characteristics in *Adventure Tales of America*. We hope you enjoy this experience in whole brain learning.

CONTENTS

PART ONE: COLONIAL AND CONFEDERATION ERAS, 1492-1789

PART TWO: THE AMERICAN REPUBLIC, 1789-1877

history—his-story; the story of the human race

"There are those, I know, who will reply that the liberation of humanity, the freedom of man and mind,
is nothing but a dream....They are right. It is the American dream."—Archibald MacLeish

AMERICAN HISTORY: WHAT'S IT ALL ABOUT?

Liberty as a human right is the central theme of American history.
American history, then, is about

THE AMERICAN DREAM—THE DREAM OF
FINDING
FREEDOM AND OPPORTUNITY
TO BE WHO YOU ARE
AND BECOME WHAT YOU MIGHT BE
AS A HUMAN BEING.

American history is an extraordinary adventure tale
about the human race and freedom.

ADVENTURE TALES OF AMERICA dramatizes the adventures of
successive waves of immigrants drawn to the
land that became the United States of America.
We are all immigrants—differing only in arrival times.
About 20,000 years ago Asians came from the West.
After 1492 Europeans and Africans came from the East.
Today immigrants from all parts of the world still come.

WHY?
Despite their diversity, a common purpose has motivated most immigrants:
the desire for freedom and opportunity—THE AMERICAN DREAM.
This common purpose continues to unite us as Americans in a multicultural society.

Not all have experienced the American Dream. Native Americans dispossessed of their land and enslaved African-Americans
stand as stark contradictions. Yet the powerful idea of LIBERTY AS A HUMAN RIGHT, codified in the United States
Constitution, has moved America slowly but surely toward its ideal of liberty and justice for all—
toward creating the land of the free and the home of the brave.

HOW DID THE UNITED STATES OF AMERICA COME TO BE? READ ON FOR THE GREATEST ADVENTURE STORY OF ALL TIME.

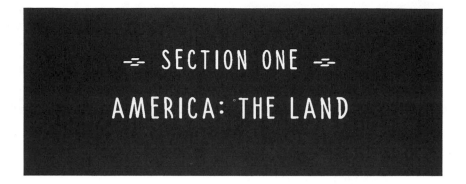
<u>America</u>—This term has two meanings: 1) the North and/or South American continents, and 2) the area that became the United States of America. The context of the narrative indicates the meaning.

PUT ON YOUR SEVEN-LEAGUE BOOTS. <u>Adventure Tales of America</u> will take you on a fascinating 500-year journey through history to re-live the exciting, daring, scary, funny adventures of the people who ventured into the unknown American wilderness and created the United States of America— what Henry David Thoreau called, "that smiling land."

TO GET WHERE WE'RE GOING, WE HAVE TO KNOW WHERE WE ARE. And that means getting our geographic bearings. History always begins with <u>GEO</u> (Earth) <u>GRAPHY</u> (to describe), for as nature shapes the land, so the land shapes the people who inhabit the land.

WHERE ON EARTH IS THE UNITED STATES OF AMERICA?

It all depends on the geological time period. The North American continent, location of the United States, continually changes position relative to other land masses. Earth scientists trace the movement to <u>plate tectonics</u>. Here's how it works.

The Earth's surface consists of <u>continents</u> (landmasses) and <u>oceans</u>. Underlying all are rigid, slow-moving <u>plates</u> on which the continents float. There are seven large plates and some smaller ones. <u>Tectonic forces</u>—conditions within the earth, such as heat energy—cause the plates and continents to move an inch or so per year.

The Earth is about 4.6 billion years old. For much of its history, continents separated and collided. Have you ever looked at a world map and imagined fitting the continents together like a jigsaw puzzle? At one time they did fit together to form one huge landmass: a supercontinent, PANGAEA (named in 1915 by Alfred Wegener, an early investigator of continental drift). About 180 million years ago Pangaea had two lobes, Laurasia and Gondwanaland. They split into continents that spread apart about one inch per year. AMERICA WAS ON THE MOVE!

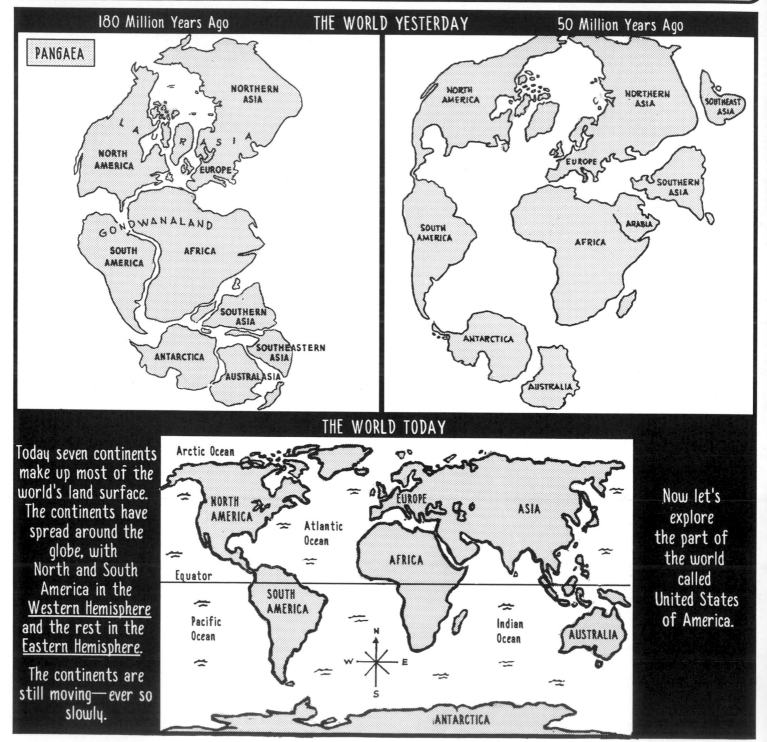

THE WORLD YESTERDAY

180 Million Years Ago — 50 Million Years Ago

THE WORLD TODAY

Today seven continents make up most of the world's land surface. The continents have spread around the globe, with North and South America in the <u>Western Hemisphere</u> and the rest in the <u>Eastern Hemisphere.</u>

The continents are still moving—ever so slowly.

Now let's explore the part of the world called United States of America.

For millions of years parts of America lay hidden under the sea or beneath giant glaciers.
Then, about 60 million years ago, the sea and ice receded, and
the land we call America emerged to begin a grand adventure.

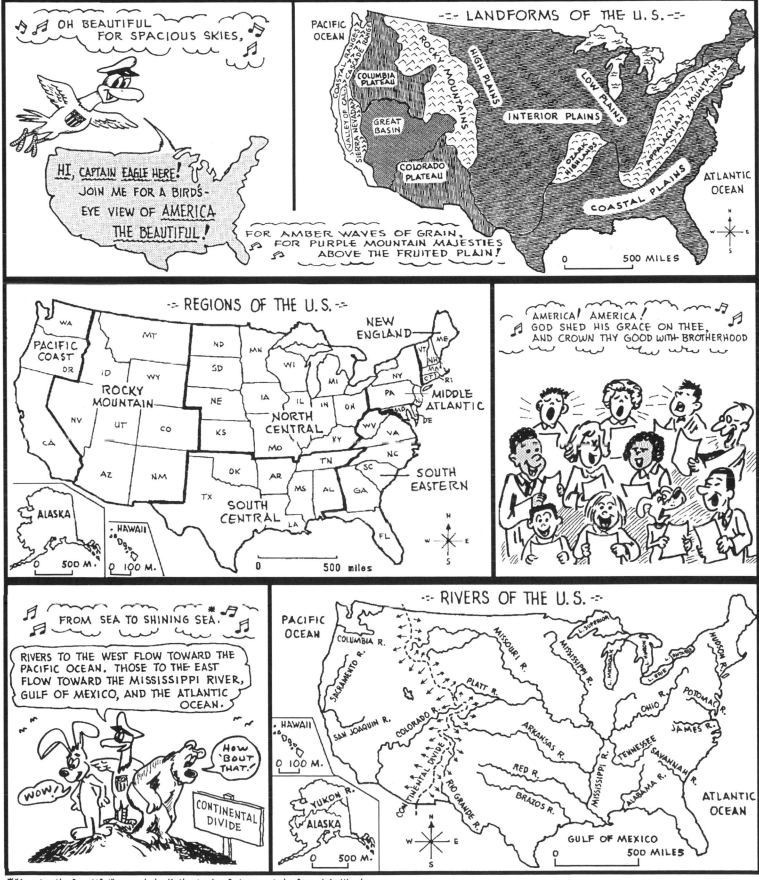

*"America the Beautiful"—words by Katharine Lee Bates; music by Samuel A. Ward

5

1492   1990s   2000

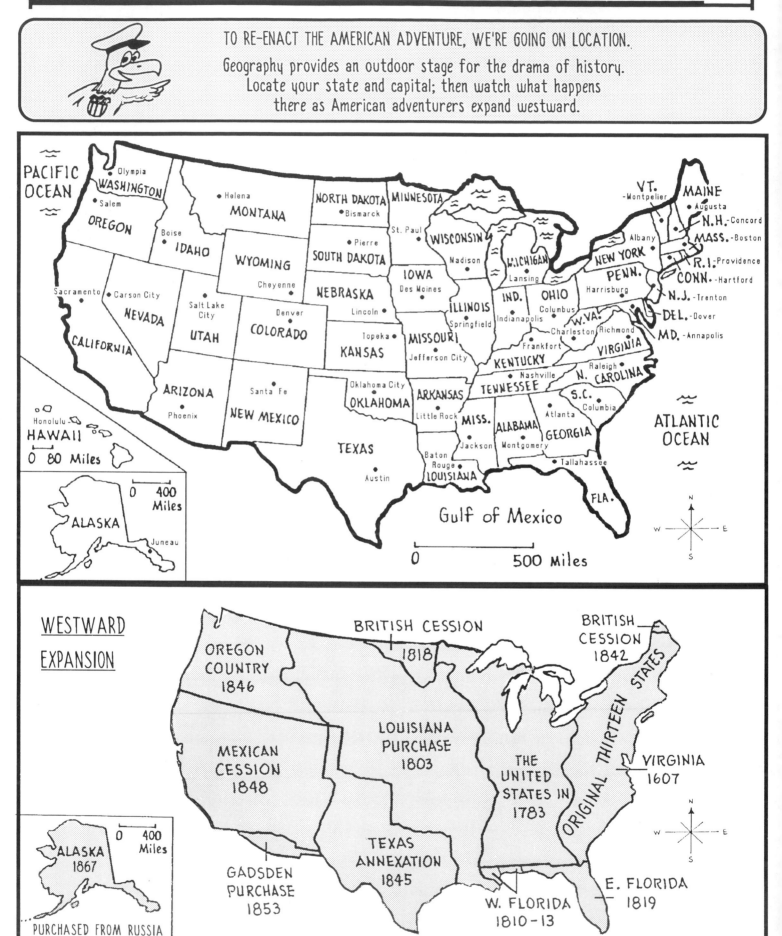

TO RE-ENACT THE AMERICAN ADVENTURE, WE'RE GOING ON LOCATION.

Geography provides an outdoor stage for the drama of history.
Locate your state and capital; then watch what happens
there as American adventurers expand westward.

WESTWARD EXPANSION

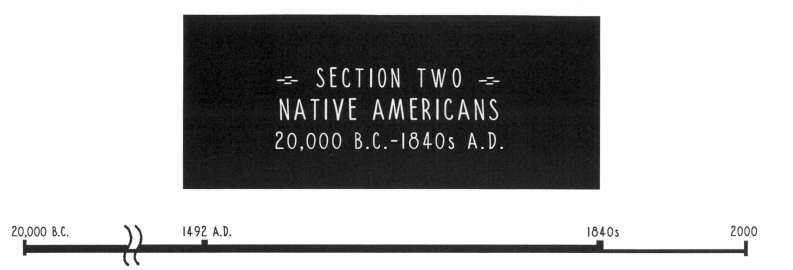

| 20,000 B.C. | | 1492 A.D. | 1840s | 2000 |

In 1492 when Christopher Columbus discovered America, he called the New World inhabitants <u>Indians</u>, for he thought, mistakenly, that he had landed in India. The name <u>Indian</u> has remained in use ever since—more than 500 years. Today we use it interchangeably with the term <u>Native American</u> (although even these earliest Americans were immigrants, not natives). Nearly every Native American group, however, called itself by a name that meant <u>people</u>.

prehistoric— refers to anything that happened before recorded history, which in America means before 1492 A.D.
immigrants—those who enter a new land, for the purpose of making it their permanent home

20,000 B.C.   1492 A.D.   2000

THE LAST GREAT ICE AGE began about 75,000 years ago when Earth's climate cooled and glaciers (giant ice sheets formed from river and ocean waters) covered northen continents. Glacier formation lowered ocean levels and exposed a strip of land 1,000 miles wide between Asia and North America. For a long time this land, called the Bering land bridge, connected Asia and Alaska.

THE BERING LAND BRIDGE made possible one of the most important human migrations in history as people from Asia, hunter-gatherers, ventured into the uninhabited North American continent, beginning about 20,000 years ago. By 8,000 B.C their descendants reached lower South America. These Asian immigrants, the first Americans, were ancestors of North and South American Indians.

THE ICE AGE ENDED 10,000 YEARS AGO. Melting ice sheets caused rising sea levels, and the Bering land bridge disappeared under water, closing the immigration route. From then until Columbus' discovery of America in 1492, America's first immigrants had the continent to themselves. Here are some of their prehistoric ADVENTURES.

10,000 B.C.—Paleo-Indian

By 10,000 B.C. some prehistoric adventurers had migrated into what is now the United States of America.

NORTH AMERICA

8,000 B.C.—Archaic

HUNTER-GATHERERS—These early Americans lived a nomadic existence, hunting and gathering their food. Because they had to follow their food supply they could not settle down in one place, and they had to travel in small groups—usually in bands of about 30 people. The dog was their only tame animal.

500 B.C.—Woodland

FARMERS—The development of agriculture led to a new village-based life for some groups. By controlling their food supply, they could live in one place and support larger populations. Corn, squash, and beans were the major crops.

SHELTER—Early Americans built homes from a variety of materials, depending on the geography and climate of their region. They used animal skins, wood, brush, dirt, clay, stone, straw, grass, and ice.

700 A.D.—Mississippian

-=- MOUND BUILDERS -=-

SOME EASTERN TRIBES BUILT MOUNDS FOR BURYING THEIR DEAD. BY 700 A.D. THEY WERE BUILDING TEMPLES ON THEIR MOUNDS TO WORSHIP THE SUN.

1492 A.D.

-=- CITY FOLKS -=-

THE RUINS OF ONCE GRAND CITIES BUILT BY THE ANASAZI AND HOHOKAM STILL DOT THE SOUTHWEST.

PUEBLO BONITO IN CHACO CANYON (1000s A.D. TO 1200s) HOUSED MORE THAN 1,000 PEOPLE IN 800 ROOMS.

PREHISTORIC CULTURES IN THE UNITED STATES

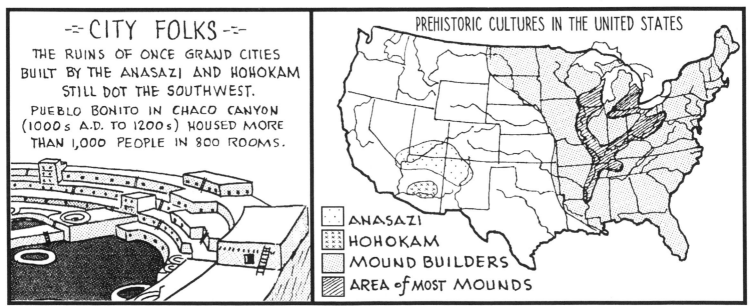

ANASAZI
HOHOKAM
MOUND BUILDERS
AREA of MOST MOUNDS

1492   1835   2000

In 1492 when Columbus discovered the New World, he did not find a vacant land.

North and South America teemed with descendants of those early adventurers who crossed the Bering Straits—beginning about 20,000 years ago. Population estimates of the two continents in 1492 range between 60,000,000 and 100,000,000.

In North America Indian groups spoke more than 300 different languages and had diverse cultures. According to their environment, they made their living by hunting, fishing, farming, herding, or some combination of these activites. Their social organization ranged from small tribes, composed of several clans (related families), to large confederacies, composed of many tribes.

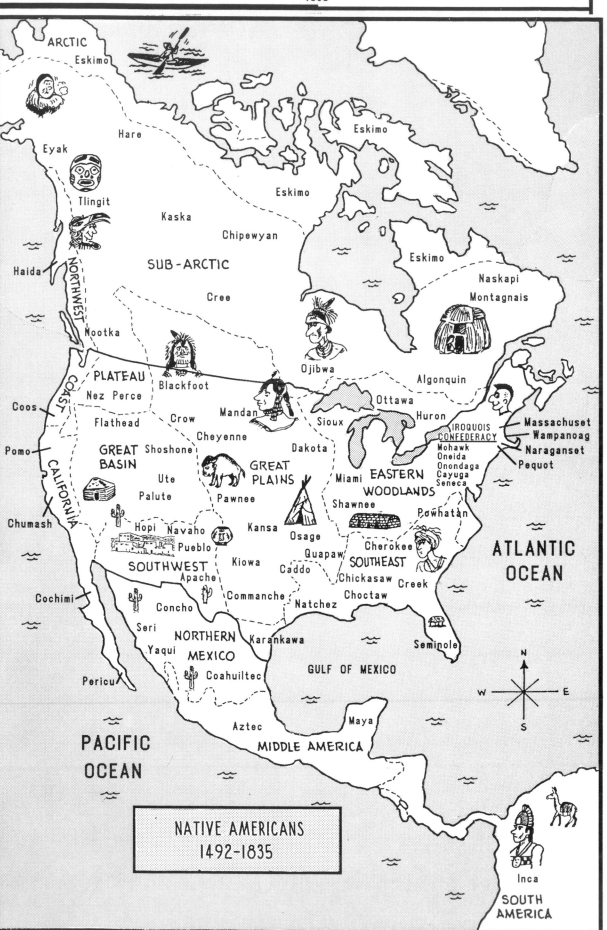

NATIVE AMERICANS
1492-1835

"If England is ever to become a great nation, she must go to school to the Iroquois. The Six Nations control this continent, not by accident, but through the triumph of their science of government."—Sir William Johnson, British High Commissioner to the Six Nations, 1765

1492   1570   1990s 2000

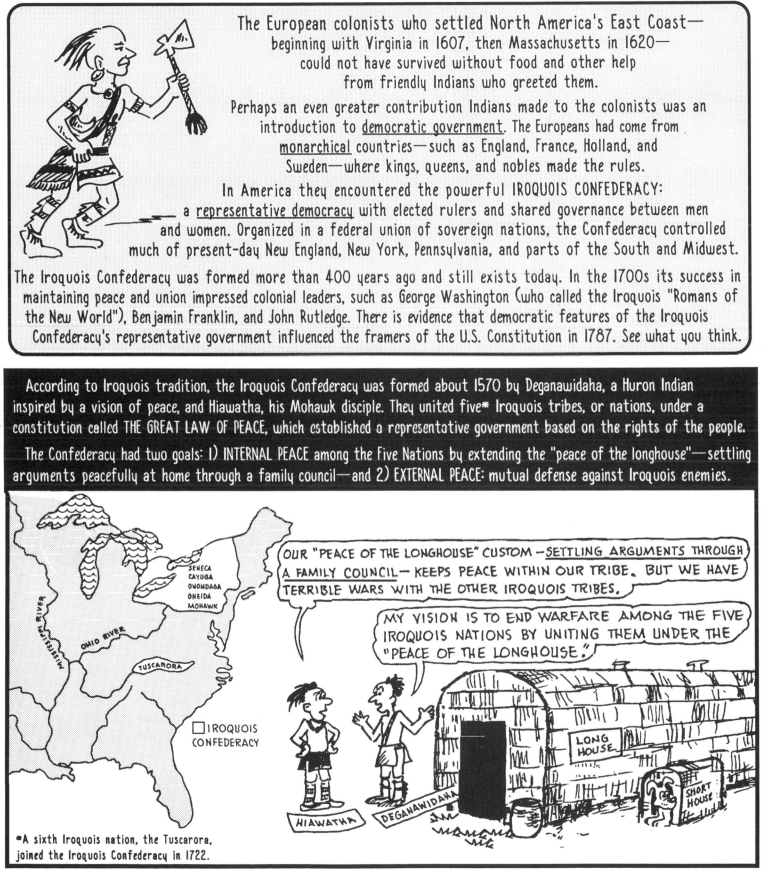

The European colonists who settled North America's East Coast—beginning with Virginia in 1607, then Massachusetts in 1620—could not have survived without food and other help from friendly Indians who greeted them.

Perhaps an even greater contribution Indians made to the colonists was an introduction to <u>democratic government</u>. The Europeans had come from <u>monarchical</u> countries—such as England, France, Holland, and Sweden—where kings, queens, and nobles made the rules.

In America they encountered the powerful IROQUOIS CONFEDERACY: a <u>representative democracy</u> with elected rulers and shared governance between men and women. Organized in a federal union of sovereign nations, the Confederacy controlled much of present-day New England, New York, Pennsylvania, and parts of the South and Midwest.

The Iroquois Confederacy was formed more than 400 years ago and still exists today. In the 1700s its success in maintaining peace and union impressed colonial leaders, such as George Washington (who called the Iroquois "Romans of the New World"), Benjamin Franklin, and John Rutledge. There is evidence that democratic features of the Iroquois Confederacy's representative government influenced the framers of the U.S. Constitution in 1787. See what you think.

According to Iroquois tradition, the Iroquois Confederacy was formed about 1570 by Deganawidaha, a Huron Indian inspired by a vision of peace, and Hiawatha, his Mohawk disciple. They united five* Iroquois tribes, or nations, under a constitution called THE GREAT LAW OF PEACE, which established a representative government based on the rights of the people.

The Confederacy had two goals: 1) INTERNAL PEACE among the Five Nations by extending the "peace of the longhouse"—settling arguments peacefully at home through a family council—and 2) EXTERNAL PEACE: mutual defense against Iroquois enemies.

SENECA
CAYUGA
ONONDAGA
ONEIDA
MOHAWK

TUSCARORA

☐ IROQUOIS
CONFEDERACY

OUR "PEACE OF THE LONGHOUSE" CUSTOM —<u>SETTLING ARGUMENTS THROUGH A FAMILY COUNCIL</u>— KEEPS PEACE WITHIN OUR TRIBE. BUT WE HAVE TERRIBLE WARS WITH THE OTHER IROQUOIS TRIBES.

MY VISION IS TO END WARFARE AMONG THE FIVE IROQUOIS NATIONS BY UNITING THEM UNDER THE "PEACE OF THE LONGHOUSE."

HIAWATHA   DEGANAWIDAHA

LONG HOUSE

SHORT HOUSE

*A sixth Iroquois nation, the Tuscarora, joined the Iroquois Confederacy in 1722.

THE IROQUOIS CONFEDERACY <u>CONSTITUTION</u>, called THE GREAT LAW OF PEACE, helped the Iroquois Indians achieve their goals of internal and external peace by settling disputes through democratic council meetings rather than warfare.

The Constitution, 117 sections long, was not in written form because the Iroquois Indians had no written language.

Instead, the Iroquois recorded their Constitution by stringing white and purple shell beads, called <u>wampum</u>, into belts. Pictorial designs in the belts symbolized parts of the Constitution.

WAMPUM BELT

WAMPUM MEMORY TECHNIQUE—Although unwritten, the Iroquois Constitution has survived 400 years. How? Each generation memorized it—all 117 sections—with the help of the pictorial wampum belts.

(Today we know why this memory technique works so well. It's easier to remember something if you turn it into a picture. In a way, you are experiencing the wampum memory technique as you read this pictorial history book.)

I CAN'T PLAY NOW, RUNNING FOX. I HAVE TO MEMORIZE THE CONSTITUTION.

Here's how the Iroquois Confederacy's democratic government worked: The Iroquois Nations chose 50 (male) chiefs to represent them annually in a <u>Grand Council of Peace</u> at Onondaga, the Iroquois capital in present-day New York.

<u>The Grand Council of Peace was based on a separation and balance of powers.</u> The chiefs sat in two decision-making groups—one on either side of a council fire—with a third group exercising veto power over both.

No question was decided until it had been discussed on both sides of the fire. All decisions had to be unanimous.

SO THAT'S WHAT WE THINK. NOW LET'S ADJOURN.

YOU KNOW THE RULES. THE QUESTION MUST ALSO BE DISCUSSED ON THIS SIDE OF THE FIRE.

FINALLY— OUR TURN!

A chief appointed as KEEPER OF THE WAMPUM created wampum belt designs that recorded all decisions and treaties. He was expected to memorize these.

<u>Free expression was allowed in the Grand Council.</u> Each Nation brought its own string of wampum belts, and these were all put in one big circle. When a chief wanted to speak, he picked up one of his Nation's belts. No one else would speak until he put it down.

<u>One communication rule prevailed.</u> Before stating his own view of an issue, a chief had to:

1) restate the issue being discussed—to make sure he understood it, and then

2) repeat the positions stated by previous speakers—to make sure he had understood them correctly.

LET'S SEE NOW. THE <u>ISSUE</u> IS WHETHER TO MAKE WAR ON THE HURONS. <u>RUNNING ELK</u> SAYS WE SHOULD BECAUSE THEY'VE INSULTED US. <u>BRAVE FOX</u> SAYS WE SHOULD IGNORE THEM BECAUSE THEY'RE JUST BAITING US. <u>I</u> SAY LET'S FIRST DEMAND AN APOLOGY AND THEN....

Each of the six Iroquois nations had a distinctive head piece, as shown above. 12

The eldest women of the Five Nations formed the Council of Women. They appointed the chiefs, advised them, and removed from office any who did not follow the will of the people.

Surprised? Europeans were shocked. The Iroquois, like most Pueblo Indians, were a matrilineal society, meaning women were the heads of their households. When a man married, he moved into the home of his wife's family, where the eldest woman was in charge. Unlike Pueblo women, however, Iroquois women had political as well as domestic power. They were the most powerful women in North America.

In the 1700s the Iroquois Confederacy's success in achieving peace and strength in union while preserving each nation's sovereignty impressed America's Founding Fathers, particularly Benjamin Franklin (Pennsylvania's Indian commissioner in the 1750s). He said:

In 1744 Benjamin Franklin published in his Philadelphia newspaper a speech by Iroquois Chief Canasatego to an Indian-British Assembly in Pennsylvania. Canasatego 1) complained of the difficulty in dealing with 13 separate colonies, and 2) advised the colonies to form a federal, democratic union like that of the Iroquois League.

In 1754 Franklin reflected Iroquois influence in drafting the Albany Plan of Union, proposing that the 13 American colonies form a union promoting peace and strength, with a 50-man legislature called the Grand Council.

In 1754 the Albany Plan was rejected by the colonies and England, but it paved the way for union under the 1781 Articles of Confederation and the 1787 U.S. Constitution, which you will read about later.

The United States Constitution begins: "We the people of the United States, in order to form a more perfect union, establish justice, ensure domestic tranquility, provide for the common defense...."

cede— to yield or transfer to another, as by treaty; to surrender, as through force

1492   1607   1890   2000

You'll be reading more of Native Americans later. To give perspective, here is an overview of what happened to the land they once inhabited.

United States history is marked by steady territorial expansion westward—by British-American colonists from 1607 to 1776 and by United States citizens after 1776. Expansion came at a terrible cost to Native Americans, for they were dispossessed of their land. How? mainly through 1) purchase, 2) treaties (inevitably broken by the white negotiators), or 3) force.

At first Native Americans were puzzled when colonists, such as Pennsylvania's founder William Penn, offered to buy their land, for they did not consider land private property. They viewed the land beneath them as the air about them: available to all and impossible to buy. But puzzlement turned to anger as they lost more and more land. They retaliated with periodic warfare against white settlers, beginning as early as 1622 in Virginia.

In 1810 Shawnee Chief Tecumseh spoke the following words—but to no avail.
"The only way to stop this evil, is for the red men to unite in claiming a common and equal right in the land, as it was at first, and should be now—for it was never divided, but belongs to all. No tribe has the right to sell, even to each other, much less to strangers. Sell a country! Why not sell the air, the great sea, as well as the earth? Did not the Great Spirit make them all for the use of his children?"

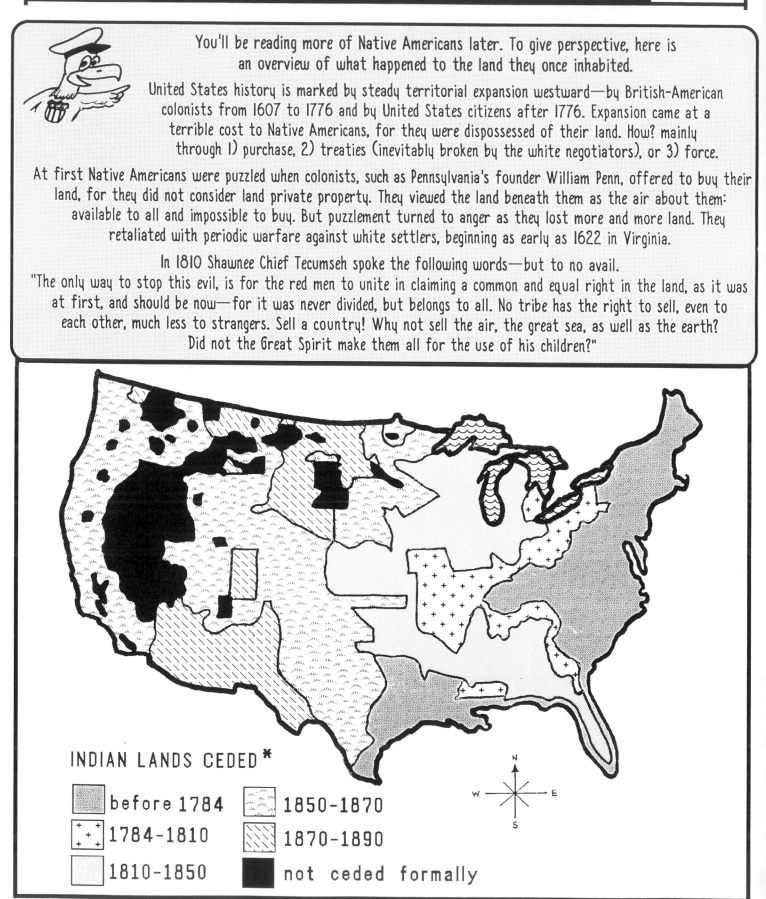

INDIAN LANDS CEDED *

before 1784   1850-1870
1784-1810   1870-1890
1810-1850   not ceded formally

* Map adapted from Carl Waldman, Atlas of the North American Indian.

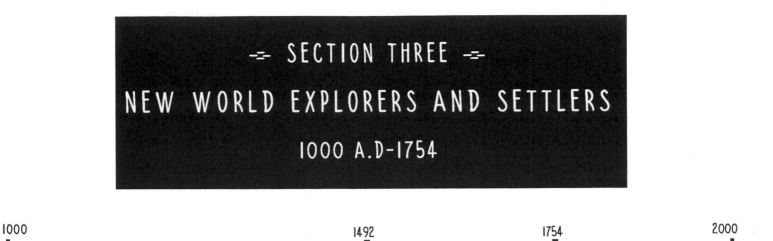

SECTION THREE
NEW WORLD EXPLORERS AND SETTLERS
1000 A.D-1754

1000   1492   1754   2000

"It is lawful to call it a new world...because none of these countries were known to our ancestors."
—Amerigo Vespucci (1497), Italian explorer for whom America is named

NORTH AMERICA by 1754

1741—Vitus Bering, a Dane in the Russian navy, gave Russia its North American claim by exploring islands off present-day Alaska. The Bering Sea, Bering Strait, and Bering land bridge bear his name.

RUSSIAN

UNEXPLORED

BRITISH

FRENCH

BRITISH

SPANISH

MAP 1000 A.D.

CHRIS COLUMBUS 1492

SPANISH CONQUISTADORES 1492—

FRENCH EXPLORERS 1524—

EUROPE

England

France

Spain

AFRICA

N W E S

"...man is usually a wandering and enterprising animal, for whom there exist few insurmountable barriers."—H.G. Wells

Europeans explored the New World for some or all of these reasons:

1. CURIOSITY

2. WEALTH

3. FAME

4. NATIONAL PRIDE

5. RELIGION

6. FOREIGN GOODS

7. FASTER, CHEAPER TRADE ROUTES

1000   1492   2000

AMERICA,

with its two continents—North and South, is four times larger than Europe.

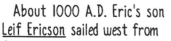

Yet 1,000 years ago, Europeans did not know this land—or its millions of people—existed.

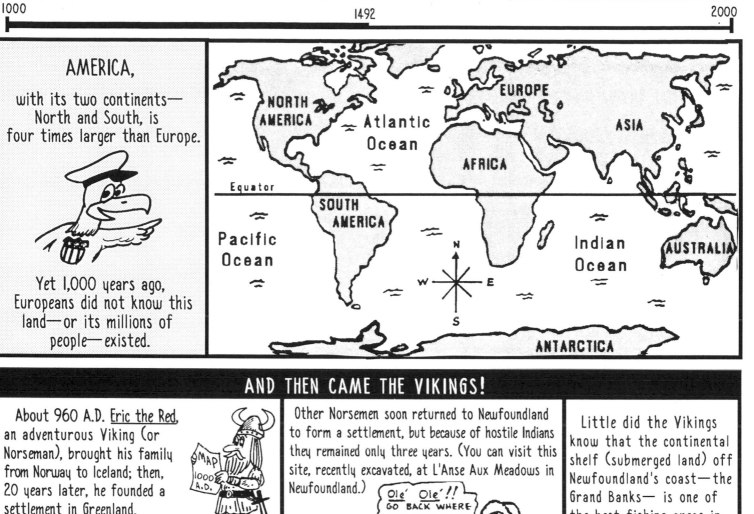

AND THEN CAME THE VIKINGS!

About 960 A.D. <u>Eric the Red</u>, an adventurous Viking (or Norseman), brought his family from Norway to Iceland; then, 20 years later, he founded a settlement in Greenland.

About 1000 A.D. Eric's son <u>Leif Ericson</u> sailed west from Greenland in search of a strange coastline, sighted earlier by another Norseman. Leif and his crew of 35 men landed on the coast of present-day <u>Newfoundland</u>, which they named <u>Vinland</u>. After wintering there, they sailed back to Greenland with a load of grapes and lumber.

Other Norsemen soon returned to Newfoundland to form a settlement, but because of hostile Indians they remained only three years. (You can visit this site, recently excavated, at L'Anse Aux Meadows in Newfoundland.)

Ole' Ole'!! GO BACK WHERE YOU CAME FROM.

Little did the Vikings know that the continental shelf (submerged land) off Newfoundland's coast—the Grand Banks— is one of the best fishing areas in the world and that its cod, mackerel, herring, and halibut would someday become New England's "gold."

And little did the Vikings know they had been to America!

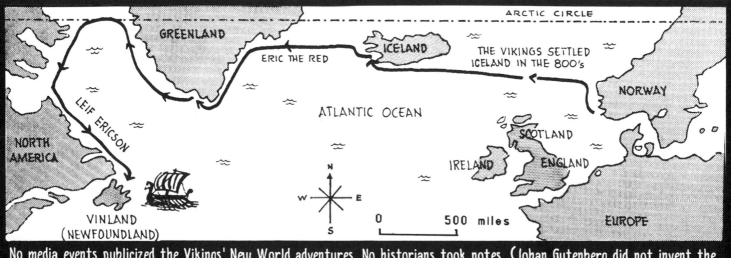

No media events publicized the Vikings' New World adventures. No historians took notes. (Johan Gutenberg did not invent the printing press until the 1450s.) No one remembered the Vikings' discovery of North America.

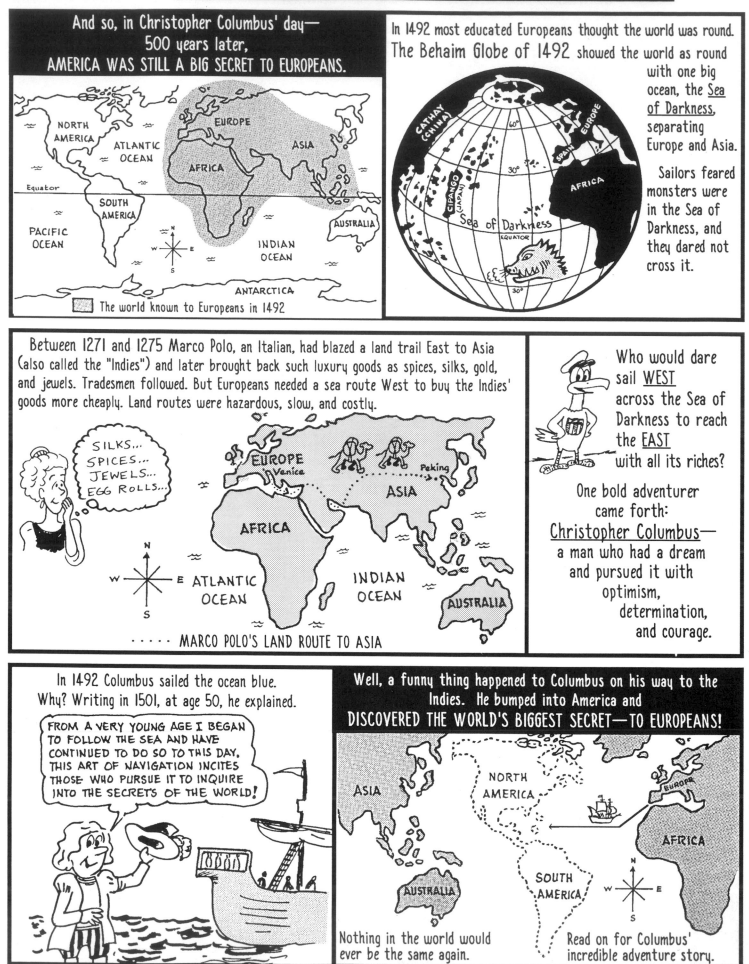

And so, in Christopher Columbus' day—500 years later, AMERICA WAS STILL A BIG SECRET TO EUROPEANS.

The world known to Europeans in 1492

In 1492 most educated Europeans thought the world was round. **The Behaim Globe of 1492** showed the world as round with one big ocean, the <u>Sea of Darkness</u>, separating Europe and Asia.

Sailors feared monsters were in the Sea of Darkness, and they dared not cross it.

Between 1271 and 1275 Marco Polo, an Italian, had blazed a land trail East to Asia (also called the "Indies") and later brought back such luxury goods as spices, silks, gold, and jewels. Tradesmen followed. But Europeans needed a sea route West to buy the Indies' goods more cheaply. Land routes were hazardous, slow, and costly.

SILKS... SPICES... JEWELS... EGG ROLLS...

· · · · · MARCO POLO'S LAND ROUTE TO ASIA

Who would dare sail <u>WEST</u> across the Sea of Darkness to reach the <u>EAST</u> with all its riches?

One bold adventurer came forth: <u>Christopher Columbus</u>— a man who had a dream and pursued it with optimism, determination, and courage.

In 1492 Columbus sailed the ocean blue. Why? Writing in 1501, at age 50, he explained.

FROM A VERY YOUNG AGE I BEGAN TO FOLLOW THE SEA AND HAVE CONTINUED TO DO SO TO THIS DAY. THIS ART OF NAVIGATION INCITES THOSE WHO PURSUE IT TO INQUIRE INTO THE SECRETS OF THE WORLD!

Well, a funny thing happened to Columbus on his way to the Indies. He bumped into America and **DISCOVERED THE WORLD'S BIGGEST SECRET—TO EUROPEANS!**

Nothing in the world would ever be the same again.

Read on for Columbus' incredible adventure story.

18

The main source for this chapter is <u>The Life of the Admiral Christopher Columbus</u>, a biography by his son Ferdinand Columbus (1488-1539), who at age 13 sailed with his father on Columbus' 4th voyage to America (1502-04). Ferdinand grew up to be a noted scholar, with a library of 15,000 books.

Ferdinand began the biography of his father with these words:

I, FERDINAND COLUMBUS, BEING THE SON OF ADMIRAL CHRISTOPHER COLUMBUS, A PERSON WORTHY OF ETERNAL GLORY FOR HIS DISCOVERY OF THE WEST INDIES, IT SEEMS FITTING THAT I, WHO SAILED WITH HIM FOR SOME TIME... SHOULD WRITE THE HISTORY OF HIS LIFE. I PROMISE TO TELL THE ADMIRAL'S LIFE ONLY FROM HIS OWN WRITINGS AND LETTERS AND WHAT I MYSELF OBSERVED.

Christopher Columbus was born in 1451 in Genoa, an Italian seaport. The eldest of five children, he helped his father, a wool weaver, but he longed to be a sailor.

HEY, CHRIS LET'S GO FOR A PIZZA.

NO THANKS, TONY--I'D RATHER WATCH THE SHIPS.

At age 14—tall and strong, with blond hair (turned white by age 30), blue eyes, and ruddy skin—he went to sea. He eventually became one of the most skilled seamen and navigators of all time.

LOOK! NO HANDS!

According to Ferdinand, Christopher (a Catholic) was devoted to God and so great an enemy to cursing and swearing that, "I never heard him utter any other oath than 'By San Fernando!'"

Shipwrecked off the Portugal coast in 1476, Columbus settled in Lisbon and worked in his brother Bartholomew's map-making shop.

LISBON PORTUGAL SPAIN

BART, WHY DON'T YOU JUST BUY AN ATLAS?

CHRIS, YOU HAVE A LOT TO LEARN.

In 1479 he married Felipa Muniz, daughter of a Portuguese nobleman who had discovered the Madeira islands (and whose exploration charts Columbus read eagerly). The next year they had a son, Diego.

SINCE YOU'RE STAYING UP TO PLOT VOYAGES AND THINGS, YOU CAN TAKE CARE OF DIEGO'S 2 A.M. FEEDING.

SEA STORIES

Portugal was a great place for seamen because in 1419 Prince Henry the Navigator had founded a center for studying the new science of navigation, in hopes of finding a sea route to the Indies around the tip of Africa.

SAILOR SCHOOL

I WONDER IF PRINCE HENRY MAKES YOU STAY AFTER SCHOOL FOR NAUTICAL BEHAVIOR. YUK! YUK!

AWWK

In Portugal, Columbus taught himself Latin, the language of geography books, so he could begin the exciting study of geography. He also learned drawing, the tool of a geographer's trade.

GOLLY POP! YOU'RE STUDYING WHEN YOU DON'T EVEN HAVE TO?

Books that sparked Columbus' imagination included that of Italian Marco Polo, which described Polo's 1271-95 journey to China (with its wondrous gold, jewels, and spices) and his adventures with the Chinese ruler Kublai Khan. Columbus had an idea!

MARCO POLO WENT <u>EAST</u> TO CHINA. WHAT ABOUT MY GOING <u>WEST</u>?

NOW, CHRIS!

THE BIG QUESTION: HOW WIDE IS THE OCEAN SEPARATING EUROPE AND ASIA? THIS LETTER FROM TOSCANELLI, THE ITALIAN ASTRONOMER, SAYS THE OCEAN IS ONLY 3,000 MILES WIDE!

WELL, THAT'S ENCOURAGING.

A SLIGHT ERROR—OFF THE MARK BY ABOUT 8,000 MILES!

In 1484 Columbus gave his idea a big name, Enterprise of the Indies, and tried to sell it to Portugal's King John II. The king and his committee of experts said, "No!"

IT MAKES PERFECT SENSE! WE CAN REACH THE EAST BY SAILING WEST! THINK OF ALL THE SPICES AND GOLD! PORTUGAL COULD BECOME A WORLD POWER.

I BET OTHER COUNTRIES WOULD JUMP AT THE CHANCE TO BEAT THE PORTUGUESE TO THE ORIENT. BARTHOLOMEW, YOU GO ASK HENRY VII OF ENGLAND AND CHARLES VIII OF FRANCE IF THEY WILL FINANCE OUR VOYAGE. I'LL GO ASK THE KING AND QUEEN OF SPAIN.

CAN'T WE DRAW STRAWS?

So in 1485 Columbus and little five-year-old Diego (whose mother had died) sailed into the Spanish harbor of Palos and started up the road.

HOW CAN I MEET THE KING AND QUEEN, AND WHO WILL TAKE CARE OF DIEGO?

ARE WE THERE YET?

At La Rábida, a Catholic monastery overlooking the harbor, Fray Juan Perez, a kindly friar, provided help.

SO THAT'S MY IDEA, PEREZ...

SOUNDS GREAT! THE QUEEN IS MY FRIEND. I'LL ASK HER TO SEE YOU, AND I'LL TAKE GOOD CARE OF DIEGO.

In 1486 King Ferdinand and Queen Isabella received Columbus at court in Cordoba. Isabella—age 35, the same as Columbus—expressed interest, but Ferdinand had his doubts. They asked a committee of geographers to study the Enterprise of the Indies proposal.

YOUR PLAN HAS POSSIBILITIES.

BUT FIRST LET'S HAVE A FEASIBILITY STUDY!

The committee took its time: four years. Meanwhile, Columbus fell in love with Beatriz Enriquez de Arana of Cordoba, who in 1488 bore him a son, Ferdinand. (As young boys, both Ferdinand and Diego served as pages to Queen Isabella.)

In 1490 the committee gave a negative report, observing that, "since creation no learned man has tried such an idea." The men added:

WHAT MAKES COLUMBUS THINK HE IS SO SMART!

YOU'D HAVE TO SAIL UP HILL COMING BACK.

THE OCEAN IS SO WIDE, IT WOULD TAKE 3 YEARS TO CROSS IT.

IT'S NEVER BEEN DONE BEFORE.

IN OTHER WORDS, "NO."

Disappointed, Columbus decided to go ask the French King for support. (Bartholomew had not succeeded there.) But at Palos, where he went to get Diego, Fray Perez advised him:

FORGET FRANCE. GO BACK AND ASK ISABELLA ONE MORE TIME.

YOU'RE RIGHT, FRAY PEREZ. DIEGO, START PACKING.

RATS! YOU MEAN WE AREN'T GOING TO PARIS?

In January 1492, Columbus went to the camp of Santa Fe, where the Catholic monarchs had just defeated the Moors, ending seven centuries of Moslem power in Spain. King Ferdinand and Queen Isabella were in a good mood.

YOUR MAJESTY, I'VE FIGURED OUT THE SECRET OF THE OCEAN TRADE-WINDS. NOW WILL YOU SUPPORT MY VOYAGE TO THE INDIES?

WELL, IT'S MAKING MORE SENSE NOW.

SPAIN
PORTUGAL
PALOS

Isabella finally said, "Yes," causing Columbus to write later: "Everyone else was disbelieving, but to the Queen, my Lady, God gave the spirit of understanding...."

WE CAN CONVERT MANY HEATHENS TO CHRISTIANITY.

ALSO GRAB PLENTY OF ASIAN RICHES BEFORE SOME OF THOSE GREEDY NATIONS CAN GET THERE! SOUNDS FEASIBLE TO ME, MY DEAR.

The Spanish monarchs appointed Columbus "Admiral of the Ocean Sea" and governor of any lands he might discover on the way to the Indies.

PLUS, YOU GET 10 PER CENT OF ANY WEALTH YOU FIND.

WILL THAT BE AFTER TAXES, SIRE?

On August 3, 1492, the Niña, Pinta, and Santa Maria sailed with Columbus and ninety crewmen first to the Canary Islands and then due west—to the edge of the unknown.

HEY, I CAN SEE JAPAN ALREADY.

AFRAID NOT SIR -- YOU'RE LOOKING BACK AT THE CANARY ISLANDS, JAPAN IS THAT WAY.

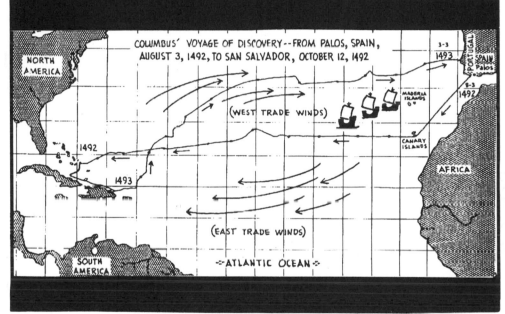

COLUMBUS' VOYAGE OF DISCOVERY -- FROM PALOS, SPAIN, AUGUST 3, 1492, TO SAN SALVADOR, OCTOBER 12, 1492

NORTH AMERICA

(WEST TRADE WINDS)

1492

1493

(EAST TRADE WINDS)

SOUTH AMERICA

-- ATLANTIC OCEAN --

MADEIRA ISLANDS 0°

CANARY ISLANDS

AFRICA

PORTUGAL SPAIN Palos

3-3 1493

8-3 1492

October 10, after seeing no land for a month, the sailors threatened mutiny. But Columbus—true to his dream—convinced them their goal was within reach. They agreed to sail onward three more days.

BY SAN FERNANDO, WE'RE GOING TO FIND THE INDIES! SAIL ON !!

"SAN FERNANDO" - I GUESS HE MEANS BUSINESS.

Two days later, Rodrigo Triana on the Pinta cried out, "tierra, tierra!" ("land, land!"). And so, on October 12—71 days out of Spain— Columbus and his crew landed on a small island in the Bahamas. Giving thanks to God, Columbus named the island San Salvador (Holy Savior).

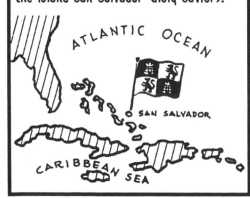

ATLANTIC OCEAN

SAN SALVADOR

CARIBBEAN SEA

Certain he had arrived in the Indies, Columbus named the peaceful natives who greeted him "Indians." They thought the Spaniards were "men from Heaven."

GREETINGS, INDIANS. I CLAIM THIS LAND FOR SPAIN!

CAN HE DO THAT?

Columbus then explored the island of Haiti (which he named Hispaniola) and Cuba (which he thought was China). He searched for gold and the Chinese ruler Kublai Khan. (Isabella had given him a letter for the great Khan.) But all he found were Indians smoking tobacco.

I HAVE AN IMPORTANT LETTER. CAN YOU SEE THAT IT REACHES THE KHAN?

NO KHAN DO, HA! HA!

After ten weeks of exploring, Columbus sailed back to Spain, bringing home seven Indians, parrots, corn, tobacco, hammocks, and only a little gold.

SQUAWK, DON'T TALK! OR THEY'LL PUT US ON EXHIBIT AND WE'LL NEVER GET BACK HOME.

GOTCHA!

Tobacco CORN

Spain welcomed Columbus as a hero; he had done the impossible! Listening to his triumphant report, King Ferdinand and Queen Isabella allowed the Admiral of the Ocean Sea to sit in their presence, a rare tribute.

HEY, I LIKE THIS RELAXED, INFORMAL SETTING — MIND IF I KICK OFF MY SHOES?

DON'T PRESS YOUR LUCK, ADMIRAL!

Portugal tried to claim the islands Columbus had discovered. So in 1493 Spain asked Pope Alexander VI (a Spaniard) to intervene. The Pope drew a line of demarcation 100 leagues (300 miles) west of the Azores Islands, giving Spain all non-Christian lands to the West and Portugal those to the east.

YEAH, IT'S TRUE. THE POPE HAS DIVIDED THE NEW WORLD BETWEEN SPAIN AND PORTUGAL.

CAN HE DO THAT???

TREATY

In 1494 the Treaty of Tordesillas confirmed the pope's decision, with one change: Portugal felt cheated out of South America, so the Pope moved the dividing line 270 leagues farther west, giving her Brazil.

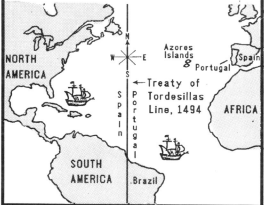

NORTH AMERICA

Azores Islands Portugal Spain

←Treaty of Tordesillas Line, 1494

AFRICA

SOUTH AMERICA Brazil

Meanwhile, Columbus made a return voyage (with 17 ships and about 1300 men) to establish a trading colony on Hispaniola. The Arawak Indians on Hispaniola—enslaved to work in gold mines and infected with European diseases—suffered terribly at the hands of the Spaniards; within twenty years, only about 250 of 5,000,000 survived.

Columbus, although a brilliant seaman, managed poorly on land. Unable to control cruelty toward the Indians, and participating in it, he was accused by rivals of unfitness and brought to Spain in chains. The monarchs restored his freedom and his status as an explorer but not his titles and glory.

Between 1492 and 1504, Columbus made four voyages to the New World. All his life, however, he remained convinced he had reached Asia.

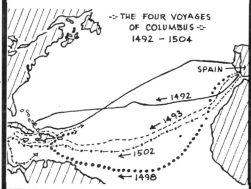

→ THE FOUR VOYAGES OF COLUMBUS → 1492 - 1504

SPAIN

← 1492

← 1493

← 1502

← 1498

And so, when the Italian Amerigo Vespucci sailed the South American coast in 1497 and called it a New World, a German mapmaker in 1507 named the New World America.

DIEGO, I DON'T UNDERSTAND WHY THEY DIDN'T NAME IT AFTER POP.

BUT FERDINAND, WOULD "THE UNITED STATES OF COLUMBUS" SOUND FUNNY?

LATER FERDINAND HONORED HIS FATHER IN A UNIQUE WAY: AFTER READING IN SENECA'S MEDEA (2ND CENTURY), "AN AGE WILL COME AFTER YEARS WHEN THE OCEAN WILL LOOSE THE CHAINS OF THINGS, AND A HUGE LAND LIE REVEALED...." FERDINAND WROTE IN THE MARGIN, "THIS PROPHECY WAS FULFILLED BY MY FATHER... THE ADMIRAL IN THE YEAR 1492."

Columbus died in 1506. But his adventurous spirit lives on, inspiring all who read of him to dream big dreams—and with optimism, determination, and courage make them come true.

WHEN I SET OUT ON THIS ENTERPRISE, THEY SAID IT WAS IMPOSSIBLE. NOW EVERY TAILOR WANTS TO BE AN EXPLORER. MAY IT ALWAYS BE SO!

Tailor Shop

CLOSED (GONE EXPLORING)

Columbus was right! The spirit of adventure brought many explorers to America. Here is an overview of Spanish explorers, who came first.

1492   1610   2000

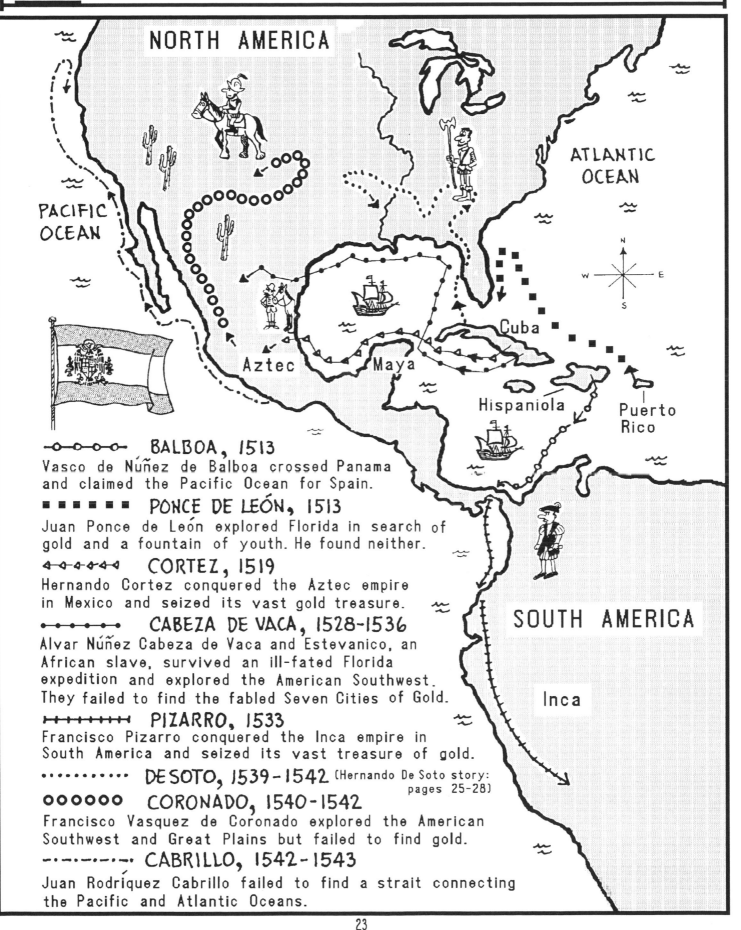

BALBOA, 1513
Vasco de Núñez de Balboa crossed Panama and claimed the Pacific Ocean for Spain.

PONCE DE LEÓN, 1513
Juan Ponce de León explored Florida in search of gold and a fountain of youth. He found neither.

CORTEZ, 1519
Hernando Cortez conquered the Aztec empire in Mexico and seized its vast gold treasure.

CABEZA DE VACA, 1528-1536
Alvar Núñez Cabeza de Vaca and Estevanico, an African slave, survived an ill-fated Florida expedition and explored the American Southwest. They failed to find the fabled Seven Cities of Gold.

PIZARRO, 1533
Francisco Pizarro conquered the Inca empire in South America and seized its vast treasure of gold.

DE SOTO, 1539-1542 (Hernando De Soto story: pages 25-28)

CORONADO, 1540-1542
Francisco Vasquez de Coronado explored the American Southwest and Great Plains but failed to find gold.

CABRILLO, 1542-1543
Juan Rodríquez Cabrillo failed to find a strait connecting the Pacific and Atlantic Oceans.

THE RACE TO CLAIM AMERICA WAS ON!

Excitement about Columbus' discovery spread throughout Europe. <u>Spain</u>, <u>France</u>, <u>England</u>, <u>Portugal</u>, and <u>Holland</u>—all competing for wealth and power—began staking their claims.

By 1550 bold Spanish conquistadors (conquerors) had founded a vast empire, NEW SPAIN and PERU, conquering the gold-rich Aztecs and Incas in the process. By 1610 Spain's empire stretched larger than the ancient Roman Empire.

Meanwhile, in 1519 Spain hired Portuguese <u>Ferdinand Magellan</u> to sail westward around the world to find the Indies. He was killed in the Philippine Islands, which he claimed for Spain, but in 1522 one of his 5 ships completed the historic, first trip around the world —with only 18 of 239 men surviving.

Three G's motivated the remarkable Spanish conquest of America:
1. GOLD—the search for wealth
2. GLORY—the search for fame
3. GOD— the aim to convert Indians to Catholic Christianity, Spain's official religion.

<u>Bernal Diaz</u> a colonist of Hispaniola, wrote:

"I came to America to serve God and His Majesty, to give light to those who were in darkness, and to grow rich, as all men desire to do."

Spanish colonizers enslaved the Indians they conquered and used their labor to farm, mine, and build cities. In 1542 <u>Bartolome de Las Casas</u>, a humane Spanish priest in Hispaniola, persuaded the King to end Indian slavery, but Indian abuse continued.

VERY WELL, BART. I'LL ABOLISH INDIAN SLAVERY <u>AT ONCE!</u>

European diseases proved fatal to the Indians, for they had no immunity. Millions died; they were replaced by enslaved Africans.

Spain ruled New Spain and Peru with a tight fist, allowing no representative government, no free trade, no freedom of religion—all the while growing rich from New World gold and silver.

DOGGONE IT, THESE ARBITRARY DECREES FROM THE KING ARE A REAL INCONVENIENCE.

GOLD ORE

YOU THINK YOU'VE GOT TROUBLES

Yet Spain gave New Spain and Peru a rich endowment of western civilization in terms of people, language, law, literature, universities, religion, plants, and livestock (horses, cows, pigs).

¿HABLA USTED ESPAÑOL?

WHAT'D HE SAY?

BEATS ME.

The empire founded by Columbus in 1492 ended for Spain three centuries later, when her American colonies won their independence. But even by 1600, Spain had lost her monopoly in America, as rival nations challenged her lead.

Before we check on France, let's explore the footsteps of one of Spain's North American conquistadors: Hernando De Soto.

Three men accompanying Hernando De Soto wrote narratives of their four-year expedition through the present-day southeastern United States: Luys de Beidma, Gentleman of Elvas, and Rodrigo Ranjel (see Edward Bourne, Narratives of the Career of Hernando de Soto, 2 vols.). These narratives, which are primary sources for this chapter, plus narratives describing the explorations of Cabeza de Vaca and Coronado, comprise the first histories of North America.

1492   1539-1542   2000

A SPIRIT OF ADVENTURE lured one of the first Spaniards to North America.

The year: 1539 — 68 years before the English settled Jamestown, Virginia.

The man: Hernando De Soto — a bold, Spanish Conquistador, eager to win fame and fortune in the New World.

North America
ATLANTIC OCEAN

IN 1492 COLUMBUS DISCOVERED A NEW WORLD. NOTHING WOULD EVER BE THE SAME AGAIN, FOR EUROPE — OR AMERICA — OR HERNANDO DE SOTO!

NORTH AMERICA
San Salvador
ATLANTIC OCEAN
SOUTH AMERICA
Spain

Eight years later, in 1500, Hernando De Soto was born in Jerez de los Caballeros, Province of Estremadura, Spain.

ATLANTIC OCEAN
FRANCE
SPAIN
JEREZ
MEDITERRANEAN SEA

This province was "Hog Country," sort of. In fact, Pizarro — who conquered Peru — was a hog herder from this area.

De Soto grew up dreaming of the New World. Do you suppose he ever dreamed that he would:
1) explore America?
2) be the first to record its history?
3) bring the first hogs to Arkansas?

LAND OF OPPORTUNITY
ZZZ

De Soto's family was of the nobility --but poor. So a wealthy count, Don Pedro de Avila, adopted him and sent him to school to become a great man.

But Hernando, age 19, had something else on his mind: Isabella, Don Pedro's beautiful daughter.

Enraged, Don Pedro ordered De Soto to leave.

DO YOU DARE TO COURT MY DAUGHTER? YOU'RE TOO POOR, HERNANDO!

De Soto's probable route through Arkansas: June 1541 - May 1542

THE SPANIARDS PASSED THROUGH LOTS OF INDIAN VILLAGES WITH LARGE POPULATIONS. TODAY YOU CAN VISIT MANY OF THESE PLACES ALONG DE SOTO'S ROUTE.

Unable to find gold in the Arkansas delta villages, De Soto traveled into the mountains.

I AM A CHILD OF THE SUN. OBEY AND SERVE ME—AND GIVE ME GOLD.

IF THE CHILD OF THE SUN WILL DRY UP THE RIVER, WE WILL BELIEVE.

I WISH THEY BOTH WOULD DRY UP.

De Soto and his men visited the Hot Springs area.

MAYBE WE CAN BOTTLE THIS STUFF AND SELL IT.

SURE, CHIEF! WE CAN CALL IT "DE SOTO POP."

In Caddo Gap, near Hot Springs, Indians attacked De Soto and his men. Fearing he would be killed, the Conquistador decided to abandon his search for gold. De Soto followed the Ouachita River into Louisiana, heading for the Gulf of Mexico and Cuba. His army numbered only 300, and they had only 40 horses. Near Ferriday, La., De Soto died from a fever.

De Soto's men buried him in the Mississippi River, fearing what the Indians would do if they learned De Soto was not a god.

REST IN PEACE H. DE SOTO

What was DeSoto's legacy to America?

GOLD?
SILVER?
DE SOTO AUTOMOBILE?
DE SOTO POP?

GROAN...

It was the SPIRIT OF ADVENTURE:

daring to venture into the unknown and explore new worlds.

And the symbol of this spirit is familiar to all Arkansans...

It is The Razorback Hog...

WOOO, PIG! SOOIE!

A descendant (we think) of The Spanish Hog.

28

1492 1524   1763   2000

Now back to the BIG RACE FOR NORTH AMERICA:

France—envious of Spain's American wealth and eager to find a northwest passage to the riches of Asia—ignored the Pope's division of the New World between Spain and Portugal in the Treaty of Tordesillas and claimed rights of discovery in North America with the voyages of three adventurers.

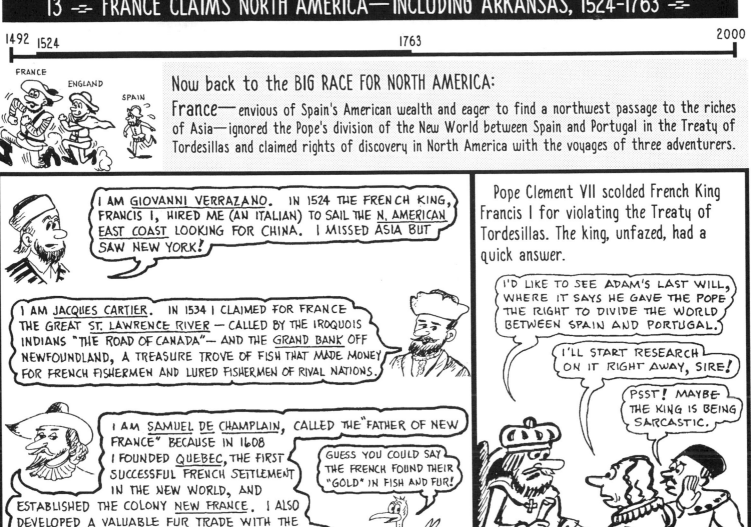

I AM GIOVANNI VERRAZANO. IN 1524 THE FRENCH KING, FRANCIS I, HIRED ME (AN ITALIAN) TO SAIL THE N. AMERICAN EAST COAST LOOKING FOR CHINA. I MISSED ASIA BUT SAW NEW YORK!

I AM JACQUES CARTIER. IN 1534 I CLAIMED FOR FRANCE THE GREAT ST. LAWRENCE RIVER — CALLED BY THE IROQUOIS INDIANS "THE ROAD OF CANADA"— AND THE GRAND BANK OFF NEWFOUNDLAND, A TREASURE TROVE OF FISH THAT MADE MONEY FOR FRENCH FISHERMEN AND LURED FISHERMEN OF RIVAL NATIONS.

I AM SAMUEL DE CHAMPLAIN, CALLED THE "FATHER OF NEW FRANCE" BECAUSE IN 1608 I FOUNDED QUEBEC, THE FIRST SUCCESSFUL FRENCH SETTLEMENT IN THE NEW WORLD, AND ESTABLISHED THE COLONY NEW FRANCE. I ALSO DEVELOPED A VALUABLE FUR TRADE WITH THE INDIANS. (EUROPEANS JUST LOVE BEAVER HATS.)

GUESS YOU COULD SAY THE FRENCH FOUND THEIR "GOLD" IN FISH AND FUR!

Pope Clement VII scolded French King Francis I for violating the Treaty of Tordesillas. The king, unfazed, had a quick answer.

I'D LIKE TO SEE ADAM'S LAST WILL, WHERE IT SAYS HE GAVE THE POPE THE RIGHT TO DIVIDE THE WORLD BETWEEN SPAIN AND PORTUGAL.

I'LL START RESEARCH ON IT RIGHT AWAY, SIRE!

PSST! MAYBE THE KING IS BEING SARCASTIC.

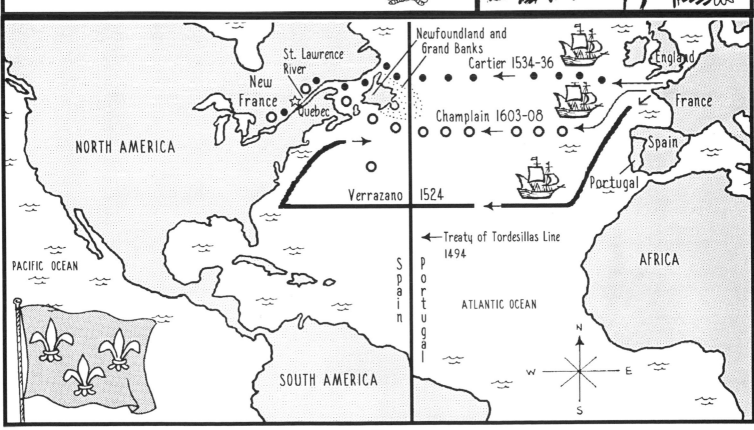

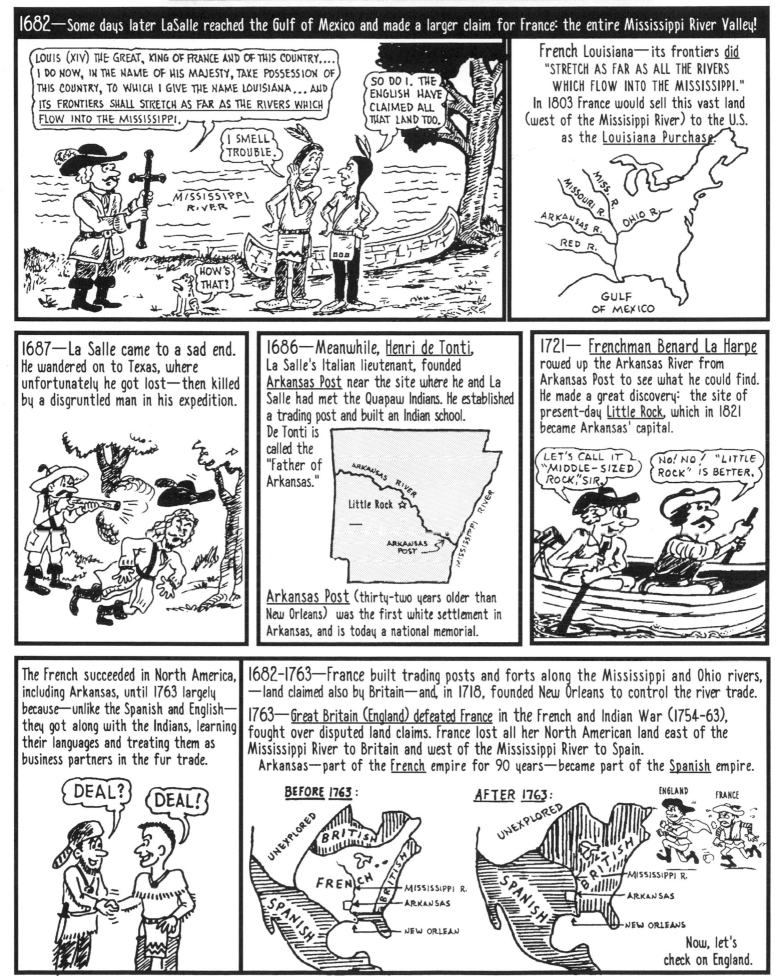

1682—Some days later LaSalle reached the Gulf of Mexico and made a larger claim for France: the entire Mississippi River Valley!

LOUIS (XIV) THE GREAT, KING OF FRANCE AND OF THIS COUNTRY.... I DO NOW, IN THE NAME OF HIS MAJESTY, TAKE POSSESSION OF THIS COUNTRY, TO WHICH I GIVE THE NAME LOUISIANA ... AND ITS FRONTIERS SHALL STRETCH AS FAR AS THE RIVERS WHICH FLOW INTO THE MISSISSIPPI.

SO DO I. THE ENGLISH HAVE CLAIMED ALL THAT LAND TOO.

I SMELL TROUBLE.

HOW'S THAT!

MISSISSIPPI RIVER

French Louisiana—its frontiers <u>did</u> "STRETCH AS FAR AS ALL THE RIVERS WHICH FLOW INTO THE MISSISSIPPI." In 1803 France would sell this vast land (west of the Mississippi River) to the U.S. as the <u>Louisiana Purchase.</u>

MISSOURI R.   MISS. R.   ARKANSAS R.   OHIO R.   RED R.

GULF OF MEXICO

1687—La Salle came to a sad end. He wandered on to Texas, where unfortunately he got lost—then killed by a disgruntled man in his expedition.

1686—Meanwhile, <u>Henri de Tonti</u>, La Salle's Italian lieutenant, founded <u>Arkansas Post</u> near the site where he and La Salle had met the Quapaw Indians. He established a trading post and built an Indian school. De Tonti is called the "Father of Arkansas."

ARKANSAS RIVER
Little Rock ☆
ARKANSAS POST
MISSISSIPPI RIVER

<u>Arkansas Post</u> (thirty-two years older than New Orleans) was the first white settlement in Arkansas, and is today a national memorial.

1721— <u>Frenchman Benard La Harpe</u> rowed up the Arkansas River from Arkansas Post to see what he could find. He made a great discovery: the site of present-day <u>Little Rock</u>, which in 1821 became Arkansas' capital.

LET'S CALL IT "MIDDLE-SIZED ROCK," SIR.

NO! NO! "LITTLE ROCK" IS BETTER.

The French succeeded in North America, including Arkansas, until 1763 largely because—unlike the Spanish and English—they got along with the Indians, learning their languages and treating them as business partners in the fur trade.

DEAL?   DEAL!

1682-1763—France built trading posts and forts along the Mississippi and Ohio rivers,—land claimed also by Britain—and, in 1718, founded New Orleans to control the river trade.

1763—<u>Great Britain (England) defeated France</u> in the French and Indian War (1754-63), fought over disputed land claims. France lost all her North American land east of the Mississippi River to Britain and west of the Mississippi River to Spain.

Arkansas—part of the <u>French</u> empire for 90 years—became part of the <u>Spanish</u> empire.

BEFORE 1763:
UNEXPLORED   BRITISH   FRENCH   BRITISH   SPANISH
MISSISSIPPI R.   ARKANSAS   NEW ORLEAN

AFTER 1763:
UNEXPLORED   BRITISH   SPANISH
ENGLAND   FRANCE
MISSISSIPPI R.   ARKANSAS   NEW ORLEANS

Now, let's check on England.

"...to seek new worlds for gold, for praise, for glory."—Sir Walter Raleigh

1492　　　　　1588　　　　　　　　　　　　　　　　　　　　　　2000

In 1497 English King Henry VII, regretting his refusal to back Columbus in 1492, paid John Cabot about $50 to find a North American passage to Asia. Cabot discovered Newfoundland instead.

WHAT, YOU DIDN'T GET TO ASIA?

BUT SIRE, NEWFOUNDLAND GIVES ENGLAND A CLAIM TO NORTH AMERICA.

Francis Drake (on a round-the-world voyage) and Henry Hudson (a Dutchman sailing for England) staked additional claims, but England was slow to colonize.

NORTH AMERICA
EUROPE
ASIA
ATLANTIC OCEAN
AFRICA
PACIFIC OCEAN
SOUTH AMERICA
INDIAN OCEAN

-1-1-1- CABOT (NEWFOUNDLAND) 1497
———— DRAKE (SAN FRANCISCO) 1579
- - - - HUDSON (HUDSON'S BAY) 1610

1584—Sir Walter Raleigh, with the help of geographer Richard Hakluyt, convinced Queen Elizabeth I that colonies in North America would make England as rich and powerful as Spain.

PLEASE, MR. HAKLUYT— PUT AWAY THE CHART. I'M CONVINCED!

PSSST, WAY TO GO.

REASON #19
REASON #20

1584—Virginia was founded when the Queen gave Raleigh a land grant stretching from present-day North Carolina to Maine. He named it Virginia for Elizabeth, the Virgin Queen.

WALT, I'VE GOT GOOD NEWS AND BAD NEWS. YOU CAN HAVE A LAND GRANT. BUT IF YOU WANT TO COLONIZE IN AMERICA YOU'LL HAVE TO PAY THE COSTS.

1587: THE LOST COLONY—Raleigh sent 117 people to settle Roanoke Island off North Carolina. By 1591 they disappeared, leaving the name of an Indian tribe, Croatoan, carved on a post. What do you think happened?

THEY PROBABLY STARVED TO DEATH

...OR WERE KILLED BY THE INDIANS.

OR JOINED UP WITH THEM...

CROATOAN

MAYBE THEY LEFT ON A CRUISE.

Meanwhile, dare-devil English sea dogs Francis Drake and John Hawkins pirated Spanish ships carrying American gold. England grew rich from this stolen treasure, and Spain grew angry!

I HEAR THE SPANISH ARE CALLING OUR LEADER "DRAGON DRAKE."

I GUESS THAT'S BECAUSE WE'RE "DRAGON" OFF SO MUCH OF THEIR GOLD.

GOLD

WE MAY HAVE GOTTEN TOO MUCH... OUR SHIP MIGHT SINK.

GOLD GOLD GOLD

YOUR MAJESTY - THIS MESSAGE FROM KING PHILIP II OF SPAIN DEMANDS YOU PUNISH DRAKE AND HIS PIRATES!

HMMPH! I HAVE NO CONTROL OVER THOSE BUCCANEERS... WHERE WAS I? OH, YES, SIR FRANCIS DRAKE, I HEREBY KNIGHT THEE.

FOR A PIRATE I'VE DONE OKAY.

SCOTLAND
IRELAND
ENGLAND
ATLANTIC OCEAN
FRANCE
SPAIN
N W S E

1588—Furious, Philip II built a 130-ship Armada to invade and punish England. The largest fleet in history, the Armada stretched seven miles as it sailed toward England.

1588—Defeat of the Spanish Armada came as a storm scattered the fleet, enabling crafty English sea dogs—led by Dragon Drake—to out-maneuver and sink much of the "invincible" Armada.

RULE, BRITANNIA BRITANNIA RULES THE WAVES—

THIS WAS A TURNING POINT IN HISTORY: THE SPANISH EMPIRE DECLINED AS ENGLAND BECAME RULER OF THE SEAS—POWERFUL ENOUGH TO BEGIN HER COLONIAL EMPIRE IN EARNEST.

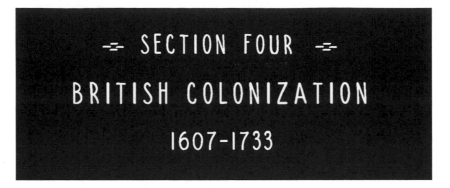

1492   1607   1733   2000

ENGLISH OR BRITISH? The proper terms are:

before 1707—ENGLISH;
after 1707—BRITISH.

In 1707 the English Parliament passed the Act of Union, uniting England and Wales with Scotland in a single kingdom called Great Britain. From this point on, all subjects of Great Britain, including English, were called British.

And so it was that
England began founding North American colonies in 1607.
A century later, in 1707, the English colonies became British colonies.

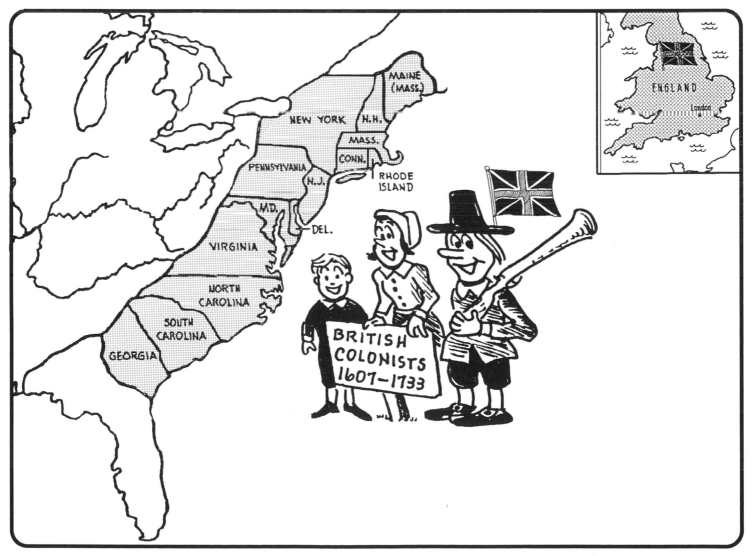

BRITISH COLONISTS 1607-1733

33

<u>colony</u>—a group of people who settle in a new land but remain subject to their original country

Between 1607 and 1733 the British founded thirteen colonies on North America's east coast and successfully ruled them for 169 years.

Other nationalities helped settle the colonies, but the population, language, laws, and culture remained predominantly British.

In 1776 the colonies broke free of their mother country and became the UNITED STATES OF AMERICA.

ENGLAND
London

THE THIRTEEN COLONIES:* DATES OF FOUNDING

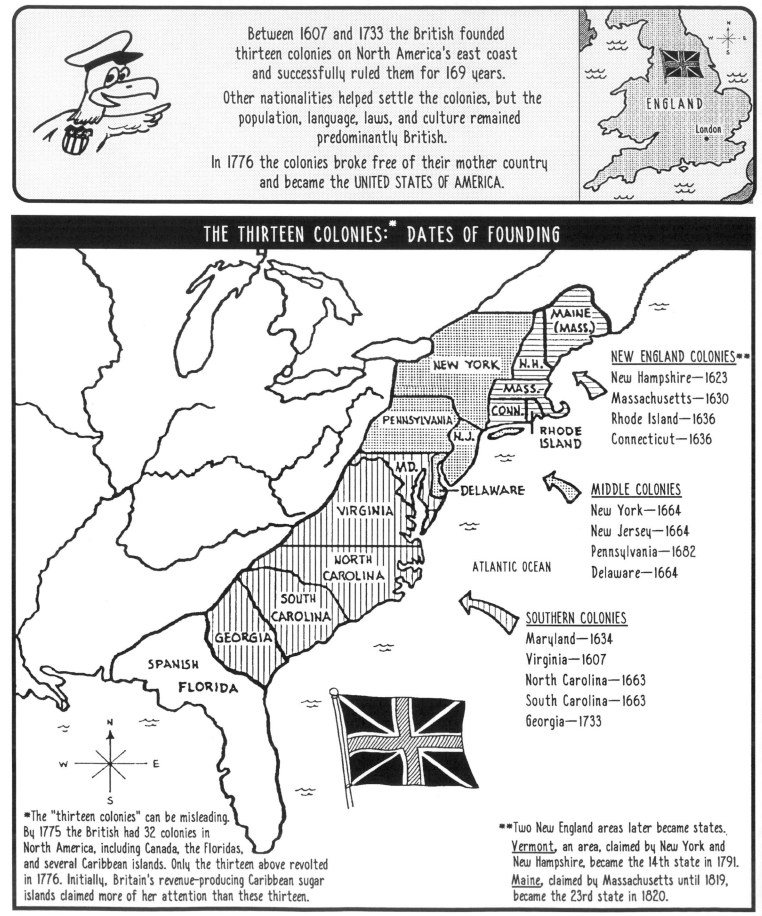

MAINE (MASS.)

NEW YORK   N.H.

MASS.

CONN.

PENNSYLVANIA

N.J.   RHODE ISLAND

MD.

DELAWARE

VIRGINIA

NORTH CAROLINA

ATLANTIC OCEAN

SOUTH CAROLINA

GEORGIA

SPANISH FLORIDA

N W E S

NEW ENGLAND COLONIES**
New Hampshire—1623
Massachusetts—1630
Rhode Island—1636
Connecticut—1636

<u>MIDDLE COLONIES</u>
New York—1664
New Jersey—1664
Pennsylvania—1682
Delaware—1664

<u>SOUTHERN COLONIES</u>
Maryland—1634
Virginia—1607
North Carolina—1663
South Carolina—1663
Georgia—1733

*The "thirteen colonies" can be misleading. By 1775 the British had 32 colonies in North America, including Canada, the Floridas, and several Caribbean islands. Only the thirteen above revolted in 1776. Initially, Britain's revenue-producing Caribbean sugar islands claimed more of her attention than these thirteen.

**Two New England areas later became states. <u>Vermont</u>, an area, claimed by New York and New Hampshire, became the 14th state in 1791. <u>Maine</u>, claimed by Massachusetts until 1819, became the 23rd state in 1820.

"There are those, I know, who will reply that the liberation of humanity, the freedom of man and mind, is nothing but a dream... they are right. It is the American Dream." —Archibald Macleish

THE AMERICAN DREAM: FREEDOM

Roller coaster upheavals in England created economic, social, religious, and political motives to colonize America—all in search of greater freedom.

OPPORTUNITY ← → HARD TIMES
MOBILITY ← → RIGIDITY
FREEDOM ← → RESTRAINT
LIBERTY ← → PERSECUTION

ECONOMIC · SOCIAL · POLITICAL · RELIGIOUS

WHO CAME—AND WHY DID THEY COME?
WOULD YOU HAVE COME?

Imagine that you were living in England between 1607 and 1775.

Would you have ventured across the 3,000-mile ocean for any of these motives?

(motive—a cause that moves a person to action.)

ECONOMIC OPPORTUNITY

1. ENGLISH MONARCHS dreamed of a favorable balance of trade by owning colonies that would sell raw materials to England at low prices and buy England's manufactured goods at high prices.

THIS REGULATED ECONOMY — MERCANTILISM— HELPS US ACCUMULATE GOLD BY SELLING MORE THAN WE BUY.

THUS ENSURING NATIONAL SECURITY. GOOD POINT, HAKLUYT!

2. A NEW MERCHANT CLASS (created by manufacturing and overseas trade) had capital to invest in colonial ventures and dreamed of striking it rich. Business boomed as English monarchs franchised trading companies, such as the East India Company.

NYET! I DO NOT WISH TO PURCHASE A CARGO OF ENGLISH MUFFINS!

EAST INDIA CO.

MUSCOVY CO.

3. MIDDLE and LOWER CLASSES dreamed of making a better living in America. Inflation (caused by New World gold flowing into Europe at 10,000 lbs. per year) sent prices sky-high and cut wages drastically.

HOW MUCH FOR A LOAF OF BREAD?

IF YOU HAVE TO ASK, YOU CAN'T AFFORD IT.

Bakery

4. UNEMPLOYED FARMERS victimized by the ENCLOSURE MOVEMENT dreamed of owning land in America. As wool manufacturing became profitable, landowners enclosed their land for sheep pastures, evicting thousands of tenant farmers.

LET'S HEAD FOR AMERICA— I HEAR THERE'S PLENTY OF LAND THERE.

ARE WE THERE YET?

SOCIAL MOBILITY

1. WORKERS AND FARMERS <u>dreamed of upward mobility</u> in America. In England a rigid class structure confined Englishmen to a <u>hierarchy</u> (a ranking from higher to lower): each person had a place in society and stayed there.

ENGLAND'S SOCIAL HIERARCHY

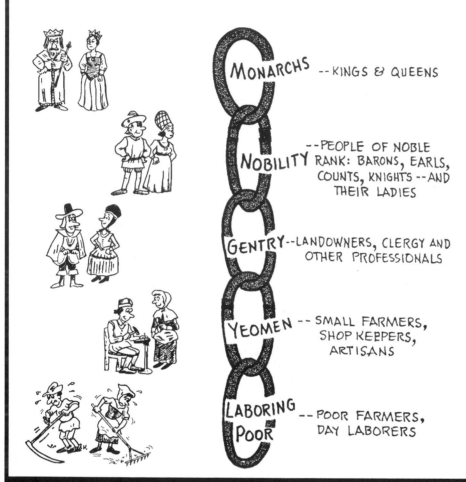

MONARCHS --KINGS & QUEENS

NOBILITY --PEOPLE OF NOBLE RANK: BARONS, EARLS, COUNTS, KNIGHTS --AND THEIR LADIES

GENTRY --LANDOWNERS, CLERGY AND OTHER PROFESSIONALS

YEOMEN -- SMALL FARMERS, SHOP KEEPERS, ARTISANS

LABORING POOR -- POOR FARMERS, DAY LABORERS

2. SOME ENGLISH LEADERS <u>dreamed of colonization as a safety valve</u>—a dumping ground for excess people (including convicts)—because increased population was draining England's resources.

POLITICAL FREEDOM

Between 1603 and 1688 MANY ENGLISH SUBJECTS <u>dreamed of greater political freedom</u> in America because of:
1) the absolutist Stuart monarchs—who claimed the <u>divine right of kings</u>, meaning that monarchs ruled in God's behalf (therefore with absolute power) and could not be disobeyed;
2) a bloody civil war (1642-49) between supporters of King Charles I (Royalists, called <u>Cavaliers</u>) and supporters of Parliament (mostly Puritans, called <u>Roundheads</u>).

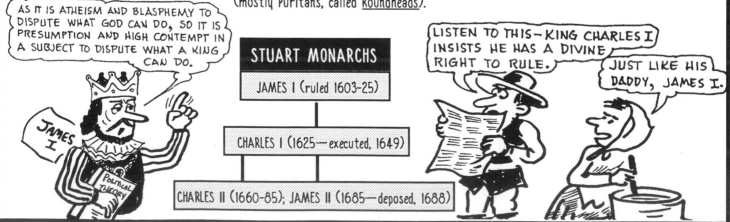

STUART MONARCHS

JAMES I (ruled 1603-25)

CHARLES I (1625—executed, 1649)

CHARLES II (1660-85); JAMES II (1685—deposed, 1688)

RELIGIOUS LIBERTY: THE PROTESTANT REFORMATION

In the 1600s ENGLISH PURITANS, persecuted by English Anglicans, <u>dreamed of religious liberty</u> in America.
Who were the Puritans? The answer involves an intriguing story.

THE PROTESTANT REFORMATION

In 1517 a revolutionary religious and political movement erupted in Europe. Beginning In the 1600's it affected settlement of the American colonies and contributed to American roots of religious liberty.

For 1,000 years the <u>Roman Catholic Church</u> had reigned supreme in Christian Europe.
Most European Christians—including kings, nobles, and commoners—accepted the pope (head of the Catholic Church) as God's ruler on earth, and they followed the pope's decrees. Then, beginning in 1517, groups protested certain Catholic beliefs and practices, questioned the pope's authority, and broke from Catholicism to form new churches which they thought would be closer to early Christian teachings. These churches soon were called <u>Protestant churches</u> because they were formed by "protesters."

Led in 1517 by <u>Martin Luther</u>, a German monk,
and later by French theologian <u>John Calvin</u> (1530s) and <u>English King Henry VIII</u> (1534),
the Protestant Reformation gave rise to LUTHERAN, CALVINIST, and ANGLICAN Protestant churches
and eventually to many other Protestant denominations.

The splintering of Catholicism shattered European unity. During the next century religious warfare raged in Europe as Catholics and Protestants fought over what to believe, how to worship, and which church should be the official one. Separation of church and state did not exist in Europe, so religious disputes often led to political warfare, specifically between <u>Catholic Spain and France</u> and <u>Protestant England and Holland.</u> These wars affected America.

But before we go further, let's check the map to get our bearings on the Protestant movement.
(Remember, before 1517 all the European countries below would have been Roman Catholic.)
Can you see why the American colonies became Protestant?

1600s—RELIGIOUS GROUPS IN WESTERN EUROPE AFTER THE PROTESTANT REFORMATION

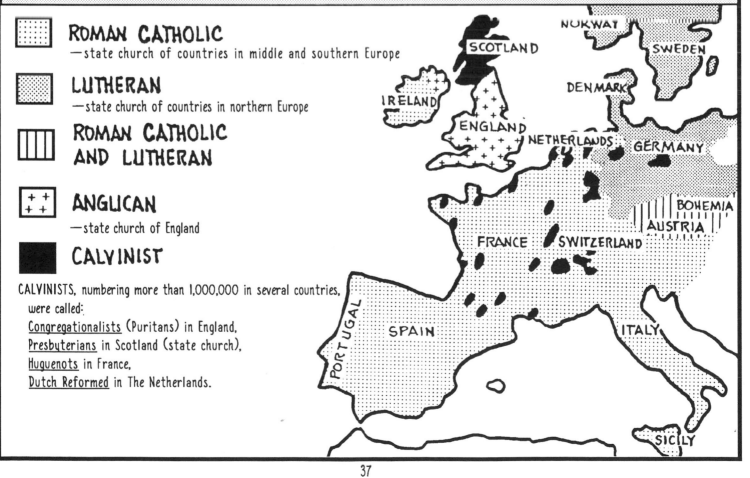

ROMAN CATHOLIC
—state church of countries in middle and southern Europe

LUTHERAN
—state church of countries in northern Europe

ROMAN CATHOLIC AND LUTHERAN

ANGLICAN
—state church of England

CALVINIST

CALVINISTS, numbering more than 1,000,000 in several countries, were called:
<u>Congregationalists</u> (Puritans) in England,
<u>Presbyterians</u> in Scotland (state church),
<u>Huguenots</u> in France,
<u>Dutch Reformed</u> in The Netherlands.

The Protestant Reformation had great impact on the American colonies, especially those in New England settled by English Puritans, so it helps to know what Protestants believed. The main Protestant doctrines fall into two categories: 1) Lutheran and Calvinist, and 2) Anglican.

PROTESTANT DOCTRINES: LUTHERAN AND CALVINIST

1. <u>SALVATION IS ATTAINED BY FAITH</u>— as opposed to the Catholic doctrine of salvation through sacraments and good works. This conclusion by Martin Luther, a German monk, started the Protestant Reformation in 1517.

2. <u>PREDESTINATION</u>—John Calvin emphasized the doctrine that only those God <u>predestined</u> (chose beforehand) would attain salvation. These were called the "elect" or "saints."

3. <u>PRIESTHOOD OF THE BELIEVER</u> (Also called "Every man his own priest")—This doctrine means that every person has <u>direct access</u> to God through the Bible, as opposed to <u>indirect access</u> through the Catholic hierarchy of church officials who act as intermediaries between individuals and God.

NOW WE CAN READ AND INTERPRET THE BIBLE FOR OURSELVES.

This doctrine is based on the idea that the <u>Bible</u>, not the pope or church, is the sole source of information about God, and that each person is free to interpret the meaning of the Bible for himself— believing what his reason and conscience tell him instead of accepting church officials' interpretations.

Watch for this doctrine to foster religious liberty and individualism in Protestant America.

PROTESTANT DOCTRINES: ANGLICAN

In 1534 English King Henry VIII broke from the Roman Catholic Church, and the Act of Supremacy established by law the Church of England—the Anglican Church. Only one change marked the difference: the <u>king</u> replaced the <u>pope</u> in the church hierarchy of officials.

King Henry VIII rejected Catholicism not for religious reasons but because the pope refused to allow the king to divorce his first wife, Catherine of Aragon. (Henry eventually had six wives.)

The king had no quarrel with Catholic doctrines; therefore, he ignored the Protestant doctrines of Luther and Calvin discussed above. He did have the Bible translated from Latin into English, so more people could read it, and he confiscated church-owned property in England, becoming considerably more wealthy.

Roman Catholic Church Hierarchy

GOD
POPE
CARDINALS
ARCHBISHOPS
BISHOPS
PRIESTS
INDIVIDUAL CHRISTIANS

Anglican Church Hierarchy

GOD
KING
ARCHBISHOPS
BISHOPS
PRIESTS
INDIVIDUAL CHRISTIANS

ENGLISH PURITANS

Some English Protestants thought the Anglican Church had not changed enough from the Catholic Church and that it needed to add the Priesthood of the Believer doctrine.

This called for "purifying" the Anglican Church by getting rid of the hierarchy.

GOD
INDIVIDUAL CHRISTIANS

Hence, these Englishmen were called PURITANS.

Unable to "purify" the Anglican Church, in 1620 Puritans began a pilgrimage to America to start their own. By 1640 more than 20,000 had formed colonies in New England.

And now, back to America to see how the British settled their colonies.

Private enterprise financed all thirteen British colonies, but all were required to govern by English law. Three kinds of colonies received charters from the king.

1. CORPORATE COLONIES (C)
The King gave charters to joint stock companies (formed by investors) to found and govern colonies for profit, with the king getting a percentage.

INCLUDE SELF-GOVERNMENT, BUT TELL THEM NOT TO FORGET MY "CUT."

Charter

2. PROPRIETARY COLONIES (P)
The King gave charters to individuals (usually his friends or relatives) to colonize and govern. He claimed a percentage of their profits.

HE'S A PROPRIETOR

OH --- I THOUGHT HE WAS A QUAKER

WM. PENN.

3. ROYAL COLONIES (R)
By 1775 most of the colonies had become royal colonies, with a governor appointed by the king.

SO THE KING THOUGHT YOU'D JUST LOVE BEING GOVERNOR...

NEW YORK OR BUST

	COLONY	FOUNDED	REASONS	CHARTERED	STATUS in 1775
1.	VIRGINIA	1607, Virginia Company	Economic	C—1606, 09, 12	Royal. since 1624
	PLYMOUTH	1620, Pilgrims (Separatists)	Religious	None	Merged w/ Mass., 1691
	MAINE	1623, Fernando Gorges	Economic	P—1639	Bought by Mass., 1677
2.	NEW HAMPSHIRE	1623, John Mason	Religious, Political	R—1679	Royal
3.	NEW YORK	1624, Dutch West India Company	Economic		
		1664, English, Duke of York	Economic	P—1664	Royal, since 1685
4.	MASSACHUSETTS	1630, Puritans	Religious	C—1629	Royal, since 1691
5.	MARYLAND	1634, Lord Baltimore	Religious	P—1632	Proprietary
6.	RHODE ISLAND	1636, Roger Williams	Religious	C—1644, 1663	Self-governing
7.	CONNECTICUT	1636, Thomas Hooker	Religious, Economic	C—1662	Self-governing
8.	DELAWARE	1638, Swedes; 1664, English	Economic	None	Proprietary
9.	NORTH CAROLINA	1663, eight English nobles	Economic	P—1663	Royal, since 1729
10.	SOUTH CAROLINA	1663, eight English nobles	Economic	P—1663	Royal, since 1729
11.	NEW JERSEY	1664, John Berkeley, Geo. Carteret	Economic,	None	Royal, since 1702
12.	PENNSYLVANIA	1682, William Penn	Religious	P—1681	Proprietary
13.	GEORGIA	1733, James Oglethorpe	Economic, Political	P—1732	Royal, since 1752

HERE'S SOMETHING TO THINK ABOUT....

Our colonial history as British subjects—169 years—is almost as long as our 200+ year history as a republic.

1607   1776   1990s

To understand the early ideas and events that shaped our American character, we'll explore America's intriguing colonial adventures—beginning with JAMESTOWN, VIRGINIA.

"In the beginning, all America was Virginia." —William Byrd

1492　　　　1607　　　　　　　　　　　　　　　　　　　　　　2000

VIRGINIA　Jamestown

JAMESTOWN, VIRGINIA—England's first permanent colony in America—was planned as a trading settlement by the Virginia Company of London (a joint stock company).

The purpose: to make money for the 650 investors who each paid twelve pounds, ten shillings per share for stock in the Virginia Company.

Adventurers—the investors were called, because they were venturing (risking) their money (capital) to make more money (profit).

WE CAN PROFIT FROM THE GOLD, FURS, LUMBER, AND FISH....

THAT WILL BE WORTH VENTURING OUR CAPITAL!

VA. COMPANY Adventurers

The Virginia Company's charter, granted by King James I, created Virginia's boundaries along points of the 34th and 41st parallels, running "from sea to sea," west and northwest.

No one had any idea of the distance from sea to sea. Virginia's indefinite western border caused problems later on.

VIRGINIA

1607—The Virginia Company's recruits (105 men) sailed to Virginia on three ships: Susan Constant, Discovery, and Godspeed. They landed April 26, welcomed by the spring fragrance of wild strawberries.

ENGLAND　FRANCE　SPAIN　PORTUGAL
NORTH AMERICA　Jamestown
WEST INDIES
Atlantic Ocean
AFRICA
SOUTH AMERICA

The men settled 30 miles up the James River on a marshy peninsula (defensible against Indians and Spanish raiders). They would be governed by a council of seven men, designated among them by the Virginia Company.

Chesapeake Bay
Jamestown
James River

Sir George Percy, wrote: "There wee landed and discovered...Faire meadowes and goodly tall Trees: with such Fresh-waters running through the woods, as I was almost ravished at the first sight thereof...."

LET'S NAME OUR SETTLEMENT "JAMESTOWN" IN HONOR OF THE KING.

THERE GOES THE NEIGHBORHOOD!

Virginia became a seedling of liberty, for in the Virginia Company's charter King James I granted Virginians "the same liberties...as if they had been abiding and born within this our realm of England."

THIS LITTLE TREE IS WORTH WATERING.

ISN'T THAT A SEEDLING FROM THE ENGLISH TREE OF LIBERTY!

JAMESTOWN, VIRGINIA

James River

The Virginians built a fort, dug for gold, and searched for a passage to China. However, they failed to plant enough crops for food; by winter, famine and disease killed all but 38 men.

1608—<u>Captain John Smith</u>, 27-year-old swashbuckling soldier-of-fortune, took charge and saved the colony by imposing a WORK ETHIC. (Half the settlers were gentlemen, unaccustomed to work.)

Rough work blistered the gentlemen's tender hands, causing them to swear loudly. Smith stopped the swearing by pouring cold water into an offender's sleeve—one can per swearing.

Meanwhile, <u>Powhatan</u>, Supreme Chieftain of the Powhatan Confederacy (about 9,000 Indians), discussed the Englishmen at Werowocomocotook, his village fourteen miles from Jamestown.

<u>Indian Princess Pocahontas</u>, his thirteen-year-old daughter, befriended the Englishmen—after saving Captain John Smith's life when the Powhatan Indians had captured him. This friendship began a period of good relations called the Peace of Pocahontas.

1612—Tobacco became Virginia's "gold" when <u>John Rolfe</u> discovered a new way to cure it. Smoking became the rage in England, and the Virginia Company prospered by exporting this cash crop.

1614—John Rolfe married Princess Pocahontas, who had become a Christian, taken the name Lady Rebecca, and begun wearing English clothes. The Virginia Company brought them to London in 1616 to promote a Virginia lottery and introduce Princess Pocahontas to King James I.

Pocahontas' death in 1617 ended the Peace of Pocahontas.

1618—SEEDS OF DEMOCRACY AND CAPITALISM

The Virginia Company wanted more laborers for tobacco production in order to increase profits. So to entice more settlers from England, it extended Virginia's

1) political freedom through a representative legislature (assembly): the HOUSE OF BURGESSES, and

2) economic freedom through private ownership of land: the HEADRIGHT SYSTEM.

THE BEGINNING OF SELF-GOVERNMENT—The House Of Burgesses became the colonies' first representative legislative assembly (and in 1790 a model for the U.S. House of Representatives). "Burgess" (or "burger") is an old English term meaning free citizen.

Each Virginia district elected two men to serve in the assembly which, along with the company-appointed governor and council, made laws for the colony.

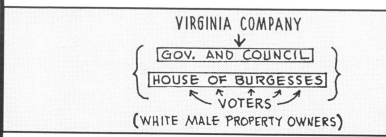

VIRGINIA COMPANY
↓
{ GOV. AND COUNCIL
HOUSE OF BURGESSES }
↑ ↑ VOTERS ↑ ↑
(WHITE MALE PROPERTY OWNERS)

By 1698 the House of Burgesses won the exclusive right to make tax laws, assuring Virginians of a bulwark of freedom: NO TAXATION WITHOUT REPRESENTATION.

The HOUSE OF BURGESSES met for the first time in July 1619 at Jamestown, Virginia. Five generations later, in 1776, leaders from the Virginia assembly, grown accustomed to political freedom, would lead the colonies to independence from England.

The HEADRIGHT SYSTEM allowed private ownership of land (as opposed to company ownership). Each pre-1616 settler received 100 acres of free land. Each thereafter received 50 acres, plus 50 acres for every person he brought from England.

I LIKE THIS CAPITALIST SYSTEM. I NOW HAVE ITS THREE BASIC PARTS: THE RIGHT TO OWN PROPERTY, THE RIGHT TO WORK AS I PLEASE, AND THE RIGHT TO MAKE A PROFIT.

1619—Ironically, at the same time the Virginia Company extended political and economic freedom to the colony, two groups not included in these freedoms were brought to Virginia.

Ninety adventurous women arrived in 1619, sent by the Virginia Company as wives for the Jamestown settlers. Each groom paid 120 pounds of tobacco for his bride's passage.

THAT YOUR NEW BRIDE?

YEAH – SHE'S WORTH HER WEIGHT IN TOBACCO.

WELL, THANKS A LOT!

Twenty kidnapped Africans were sold to the Jamestown settlers by the captain of a Dutch ship. As indentured servants, they probably were freed after several years. But by the late 1600s black servitude turned into black slavery.

TAKE HEART. WE'LL BE FREE IN 25 YEARS.

YEAH, BUT I GOT A FUNNY FEELING ABOUT WHERE ALL THIS IS HEADING....

SO YOU SEE, AMERICA'S PROGRESS TOWARD FREEDOM WAS UNEVEN, SOMETIMES 1 STEP FORWARD AND 2 BACK.

INDENTURED SERVANTS AND SLAVES

The headright system encouraged Virginians to acquire land (50 acres per person) by importing people from England who would sign a contract for three to seven years of servitude (unpaid labor), in exchange for their passage to America. After their servitude, they were free.

Many of these contract-servants were illiterate and could not read their contract. To protect them against fraud, duplicate contracts were notched, or indented. If there were any contract disputes, the notches, or indentures, had to match.

About 75 percent of Virginia's settlers in the 1600s came as indentured servants. Those surviving a high death toll (from hunger, disease, and abuse) sometimes settled on the frontier where land was more plentiful. Other colonies (mostly southern) also used indentured servants.

Africans in Virginia—at first treated as indentured servants with longer terms—were enslaved between 1650 and 1700. White indentured servants outnumbered black slaves in Virginia until 1700.

indentured servant—a person who exchanged 3 to 7 years of servitude for passage to America.

slave—a person who was bought and sold as property and forced to work.

ONLY TWO MORE YEARS AND I'M FREE!

LUCKY YOU! I'M BOUND FOR LIFE.

INDENTURED SERVANT

SLAVE

In 1622 tragedy struck Virginia!

ON GOOD FRIDAY POWHATAN INDIANS, LED BY OPECHANCANOUGH, MASSACRED 347 VIRGINIANS (¼ THE COLONY) IN A NOONTIME, SURPRISE ATTACK.

THE COLONISTS' RETALIATION, ALONG WITH DISEASE, TOOK ITS TOLL: BY 1700 ONLY ABOUT 1,000 OF 9,000 POWHATAN INDIANS SURVIVED.

1624—King James I, who disliked representative government, used the massacre and the Virginia Company's financial problems as an excuse to revoke the Company's charter and make Virginia a royal colony. He dismissed the House of Burgesses, but the members met anyway. In 1639 his son King Charles I reinstated the House of Burgesses.

Virginians prospered under royal rule, but they guarded their right to legislative self government.

THE COMPANY'S MADE A MESS OF THINGS! FROM NOW ON I'LL APPOINT THE GOVERNOR AND COUNCIL.

YES, SIRE!

KING

~~VIRGINIA COMPANY~~
↓
GOV. AND COUNCIL
HOUSE OF BURGESSES
↑ ← VOTERS → ↑
(WHITE MALE PROPERTY OWNERS)

Sir William Berkeley served as one of the first royally appointed governors of Virginia (1642). Although an able ruler, he had no use for liberty.

I THANK GOD THERE ARE NO FREE SCHOOLS, NOR PRINTING ... FOR LEARNING HAS BROUGHT DISOBEDIENCE, AND HERESY, AND SECTS INTO THE WORLD, AND PRINTING HAS DIVULGED THEM, AND LIBELS AGAINST THE BEST GOVERNMENT. GOD KEEP US FROM BOTH.

In the 1670s frontier settlers in western Virginia rebelled against the autocratic rule of Governor Berkeley. He levied high taxes, while denying frontiersmen a voice in the government and protection against invading Indians.

WHAT SEEMS TO BE THE PROBLEM?

1676—BACON'S REBELLION

Nathaniel Bacon, a frontier planter, led the frontiersmen in a rebellion against Governor Berkeley, driving him from Jamestown and burning the town. When Bacon died of a sudden illness, so did the rebellion. However, King Charles II replaced Berkeley, restoring harmony to the colony.

DEAR BILL you're Fired!

"The...large plantation...fostered habits of self-reliance in individual men; it assisted in promoting an intense love of liberty;
it strengthened the ties of family and kinship at the very time that it cultivated the spirit of general hospitality."—Phillip Bruce

1492   1700   1800   2000

TIDEWATER PLANTATIONS AND TIDEWATER GENTRY

Geography determines history.
Virginia's rich coastal plain, fingered with deep rivers, led to an agricultural economy and a rural society.
During the 1700s Virginians spread upland from Jamestown and developed large tobacco farms along the rivers.
The farms, often covering thousands of acres, were called TIDEWATER PLANTATIONS and their owners, TIDEWATER GENTRY.

Tidewater describes the ocean tides which swelled the rivers and made them navigable for sea-going ships. Ships could sail inland 80 to 100 miles —as far as the fall line, that is, the beginning of the foothills leading to the Appalachian Mountains. The foothills region is called the Piedmont.

Tidewater plantations: The choice land, of course, was along the tidewater rivers because cash crops, mainly tobacco, could be loaded directly on ships headed for England, cutting out the cost of middlemen.

Tidewater gentry, although a minority compared to small farmers, emerged as an aristocratic ruling class that dominated Virginia politics. Power remained for generations in the hands of families—such as the Byrds, Carters, Lees, Randolphs, and Harrisons—in part by the law of primogeniture: inheritance of an entire estate by the eldest son (a law Thomas Jefferson led Virginia to abandon in 1776).

Today, you can visit many James River plantations, including those of U.S. Presidents Benjamin Harrison, William Henry Harrison, and John Tyler.

TIDEWATER PLANTATIONS were self-contained economic units resembling small towns. Nearly everything consumed was produced on site by slaves, without whose labor plantations couldn't have existed. Each plantation had its own dock, where ships unloaded goods planters had ordered and loaded tobacco for sale in England. Virginians felt more in touch with England than New England.

Rural isolation had its effects. There being no public schools, planters educated their children in England or at home with hired tutors. Visits from relatives and friends were major events and hospitality became a southern trait. Neighboring planters used the rivers as transportation in visiting. Highlights of the year came with spring and fall trips to Williamsburg. Let's go there now.

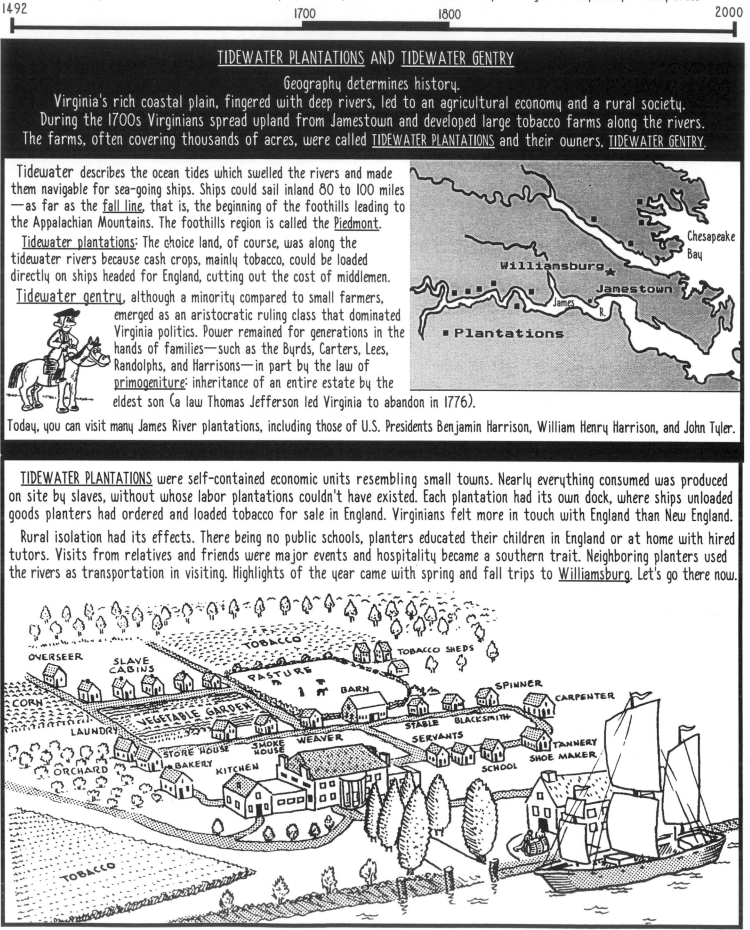

❖ VIRGINIA: SEEDLING OF LIBERTY ❖

1492   1699   1780   2000

WILLIAMSBURG—In 1699 Virginians moved the capital from Jamestown to Middle Plantation, a small village seven miles away, and renamed it WILLIAMSBURG, for King William III. Governor Francis Nicholson designed Williamsburg as a beautiful new city that would reflect Virginia's importance as the largest English colony (1700 population: 70,000). It remained the capital until 1780.

Williamsburg's population of 2,000 doubled twice annually at Publick Times when the legislature and courts were in session. Every spring and fall Virginians, a rural, agricultural people, congregated in the colony's only city for a few weeks of business, politics, shopping—and a whirlwind social season of fairs, balls, theater, music, and horseracing.

For 81 years Williamsburg served as a cosmopolitan center of learning, government, business, and religion for Virginia's plantation gentry, many of whom would lead the American Revolution in 1776 and form the American republic. Here were shaped the public lives of men who shaped American history—and thus your own life. You will read of them later, but now—imagine them here in Williamsburg as college students and/or burgesses (members of the House of Burgesses).

Colonial Williamsburg

SCENES AT WILLIAMSBURG, VIRGINIA, 1760–80

■ GOVERNOR'S PALACE—George Washington (a burgess for 15 years) dancing three hours non-stop at fancy royal balls; college student Thomas Jefferson dining and playing in musical quartets with the royal governor; Jefferson and Patrick Henry each living here as governor, following American independence.

■ COLLEGE OF WILLIAM AND MARY—Students Thomas Jefferson, James Monroe, and John Marshall reading John Locke's Enlightenment ideas about natural law in human society: the right to life, liberty, and property.

■ BRUTON PARISH CHURCH—(Anglicanism was the official religion of Virginia.) Burgesses James Madison Richard Henry Lee, George Mason, and George Washington worshipping; Washington also serving as vestryman.

■ DUKE OF GLOUCESTER STREET—Burgess Thomas Jefferson jogging his daily mile down the broad, nearly-mile-long avenue.

■ HOUSE OF BURGESSES, CAPITOL BUILDING— 1765—Burgess Patrick Henry thunderously protesting the Stamp Act; 1776—Burgesses voting for independence.

Today, you can visit Williamsburg and experience life as it was in the 1700s, thanks to the generosity of John D. Rockefeller, Jr. who, in the 1920s, restored Williamsburg to its colonial splendor—and to the vision of the Reverend W.A.R. Goodwin, rector of Bruton Parish Church, who inspired him to do so.

45

1776–83: REVOLUTIONARY WAR—Virginians in the House of Burgesses and the Continental Congress spearheaded the colonies' struggle for independence from Britain. Thomas Jefferson wrote the Declaration of Independence, and George Washington won the war as commander in chief of the Continental Army.

FROM JAMESTOWN TO YORKTOWN—In one of the great ironies of history, the British in 1781 lost their North American colonial empire at the Battle of Yorktown—12 miles from Jamestown where they had launched it in 1607.

THE SEEDLING TREE OF LIBERTY HAD TAKEN ROOT IN VIRGINIA SOIL.

[present-day boundaries]

VIRGINIA
Richmond ★ — Williamsburg — Jamestown

STATEHOOD (western boundary variable until 1863)

1776—Virginia wrote a state constitution and became an independent commonwealth. The militia forced Lord Dunmore, the royal governor, to leave Virginia.

1776–79—Patrick Henry served as governor.

1779–80—Thomas Jefferson served as governor.

1780—The capital was moved to Richmond.

1788—Virginia ratified the United States Constitution

1861—Virginia seceded from the Union, joined the Confederate States of America, and became a major battleground in the Civil War.

1861—Richmond became the capital of the Confederate States of America

1870—Virginia was admitted back into the Union.

Chesapeake Bay

Richmond

Williamsburg · Yorktown · Jamestown

· Plantations

UNITED STATES PRESIDENTS FROM VIRGINIA

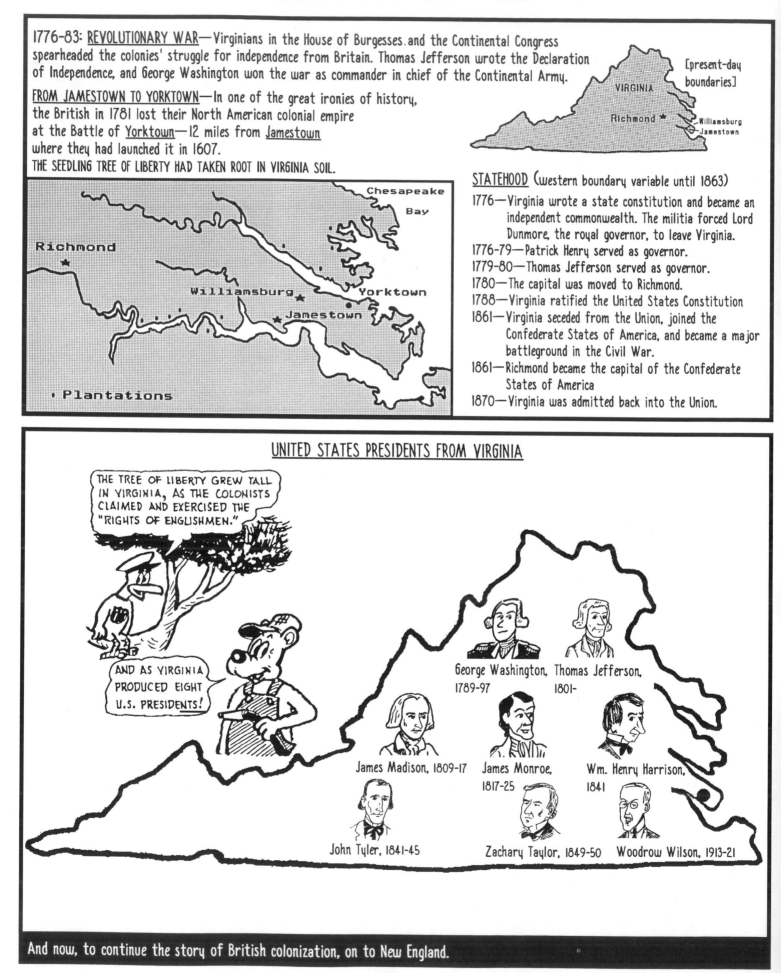

THE TREE OF LIBERTY GREW TALL IN VIRGINIA, AS THE COLONISTS CLAIMED AND EXERCISED THE "RIGHTS OF ENGLISHMEN."

AND AS VIRGINIA PRODUCED EIGHT U.S. PRESIDENTS!

George Washington, 1789-97

Thomas Jefferson, 1801-

James Madison, 1809-17

James Monroe, 1817-25

Wm. Henry Harrison, 1841

John Tyler, 1841-45

Zachary Taylor, 1849-50

Woodrow Wilson, 1913-21

And now, to continue the story of British colonization, on to New England.

"They knew they were pilgrimes, and looked not much on those things, but lift up their eyes to the heavens, their dearest country."
—William Bradford, second governor of Plymouth

1492   1620   2000

pilgrim—one who makes a relgious journey

In contrast to Jamestown, a business venture, Plymouth Colony was founded for religious reasons. On September 6, 1620, the Mayflower sailed from Plymouth, England, bringing 102 English men, women, and children to found

PLYMOUTH COLONY IN MASSACHUSETTS, the 2nd permanent English colony in America.

About 35 were Puritan Pilgrims from Scrooby, England, who—after a decade in Holland— were seeking religious freedom in America. These Puritans are called Pilgrims because of their religious journey. They also are called Separatists because they were separating from the Anglican Church.

The rest on board were Anglicans (including John Alden, Priscilla Mullins, and Miles Standish) seeking economic opportunity.

Financed by 70 London merchants, the group had obtained a land grant from the Virginia Company. But a storm blew them off course—to Massachusetts instead of northern Virginia. They anchored off Cape Cod on November 10, 1620.

LUCKILY WE HAVE A MAP OF THIS AREA. IT WAS DRAWN BY CAPTAIN JOHN SMITH IN 1614, WHEN HE EXPLORED THE COAST FROM MAINE TO CAPE COD.

HE NAMED THE WHOLE AREA "NEW ENGLAND" AND THAT INDIAN VILLAGE ACROSS THE BAY, "PLYMOUTH."

PLYMOUTH HAS A WIDE HARBOR. LET'S GO EXPLORE IT.

A problem arose. The Pilgrims were outside the Virginia Company's jurisdiction, so they had no government or laws. And the Anglicans (upset at missing Virginia) threatened mutiny against the Pilgrims.

HEY! WE'RE BEYOND REACH OF THE LAW!

GREAT- WE CAN THROW BIG PARTIES, AND SO ON ....

HAVE YOU TAKEN A SERIOUS LOOK AT THAT WILDERNESS?

So, still aboard ship, Pilgrim leaders William Bradford and William Brewster invited all 41 males—Puritan Pilgrims and Anglicans alike, regardless of religious and class differences— to sign the Mayflower Compact. (Women had few legal rights, so they were excluded.)

THIS IS AN AGREEMENT TO BE SELF-GOVERNING. ALL MEN CAN ENACT LAWS AND ELECT OFFICIALS — AND EVERYONE WILL ABIDE BY THE WILL OF THE MAJORITY.

SOUNDS FAIR TO ME.

THE MAYFLOWER COMPACT

IN THE NAME OF GOD, AMEN. WE WHOSE NAMES ARE UNDERWRITTEN, THE LOYALL SUBJECTS OF OUR DREAD SOVERAIGNE LORD KING JAMES, HAVING UNDERTAKEN FOR YE GLORIE OF GOD, AND ADVANCEMENT OF YE CHRISTIAN FAITH, AND YE HONOUR OF OUR KING AND COUNTRIE, A VOYAGE TO PLANT YE FIRST COLONIE IN YE NORTHERN PARTS OF VIRGINIA, DOE... SOLEMNLY & MUTUALLY IN YE PRESENCE OF GOD, AND ONE OF ANOTHER, COVENANT & COMBINE OURSELVES TOGEATHER INTO A CIVILL BODY POLITICK... TO ENACTE, CONSTITUTE, AND FRAME SUCH JUST & EQUALL LAWES, ORDINANCES, ACTS, CONSTITUTIONS, & OFFICES FOR YE GENERALL GOOD OF YE COLONIE, UNTO WHICH WE PROMISE ALL DUE SUBMISSION AND OBEDIENCE.

The Pilgrims signed first—and waited. Would the Anglicans sign or mutiny? Finally, Captain Miles Standish, in charge of military defense, led the other Anglicans in signing.

SURE, I'LL SIGN IT. THIS MAY BECOME A HISTORIC DOCUMENT.

YOU'RE QUITE RIGHT, CAPTAIN STANDISH.

America's first adventure in democracy had begun. The men immediately elected John Carver governor, the first democratically elected governor in America.

THE MYSTERY OF PLYMOUTH

The Pilgrims went ashore to explore Plymouth and found the Indian village deserted. WHERE WERE THE INDIANS? Only their drying corn fields remained.

WE MIGHT AS WELL SETTLE HERE AND HELP OURSELVES TO THESE CROPS. LOOK'S LIKE IT'S MEANT TO BE.

On Christmas day, 1620, the Pilgrims began building their settlement of rude huts. Sleet and snow and disease took their toll. About half the group died that winter.

I DON'T KNOW ABOUT YOU, PRUDENCE, BUT I'M GETTING DISCOURAGED.

M-ME TOO.

Then on March 16, 1621, an astonishing event occurred that helped save the colony: Samoset, an Abnaki Indian from Maine, strolled into Plymouth and welcomed the settlers in English.

HELLO, ENGLISHMEN!

HUH?

THEY THOUGHT HE'D BE TALKING ALGONQUIN OR SOMETHING.

Samoset had learned English while sailing the Maine coast with English captains. He now revealed the mystery of Plymouth.

Plymouth was once an Indian village of about 2,000, named Pawtuxet. In 1617 a great plague [perhaps smallpox*] killed all its people—except my friend Squanto, who earlier had been captured by an English sea captain and sold as a slave in Spain. He escaped and went to England, where he learned English. In 1619 he sailed back to America, only to find his people gone and his village Pawtuxet deserted. He was grief-stricken.
Squanto now lives with Chief Massasoit and the Wampanoag Indians on Narragansett Bay. I will bring him to see you.

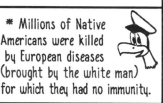

* Millions of Native Americans were killed by European diseases (brought by the white man) for which they had no immunity.

When Squanto arrived, he befriended the Pilgrims. He taught them survival skills, such as how to plant corn (a New World plant) and trap game. He lived with them and even adopted their religion.

HERE'S MY NEW CASSETTE ON HOW TO FARM IN AMERICA.

?

They were amazed that Squanto had lived in their homeland and spoke English. He became their interpreter and arranged a peace treaty with the Wampanoag Indians.

THANKSGIVING

The New England autumn brought a good 20-acre corn harvest, so the grateful Pilgrims (about sixty by then) set aside a day for feasting and giving thanks to God.

They had invited the Wampanoags, and Chief Massasoit arrived with 90 hungry Indians!

☆ ☆ ☆

(In 1863 President Abraham Lincoln proclaimed Thanksgiving a national holiday.)

Chief Massasoit and the 90 Wampanoags had such a good time that they stayed on for three days of feasting and games of skill and chance.

THEY'RE HAVING A THANKSGIVING FEAST. (GULP) NOW WE KNOW WHAT HAPPENED TO UNCLE LOUIE....

PLYMOUTH VILLAGE: A FREE ENTERPRISE ADVENTURE

By 1627 Plymouth was a thriving village of about 200. At first the settlers had owned land collectively, but when complaints arose because some worked harder than others, private ownership of land was allowed (1623), making all hands very industrious. Plymouth had learned the lesson of Jamestown: people work harder when they own their own property. By working hard at farming, fishing, and fur trading, the Pilgrims earned enough money to buy out their London investors (1627). They became self-supporting and independent.

In 1622 the Pilgrims heard of the Virginia massacre by Powhatan Indians, and they built a fort around the village.

A SELF-GOVERNING COMMONWEALTH

By 1643 Plymouth Colony had 10 towns. Each elected two representatives to a legislature, called the General Court, which enacted colonial laws.

And each held democratic town meetings, where all freemen could discuss and vote on local affairs.

In 1621 Plymouth Colony elected 32-year old William Bradford as governor. A man of energy, courage, and wit, he served for 30 years

A SELF-GOVERNING CHURCH

Based on the democratic Reformation doctrine "priesthood of every believer," each church congregation was independent, holding yearly elections to choose its pastor and other officers. This democratic practice in church government became the model for New England's local civil government, the town meeting.

Plymouth and other New England towns lived at peace with New England Indians until the 1670's, except for a defensive attack against the Pequot Indians in 1637.

But by 1675 the New England population of 40,000—double that of the Indian population—had taken so much Indian land that Chief Massasoit's heir Metacomet, called "King Philip" by the Puritans for his princely ways, warned:

Little remains of my ancestors' domain. I am resolved not to see the day when I have no country.

KING PHILIP

AND THEN CAME KING PHILIP'S WAR: 1675-76.

IN 1675 TRAGEDY STRUCK PLYMOUTH AND OTHER NEW ENGLAND COLONIES. KING PHILIP (METACOMET) LED THE WAMPANOAG FEDERATION IN WARFARE AGAINST PLYMOUTH AND OTHER NEW ENGLAND COLONIES. WHY?

I DON'T GET IT. FIFTY-FOUR YEARS AGO THEY WERE REAL CHUMMY AT THANKSGIVING.

WELL, THE INDIANS WERE ANGRY AT LOSING THEIR LAND! THEY KILLED HUNDREDS OF SETTLERS AND DESTROYED MANY TOWNS.

The New England Confederation, a colonial defense league (1643-84), sent 1,000 soldiers to fight the Indians. In 1676 they killed King Philip and won the war. Of 90 New England towns, 40 were burned and 12 destroyed.

But the Indians' loss was greater: The land of their ancestors now clearly belonged to the white man. Such would be the story for the next two centuries.

• Towns attacked by Indians
INDIAN TRIBES
PLYMOUTH COLONY

In 1691 Plymouth Colony (pop. 7,000) was incorporated by its larger Puritan neighbor: Massachusetts Bay Colony, founded in 1630.

MASSACHUSETTS BAY COLONY

Today, we still honor the Pilgrims for their faith and courage—and for nurturing the American Tree of Liberty with their democratic practices.

TREE OF LIBERTY

YES... SOMEONE GOT IT OFF TO A FINE START LONG AGO.

WHAT A NEAT TREE!

"...and as one small candle may light a thousand; so the light here kindled hath shone unto many, yea...to our whole nation."
—Governor William Bradford

YOU CAN READ FIRST-HAND ABOUT THE PILGRIMS IN HISTORY OF PLYMOUTH PLANTATION, WRITTEN IN 1647 BY WILLIAM BRADFORD, GOVERNOR OF PLYMOUTH COLONY FOR 30 YEARS.

1492   1630   **THE PURITANS' HOLY COMMONWEALTH**   2000

Within a decade of founding Plymouth, the English Pilgrims, or Separatists, had new neighbors: English Puritans. What brought them over?

Panel 1: KING CHARLES I disliked English Puritans because they insisted on purifying the Anglican church (unlike the Separatists who cut all ties). When he ruled without Parliament (1629-1640), he harrassed these dissenters, or non-conformists, aiming to "harrie them out of the land."

ARCHBISHOP LAUD, LET'S MAKE THOSE PURITANS CONFORM TO THE CHURCH OF ENGLAND.

LEAVE IT TO ME, SIRE.

Panel 2: The result: a Great Migration of more than 20,000 English Puritans to New England between 1629 and 1640.

ENGLAND · BOSTON · PLYMOUTH · JAMESTOWN · ATLANTIC OCEAN · SPAIN

Among the first to migrate were Puritans who in 1629 formed the Massachusetts Bay Company, a trading company.

Panel 3: In 1630 the Massachusetts Bay Company Puritans sailed 1,000 strong on 17 ships into Boston Harbor to found the Massachusetts Bay Colony. With Boston a hub, they spread to several small communities.

MASSACHUSETTS BAY COLONY · Boston ☆ · Plymouth · PLYMOUTH COLONY

Panel 4: Led by John Winthrop, an English lawyer, they brought their Company charter with them and transformed the Company into a self-governing commonwealth, based on Puritan religious ideas. Winthrop served as governor for 12 years.

WE'LL BUILD A "CITY ON A HILL" — A MODEL CHRISTIAN COMMUNITY FOR ALL ANGLICANS TO COPY.

YEA! HEAR, HEAR! RIGHT ON!

Panel 5: ONLY THE MEN ABLE TO INTERPRET GOD'S WILL SHOULD BE IN CHARGE.

AND THAT MEANS ALL OF US, GOVERNOR!

ASST. ASST.

Governor Winthrop distrusted democracy. He thought God's will—not the people's—should determine laws. So he misrepresented the charter to the colonists, saying only he and 18 assistants could make laws and govern.

Panel 6: But in 1634 Puritans from Watertown—protesting taxation without representation—asked to read the charter for themselves. They made quite a discovery.

HEY! IT SAYS HERE THAT AS FREEMEN WE HAVE THE RIGHT TO MAKE THE LAWS FOR THE COLONY!

CHARTER for MASS. BAY

Panel 7: Winthrop reluctantly agreed to a representative assembly, the second in British America. Each town would elect two deputies to meet as a legislative body with the governor and assistants in the General Court.

VOTE FOR ME!

Panel 8: FREEMEN—ALL ADULT MALES, EXCEPT INDENTURED SERVANTS—WHO TOOK A LOYALTY OATH TO THE COLONY COULD VOTE ON DEPUTIES AND LOCAL ISSUES IN TOWN MEETINGS.

BUT ONLY FREEMEN WHO WERE CHURCH MEMBERS COULD ALSO VOTE FOR THE GOVERNOR AND ASSISTANTS. (AT FIRST MOST COLONISTS WERE CHURCH MEMBERS.)

? ? ? ?

Panel 9: The Puritans' church, based on the protestant doctrine, "priesthood of the believer," also had self-government. The name of the church, Congregational, reflects this democratic approach.

WE PURITANS ARE ACCUSTOMED TO SELF-GOVERNMENT BECAUSE OUR CHURCHES ARE DEMOCRATIC. MEMBERS OF THE CONGREGATION ELECT THEIR OWN MINISTERS AND OTHER OFFICIALS.

GREAT! CAN WE VOTE ON HOW LONG THE MINISTERS PREACH?

Church and state were closely entwined in Puritan Massachusetts.

The state's purpose, according to the Puritans, was to encourage a godly community by supporting the church.

The state government supported the church by:

1. requiring every person to attend church, whether a member or not,

"READ MY LIPS" — LET'S RAISE TAXES

2. requiring every town to support its church minister through taxes,

AHA!

3. enforcing moral codes, as well as "blue laws" that prohibited frivolity on Sunday (dancing, drinking, card-playing).

However, church and state were separate in these ways:
1. Ministers could not hold public office.
2. Public officials could not hold church offices.

REVEREND, I HAVE TO SHOW YOU SOMETHING...

MASS. LAWS

WATTS FOR GOVERNOR VOTE
ELECT Rev. W WATTS
VOTE WATTS
PAIN

The Puritans made the Congregational church the established (official) church of the colony. They persecuted other sects.

THOSE PURITANS HAVE MADE CONGREGATIONALISM THE OFFICIAL STATE CHURCH. THAT MEANS IT'S TAX-SUPPORTED.

AND THEY RAN THE BAPTISTS OUT OF TOWN BECAUSE THEY DON'T BELIEVE IN STATE CHURCHES.

AND I HEAR THEY HANGED 4 QUAKERS FOR THEIR BELIEFS.

By 1684 Massachusetts operated as an almost independent republic, ignoring even England's trade laws; so King James II revoked its charter and made it a royal colony.

In 1686 England sought greater control by creating the Dominion of New England (including colonies from Maine to Delaware), governed by Sir Edmund Andros. The autocratic governor dismissed Massachusetts' assembly, restricted town meetings, and introduced Anglican worship.

THOSE TOWN MEETINGS ARE SEED PLOTS OF DEMOCRACY!

LOVE YOUR PERM, GOV. ANDROS.

In 1688-89 England's Glorious Revolution dethroned despotic King James II, and the Dominion of New England collapsed. Angry Puritans turned on Andros, who fled—disguised as a woman. Betrayed by his boots, he was captured and imprisoned.

In 1691 Massachusetts received a new royal charter, ending Puritan rule with:

1. a royally appointed rather than an elected governor,

2. voting rights based on property rather than religion,

3. incorporation of Plymouth Colony,

4. freedom of worship for all Protestants. (However, the Congregational church remained the established church until 1820.)

1692—Belief in witches, a common European superstition for centuries, also infected the colonies. Massachusetts' unsettling times helped spawn mass hysteria in Salem, where 19 women and one man accused as witches were executed. When Governor Phipps' wife and other prominent people were accused, the Salem witch hunt stopped.

WITCH LIST

And now, on to other New England colonies.

HERE IS A PARADOX: THE PURITANS CAME TO AMERICA FOR RELIGIOUS LIBERTY; BUT THEY DID NOT EXTEND THIS LIBERTY TO OTHERS, WHOSE BELIEFS DIFFERED FROM THEIR OWN.

CONSEQUENTLY, SOME DISSENTERS (THOSE WHO DIFFER) FOUNDED OTHER COLONIES IN NEW ENGLAND. HERE'S THEIR STORY...

21 ⟺ NEW ENGLAND: RHODE ISLAND, CONNECTICUT, AND NEW HAMPSHIRE ⟺

1492   1623   1679   2000

1636—RHODE ISLAND

In 1636 Roger Williams, a Separatist minister, was banished from Massachusetts for his belief in separation of church and state and for saying that the colonists should have paid the Indians for their land.

AND DON'T COME BACK!

MASSACHUSETTS

After wintering with the Narragansett Indians, he bought land from them and settled Providence. Later he founded the colony of Rhode Island, creating a democratic government with religious freedom and separation of church and state.

??

WELCOME TO RHODE ISLAND
CONGREGATIONALIST CHURCH
QUAKER ASSEMBLY →
BAPTIST CHURCH →
MISCELLANEOUS STRAIGHT AHEAD

State religions have prevailed throughout history. Williams challenged America to an adventure in freedom few in the world have dared: the freedom of religious belief.

ALL RELIGIONS, BE THEY TURKISH, JEWISH, PAGANIST OR ANTICHRISTIAN, MUST BE TOLERATED. NO PERSON IN THIS COLONY SHALL BE MOLESTED OR QUESTIONED FOR THE MATTER OF HIS CONSCIENCE TO GOD. WE MUST PART WITH LAND AND LIVES BEFORE WE PART WITH SUCH A JEWEL.

Roger Williams set the precedent for freedom of religion and separation of church and state, later supported by Thomas Jefferson and James Madison and guaranteed by the First Amendment of the U.S. Constitution.

• HALL OF FAME •
ROGER WILLIAMS

The American Hall of Fame honors him for this unique contribution to human freedom—your freedom to think and believe as you choose.

In 1638 Anne Hutchinson joined Williams in Rhode Island and founded Portsmouth. Banished from Massachusetts for teaching that God spoke to people directly, not just through the Bible, she also had violated a belief about woman's role.

AND ANOTHER THING—THE BIBLE SAYS WOMEN ARE NOT TO SPEAK PUBLICLY.

1636—CONNECTICUT

In 1636 Thomas Hooker—and other Puritans who disagreed with Massachusetts' requirement of church membership for voting—settled the fertile Connecticut River valley.

BUT HOW WILL WE EVER TEACH THE CHILDREN TO SPELL CONNECTICUT?

The Fundamental Orders of Connecticut, written by Connecticut Puritans in 1639, became America's first written constitution. It created a democratic government, with voting rights based on property ownership rather than religious beliefs.

YOU'RE GOING TO VOTE FOR GOVERNOR? YOU HAVEN'T BEEN TO CHURCH IN WEEKS!

SO WHAT? I OWN A FARM AND SOME LIVESTOCK!

1623—NEW HAMPSHIRE

In 1623 Fernando Gorges and John Mason received from the Council of New England a land grant between the Kennebec and Merrimac Rivers. Mason took the western half and named it New Hampshire; Gorges named his eastern half Maine. Neither man was very successful in establishing settlements.

During the 1630s Puritans from Massacusetts settled in both areas, and by the 1650s Massachusetts claimed the regions by right of settlement.

In 1679 NEW HAMPSHIRE became a colony.

In 1820 MAINE, never a separate colony, became a state.

MAINE (MASS.)
N.H.
MASS.
CONN.
RHODE ISLAND

"...[God] shall make us a praise and glory that men shall say of succeeding plantations, 'The Lord make it like that of <u>New England</u>.'"—John Winthrop, 1630
Puritanism declined after Massachusetts became a royal colony in 1691, but a 3-fold Puritan legacy makes John Winthrop's hope a reality.

1. DEMOCRATIC GOVERNMENT: RELIGIOUS AND POLITICAL

The Puritans were not democrats, but paradoxically, they carried the seeds of democracy in their Protestant religious doctrine, <u>"the priesthood of the believer,"</u> sometimes expressed as <u>"every person his own priest."</u> This belief—that individuals were capable of reading and interpreting the Bible for themselves, without any intervening authority—led to 1) individualism, 2) freedom of conscience, and 3) self-government in both church and state. In turn, Puritan self-government—based on a covenant (agreement) among men and deriving its powers from the consent of the governed—set the framework for American democracy.

CHURCH MEETING

Thomas Jefferson called New England towns "little republics, the best schools for political liberty the world ever saw."

By 1776 their "graduates" included leaders of American independence, such as Samuel Adams, John Adams, and John Hancock.

TOWN MEETING

2. FREE, PUBLIC EDUCATION

For centuries, only the wealthy few could go to school. Today, if you have learned to read, write, count, and think in a public school—free of charge—you can thank the Puritans. In the 1640s Massachusetts Puritans pioneered in establishing tax-supported public education, free and available to all. The other New England colonies quickly followed suit. Not until the 1830s, however, did other sections of the country have a state public school system. The South had none until after the Civil War.

What motivated the Puritans to so value learning?

Puritans emphasized intellect as well as emotion in their religion because they viewed education as a means to understanding the Bible. With "every person his own priest," each individual bore the awesome responsibility for his own salvation, which involved reading and interpreting the Bible. This made <u>literacy</u>—the ability to read and write—and <u>scholarship</u> (knowledge through study) essential. Samuel Willard explained, "Faith doth not...cast out reason, for there is nothing in religion contrary to it...." In the 1600s the majority of New England's ministers were graduates of Oxford and Cambridge Universities in England, and many were outstanding scholars—including John Cotton, said to be a walking library; Increase Mather, president of Harvard College (1685-1701); and his son Cotton Mather, author of 450 books.

Secular as well as religious reasons stirred Puritan interest in education. The Massachusetts Code of 1648 stated that, "...the good education of children is of singular...benefit to any Common-wealth." Specifically, it enabled them to read and understand the laws.

Scarcely five years after carving Boston from the wilderness, Massachusetts Puritans founded two educational institutions, which still exist today:

■ 1635—<u>Boston Latin School</u>, for boys preparing for college.

■ 1636—<u>Harvard College</u>, a private school to train ministers. As one Puritan wrote, "After God had carried us safe to New-England, one of the next things we longed...after was to advance learning and perpetuate it to prosperity; dreading to leave an illiterate ministry to the churches, when the present ministers shall lie in the dust."

Next, Massachusetts passed ground-breaking legislation:

■ 1642—<u>a law requiring families to teach their children to read</u>. This became the first such law in the English-speaking world.

■ 1647—<u>a law requiring that towns of 50+ families maintain a primary school</u> for girls and boys, and towns of 100+ families, a Latin grammar school for boys. Parents whose children did not attend were required to teach them to read at home, else pay a fine. In effect, juvenile illiteracy became illegal.

America's intellectual roots, established in free, public schools under local control, are a priceless Puritan legacy.

A person should have a calling, or vocation, "so he may Glorify God by doing Good for Others, and getting of Good for himself."—Cotton Mather

3. THE PROTESTANT WORK ETHIC: INDUSTRY+VIRTUE+FRUGALITY = SUCCESS

Do you feel guilty when you're not working—even if your work is finished?

Then you have experienced the PROTESTANT WORK ETHIC, perhaps our strongest Puritan legacy, and for 300 years the most influential force in shaping the American character. Here's what it all means.

Puritans faced a constant religious dilemma: "Am I saved or not? Will I go to heaven or not?"

The troubling question arose from the Protestant doctrine of predestination, set forth in the 1500s by John Calvin. According to Calvin a person, through free choice, could attain salvation from mankind's sinful state through faith in Jesus. However (here's the catch), the choice actually was pre-determined, or predestined, because God has known since creation the choice of every person.

And so, the unanswerable question: "Am I predestined for salvation?" New England Puritans relieved their anxiety by following John Calvin's advice:

> Glorify God as if you were saved.
> Then, if so, you'll go to heaven anyway when you die.
> If not, at least you made the world a better place.

And how might one glorify God? Through the following steps, which came to be called:

THE PROTESTANT WORK ETHIC

1) INDUSTRY—Work hard at your calling, or vocation, whether a day laborer or doctor.

2) VIRTUE—Be honest: maintain righteous conduct in all ways.

3) FRUGALITY—Spend money not on yourself (indulgence diverts you from glorifying God) but on charity and reinvestment in your work.

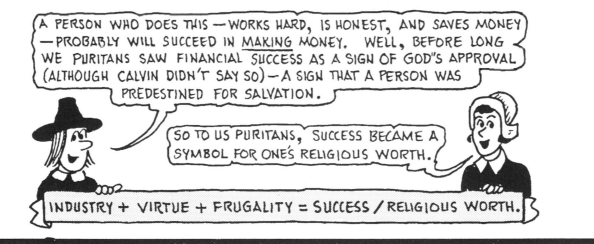

A PERSON WHO DOES THIS —WORKS HARD, IS HONEST, AND SAVES MONEY —PROBABLY WILL SUCCEED IN MAKING MONEY. WELL, BEFORE LONG WE PURITANS SAW FINANCIAL SUCCESS AS A SIGN OF GOD"S APPROVAL (ALTHOUGH CALVIN DIDN'T SAY SO) —A SIGN THAT A PERSON WAS PREDESTINED FOR SALVATION.

SO TO US PURITANS, SUCCESS BECAME A SYMBOL FOR ONE'S RELIGIOUS WORTH.

INDUSTRY + VIRTUE + FRUGALITY = SUCCESS / RELIGIOUS WORTH.

In the 1700s Benjamin Franklin gave "success" a secular rather than religious meaning. In this form, the Protestant Work Ethic has become a measure of the American character. Leave off any of the three parts, and one's character is questioned.

TO ME, SUCCESS IS A SYMBOL OF MORAL WORTH: CHARACTER.

INDUSTRY + VIRTUE + FRUGALITY = SUCCESS / CHARACTER

1492   1609   1684   2000

The Middle Colonies were all _proprietary_ colonies, given by the king to favored individuals who could dispose of the land as they wished, appoint officials, and make laws—in accordance with the laws of England and subject to their colonists' agreement.

Unlike the New England and Southern colonies, the Middle colonies had some non-English origins—such as the Dutch on the Hudson River, the Swedes on the Delaware River, the Germans in Pennsylvania—and were characterized by ethnic diversity and religious toleration. Rich soil led to commercial farming. With grain the chief crop, the Middle Colonies were called "Bread Colonies."

1624—NEW YORK: A DUTCH COLONY

1609—_Henry Hudson_, an English seaman hired by the Dutch, claimed the Hudson River for Holland.

1624—_The Dutch West India Company established the colony of New Netherland_ along the Hudson River valley to develop fur trading. It granted large estates to _patroons_, anyone bringing 50 settlers. Only the Van Rensselaer patroonship succeeded.

1626—_Dutch Governor Peter Minuit bought Manhattan Island_ from the Canarsie Indians for trinkets worth about $24. There the Dutch established a trading post, New Amsterdam; later named _New York City_, it became a thriving seaport.

WHAT!? YOU GAVE MY BEST TRINKETS FOR AN ISLAND?

The Dutch West India Co. encouraged settlers of many nationalities and faiths (although the Dutch Reformed Church was the official church). A visiting French priest observed:

MAY 1, 1643... DEAR DIARY: ON MY VISIT TO NEW NETHERLAND, I DISCOVERED THERE ARE 18 LANGUAGES SPOKEN THERE.

1664—NEW YORK: AN ENGLISH COLONY

1664—English King Charles II, desiring the land between Virginia and Massachusetts, made his brother _James, Duke of York_ (later, King James II), proprietor of New Netherland—if he could take it from the Dutch!

When James sent four ships to conquer New Netherland, the Dutch colonists ignored autocratic _Governor Peter Stuyvesant's_ order to resist. They surrendered and became an English colony—renamed New York—with all the rights of Englishmen.

Anglicanism became the official religion.

COME ON, LET'S FIGHT LIKE TRUE DUTCHMEN

OOPS! --WHERE DID EVERYBODY GO?

BYE NOW.

The Dutch lost New York to England, but they left their mark on America through:

famous people—Roosevelts, Vanderbilts;

words—fun, cookie, boss, yacht, yankee (from _Janke_, or _Johnny_, a Dutch term for New Englanders);

customs—Easter eggs and Santa Claus.

JUST THINK, ROOSEVELT, SOME OF OUR DESCENDANTS WILL LIKELY BECOME FAMOUS.

YES, CLAUS, IT'S HIGHLY POSSIBLE.

1664—NEW JERSEY

In 1664 the Duke of York gave land between the Hudson and Delaware rivers to two friends, John Berkeley and George Carteret, who named their colony New Jersey (after the Isle of Jersey in England). They divided their grant into East Jersey and West Jersey, and established religious and political freedom to attract colonists. In 1702 New Jersey united and became a royal colony.

1682—PENNSYLVANIA

William Penn had a nice surprise!

I GRANT YOU LANDS IN AMERICA IN PAYMENT OF MY £16,000 DEBT TO YOUR FATHER. YOU WILL BE PROPRIETOR OF A WOODED DOMAIN BIGGER THAN ENGLAND. YOU COULD NAME IT "PENN'S WOODS." IN OTHER WORDS, "PENNSYLVANIA."

YEAH, GEORGE. PROVIDING RELIGIOUS LIBERTY AND A REPRESENTATIVE ASSEMBLY WILL SURELY ATTRACT COLONISTS.

Penn, an English Quaker, made Pennsylvania a haven for persecuted Quakers, a religious group that believed all people had the Inner Light of God within them; thus all were equal—including women, blacks, and Indians.

Penn's Frames of Government guaranteed political and religious freedom and also provided economic opportunity: every male settler received 50 acres of land. The colony's elected unicameral (one house) legislature had greater autonomy than other colonial assemblies.

WELCOME TO PHILADELPHIA, THE CITY OF BROTHERLY LOVE!

Penn advertised his Holy Experiment (based on tolerance, truth, and peace) in Europe, attracting thousands of Germans and Scotch-Irish, as well as French, Dutch, Swedes, Danes, Finns, and English.

STRANGER, I WANT TO SETTLE WHERE I CAN SPEAK MY OWN MIND, AND MAYBE START A NEW CHURCH.

THEN PENNSYLVANIA IS THE PLACE FOR YOU. IT'S THAT-A-WAY.

1664—DELAWARE

In 1638 the New Sweden Company founded New Sweden on Delaware Bay. The colony was taken over by New Netherland in 1655, then lost to England's Duke of York in 1664.

GOT THAT?

In 1682 William Penn bought Delaware from New York and in 1702 allowed it to elect its own assembly as the colony of Delaware. However, Pennsylvania governed Delaware until the Revolution.

I'M THE BOSS!

NOT FOR LONG.

The Swedes of Delaware made two important contributions to America:

1. introduction of the Lutheran Church;

2. log cabin design and construction, used by westward-moving frontiersmen.

1492   1607   1733   2000

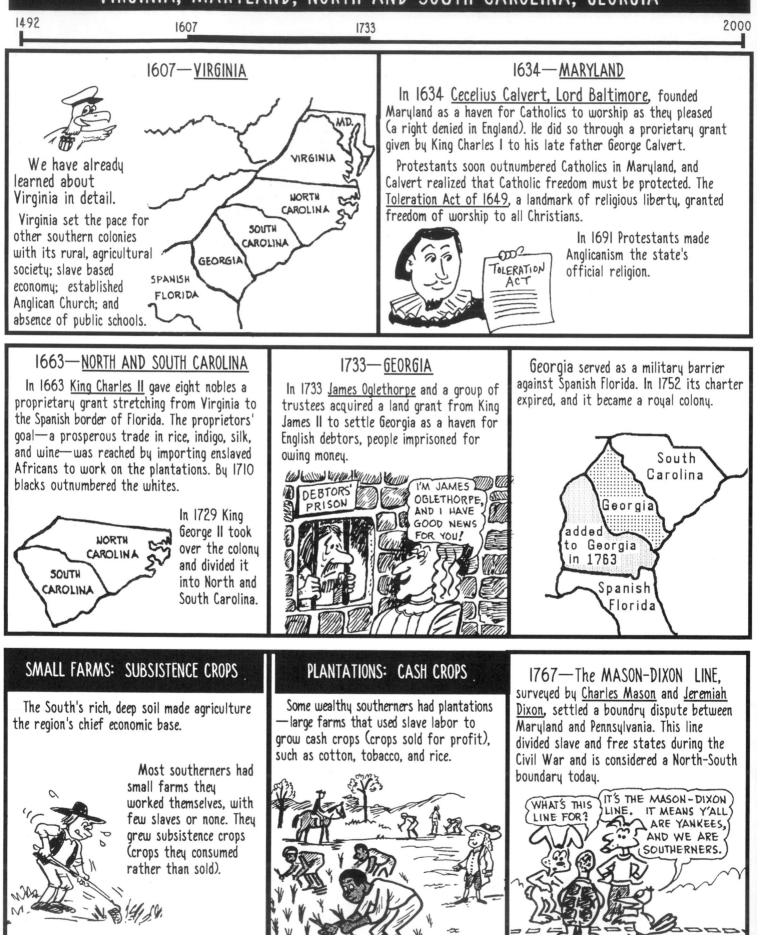

1607—VIRGINIA

We have already learned about Virginia in detail.

Virginia set the pace for other southern colonies with its rural, agricultural society; slave based economy; established Anglican Church; and absence of public schools.

1634—MARYLAND

In 1634 Cecelius Calvert, Lord Baltimore, founded Maryland as a haven for Catholics to worship as they pleased (a right denied in England). He did so through a proprietary grant given by King Charles I to his late father George Calvert.

Protestants soon outnumbered Catholics in Maryland, and Calvert realized that Catholic freedom must be protected. The Toleration Act of 1649, a landmark of religious liberty, granted freedom of worship to all Christians.

In 1691 Protestants made Anglicanism the state's official religion.

1663—NORTH AND SOUTH CAROLINA

In 1663 King Charles II gave eight nobles a proprietary grant stretching from Virginia to the Spanish border of Florida. The proprietors' goal—a prosperous trade in rice, indigo, silk, and wine—was reached by importing enslaved Africans to work on the plantations. By 1710 blacks outnumbered the whites.

In 1729 King George II took over the colony and divided it into North and South Carolina.

1733—GEORGIA

In 1733 James Oglethorpe and a group of trustees acquired a land grant from King James II to settle Georgia as a haven for English debtors, people imprisoned for owing money.

DEBTORS' PRISON

I'M JAMES OGLETHORPE, AND I HAVE GOOD NEWS FOR YOU!

Georgia served as a military barrier against Spanish Florida. In 1752 its charter expired, and it became a royal colony.

South Carolina

Georgia

added to Georgia in 1763

Spanish Florida

SMALL FARMS: SUBSISTENCE CROPS

The South's rich, deep soil made agriculture the region's chief economic base.

Most southerners had small farms they worked themselves, with few slaves or none. They grew subsistence crops (crops they consumed rather than sold).

PLANTATIONS: CASH CROPS

Some wealthy southerners had plantations —large farms that used slave labor to grow cash crops (crops sold for profit), such as cotton, tobacco, and rice.

1767—The MASON-DIXON LINE,

surveyed by Charles Mason and Jeremiah Dixon, settled a boundry dispute between Maryland and Pennsylvania. This line divided slave and free states during the Civil War and is considered a North-South boundary today.

WHAT'S THIS LINE FOR?

IT'S THE MASON-DIXON LINE. IT MEANS Y'ALL ARE YANKEES, AND WE ARE SOUTHERNERS.

58

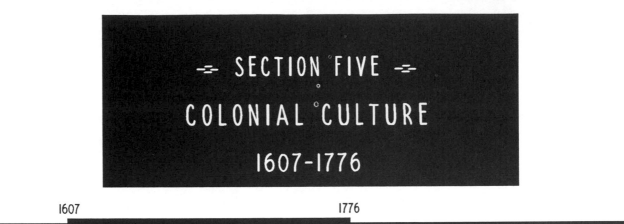

1492   1607   1776   2000

"Whence come all these people? They are a mixture of English, Scotch, Irish, French, Dutch, German, and Swedes.
From this promiscuous breed that race now called American has now arisen....

"What then is an American, this new man?....
He is an American who leaving behind him all his ancient prejudices and manners,
receives new ones from the new mode of life he has embraced, the new government he obeys, and the new rank he holds."
—J. Hector St. John de Crevecoeur, 1782

culture—the sum total of a group's ways of living

The P E R S I A acronym is convenient for organizing the ways people live in a society, and thus understanding their culture.

People throughout history—no matter when or where they lived—have had six human concerns, expressed in the these six questions. ⟶

Their answers—in different times and places—have created different kinds of political, economic, relgious, social, intellectual, and artistic institutions, the sum of which is their culture.

P olitical: Who shall be in charge?
E conomic: How shall we eat?
R eligious: What is the meaning of life—its origin, destination, purpose?
S ocial: How shall we relate to each other?
I ntellectual: How shall we learn?
A rtistic: How shall we express ourselves: our emotions, thoughts, ideas?

Below are some (but not all) of the ways people have answered the six questions through centuries of history. How have their answers shaped our institutions? How do you answer the questions? On the next page we'll apply the P E R S I A acronym to the colonies.

POLITICAL
Who shall be in charge?

I WILL! I'M THE STRONGEST
BUT I'M THE WISEST!
WHAT ABOUT US? THE PEOPLE?

BASED ON POWER
head of clan
oligarch
monarch
dictator

BASED ON SOCIAL CONTRACT
the people—in a democracy,
1) direct, or
2) representative

ECONOMIC
How shall we eat?

AGRICULTURE   COMMERCE

TRADES AND PROFESSIONS

INDUSTRY:

COMPUTER SHOP

manufacturing

electronic

RELIGIOUS
What is the meaning of life?

ORIGIN: Where did we come from?
DESTINATION: What happens when we die?
PURPOSE: How shall we spend our lives?

WHAT DO YOU MEAN YOU DON'T HAVE A CLUE?

GURU

SOCIAL
How shall we relate?

AUTHORITARIAN SOCIETY, based on servitude and/or slavery

ONLY TWO MORE YEARS AND I'M FREE!
LUCKY YOU! I'M BOUND FOR LIFE.
INDENTURED SERVANT
SLAVE

DEFERENCE SOCIETY, based on rank

EGALITARIAN SOCIETY, based on equal rights under the law.

INTELLECTUAL
How shall we learn?

ALL YOU NEED TO KNOW ABOUT THE FUZZY HEADED WARBLER IS IN THIS AUTHORITATIVE WORK.
ALL THE SAME, I WANT TO OBSERVE FOR MYSELF.

AUTHORITY: Someone tells you.

DISCOVERY: You find out for yourself.

ARTISTIC
How shall we express ourselves?

SINGING

PAINTING

DANCING

WRITING

INSTITUTIONS	NEW ENGLAND COLONIES	MIDDLE COLONIES	SOUTHERN COLONIES
POLITICAL Who shall be in charge?	Town meetings were the most direct form of democracy in the colonies.	As in Virginia, ⟶ all the colonies eventually had a representative legislature (called assembly), with the power to vote on taxes. Members were elected by white male property owners (and in a few colonies, female property owners).	King ↓ GOV. AND COUNCIL ↓ HOUSE OF BURGESSES ↑↓ VOTERS (WHITE MALE PROPERTY OWNERS) The king made appointments only in the royal colonies, though he ruled all.
ECONOMIC How shall we eat?	Fishing, shipbuilding, sea trade, naval stores, furs. Thin, rocky soil made farming unproductive.	Grain farms, seaports, iron works.	Plantations and small farms. Tobacco, rice, indigo, cotton.
RELIGIOUS What is the meaning of life? —origin? —purpose? —destination?	Congregational Church the state, tax-supported church (except in R.I.).	MIND IF I START A NEW CHURCH? VHY NOT? Many churches; religious tolerance. WELCOME TO NEW NETHERLAND	Anglican Church the state church: taxes and membership required.
SOCIAL How shall we relate?	Urban; towns surrounded by fields. Strong sense of community. Deference society.	The most egalitarian of the colonies (a matter of degree).	Rural; few towns. Plantation life modeled on English country life. Authoritarian and deference societies. INDENTURED SERVANT SLAVE
INTELLECTUAL How shall we learn?	In 1647 Massachusetts started the first compulsory public schools. Scientific pursuits in all three regions. BOSTON LATIN SCHOOL 1635	No public schools. Private schools run by churches and individuals. As in all colonies, girls had less education.	No public and few private schools. Wealthy people hired tutors for plantation schools. SERVANTS SCHOOL
ARTISTIC How shall we express ourselves?	John Singleton Copley John Trumbull Gilbert Stuart Anne Bradstreet Phyllis Wheatley William Bradford Mercy Otis Warren Cotton Mather	Hudson River Valley painters Benjamin West Charles Willson Peale Benjamin Franklin Thomas Paine Philip Freneau Alexander Hamilton	Architecture, theatre, music, and dancing. Thomas Jefferson James Madison William Byrd II

1750—BLACK AND WHITE POPULATION OF THE COLONIES
Total 1750 Population: 1,170,760

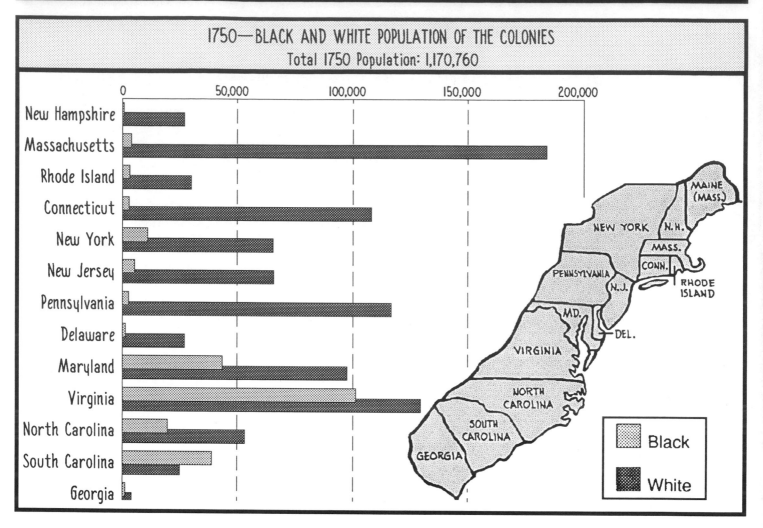

1790—ETHNIC POPULATION OF THE NEW UNITED STATES
Total 1790 Population: 3,929,214

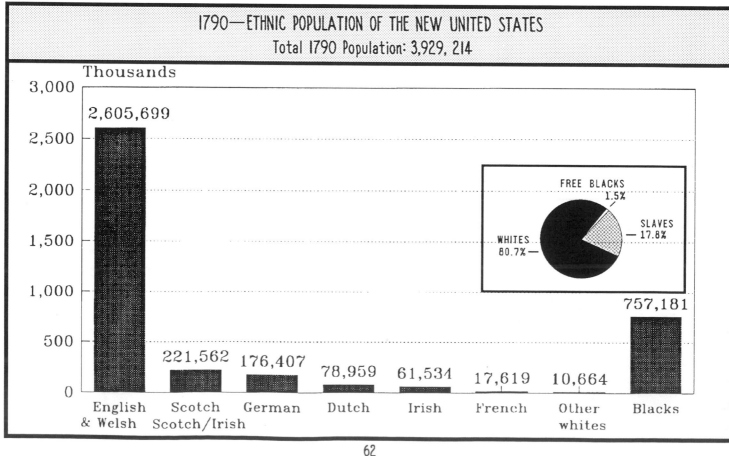

"In America, people don't ask 'What is he?' but 'What can he do?'"—Benjamin Franklin

America has always had social classes.
But unlike Europe's tradition of closed social ranks, fixed by birth,
America's open social ladder—climbed through wealth and talent,—offers upward mobility.
Abundant land plus hard work put wealth within reach of the colonists, and America's economic opportunities
beckoned them up the ladder. Benjamin Franklin, about whom you'll read later, is one example of the response.

Freedom to climb the social ladder, to better one's self, is the American Dream.
To catch the spirit of the American Dream in the colonial era, read the words of
Hector St. John de Crevecoeur, a French immigrant living in New York, who wrote
<u>Letters From an American Farmer</u> in 1782. The selection below is from his most famous letter.

"WHAT IS AN AMERICAN?

"In this great American asylum, the poor of Europe have by some means met together....Urged by a variety of motives, here they came. Everything has tended to regenerate them; new laws, a new mode of living, a new social system; here they are become men: in Europe they were as so many useless plants...they withered, and were mowed down by want, hunger, and war; but now by the power of transplantation...they have taken root and flourished!

"Here are no aristocratical families, no courts, no kings, no bishops...no great...luxury. The rich and the poor are not so far removed from each other as in Europe....

"We are all animated with the spirit of industry which is unfettered and unrestrained, because each person works for himself...without any part being claimed by a despotic prince, a rich abbot, or a mighty lord.

"We have no princes for whom we toil, starve, and bleed; we are the most perfect society now existing in the world. Here man is free as he ought to be....

"Whence come all these people? They are a mixture of English, Scotch, Irish, French, Dutch, German, and Swedes. From this promiscuous breed that race now called American has now arisen....

"What then is the American, this new man?....I could point out to you a family whose grandfather was an Englishman, whose wife was Dutch, whose son married a French woman, and whose present four sons have now four wives of different nations.

"He is an American, who leaving behind him all his ancient prejudices and manners, receives new ones from the new mode of life he has embraced, the new government he obeys, and the new rank he holds.

"Here individuals of all nations are melted into a new race of men, whose labours and posterity will one day cause great changes in the world."

<u>UPPER CLASS</u>: <u>GENTRY</u>
(upper 5%)
   planters
   merchants
   royal officials
   ministers
   professionals

Called "Mister" and "Mistress" and given deference, the gentry dressed in silks with lace ruffles and wore wigs, earning the name "bigwigs"; they had front pews in churches. At Harvard College, wealth not grades set class rank.

<u>MIDDLE CLASS</u> (largest percent)
   farmers
   tradespeople
   artisans (skilled workers in crafts, such as weaving and carpentry)

Called "Goodman" and "Goodwoman," they both gave and received deference and wore simple clothes.

<u>LOWER CLASS</u>
   hired hands
   indentured servants
   enslaved African-Americans

Called the "meaner sort," they deferred to middle and upper classes. They wore clothes of homespun <u>linsey-wolsey</u> (linen and wool) and were subject to fines for dressing like the gentry.

A large number of colonists came as indentured servants; many rose to the middle class, some to the upper class. (A section on enslaved African-Americans follows.)

1492   1720s-40s   2000

THE GREAT AWAKENING
was a movement

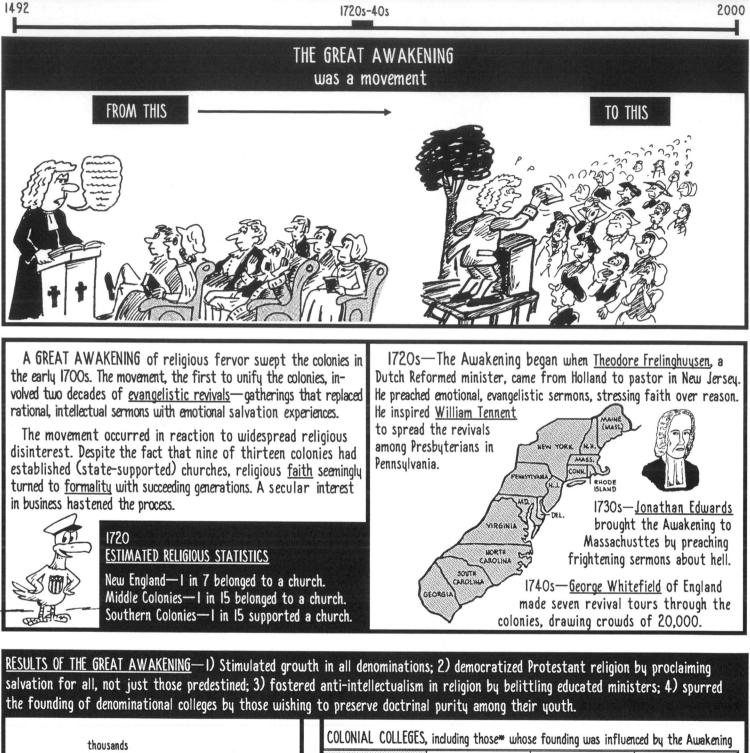

FROM THIS   ⟶   TO THIS

A GREAT AWAKENING of religious fervor swept the colonies in the early 1700s. The movement, the first to unify the colonies, involved two decades of <u>evangelistic revivals</u>—gatherings that replaced rational, intellectual sermons with emotional salvation experiences.

The movement occurred in reaction to widespread religious disinterest. Despite the fact that nine of thirteen colonies had established (state-supported) churches, religious <u>faith</u> seemingly turned to <u>formality</u> with succeeding generations. A secular interest in business hastened the process.

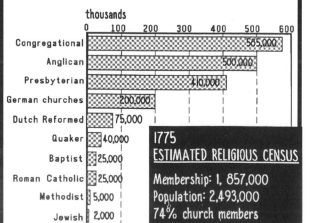

1720
ESTIMATED RELIGIOUS STATISTICS

New England—1 in 7 belonged to a church.
Middle Colonies—1 in 15 belonged to a church.
Southern Colonies—1 in 15 supported a church.

1720s—The Awakening began when <u>Theodore Frelinghuysen</u>, a Dutch Reformed minister, came from Holland to pastor in New Jersey. He preached emotional, evangelistic sermons, stressing faith over reason. He inspired <u>William Tennent</u> to spread the revivals among Presbyterians in Pennsylvania.

1730s—<u>Jonathan Edwards</u> brought the Awakening to Massachusttes by preaching frightening sermons about hell.

1740s—<u>George Whitefield</u> of England made seven revival tours through the colonies, drawing crowds of 20,000.

<u>RESULTS OF THE GREAT AWAKENING</u>—1) Stimulated growth in all denominations; 2) democratized Protestant religion by proclaiming salvation for all, not just those predestined; 3) fostered anti-intellectualism in religion by belittling educated ministers; 4) spurred the founding of denominational colleges by those wishing to preserve doctrinal purity among their youth.

thousands
0   100   200   300   400   500   600

Congregational — 585,000
Anglican — 500,000
Presbyterian — 410,000
German churches — 200,000
Dutch Reformed — 75,000
Quaker — 40,000
Baptist — 25,000
Roman Catholic — 25,000
Methodist — 5,000
Jewish — 2,000

1775
ESTIMATED RELIGIOUS CENSUS

Membership: 1, 857,000
Population: 2,493,000
74% church members

COLONIAL COLLEGES, including those✳ whose founding was influenced by the Awakening

1. Harvard	Congregational	1636	Cambridge, Mass.
2. William and Mary	Anglican	1693	Williamsburg, Va.
3. Yale	Congregational	1701	New Haven, Conn.
4. ✳Princeton	Presbyterian	1746	Princeton, N.J.
5. Pennsylvania	Nondenominational	1751	Philadelphia, Pa.
6. ✳Columbia	Anglican	1754	New York, N.Y.
7. ✳Brown	Baptist	1764	Providence, R.I.
8. ✳Rutgers	Dutch Reformed	1766	New Brunswick, N.J.
9. ✳Dartmouth	Congregational	1769	Hanover, N.H.

The economic golden rule: He who has the gold makes the rules.

1492   1607   1776   2000

MERCANTILISM

What makes a nation powerful? Gold in the treasury!

So said the <u>mercantile</u> economic theory guiding England and most European nations in the 17th and 18th centuries.

That meant having a favorable balance of trade: more gold coming in than going out of a country—or just plain "selling more than you buy."

And that meant a nation must <u>regulate its trade</u>—to sell more than it bought—for the good of the nation.

TRADE REGULATIONS

<u>TRADE REGULATIONS</u>—Colonies were a great asset, for they provided <u>controlled markets</u> for the mother country. England attempted such control with <u>navigation laws</u> that:

1. required her 13 colonies to trade mainly with England, buying her manufactured goods and selling her their raw products (Manufactured goods cost more than raw goods, thus bringing more gold to England.);
2. required the use of ships made in England or the colonies;
3. forbade colonial manufactures that competed with England's;
4. required tax-stops in England when trading with other nations.

SALUTARY NEGLECT

<u>SALUTARY NEGLECT</u>—Actually, until 1763, England neglected to enforce these laws, a situation the colonists liked; they called it <u>salutary</u> (beneficial) <u>neglect</u>.

The colonists often evaded the navigation laws, sometimes through bribery and smuggling. They developed a profitable <u>triangular trade</u> with Africa and the West Indies sugar islands (several of which were England's, including the Bahamas, Jamaica, and Barbados).

The colonists grew accustomed to <u>de facto</u> (in fact) free trade, and when England enforced the trade laws after 1763—sparks flew!

TRIANGULAR TRADE ROUTES

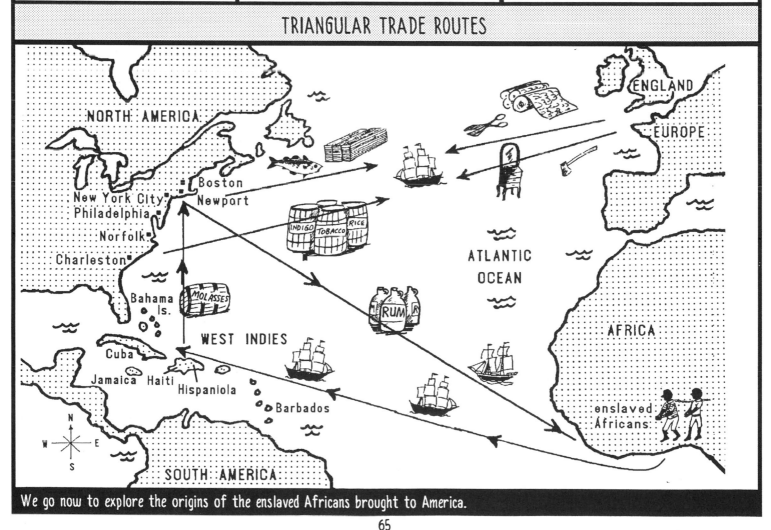

We go now to explore the origins of the enslaved Africans brought to America.

In the 1600s Abd-al-Rahman as-Sadi, a black historian from Timbuktu, Africa, wrote a history of West Africa titled Tarikh as-Sudan (Arabic for History of the Sudan). He explained his reason for writing the history:

And because learning is rich in beauty and fertile in its teaching, since it instructs men about their fatherland, their ancestors, their history, the names of their heroes and what lives they lived, I asked God's help and decided to set down all that I myself could learn on the subject of the Songhay princes of the Sudan, their adventures, their story, their achievements and their wars. Then I added the history of Timbuktu from the time of its foundation, of the princes who ruled there and the scholars and saints who lived there, and of other things as well.

As-Sadi's words give meaning and context to the following section on African-American origins in West Africa.

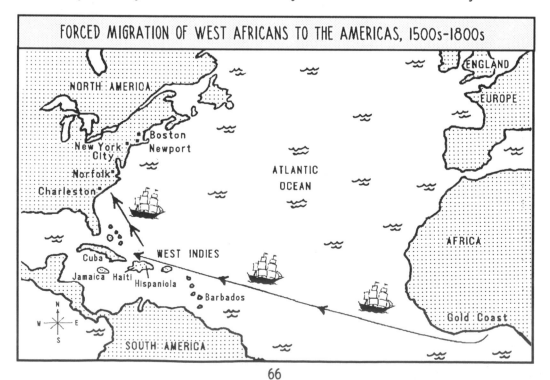

FORCED MIGRATION OF WEST AFRICANS TO THE AMERICAS, 1500s-1800s

66

31 ⇌ SLAVERY: A BRIEF HISTORY ⇌

slave—one who is the property of and subject to another person
"Although all men are born free, slavery has been the general lot of the human race."—James Madison
"Whenever I hear anyone arguing for slavery, I feel a strong impulse to see it tried on him personally. As I would not be a slave, so would I not be a master. This expresses my idea of democracy. Whatever differs from this, to the extent of the difference, is no democracy."—Abraham Lincoln

 Unlike those who came to North and South America seeking opportunity, Africans arrived in the Western Hemisphere as captives who had been enslaved. African slaves accompanied the first Spanish, Portuguese, and French explorers of North and South America, and in 1502 Columbus brought the first enslaved African to live in the New World. After that, slavery existed in the Western Hemisphere until 1889 when Brazil outlawed the institution. Slavery, however, did not begin in the New World. It is as ancient as humankind.

WHY DO PEOPLE PRACTICE SLAVERY—THE OWNING OF ANOTHER PERSON? AND WHEN DID SLAVERY BEGIN?

IS THE REASON FOR SLAVERY A DESIRE TO GAIN EASE BY FORCING SOMEONE ELSE TO DO THE WORK?
If so, slavery probably began when farming did, about 10,000 years ago.
Unlike hunting and gathering, tilling the soil was back-breaking work,
an incentive to enslave prisoners of war instead of killing them.
Throughout history war captives have remained the chief slave
source, supplemented by criminals and debtors.

From written historical records beginning 5,000 years ago, we know that slavery existed in the earliest civilizations—Egypt, Mesopotamia, Persia, China, India, Arabia—and has been practiced ever since, reaching a peak with ancient Greece and Rome, and declining during the Middle Ages. During these centuries slavery existed also among blacks in Africa and Native Americans in the Western Hemisphere. In these cultures, unlike those of the Americas after 1500, slaves sometimes could win their freedom and become integrated into the society of the slave masters, without a stigma of inferiority from their slave origins.

IS THE REASON FOR SLAVERY THE DESIRE TO GAIN WEALTH FROM THE FORCED LABOR OF OTHERS?
If so, this explains why the discovery and colonization of the New World
(1400s-1800s) caused the greatest expansion of slavery the world has
ever known—and at a time when slavery was declining elsewhere. The
soil of half the known world needed tilling and mining, and prospects
of wealth gained from slave labor proved irresistible.

European colonizers of the West Indies first enslaved Native Americans to work the soil, but harsh treatment and European diseases quickly destroyed the native population. Portuguese and Spanish colonizers then looked to Africa for slave labor, as did the British, Dutch, and French.

For centuries Africans had enslaved other Africans captured in warfare or had sold the captives to Arab slave traders. In the 1500s Europeans tapped into this African slave trade by establishing commercial slaving relations with West African chiefs on the Guinea Coast, mostly on the chief's terms. The Europeans stayed on the coast, paying rent for the trading forts they built there. The African chiefs raided African communities in the interior, marched their captives in chains to the coast, and sold them to the Europeans for guns—which the chiefs used to capture more Africans from the interior. This business arrangement lasted almost 400 years. In the 1800s, Europeans gained the upper hand and began colonizing Africa.

From the 1500s through the 1800s European slave traders shipped to the New World about 12,000,000 Africans. Some they kidnapped; about 80 percent they bought from African chiefs. In time, the African chiefs became wary of continuing to raid neighboring territories for captives. However, they were locked into a vicious cycle: They needed guns to protect their own kingdoms from slave-raiding African neighbors, but lacking the technology to make guns they had to buy them from the Europeans—in exchange for more African captives.

And so, between the 1500s and 1800s, there took place a tragic diaspora of twelve million Africans, exported as slaves to a strange New World.

1492 1502   1889   2000

Between the 1500s and 1800s European traders transported 12,000,000 Africans across the Atlantic Ocean under horrible conditions—a cruel "middle passage" during which nearly 2,000,000 died—and sold them into slavery. Ninety-five percent of the 10,000,000 survivors went to plantations in Brazil and the West Indies, where they were used for labor-intensive sugar production.

About 500,000 Africans—five percent of the 10,000,000 total—were brought to colonies that became the United States. In 1619, a year before the Pilgrims came to Massachusetts on the Mayflower, the first Africans arrived in Virginia as indentured servants. Until the 1650s Virginia law did not recognize slavery. After that, Virginia laws instituting slavery gradually were enacted, and by 1700 a full-blown slave code had evolved that spread to all the colonies. From 1700 on, enslaved Africans constituted the major labor force on the tobacco plantations of Virginia and Maryland; by 1750 they outnumbered whites in South Carolina.

In 1776 an estimated 500,000 African-Americans lived in Britain's thirteen North American colonies (20 percent of the population), with about 90 percent enslaved in the agricultural South. The few free blacks, in both North and South, suffered discrimination. The American Revolution of 1776-83 did nothing to change the institution of slavery.

The Founding Fathers who wrote the U.S. Constitution in 1787, several of whom opposed slavery, failed to end this tragic institution; they knew the South would not join the Union under such terms. They compromised by including a provision ending the slave trade by 1807. Most thought slavery would gradually end thereafter because it was not profitable.

Not so. Eli Whitney's invention of the cotton gin in 1793 made cotton a profitable southern crop. Slave labor yielded large cotton crops; therefore, slavery became entrenched in the southern states. The Civil War (1861-65) finally ended slavery in the United States. However, not until the Civil Rights movement of the 1960s did African-Americans gain the rights of citizenship won in the Civil War.

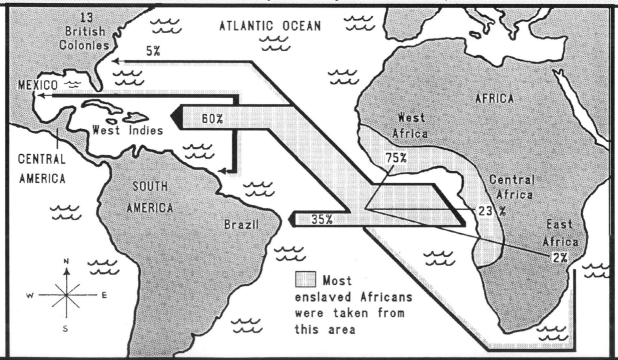

African-Americans contributed significantly to developing the New World, not only through their tragic forced labor, but also through the rich culture they brought from Africa. Let's go now to Africa to explore the heritage of African-Americans.

If you were to visit Africa today, you would find a continent of 450,000,000 people representing countless ethnic groups who speak between 800 and 1,000 different languages.

The Africa you see on the 1992 map below is, in a sense, a young continent, for it is made up of self-governing nations newly freed from European colonial domination which lasted from the 1880s to the 1960s.

In reality Africa is an ancient land with an intriguing past. As we search there for the African-American heritage, we'll also find humankind's deepest roots.

AFRICA: 1992

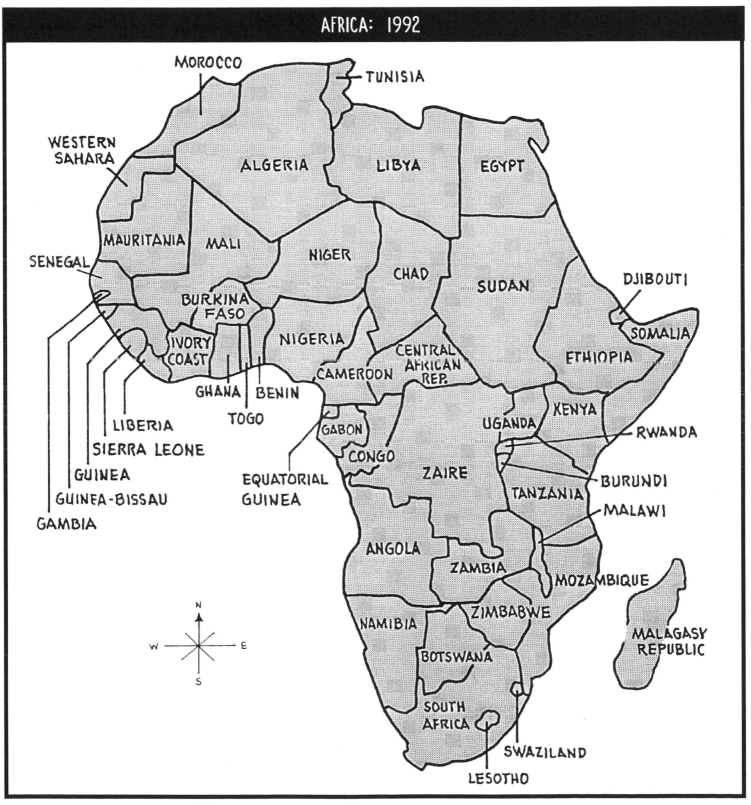

Until the 1800s Europeans knew little about the African continent because few had explored it.

Why?

1) Europeans had no natural immunity to tropical diseases.

2) Arab middlemen had a near monopoly on trade between Africa and the rest of the world.

3) Africa has a formidable geography.

Africa is a huge continent, second only to Asia in size. It stretches 5,000 miles in length and breadth. The United States could fit into Africa three times.

The SAHARA DESERT (nearly the size of the United States) is the largest desert in the world. It formed both a <u>physical barrier</u> and a <u>knowledge barrier</u> between Europe and the vast sub-Saharan region to the south of it. Not until the 1400s—when the Portuguese developed navigation technology to sail the African coastline—did Europeans begin to learn firsthand of what they considered a mysterious land. It took Europeans four more centuries—until the 1800s—to penetrate Africa's interior. Africans, of course, knew where they were all along.

<u>AFRICAN GEOGRAPHY</u> has an unusual balance: its upper and lower halves are almost mirror images. Imagine that you and a friend start a journey from each end of the continent, northern and southern, and meet in the middle. You will have similar experiences:

<u>FERTILE COASTLANDS</u> forming Africa's northern and southern borders will give you a friendly send-off.

<u>BARREN DESERTS</u> with hot, shifting sand dunes and stark mountains will test your endurance and courage.

Relief comes with an occasional <u>oasis</u>, a patch of land with green grass and palm trees, watered by underground springs. Oases are scattered through the deserts. They range in size from less than a square mile to an area large enough to support a million palm trees. Oases line part of the 4,160-mile Nile River, the longest river in the world.

<u>STEPPES AND BUSHLAND</u>—with short grasses and thorny bushes— border the deserts and soon lead you to fertile land.

<u>SAVANNAHS OR GRASSLANDS</u>—with grasses as high as six feet— cover two-fifths of Africa and are the most favorable areas for agriculture. You'll hear the <u>northern savannah</u> referred to as the <u>SUDAN</u> because several centuries ago North African Arabs began calling this area "bilad al-Sudan," Arabic for "land of the blacks." (Don't confuse the <u>Sudan region</u> with the modern <u>country of Sudan</u>.)

<u>TROPICAL RAIN FORESTS</u> along the equator in central Africa are so dense they'll slow your progress.

<u>MOUNTAINS, LAKES, AND VALLEYS</u>—You can detour eastward and find adventures climbing Mount Kilimanjaro, among Africa's tallest mountains; swimming in Lake Victoria, the world's second largest fresh water lake; and exploring the Great Rift Valley, site of the earliest human fossils.

SAHARA DESERT

NILE R.

Equator

Lake Victoria

KALAHARI DESERT

N
W   E
S

For centuries Africans' food supply has come from animals, such as cattle and goats; fruit trees; and farm crops, including grains, legumes, and vegetables. (The words <u>goober</u> and <u>yam</u> came from Africa.) Many Africans brought to America as slaves had advanced agricultural skills.

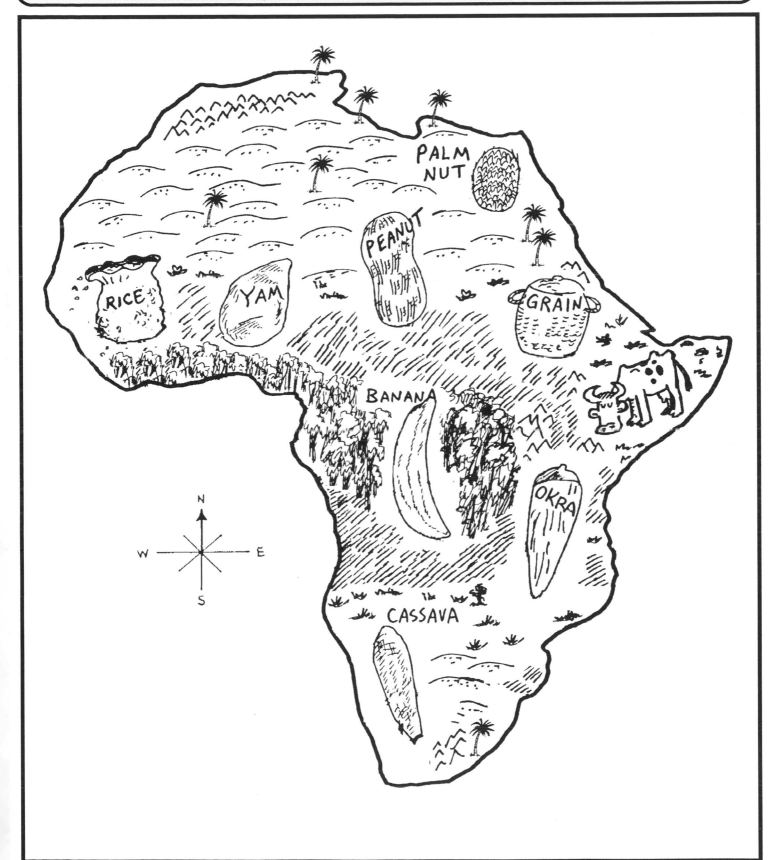

In the 1800s European explorers told of Africa's exotic wild animals. Their tales attracted big game hunters to Africa from all over the world. Continuous hunting has reduced the numbers of animals and endangered some. Elephants, killed by the thousands for their ivory tusks, once roamed most of the continent but now live mainly in eastern Africa. Today, large national parks are attempting to protect Africa's wild animals.

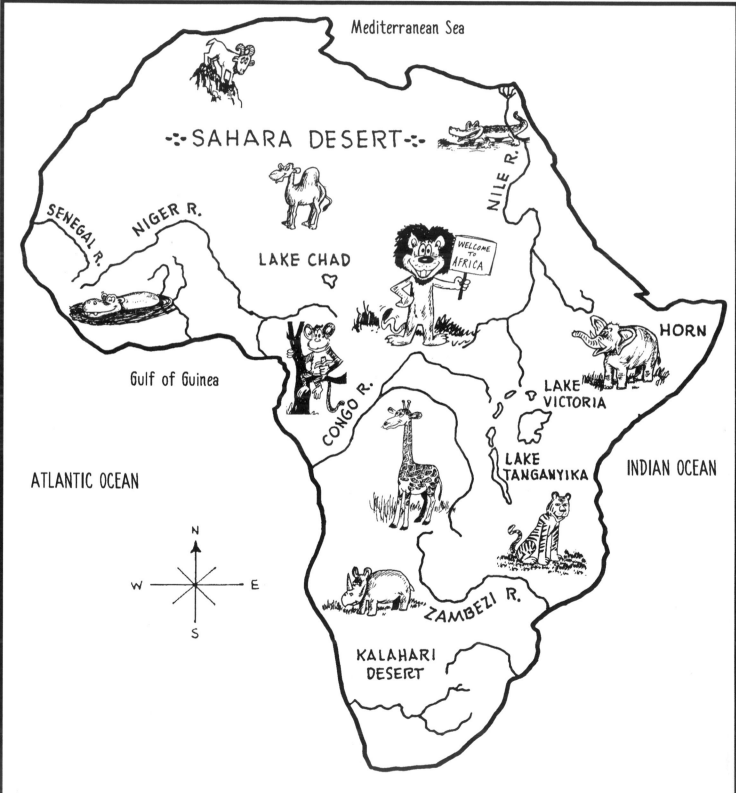

ethnic—pertaining to a group of people who share distinctive physical and cultural traits
"It seems that we all belong, ultimately, to Africa."—Roland Oliver, The African Experience, 1991

AFRICA: CRADLE OF HUMANKIND

As recently as 1930, textbooks portrayed Africa with a blank center labeled: UNEXPLORED TERRITORY. Much of Africa's history was blank, too—unexplored and unwritten. Scholars now think Africa may have the longest human history in the world, for archeological evidence points to it as the birthplace of humankind.

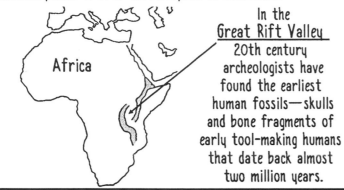

In the Great Rift Valley 20th century archeologists have found the earliest human fossils—skulls and bone fragments of early tool-making humans that date back almost two million years.

ETHNIC GROUPS

As humans developed and multiplied, they spread slowly through Africa, Asia, Europe, and other parts of the world. Varying climate conditions, geography, beliefs, and customs resulted in ethnic groups with:

1) diverse physical characteristics such as stature, facial structure, skin color (People near the hot Equator developed darker skin from melanin, the pigment or coloring matter in skin cells which protects skin from sun damage.);

2) diverse cultures in regard to language and ways of organizing societal institutions: political, religious, economic, social, intellectual, and artistic.

Ethnic groups and identities are not static; over time and in different contexts they may change. (Classification of ethnic groups differs according to various anthropologists.)

LANGUAGE GROUPS IN AFRICA DURING THE AFRICAN-AMERICAN SLAVE TRADE ERA, 1500s-1800s

Various groups of people speaking between 800 and 1,000 languages populated Africa during the four centuries of African-American slave trading. They can be divided into four major language groups and various sub-groups.

North Africa ⟶

⟿ SAHARA DESERT ⟶

The Sahara Desert separated Africans into two major cultural regions:
1) North Africa, and 2) sub-Saharan Africa.

Sub-Saharan Africa ⟶

In the 1400s Portuguese sailors exploring Africa's sub-Saharan western coast—the ancestral home of most African-Americans—called the people there Negroes (Portuguese and Spanish for "blacks") because of their dark skin.

Africans brought to the Americas by Portuguese, French, British, and Dutch slave traders also were called Negroes, as well as coloreds. In the United States these terms referred to them and their descendants until the 1960s. Since then most African-Americans have preferred three other terms, which express pride in their African origins: blacks, Afro-Americans, and African-Americans.

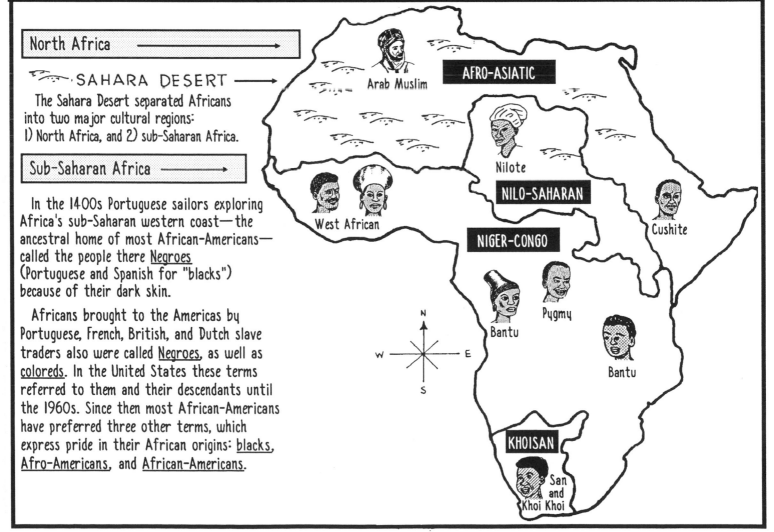

WEST AFRICAN RELIGIONS

Most West Africans were polytheists—believers in many gods: a High God (the creator) and lesser gods. Some gods controlled and resided within nature (animism) and some gods were the spirits of their ancestors.

Ancestor worship regulated all of life because of the belief that forefathers' spirits had great power over their living families and must be obeyed and pleased. This meant observing laws and rules of behavior the ancestors had established while alive—that is, living as the dead relatives had once lived. Change was suspect, if not deviant, behavior. Polygyny, the practice of having many wives, was allowed.

Religion and politics were one: kings, chiefs, and family heads were considered the ancestors' earthly representatives, and thus the religious as well as political leaders. Like other pre-scientific peoples, including European Christians, West Africans believed in witchcraft, the use of supernatural powers, usually for evil; in defense they relied on witch doctors and magic charms.

West Africans worshipped at simple shrines. A sacred altar might be a collection of rocks, wood, and everyday objects.

MASKS associated with ancestors were worn in religious rituals.

ISLAM

By 1100 many West Africans had converted to Islam, a monotheistic religion (belief in one god) founded in 622 by Muhammed in Mecca, Arabia.
In Arabic: <u>Islam</u> means "submission to the will of God." <u>Muslim</u> means "a believer in Islam." <u>Koran</u>, the name of Islam's holy book, means "the reading."

Muhammed taught that there was only one God, Allah; that Muhammed was his prophet; and that Islam must be spread to other peoples. He taught that Muslims must practice ethical behavior, such as honesty, fairness, courage, honor, charity, and kindness—including to slaves; that evildoers must be punished on the Old Testament basis of retribution: "an eye for an eye, a tooth for a tooth." Islam allowed polygyny, with a limitation of four wives.

Arabic became the language of West African literature, and the Arabic alphabet was used to write some African languages. This paralleled events in Europe, where Latin was the language of literacy and the Latin alphabet was used to write European languages.

A Muslim mosque

Spread of Islam by 1200

Mecca

CHRISTIANITY

By the 300s Christianity spread to parts of North and East Africa, but it had no impact in West Africa until the 1500s when European Christians started missions there in the wake of European slave-traders. It made little progress until the 1800s.

Christianity is a monotheistic religion based on the life and teachings of Jesus Christ, a Jew born in Palestine almost 2,000 years ago. The year of his birth marks the beginning of the Christian era, signified by "A.D."—<u>Anno Domini</u>, the year of our Lord.

Jesus' ethical teachings emphasized two principles:
1) the Golden Rule: "Do unto others as you would have them do unto you." (Luke 6:31)
2) non-retribution: "Ye hath heard that it hath been said 'Thou shalt love thy neighbor and hate thine enemy.' But I say unto you, love [also] your enemies...do good to them that hate you...." (Matthew 5:43-44)

European Christians stressed the importance of reading the Bible and thus reinforced the techniques of literacy which Arab Muslims had brought to West Africa. Christianity allowed only monogamy—marriage to one person.

Church of St. George
Ethiopia, East Africa (1200s)

In exploring the rich heritage of African-Americans, WEST AFRICAN HISTORY is of central interest, for the roots of most blacks in the United States are in the Sudan (savannah) and the coastal (forest) regions of West Africa. (Sudan, meaning "land of the blacks," is the term North African Arab Muslims gave the savannah area below the Sahara Desert.) NORTH AFRICAN HISTORY provides a vital context because trans-Saharan trade brought North African Arab Muslim influences to the West African Sudan.

The timelines of both regions give perspective to West African history.

(You'll enjoy reading more about West African history in Basil Davidson's The African Past, 1964, and African Kingdoms, 1966, and Roland Oliver's Africa in the Days of Exploration, 1965, and The African Experience, 1991—all used as sources for this chapter.)

NORTH AFRICAN CIVILIZATIONS

3100 B.C.—KINGDOM OF EGYPT unified. Egypt's recorded history, the oldest of any civilization, begins about this time. Egypt's empire, lasting 25 centuries, is conquered by Persia (525 B.C.), Greece (332 B.C.), and Rome (30 B.C.).

1100 B.C.—PHOENICIA begins colonizing North African coast.
814 B.C.—Phoenicia founds Carthage. Carthage controls Mediterranean trade for 600 years.

146 B.C.—ROMANS defeat Carthage in Punic Wars. ROMAN EMPIRE expands into North Africa

640 A.D.-711 —ARAB MUSLIMS from Arabian Peninsula conquer North Africa and Spain; introduce Islamic religion and Arabic language. By 1000 A.D. Muslim influence reaches the West African Sudan.

WEST AFRICAN KINGDOMS:
African kingdoms were political states, of widely varying sizes, formed as tribal chiefs conquered neighboring tribes and assumed the title "king." Kingdoms of vast size also were called empires.

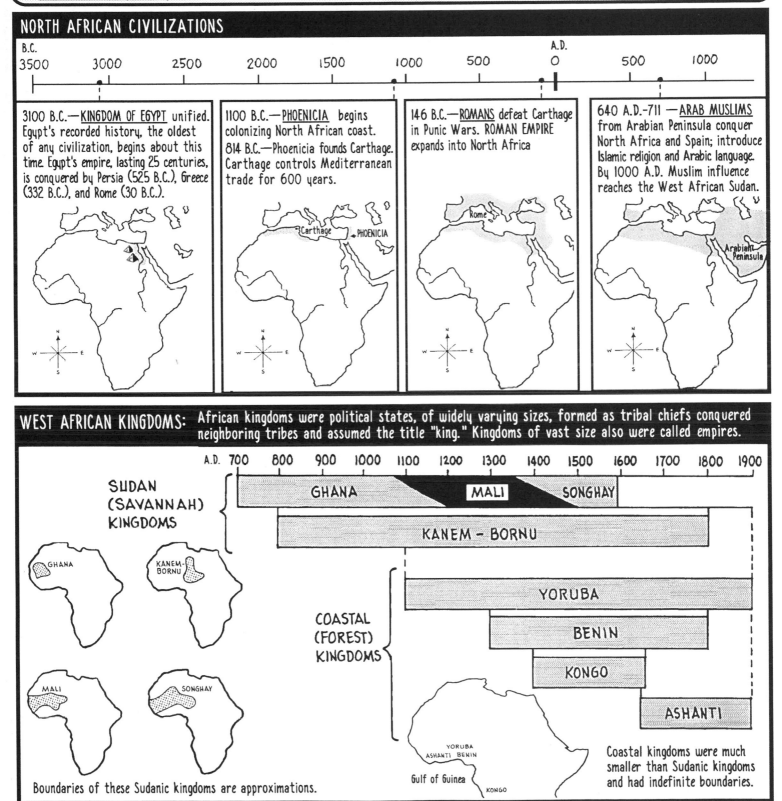

SUDAN (SAVANNAH) KINGDOMS

GHANA   MALI   SONGHAY

KANEM - BORNU

COASTAL (FOREST) KINGDOMS

YORUBA

BENIN

KONGO

ASHANTI

Boundaries of these Sudanic kingdoms are approximations.

Coastal kingdoms were much smaller than Sudanic kingdoms and had indefinite boundaries.

West Africa's historical record is incomplete because few written records exist prior to the 1800s. The earliest—beginning in the 900s—are travel accounts by Arab Muslims from <u>North Africa</u> and <u>Spain</u>.

During centuries of trade across the Sahara Desert (trans-Saharan trade), Muslim merchants and scholars from North Africa brought literacy to West African cities in the Sudan, such as <u>Timbuktu</u>, and by the 1600s some West Africans were writing their own history. An example is Abd al-Rahman as-Sadi of Timbuktu who wrote <u>Tarikh as-Sudan</u> (Arabic for <u>History of the Sudan</u>) in the 1600s.

From these written records, plus archaeology and oral tradition, we know of wealthy, powerful kingdoms—such as Ghana, Mali, and Songhay—existing in West Africa during the medieval period and the American slave-trade era.

1200 A.D.—Extent of Arab Muslim influence: spread of Islamic religion, Arabic language

GOLD TRADE CREATES WEST AFRICAN EMPIRES

GOLD—this precious metal located in West Africa fueled a highly organized trans-Saharan trade system between North African Arab Moslems and West African blacks which gave rise to three great West African empires.

A demand for West African gold motivated North African Arab merchants to brave the dangerous, 1,200 mile Sahara Desert to trade salt for gold. The demand for gold came from Europe as well as North Africa, for European and Asian gold mines were nearly depleted by 1000 A.D. For 500 years, until Spain's discovery of the New World's gold, West Africans controlled the western world's gold supply.

TRADE ROUTES ACROSS THE SAHARA DESERT

Centuries of trade between North African Arabs and West African blacks created wealthy black cities along the Sudan trade routes. Rulers of the cities controlled trans-Saharan trade as middlemen, taxing both imported salt and exported gold. Using their trade wealth, successive West African rulers built military strength (based on iron weapons), conquered their neighbors, and devoloped large kingdoms. Read on for the adventures of the first powerful West African kingdom: Ghana.

Arabs traded: salt, copper, horses, silks, books.

West Africans traded: gold, ivory, slaves

As many as 12,000 camels might be in one caravan. They couldn't have done it without us! We could go days without water on the Sahara Desert.

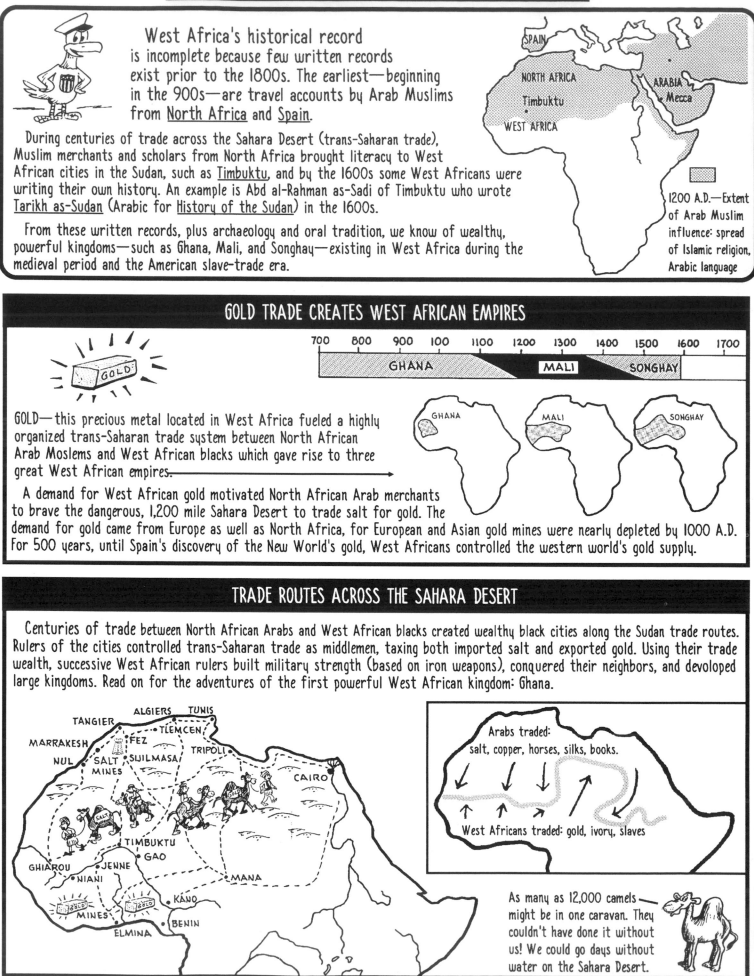

700 800 900 100 1100 1200 1300 1400 1500 1600 1700 1800 1900

| GHANA | MALI | SONGHAY |

The West African kingdom of Ghana flourished from the 700s to about 1100, although its origin dates back to the 300s, and it survived until about 1200. Ghana's founders were the first West Africans to smelt iron ore. This technological advance, along with control of West African gold mines and the trans-Saharan trade in the Sudan, enabled Ghana to expand its power over many tribes and chieftains to create the first West African empire. (The empire's name came from the title of its king, the ghana, meaning "war chief." The modern country of Ghana, formed in 1957, was named for the ancient empire.)

Koumbi, Ghana's recently excavated capital, (population about 15,000) consisted of two towns enclosed by a wall, one built for Muslim Arab merchants. While Ghana blacks welcomed Muslims as residents, they practiced their own traditional religion: the worship of ancestors and tribal gods. They regarded the king as a divine ruler, the earthly representive of their ancestors. In 1076, however, reformist Muslim Arabs, called the Almoravids, invaded Ghana and established the religion of Islam: the worship of one God, Allah, and his prophet Mohammed. Ghana soon regained its independence, but declined in power by 1200. Islam remained a strong influence and became the official religion of Mali and Songhay, kingdoms which in turn displaced Ghana.

The splendor of Ghana in 1067 was recorded by an Arab visitor to the court of King Tankamanin.

In 1076 the account was published in _Book of Roads and Kingdoms_, by al-Bakri, a noted Arab geographer from Cordoba, Spain.

Here is an excerpt:

GHANA

KOUMBI

GOLD

"This [King] Tankamanin is powerful, rules an enormous kingdom and possesses great authority.

"The city...consists of two towns lying in a plain. One...is inhabited by Muslims. It is large and possesses twelve mosques....There are imams, muezzins, jurists and...learned men. Around the town are wells of sweet water from which they drink and near which they grow vegetables. The town in which the king lives is six miles from the Muslim one. The land between the two towns is covered with houses...made of stone and acacia wood. The king has a palace and a number of dome-shaped dwellings, the whole surrounded by an enclosure like the defensive wall of a city. In the town where the king lives...is a mosque where pray the Muslims who come on visiting diplomatic missions. Around the king's town are domed buildings, woods, and copses where live the sorcerers of these people, the men in charge of the religious cult....The king's interpreters, his treasurer, and the majority of his ministers are Muslims.

"The court of appeal is held in a domed pavillion, around which stand ten horses with gold embroidered trappings. Behind the king stand...pages holding shields and swords decorated with gold, and on his right are the sons of the subordinate kings of his country, all wearing splendid garments....The audience is announced by the beating of a drum which they call 'daba'....When the people who profess the same religion as the king approach him, they fall on their knees and sprinkle their heads with dust, for this is their way of showing him respect. As for the Muslims, they greet him only by clapping their hands.

"When the king of Ghana calls up his army, he can put 200,000 men in the field, more than 40,000 of whom are bowmen. The horses in Ghana are very small."

A later visiter to Ghana wrote that the king's horses slept on carpets, wore silk halters, and had three attendants each.

700 800 900 100 1100 1200 1300 1400 1500 1600 1700 1800 1900

GHANA   MALI   SONGHAY

The West African Kingdom of Mali rose to power in the 1200s and exceeded Ghana in wealth and power before gradually being conquered by Songhay.

Larger than Western Europe, wealthier than Egypt, Mali was one of the fourteenth century's great empires. It was known in Europe for its control of the gold trade, for its intellectual capital Timbuktu—center of Muslim scholarship, and for its virtuous king MANSA MUSA, who had a love of learning.

MALI

TIMBUKTU

GOLD

MANSA MUSA
Reigned: 1312-1337

Several European maps of the 1300s marked Mali. The Catalan map of 1375 showed Mali's gifted ruler MANSA MUSA seated on a gold throne, receiving tributes of gold. The caption:

"This Negro lord is called Musa Mali, Lord of the Negroes of Guinea. So abundant is the gold which is found in his land that he is the richest and noblest king in all the land."

1324-25—FROM MALI TO MECCA: MANSA MUSA'S FAMOUS PILGRIMAGE

ISLAM was the state religion of Mali, and Mali's rulers (mansas) were devoted Muslims.

In 1324 MANSA MUSA—known for his justice, generosity, and love of learning—demonstrated his devotion to Islam with a spectacular 3,000-mile pilgrimage to Mecca, Islam's holy city in Arabia. Accompanied by thousands—some said 60,000—including 500 slaves, each carrying a four-pound staff of gold, Mansa Musa crossed the Sahara Desert with a caravan of camels bearing two tons of gold, which he distributed as gifts along the way. (His generosity was so great it devalued gold for 12 years in Egypt, one of his stops.) Mansa Musa's fame spread as far as Europe and Baghdad.

Baghdad

Mecca

Timbuktu

When Mansa Musa returned home, he brought several learned men who added to Mali's intellectual and cultural life. The most important was Ibrahim Es Saheli, an Arab Muslim from Granada, Spain. A scholar, poet, and architect, Es Saheli built many beautiful buildings using Spanish and North African architecture: a palace for Mansa Musa and mosques in Gao, Jenne, and Timbuktu. The Sankore Mosque in Timbuktu became a renowned learning center, the University of Sankore.

In 1353 Ibn Battuta, a North African Arab, visited Mali. He observed:
"...Mansa Musa [was] a generous and virtuous prince....The Negroes possess some admirable qualities. They are seldom unjust and have a greater abhorrence of injustice than any other people. The sultan shows no mercy to anyone who is guilty of the least act of it. There is complete security in the country. Neither traveler nor inhabitant in it has anything to fear from robbers or men of violence...."

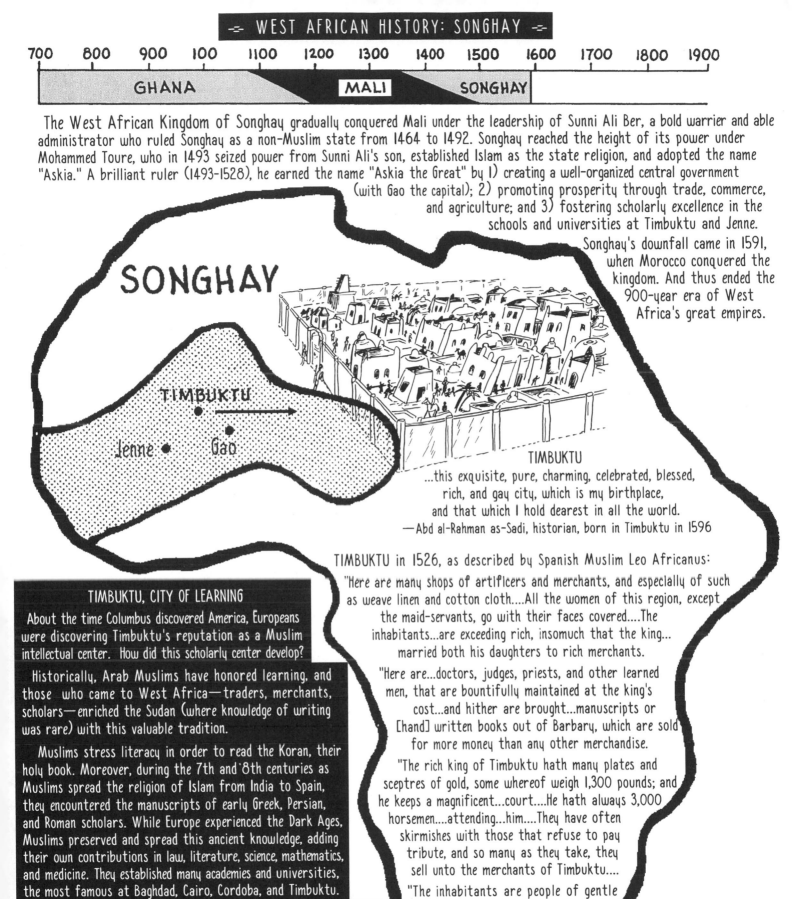

700 800 900 100 1100 1200 1300 1400 1500 1600 1700 1800 1900

GHANA   MALI   SONGHAY

The West African Kingdom of Songhay gradually conquered Mali under the leadership of Sunni Ali Ber, a bold warrier and able administrator who ruled Songhay as a non-Muslim state from 1464 to 1492. Songhay reached the height of its power under Mohammed Toure, who in 1493 seized power from Sunni Ali's son, established Islam as the state religion, and adopted the name "Askia." A brilliant ruler (1493-1528), he earned the name "Askia the Great" by 1) creating a well-organized central government (with Gao the capital); 2) promoting prosperity through trade, commerce, and agriculture; and 3) fostering scholarly excellence in the schools and universities at Timbuktu and Jenne.

Songhay's downfall came in 1591, when Morocco conquered the kingdom. And thus ended the 900-year era of West Africa's great empires.

SONGHAY

TIMBUKTU

Jenne ● Gao

TIMBUKTU

...this exquisite, pure, charming, celebrated, blessed, rich, and gay city, which is my birthplace, and that which I hold dearest in all the world.
—Abd al-Rahman as-Sadi, historian, born in Timbuktu in 1596

TIMBUKTU in 1526, as described by Spanish Muslim Leo Africanus:

"Here are many shops of artificers and merchants, and especially of such as weave linen and cotton cloth....All the women of this region, except the maid-servants, go with their faces covered....The inhabitants...are exceeding rich, insomuch that the king... married both his daughters to rich merchants.

"Here are...doctors, judges, priests, and other learned men, that are bountifully maintained at the king's cost...and hither are brought...manuscripts or [hand] written books out of Barbary, which are sold for more money than any other merchandise.

"The rich king of Timbuktu hath many plates and sceptres of gold, some whereof weigh 1,300 pounds; and he keeps a magnificent...court....He hath always 3,000 horsemen....attending...him....They have often skirmishes with those that refuse to pay tribute, and so many as they take, they sell unto the merchants of Timbuktu....

"The inhabitants are people of gentle and cheerful disposition, and spend a great part of the night singing and dancing through all the streets of the city...."

TIMBUKTU, CITY OF LEARNING

About the time Columbus discovered America, Europeans were discovering Timbuktu's reputation as a Muslim intellectual center. How did this scholarly center develop?

Historically, Arab Muslims have honored learning, and those who came to West Africa—traders, merchants, scholars—enriched the Sudan (where knowledge of writing was rare) with this valuable tradition.

Muslims stress literacy in order to read the Koran, their holy book. Moreover, during the 7th and 8th centuries as Muslims spread the religion of Islam from India to Spain, they encountered the manuscripts of early Greek, Persian, and Roman scholars. While Europe experienced the Dark Ages, Muslims preserved and spread this ancient knowledge, adding their own contributions in law, literature, science, mathematics, and medicine. They established many academies and universities, the most famous at Baghdad, Cairo, Cordoba, and Timbuktu.

Timbuktu's University of Sankore drew students from Africa, Europe and Asia to study law, science, literature, philosophy, and music with such scholars as Ahmad Baba, who wrote 40 books and had a library of 1,600 books.

Timbuktu produced many scholars. In the 1660s two completed important histories of West Africa: Mahmud Kati, Tarikh al-Fattash, and Abd al-Rahman as-Sadi, Tarikh as-Sudan.

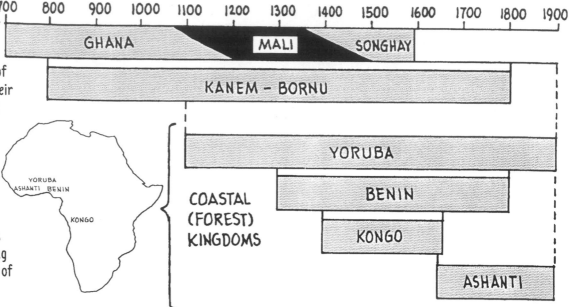

| 700 | 800 | 900 | 1000 | 1100 | 1200 | 1300 | 1400 | 1500 | 1600 | 1700 | 1800 | 1900 |

GHANA · MALI · SONGHAY

KANEM - BORNU

COASTAL (FOREST) KINGDOMS
- YORUBA
- BENIN
- KONGO
- ASHANTI

The coastal kingdoms of West Africa had little contact with Muslim North Africans until the 1500s and thus had no knowledge of writing until Europeans came to their shores, beginning in the 1400s:

Consequently, the region's history before then comes from archaeology and oral tradition. From the late 1400s to the 1800s, written reports from European traders also provide information about West Africa's numerous coastal kingdoms, among which were YORUBA (a confederacy of states), BENIN, KONGO, AND ASHANTI.

YORUBA ASHANTI BENIN · KONGO

BENIN, one of the most advanced coastal kingdoms, impressed European traders from Portugal, Holland, and Britain who—beginning with Portugal in 1486—established diplomatic and trading ties with the coastal kingdoms.

In 1602 a collection of West African travel accounts, <u>Description of Guinea</u>, contained a Dutch trader's impression of Benin, capital city of Benin: "[It is] very great when you go into it [for] you enter a great broad street, not paved, which seems to be seven or eight times broader than Warmoes street in Amsterdam." He described other streets pf great length with houses that "stand in good order...as the houses in Holland stand. Those belonging to men of quality...have two or three steps to go up...."

In 1662 Dutchman Olfert Dapper wrote that the Benin king's palace compound was as big as the Dutch town of Haarlem. In it were "fine galleries...as big as those on the Exchange at Amsterdam," which contained bronze plaques depicting Benin's history (including the arrival of the Portuguese in heavy armor). The plaques were used as memory devices by the king's "court remembrancers."

Olfert Dapper also described Benin's people: "They are people who have good laws and a well-organized police; who live on good terms with the Dutch and other foreigners who come to trade among them, and to whom they show a thousand marks of friendship."

BENIN

Benin's kings, called Obas, were absolute monarchs who reigned as the earthly representatives of Benin's gods. Religion and politics were one, and anyone who questioned the Oba's authority was executed as a heretic.

Ewuare the Great (1440-73), said to be courageous and wise, was one of Benin's outstanding kings. According to oral tradition he expanded Benin by conquering 201 cities and forcing tribute from them. He then created a central government with a state council and local governors. He built good roads in Benin City, and built a great wall around the city.

THE QUEEN MOTHER OF BENIN

The people of West Africa's coastal kingdoms produced magnificent sculptures, such as this Benin 16th century bronze sculpture of the Queen Mother, whose elaborate headdress indicates her high rank.

ETHNIC GROUPS

We can only generalize about how West Africans lived during the slave-trade era, for there were numerous black ethnic groups with different languages, religions, and customs.

Berabish Kunta
Trarza Quaish Oulliminden Assen
Tukulor Masina Adarawa Beriberi
Wolof Soninke Songhai Tazarawa
Serer Malinke Mossi Hausa Manga
Susu Fula Bobo Busa Angas Kanuri
Temne Senufo Bariba Nupe Jukun
Mende Baule Yoruba Tiv
Ngere Asante Edo Igbo
Bassa Ijo Ibibio

CITY LIFE

Several West African communities on the trans-Sahara trade routes grew into cities populated by thousands; some were capitals of empires populated by millions. The cities were thriving commercial and cultural centers that promoted an exchange of goods—and ideas—between West Africans and North Africans.

SALT MINES
WALATA TIMBUKTU
GHIAROU JENNE GAO TAKEDDO
NIANI MANA
KANO
ELMINA BENIN

Timbuktu

VILLAGE LIFE

The majority of West Africans lived in rural villages, varying in size, composed of families and clans. (A <u>clan</u> is an extended family; all the relatives of a common ancestor.) Village populations might also include slaves, usually captives from other villages.

THE FAMILY was the basic unit of village society. Kinship ties undergirded the total organization of village life, and kinship loyalty was of utmost value. In disputes a person sided with the closest kin, regardless of agreement.

Kinship ties in most ethnic groups were <u>patrilineal</u>: kinship and property were linked through <u>male</u> family members. The head of a family was its oldest male member. Village chiefs were chosen usually from the oldest male descendants of village founders.

Some ethnic groups were <u>matrilineal</u>: kinship and property were linked through <u>female</u> family members. The head of a family was the mother's oldest brother; he had legal guardianship of the children. Village chiefs were chosen usually from the oldest brothers of the oldest women descended from village founders.

Villagers lived mainly by farming and, to a lesser extent, hunting.

MASTER OF THE GROUND—Agriculture was so vital to survival that most villagers owned land collectively and assigned farm acreage to individuals through an official called <u>Master of the Ground</u>. Land not used productively had to be returned to the public domain. Consequently, many West Africans became expert farmers. The Master's role in administering wise use of the soil carried such weight, not even the chief could overrule him.

Highly developed tracking skills, along with courage and stamina, enabled West Africans to successfully hunt dangerous wild game for food.

Both urban and rural West African communities had skilled artisans, male and female Women, in addition to being artisans, typically played important roles in commerce and trade.

West Africans were among the first people to enter the iron age (about 200 A.D.). They were pioneers in iron smelting and by the 1500s had become expert metal craftspersons. Later, in American cities such as Charleston and New Orleans, African-Americans used their ancestral metal-working skills in creating beautiful, hand-wrought iron grills and balconies for Southern mansions.

BLACKSMITHS, highly respected for their expertise, smelted iron and forged implements such as farm tools, knives, axes, and saws. Some worked also in gold, silver, copper and bronze.

POTTERY, one of the oldest crafts, dates back probably to the late stone age in West Africa. The earliest examples are from the early iron-age Nok culture (present-day Nigeria) about 200 A.D.

TEXTILE WEAVING AND DYING were major crafts. West Africans grew cotton, from which they produced brightly colored cloth with geometric designs. They also grew <u>indigo</u> and used it to dye cloth a beautiful blue.

FURNITURE-MAKING involved carpentry skills and carving artistry. West Africans made household items as beautiful as possible to please the spirits, which they believed inhabited all objects. Geometric designs, carved or woven, were thought to hold mystical powers.

In pre-Civil War America blacks (such as Milton Day of North Carolina) created handsome furniture, pieces that today rank as prized antiques.

IN AMERICA: Not all Africans brought to America as slaves were artisans, but those who were made unique contributions to the American economy.

BACK IN AFRICA I WAS A CARPENTER AND A WOOD CARVER.

MY FATHER WAS A WEAVER, AND I WAS A CLOTH DYER.

West African art is best known for its splendid sculptures, such as this 16th century bronze, QUEEN MOTHER OF BENIN. (Terra cotta sculptures date back to 200 A.D.

West Africans sculpted in wood, metals and ivory. Subjects included figures, masks, and ceremonial objects.

Equisite gold-work, such as this pendant, typified the art of Ashanti.

Art was part of everyday life, as seen in intricately carved combs.

Body art was used to identify one's clan and to help commune with spirits.

About 1900 Europeans first exposed to African art labeled it primitive. Ironically, it influenced the modern art of Pablo Picasso, Georges Braque, Henry Moore and other abstract artists.

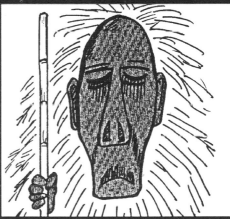

STORYTELLING was a highly developed art form for West Africans, as it had been for Europeans before they were introduced to literacy. Lacking the techniques of reading and writing, West Africans created an oral tradition by telling their history, stories, fables, parables, and proverbs over and over to each generation.

The storyteller, called griot, would act out the parts, joke, and sing—and all would join in. As you can imagine, storytelling educated families in creative ways.

Folk tales about animals were favorites. In America these tales influenced southern writers such as Joel Chandler Harris, author of the Br'er Rabbit stories.

Listen as the griot tells an African folk tale about the Great Spider, Ananse Kokrofo.

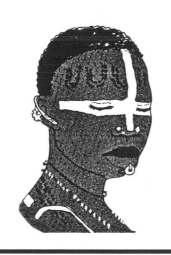

One day Ananse the Spider, determined to be the Great Spider, collected all the wisdom in the world, tucked it in a gourd tied to his stomach, and scrambled up a tree to hide it.

He had trouble half way up because the gourd got in his way.

Ntikuma, his son watching from below, said, "Father, if you truly had all the wisdom of the world, you would have put the gourd on your back. Ha! Ha!"

Hearing the truth, Ananse threw the gourd down in a fit of temper. The gourd broke, scattering wisdom everywhere. Men rushed to gather what they could, but no man got more than just a little bit.

"We are almost a nation of dancers, musicians and poets. Thus every great event...is celebrated in public dances, which are accompanied with songs and music suited to the occasion....We have many musical instruments, particularly drums of different kinds...."—Olaudah Equiana of Benin, 1789

MUSIC, accompanied by dancing and responsive choral singing, occupied a central role in West African life—in religious rituals, aesthetic expression, and entertainment. Musical instruments included harp, flute, xylophone, guitar, banjo, zither, and drum.

HARP

FLUTE

XYLOPHONE (with gourds)

THE TALKING DRUM—Drumming, the heart and soul of West African music, utilized instruments as simple as rocks or hollow logs with stretched hides and as sophisticated as the <u>talking drum</u> that simulated speech. The remarkable talking drum was strung with cords that created tension on the drumhead. Manipulation of the cords while striking the drumhead with a curved stick could produce changes in pitch ranging more than an octave. Skilled talking drummers could create the sounds of speech and relay words and sentences 100 miles in two hours, according to an 1899 account by British traveller A.B. Lloyd.

TALKING DRUM

DANCE—Dancing to drummers' complex polyrhythmic patterns, West Africans did complicated movements—following one rhythmic pattern with their feet, adding another with their hands, then another with their shoulders, and still another with their heads. The rhythmic drum beat often sent dancers into a trance.

In America, African music has had great impact, as African-American musicians developed new musical forms:

<u>JAZZ</u>, one of America's few original art forms, derives from African drummers' polyrhythmic patterns, whereby the first drummer sets a theme and other drummers spontaneously join in with complementary variations. Jazz musicians do the same with their various instruments.

<u>RHYTHM AND BLUES</u> music features the flattened, "blue" notes of African music.

<u>RAGTIME</u> music is based on African syncopated rhythms, which stress normally unaccented beats.

<u>SPIRITUALS</u> and other African-American church songs reflect African musical traditions.

The life of Africans changed drastically with the beginning of European trade in the 1400s. You learned earlier that Europeans depended on West Africa for their gold supply. They resented having to pay heavy gold duties (taxes) to North African Arabs who controlled the trans-Saharan gold trade with West Africa. Unable to break the Arabs' gold trade monopoly, the Portuguese— under the leadership of Prince Henry the Navigator—finally developed the navigational technology to sail around the bulge of Africa and trade for gold directly with West Africans.

Portugal, followed by other European countries, discovered that West Africans had things for sale other than gold: pepper, ivory, and their fellow Africans, captured in warfare. Commerce in slaves proved profitable, and so began the forced migration of Africans to the Americas.

PARTICIPANTS IN THE NEW WORLD SLAVE TRADE

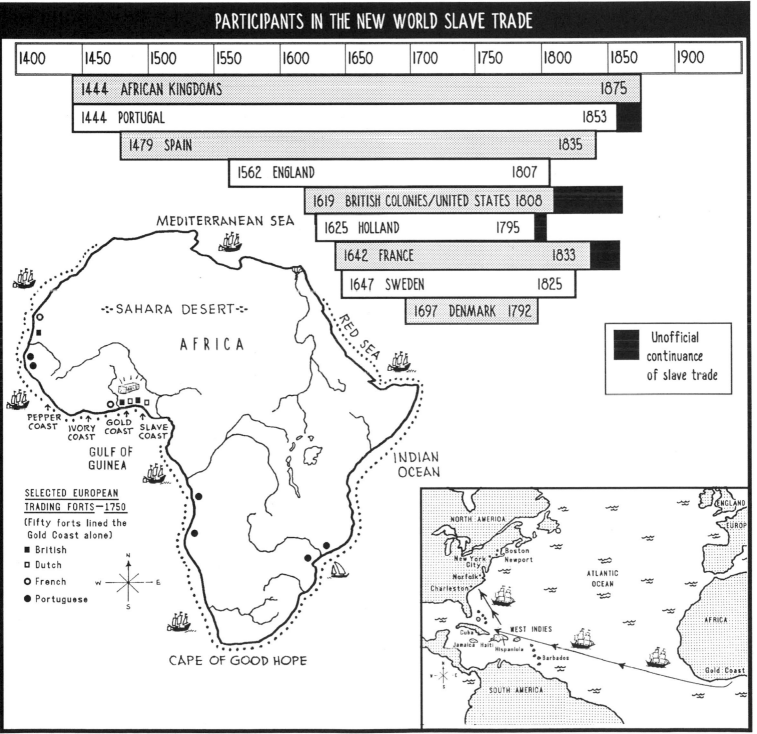

| 1400 | 1450 | 1500 | 1550 | 1600 | 1650 | 1700 | 1750 | 1800 | 1850 | 1900 |

1444 AFRICAN KINGDOMS 1875
1444 PORTUGAL 1853
1479 SPAIN 1835
1562 ENGLAND 1807
1619 BRITISH COLONIES/UNITED STATES 1808
1625 HOLLAND 1795
1642 FRANCE 1833
1647 SWEDEN 1825
1697 DENMARK 1792

■ Unofficial continuance of slave trade

MEDITERRANEAN SEA

SAHARA DESERT
AFRICA
RED SEA
INDIAN OCEAN

PEPPER COAST   IVORY COAST   GOLD COAST   SLAVE COAST

GULF OF GUINEA

SELECTED EUROPEAN TRADING FORTS—1750
(Fifty forts lined the Gold Coast alone)
■ British
□ Dutch
○ French
● Portuguese

N
W   E
S

CAPE OF GOOD HOPE

NORTH AMERICA   ENGLAND   EUROPE
New York City   Boston   Newport
Norfolk
Charleston   ATLANTIC OCEAN
Cuba   WEST INDIES   AFRICA
Jamaica Haiti Hispaniola
Barbados   Gold Coast
SOUTH AMERICA

1492   1740   1800   2000

"Nature and nature's laws lay hid in night.
God said, 'Let Newton be!' and all was light."
—Alexander Pope

41 ÷ THE AMERICAN ENLIGHTENMENT: AGE OF REASON, 1740-1800 ÷

enlighten—to shed light on truth: to free from ignorance
truth—how things are

intellect—power of the mind to understand through the use of reason
reason—to explore the cause and effect of things

1492   1740   1800   2000

THE ENLIGHTENMENT was a European and American intellectual revolution of the 18th century. It overthrew a long era of absolute ideas revealed through priests and kings; it affirmed man's capacity to reason and thus discover for himself truths about God, man, and the universe. The Enlightenment period emphasized man's <u>freedom</u>, as well as his ability, to think for himself. The 18th century, called the AGE OF REASON, gave birth to the American republic, founded by men of the Enlightenment.

I CAN TELL YOU ALL YOU WANT TO KNOW ABOUT THE PLANETS. I'VE HAD A <u>VISION</u>, AND THE KING HAS ENDORSED IT.

WELL, I'M GOING TO LEARN EMPIRICALLY—THROUGH OBSERVATION, REASON, AND LOGIC.

FROM THIS
REVELATION

TO THIS
DISCOVERY

From where did this new confidence in reason come? It started with the <u>SCIENTIFIC REVOLUTION</u> of the 16th and 17th centuries.

In 1665 English scientist SIR ISAAC NEWTON, building on the work of Polish NICKOLAS COPERNICUS and Italian GALILEO GALILEI, discovered the laws of motion governing the universe. These were laws of nature: <u>natural laws</u> that could be learned through observation, reason, and logic. In other words, thunder was not the wrath of God but a result of physical occurances, understandable through <u>reason</u>—that is, cause and effect thinking.

<u>NATURAL LAW</u> and <u>REASON</u> became key words of the Enlightenment. Newton applied them to the physical world. JOHN LOCKE and ADAM SMITH, two other British thinkers, applied them to human society: to politics and economics. America's FOUNDING FATHERS applied them to their Revolution and Constitution.

AMERICAN ENLIGHTENMENT INSTITUTIONS

POLITICAL:
Republic

Natural law gives each human being three natural rights: LIFE, LIBERTY, and PROPERTY, according to JOHN LOCKE, an English philosopher, in <u>Two Treatises of Government</u> (1690). Reason tells us that LIFE is essential to being human; LIBERTY is essential to protecting one's life, and PROPERTY is essential for things to sustain life.

People infringe on each other's rights, so through a social contract (mutual agreement) they form a government whose sole purpose is to protect their three rights. The people elect agents to govern them but retain their sovereignty. If the agents fail to protect the people's rights to LIFE, LIBERTY and PROPERTY, they may be deposed. Locke's ideas influenced THOMAS JEFFERSON in the Declaration of Independence.

ECONOMIC:
Capitalism

The law of supply and demand is the natural law of the market place, according to Scottish economist ADAM SMITH in <u>Wealth of Nations</u> (1776). With no government interference in business, neither aid nor regulation, the invisible hand of supply and demand competition leads to the best product at the lowest price.

<u>Capitalism</u>, an economic system based on the law of supply and demand, was adopted by the Founding Fathers. Capitalism involves three rights: 1) private property, 2) free enterprise, and 3) profit. BENJAMIN FRANKLIN, about whom you will read later, was one of the greatest exponents of capitalism.

RELIGIOUS:
Deism

According to THOMAS PAINE in his book <u>Age of Reason</u> (1794), God created a universe governed by natural laws; therefore, nature is mankind's Bible. This is the basic concept of Deism, a religious philosophy held by many 18th century American political leaders, including Thomas Jefferson and John Adams, as well as Paine. Deists believed in a rational God of goodness who wanted the best for His creation. They rejected supernatural phenomena, including heaven and hell. They believed in creating heaven on earth by doing good. Morality could be determined by reason and natural law rather than through religious authorities—the standard of morality being that which contributes to people's welfare and happiness.

INTELLECTUAL:
Science

Learning through discovery was the hallmark of the Enlightenment period. This involved a scientific approach to learning nature's laws through observation and experiment, as well as the belief that new knowledge should be used for the good of mankind. You'll see this approach to learning in the lives of two self-taught men who spent their lives investigating nature: BENJAMIN BANNEKER and BENJAMIN FRANKLIN.
Read on for the story of Benjamin Banneker.

"I consider [Banneker] as a fresh proof that the powers of the mind are disconnected with the colour of the skin."—James McHenry, U.S. Senator, 1791

1492   1731   1806   2000

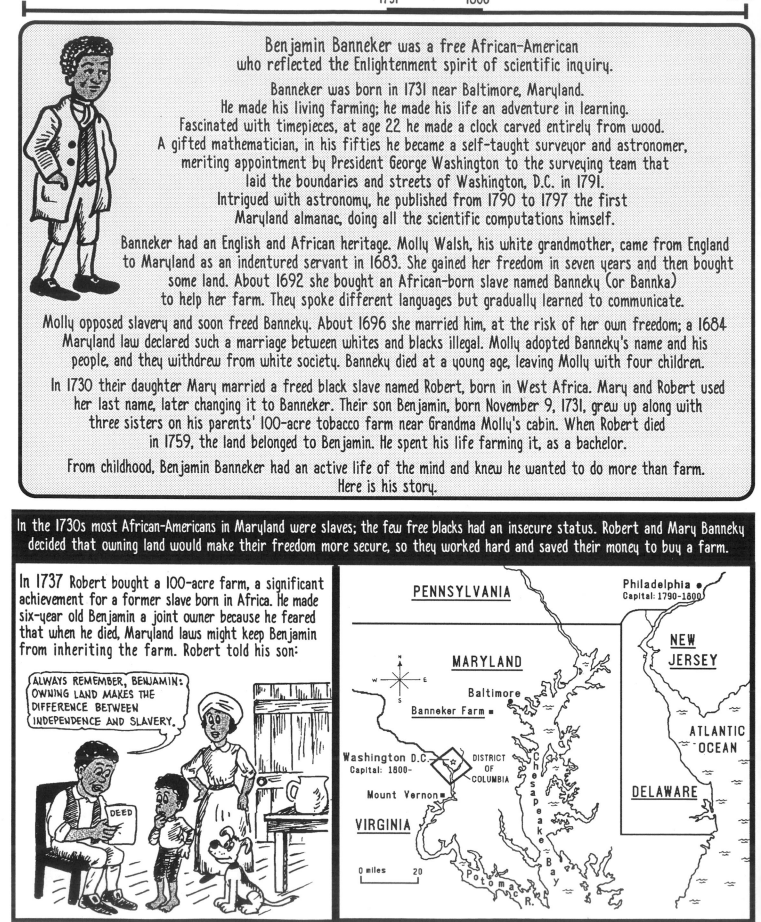

Benjamin Banneker was a free African-American
who reflected the Enlightenment spirit of scientific inquiry.

Banneker was born in 1731 near Baltimore, Maryland.
He made his living farming; he made his life an adventure in learning.
Fascinated with timepieces, at age 22 he made a clock carved entirely from wood.
A gifted mathematician, in his fifties he became a self-taught surveyor and astronomer,
meriting appointment by President George Washington to the surveying team that
laid the boundaries and streets of Washington, D.C. in 1791.
Intrigued with astronomy, he published from 1790 to 1797 the first
Maryland almanac, doing all the scientific computations himself.

Banneker had an English and African heritage. Molly Walsh, his white grandmother, came from England
to Maryland as an indentured servant in 1683. She gained her freedom in seven years and then bought
some land. About 1692 she bought an African-born slave named Banneky (or Bannka)
to help her farm. They spoke different languages but gradually learned to communicate.

Molly opposed slavery and soon freed Banneky. About 1696 she married him, at the risk of her own freedom; a 1684
Maryland law declared such a marriage between whites and blacks illegal. Molly adopted Banneky's name and his
people, and they withdrew from white society. Banneky died at a young age, leaving Molly with four children.

In 1730 their daughter Mary married a freed black slave named Robert, born in West Africa. Mary and Robert used
her last name, later changing it to Banneker. Their son Benjamin, born November 9, 1731, grew up along with
three sisters on his parents' 100-acre tobacco farm near Grandma Molly's cabin. When Robert died
in 1759, the land belonged to Benjamin. He spent his life farming it, as a bachelor.

From childhood, Benjamin Banneker had an active life of the mind and knew he wanted to do more than farm.
Here is his story.

In the 1730s most African-Americans in Maryland were slaves; the few free blacks had an insecure status. Robert and Mary Banneky
decided that owning land would make their freedom more secure, so they worked hard and saved their money to buy a farm.

In 1737 Robert bought a 100-acre farm, a significant
achievement for a former slave born in Africa. He made
six-year old Benjamin a joint owner because he feared
that when he died, Maryland laws might keep Benjamin
from inheriting the farm. Robert told his son:

ALWAYS REMEMBER, BENJAMIN: OWNING LAND MAKES THE DIFFERENCE BETWEEN INDEPENDENCE AND SLAVERY.

DEED

PENNSYLVANIA

Philadelphia ●
Capital: 1790-1800

MARYLAND

Baltimore

Banneker Farm ■

NEW JERSEY

Washington D.C. ☆ DISTRICT OF COLUMBIA
Capital: 1800-

Mount Vernon ■

VIRGINIA

Chesapeake Bay

ATLANTIC OCEAN

DELAWARE

0 miles 20

Potomac R.

Grandma Molly taught Benjamin to read and write from her only book: the Bible. And she told him stories of his Grandpa Banneky (whom a family acquaintance, Martha Tyson, described as a dignified man of "bright intelligence").

BENJAMIN, YOU HAVE A PROUD AFRICAN AND ENGLISH HERITAGE. YOUR GRANDFATHER BANNEKY WAS AN AFRICAN PRINCE, THE SON OF AN AFRICAN CHIEFTAIN. HE WAS CAPTURED BY SLAVE TRADERS, SOLD TO A SLAVETRADE COMPANY AND BROUGHT BY SHIP TO AMERICA.

Benjamin attended a one-room Quaker school for four winters, along with several white students and another free black, Jacob Hall. A gifted student, Benjamin liked to invent math puzzles, and (according to Jacob) "all his delight was to dive into his books."

GOOD ANSWER, BENJAMIN. YOU HAVE A KEEN MATHEMATICAL MIND.

1751—At age 20, Benjamin Banneker began a venture that revealed astonishing mathematical and mechanical ability. He borrowed a pocket watch for a week to see how it worked. He decided he could create his own timepiece, so after taking the watch apart, he drew the pieces and memorized how they fit together.

HOPE THIS WORKS. I JUST KNOW IT WILL.

1753—Guided only by his drawings and laboring for two years, Banneker made a clock by carving the parts from wood. It kept perfect time for 53 years. (The day Benjamin died in 1806, a fire destroyed his home and his clock.)

Throughout his life people came from miles around to see the first clock made of wood—and the remarkable man who made it.

1776—During the Revolutionary War Banneker grew wheat for American soldiers. He read with puzzlement Thomas Jefferson's words in the Declaration of Independence.

IN THE DECLARATION OF INDEPENDENCE THOMAS JEFFERSON SAID ALL MEN ARE CREATED EQUAL. WHY DOESN'T THAT INCLUDE BLACKS?

ARMY QUARTER MASTER

1789—At age 58, Banneker found a new direction for his life: astronomy.

George Ellicott, a Quaker neighbor, loaned him surveying and astronomy textbooks and instruments.

By 1790 Benjamin mastered both subjects on his own and amazed George by calculating a 1791 ephemeris (astronomical projections for the calendar year), the basic information for an almanac.

1791—Banneker sent his epihemis—the astronomical projections for a 1791 almanac—to Andrew Ellicott, George's surveyer cousin, and received the surprise of his life. President George Washington had appointed Andrew to survey the site for the nation's new capital, later named Washington, D.C. Andrew was impressed by Banneker's astronomical expertise (essential for surveying land) and recommended him for the survey team to Thomas Jefferson, who was in charge of the project. Then, at Jefferson's recommendation, Washington confirmed Banneker's appointment.

February-April 1791—Using Pierre L'Enfant's design for Washington, D.C., the surveying team went to work. Every night Banneker observed the stars from a hole in the observatory tent and then used their latitude and longitude to compute base points for the capital's streets.

On March 28, 1791, President Washington came to visit the capital site. There is no evidence that Banneker met him, but Benjamin must have been proud as Washington (himself a surveyor) reviewed the team's work.

1791—Upon returning home Banneker fulfilled his ambition to write Benjamin Banneker's Almanac.

Unlike Benjamin Franklin in Poor Richard's Almanac, he did his own computing of the tides, eclipses, sunrises and sunsets.

But like Franklin, he included proverbs and essays to entertain and instruct.

Among the essays were several on antislavery, written by members of the Maryland Society for the Abolition of Slavery.

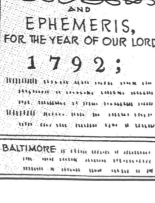

Banneker's publisher asked Dr. David Rittenhouse of Philadelphia to review the almanac before its printing. Rittenhouse, the country's foremost scientist and Benjamin Franklin's successor as president of the American Philosophical Society, reported:

1792-97—Banneker's almanac was a big success. He published one annually for six years; by 1797, twenty-eight editions had been printed. The 1793 almanac contained an exchange of letters with Thomas Jefferson.

Banneker sent a letter and a copy of his first almanac to Secretary of State Thomas Jefferson, author of the Declaration of Independence.

August 19, 1791

Sir...I suppose it is a truth too well attested to you...that we are a race of Beings who have long laboured under the abuse and censure of the world, that we have long been looked upon with an eye of contempt, and that we have long been considered rather as brutish than human, and scarcely capable of mental endowments.

Sir, I hope I may safely admit...that you are friendly and well disposed towards us...willing and ready to lend your aid....

Sir, suffer me to recall...that time in which the arms and tyranny of the British Crown were exerted...to reduce you to a state of servitude....This, Sir, was a time in which you clearly saw into the injustice of...slavery...and held forth this true and invaluable doctrine: "We hold these truths to be self-evident, that all men are created equal, and that they are endowed by their creator with certain inalienable rights, that amongst these are life, liberty, and the pursuit of happiness."

...but Sir, how pitiable it is to reflect, that...you should at the same time counteract [God's] mercies, in detaining through fraud and violence my brethren under groaning captivity and cruel oppression....

...as Job proposed to his friends, "Put your souls in their souls' stead...and thus shall you need neither the direction of myself or others in what manner to proceed herein...."

And now Sir, I shall conclude and subscribe my self with the most profound respect,

Your most obedient humble servant
Benjamin Banneker

Four days after receiving Banneker's letter, Jefferson replied.

August 30, 1791

Sir, I thank you sincerely for your letter of the 19th...and for the Almanac....Nobody wishes more than I do to see such proofs as you exhibit, that nature has given to our black brethren, talents equal to those of the other colors of men, and that the appearance of a want of them is owing merely to the degraded condition of their existence, both in Africa and America. I can add with truth, that nobody wishes more ardently to see a good system commenced for raising the condition both of their body and mind to what it ought to be, as fast as the imbecility of their present existence, and other circumstances which cannot be neglected, will admit.

I have taken the liberty of sending your Almanac to Monsieur de Condorcet, Secretary of the Academy of Sciences at Paris...because I considered it as a document to which your whole colour had a right for their justification against the doubts which have been entertained of them.

I am with great esteem, Sir, your most obedient humble servant.
Thomas Jefferson

Banneker spent his last years
observing nature and
playing his flute and violin
under a favorite pear tree.

He belonged to no church,
although he dressed as a Quaker and often
attended the Society of Friends meeting-house.
Martha Tyson, daughter of George Ellicott, said,

"His life was one of constant worship in the great
temples of nature."

1806—Benjamin Banneker died at age 74.

An obituary in the Federal Gazette described Banneker as "well known...among scientific men as an astronomer and mathematician."

His reputation as an African-American intellectual widened after his death. In 1836 Martha Tyson wrote A Sketch of Banneker's life. Other memoirs followed.

In 1852 Banneker's manuscripts, letters, and almanacs were given to the Maryland Historical Society.

In 1878 Frederick Douglass, black abolitionist, said:
"We as a people are especially in need of just such examples of mental industry and success as I believe the life of Benjamin Banneker furnish."

1854—In tribute to Banneker, African-American young men in Philadelphia who had formed the Young Men's Mutual Instruction Society named it the BANNEKER INSTITUTE.

In 1954 a plaque designated the Westchester Grade School in Oella, Maryland as the approximate location of Banneker's home.

Benjamin Banneker

1731-1806

Self-educated Negro

Mathematician—Astronomer

He made the first Maryland Almanac in 1792.

Assisted in survey of District of Columbia.

His achievements recognized

by Thomas Jefferson.

Was born, lived his entire life and

died near here.

This story is based on a biography you might like to read, The Life of Benjamin Banneker by Sylvio A. Bedini.

Enlightenment ideas shaped the thinking of many of the Founding Fathers—the dozens of men who led America from colonial status to independence and created a republic based on the human rights of life, liberty, and property. The light of reason shone brightly on and through "the big six" below. Without their wisdom, imagination, integrity and heroic efforts for the cause of freedom, the United States as we know it would not exist. They shared a vision that liberty for Americans might spread to all humankind. You'll be reading about them from now on, so here's an introduction.

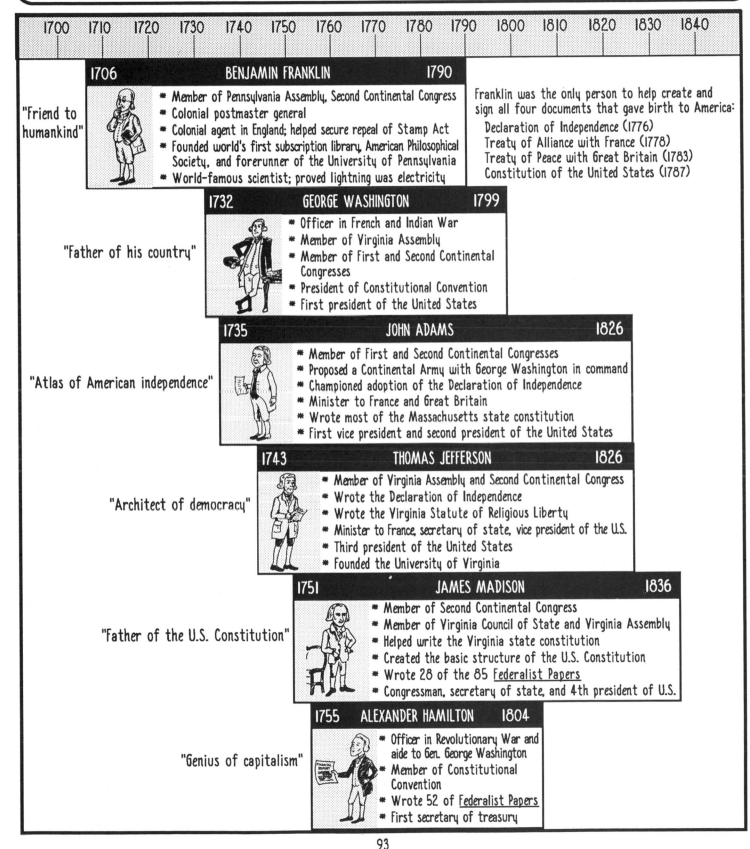

| 1700 | 1710 | 1720 | 1730 | 1740 | 1750 | 1760 | 1770 | 1780 | 1790 | 1800 | 1810 | 1820 | 1830 | 1840 |

1706 — BENJAMIN FRANKLIN — 1790

"Friend to humankind"

* Member of Pennsylvania Assembly, Second Continental Congress
* Colonial postmaster general
* Colonial agent in England; helped secure repeal of Stamp Act
* Founded world's first subscription library, American Philosophical Society, and forerunner of the University of Pennsylvania
* World-famous scientist; proved lightning was electricity

Franklin was the only person to help create and sign all four documents that gave birth to America:

Declaration of Independence (1776)
Treaty of Alliance with France (1778)
Treaty of Peace with Great Britain (1783)
Constitution of the United States (1787)

1732 — GEORGE WASHINGTON — 1799

"Father of his country"

* Officer in French and Indian War
* Member of Virginia Assembly
* Member of First and Second Continental Congresses
* President of Constitutional Convention
* First president of the United States

1735 — JOHN ADAMS — 1826

"Atlas of American independence"

* Member of First and Second Continental Congresses
* Proposed a Continental Army with George Washington in command
* Championed adoption of the Declaration of Independence
* Minister to France and Great Britain
* Wrote most of the Massachusetts state constitution
* First vice president and second president of the United States

1743 — THOMAS JEFFERSON — 1826

"Architect of democracy"

* Member of Virginia Assembly and Second Continental Congress
* Wrote the Declaration of Independence
* Wrote the Virginia Statute of Religious Liberty
* Minister to France, secretary of state, vice president of the U.S.
* Third president of the United States
* Founded the University of Virginia

1751 — JAMES MADISON — 1836

"Father of the U.S. Constitution"

* Member of Second Continental Congress
* Member of Virginia Council of State and Virginia Assembly
* Helped write the Virginia state constitution
* Created the basic structure of the U.S. Constitution
* Wrote 28 of the 85 Federalist Papers
* Congressman, secretary of state, and 4th president of U.S.

1755 — ALEXANDER HAMILTON — 1804

"Genius of capitalism"

* Officer in Revolutionary War and aide to Gen. George Washington
* Member of Constitutional Convention
* Wrote 52 of Federalist Papers
* First secretary of treasury

character: the sum of distinctive qualities describing a person or group; the stamp of individuality engraved by nature, habit, and education

| 1492 | 1706 | 1790 | 2000 |

Of all the Founding Fathers, Benjamin Franklin best symbolized the Enlightenment, for he successfully applied the light of reason to every aspect of life. His achievements as

> I grew convinced that truth, sincerity, and integrity were of the utmost importance to a happy life.

printer and businessman,
scientist and inventor,
statesman and diplomat,
philosopher and humanitarian

earned him the reputation of "the greatest American" and "a friend to humankind."

Through his talents as a thinker, writer, moralist, and humorist he applied the light of reason to shaping the American character. In 1782 J. Hector St. John de Crevecoeur asked, "What then is the American, this new man?" After Franklin, the answer would be, "Someone like Ben: industrious, honest, frugal, practical, persevering, optimistic, curious, inventive, good-natured, and generous."

INDUSTRIOUS—"Keep thy shop, and thy shop will keep thee." "He that hath a trade hath an estate."*

COMPUTER SHOP

HONEST—"Honesty is the best policy." "Avoid dishonest gain; no price can recompense the pangs of vice."

SCAM PLAN

FRUGAL—"Beware of little expenses; a small leak will sink a big ship." "...spend less than you get...."

HELP!
BILL BILL BILL BILL BILL

PRACTICAL—"Tell me and I forget. Teach me and I remember. Involve me and I learn."

PERSEVERING—"Industry, perseverance, and frugality make fortune yield."

OPTIMISTIC—"There are many sorrows in this life, but many more pleasures. That is why I love life."

CURIOUS—"The doors of wisdom are never shut."

ART   HISTORY   SCIENCE

INVENTIVE—"Necessity is the mother of invention."

COOKIES

GOOD-NATURED—"Bad humor is an uncleanness of the soul."

LIGHTEN UP HARRY!

GENEROUS—"When you are good to others, you are best to yourself." "What is serving God? 'Tis doing good to man."

ORPHAN FUND

In 1880 Mark Twain noted Franklin's far-reaching influence.

> AS A BOY I HAD TO BOIL SOAP AND STUDY GEOMETRY AT BREAKFAST AND DO EVERYTHING JUST AS FRANKLIN DID IN HOPES I WOULD BE A FRANKLIN SOMEDAY!

> GUESS IF I'VE INFLUENCED THE AMERICAN CHARACTER, IT'S ONLY FAIR TO TELL YOU WHAT SHAPED MY CHARACTER. WELL, HERE'S MY STORY—WITH A WARNING THAT AS A TEENAGER I RAN AWAY FROM HOME AND...WELL, SEE FOR YOURSELF.

* Proverbs on this page are quoted from Benjamin Franklin's Poor Richard's Almanac.

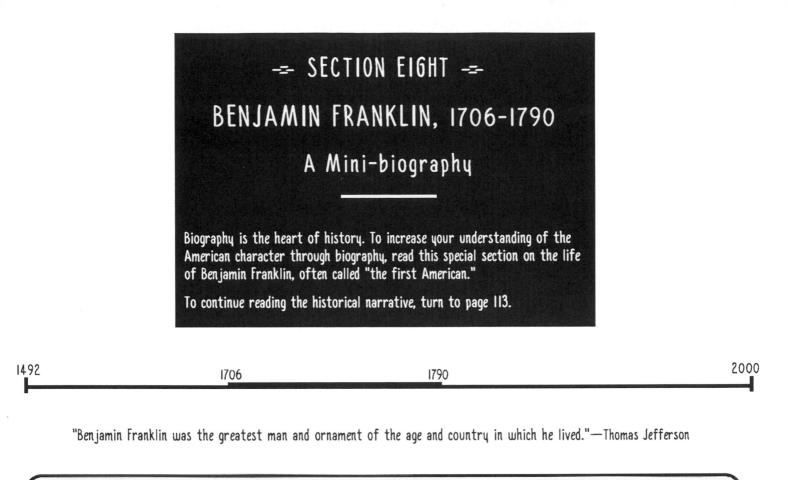

SECTION EIGHT

BENJAMIN FRANKLIN, 1706-1790

A Mini-biography

Biography is the heart of history. To increase your understanding of the American character through biography, read this special section on the life of Benjamin Franklin, often called "the first American."

To continue reading the historical narrative, turn to page 113.

1492   1706   1790   2000

"Benjamin Franklin was the greatest man and ornament of the age and country in which he lived."—Thomas Jefferson

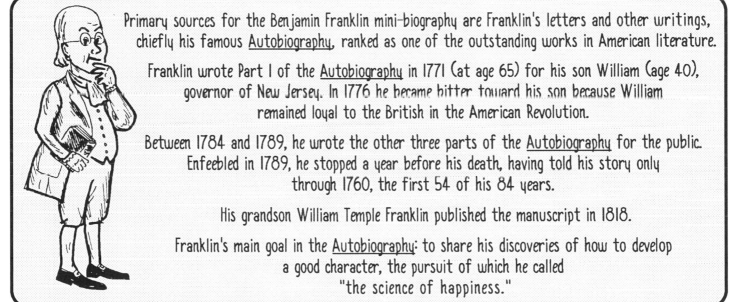

Primary sources for the Benjamin Franklin mini-biography are Franklin's letters and other writings, chiefly his famous <u>Autobiography</u>, ranked as one of the outstanding works in American literature.

Franklin wrote Part I of the <u>Autobiography</u> in 1771 (at age 65) for his son William (age 40), governor of New Jersey. In 1776 he became bitter toward his son because William remained loyal to the British in the American Revolution.

Between 1784 and 1789, he wrote the other three parts of the <u>Autobiography</u> for the public. Enfeebled in 1789, he stopped a year before his death, having told his story only through 1760, the first 54 of his 84 years.

His grandson William Temple Franklin published the manuscript in 1818.

Franklin's main goal in the <u>Autobiography</u>: to share his discoveries of how to develop a good character, the pursuit of which he called "the science of happiness."

1492   1706   1790   2000

In 1771, while serving as a colonial agent in England, Benjamin Franklin began his autobiography with these words:

Benjamin Franklin

William Franklin

GOVERNOR OF NEW JERSEY

"Dear Son:

"I have ever had a pleasure in obtaining any little anecdotes of my ancestors....Imagining it may be equally agreeable to you to know the circumstances of my life...I sit down to write them for you....

"Besides, there are some other inducements that excite me to this undertaking. From the poverty and obscurity in which I was born... I have raised myself to a state of affluence and some degree of celebrity in the world. As constant good fortune has accompanied me...my posterity will perhaps be desirous of learning the means which I employed....They may also deem them fit to be imitated, should any of them find themselves in similar circumstances....

"And lastly (I may as well confess it, as the denial of it would be believed by nobody) I shall perhaps not a little gratify my own vanity. Indeed I never heard or saw the introductory words, "Without vanity I may say," etc., but some vain thing immediately followed. Most people dislike vanity in others whatever share they have of it themselves, but I give it fair quarter wherever I meet with it, being persuaded that it is often productive of good to the possessor and to others that are within his sphere of action. And therefore, in many cases it would not be altogether absurd if a man were to thank God for his vanity among the other comforts of life.

"And now I speak of thanking God, I desire with all humility to acknowledge that I owe the mentioned happiness of my past life to his divine providence, which led me to the means I used and gave them success."

"...relating to our ancestors....the family had lived in the same village, Ecton [England] for 300 years...on a freehold [farm] of about 30 acres, aided by the smith's business...the eldest son being always bred to that business...."

"Our humble family early embraced the Reformation....[and] continued Protestants through the Reign of [Queen] Mary [Bloody Mary, 1553-58], when they were sometimes in danger of persecution on account of their zeal against Popery [Catholicism]. They had an English Bible, and to conceal it...it was fastened open with tapes under...a stool. When my great, great grandfather wished to read it to his family, he turned up the...stool upon his knees...."

"Josiah, my father, married young and carried his wife [Anne] with three children to [Boston] New England about 1682....where they expected to enjoy the exercise of their [Puritan] religion with freedom.

"By the same wife [he] had four children more born there and by a second wife [Abiah, daughter of Peter Folger, a founder of Nantucket Island] 10 more, in all 17, of which I remember often to have seen 13 sitting together at his table...."

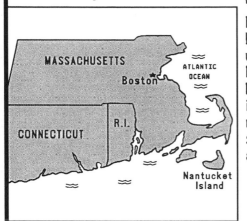

Boston: January 17, 1706—And so a crowd of brothers and sisters welcomed the birth of Benjamin Franklin, the 15th of 17 children born to Abiah and Josiah, by now an industrious, respected Boston candle and soap maker.

HERE WE ARE - MILK STREET AGAIN!

MILK STREET

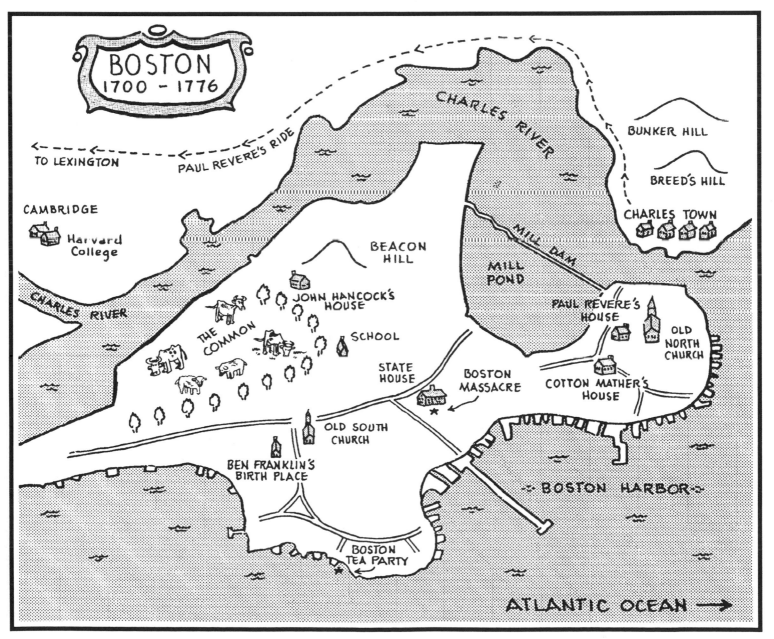

BOSTON 1700 - 1776

PAUL REVERE'S RIDE

TO LEXINGTON

CHARLES RIVER

BUNKER HILL

BREED'S HILL

CHARLES TOWN

CAMBRIDGE
Harvard College

CHARLES RIVER

BEACON HILL

MILL DAM

MILL POND

JOHN HANCOCK'S HOUSE

THE COMMON

SCHOOL

PAUL REVERE'S HOUSE

OLD NORTH CHURCH

STATE HOUSE

BOSTON MASSACRE

COTTON MATHER'S HOUSE

OLD SOUTH CHURCH

BEN FRANKLIN'S BIRTH PLACE

BOSTON HARBOR

BOSTON TEA PARTY

ATLANTIC OCEAN →

Ben described his mother as "a discreet and virtuous woman." He added, "I think you might like to know something of [my father's]...character....He was...well set and very strong, could draw...and was skilled a little in music and had a clear pleasing voice....But his great excellence lay in sound understanding and solid judgment....I remember his being...visited by leading people, who consulted him for his opinion in affairs of the town or of the church....He was...frequently chosen an arbiter between contending parties.

"At his table he liked to have some sensible friend...,to converse with, and always took care to start some ingenious or useful topic which might tend to improve the minds of his children....[turning] our attention to what was good, just, and prudent in the conduct of life." Josiah believed in the Puritan concept of learning as expressed by Samuel Sewell, his pastor at Old South Church, "without knowledge the mind of man cannot be good...."

THE <u>WHISTLE LESSON</u> was one of Ben's earliest memories.

"When I was a child of seven years...being charmed with the sound of a whistle...in the hands of another boy, I voluntarily offered and gave all my money for one. I then came home and went whistling all over the house, much pleased....My brothers and sisters, understanding the bargain I had made... laughed so much at me for my folly that I cried...."

"As I grew up...and observed the actions of men, I thought I met many who gave too much for the whistle....In short, I conceived that the great part of the miseries of mankind were brought upon them by the false estimates they had made of the value of things, and by their giving too much for the whistle."

"I had a strong inclination for the sea [Boston was a thriving seaport; its population, 10,000.]; but my father declared against it; however...I learned early to swim well, and to manage boats, and when in a boat...with other boys I was commonly allowed to govern...." "I amused myself one day...with my kite...enjoying at the same time the pleasure of swimming."

"I was generally a leader among the boys, and sometimes led them into scrapes, of which I will mention one...as it shows an early...public spirit, though not then justly conducted. There was a salt marsh...[where] we used to...fish....My proposal was to build a wharf there [from] a heap of stones...intended for a new house. The next morning...we were discovered...and corrected by our fathers."

"Genius without education is like silver in the mine." —Poor Richard's Almanac

"I have from my youth been indefatigably studious to gain and treasure up in my mind all useful and desirable knowledge...."—Benjamin Franklin

1716-1718—Between the ages of 10 and 12, Ben read five books that influenced him forever.

1) John Bunyan, *The Pilgrims's Progress*
2) R. Burton, *Historical Collections*
3) Plutarch, *Parallel Lives of the Noble Greeks and Romans*
4) Daniel Defoe, *Essay on Projects*
5) Cotton Mather, *Essays to Do Good*

1) *The Pilgrim's Progress,* written in 1678 by John Bunyan, an English Puritan preacher, is a famous allegory (published in 100 languages) in which the characters represent virtues and vices. Christian, the hero laden with burdens, progresses through life toward the Celestial City (heaven), crossing hazardous places along the way.

"From a child I was fond of reading, and all the little money that came into my hands was ever laid out in books. Pleased with *The Pilgrim's Progress,* my first collection was of John Bunyan's works."

Christian meets people who try to hurt him: VICES such as Pride, Envy, Giant Despair and his wife Diffidence—and people who help him: VIRTUES such as Old Honest, Faithful, Hopeful, and Courage.

Ben learned valuable tips from Christian's progress.

VANITY FAIR

SLOUGH OF DESPOND

HILL OF DIFFICULTY

CELESTIAL CITY

Bunyan wrote in his preface, "Wouldst thou see a truth within a fable? ....Then read my fancies: they will stick like burrs...."

THEY DID STICK LIKE BURRS FOR BEN, ESPECIALLY THE OPTIMISTIC IDEA OF PROGRESS — FORWARD MOVEMENT TOWARD GOODNESS. HE WOULD LIVE LIFE AS AN ADVENTURE: DOING BATTLE WITH VICES (SOMETIMES LOSING) AND BEFRIENDING VIRTUES, STRIVING TOWARD THE GOAL OF BEING GOOD AND DOING GOOD.

virtue—goodness that is consciously maintained; moral excellence

2) R. Burton's Historical Collections

became Ben's next purchase. "Burton" was an alias for Nathan Crouch, an English printer who popularized history in brief volumes (40 or 50 in all), such as "Admirable Curiosities, Rarities, and Wonders in England" and "Unfortunate Court Favorites of England," for twelve pennies each.

BEN, WHERE'D YOU GET THOSE POP HISTORY BOOKS? THEY'RE HARDLY SCHOLARLY.

BUT THEY'RE FACTUAL—AND LIVELY! THEY MAKE HISTORY COME ALIVE. JAMES BOSWELL SAID SAMUEL JOHNSON, THE ENGLISH WRITER AND CRITIC, ORDERED A WHOLE SET. HE TOLD HIS BOOKSELLER, "... THEY SEEM VERY PROPER TO ALLURE BACKWARD READERS; BE SO KIND AS TO GET THEM FOR ME...."

"My Father's little library consisted chiefly of books in polemic divinity, most of which I read, and have since often regretted that at a time when I had such a thirst for knowledge, more proper books had not fallen in my way....

"Plutarch's Lives there was, in which I read abundantly, and I still think that time spent to great advantage."

3) In Parallel Lives of the Noble Greeks and Romans

(an important book read by all the Founding Fathers), Plutarch, a Greek writing in the first century A.D., made Greek and Roman history personal, vibrant, and exciting by telling it through the lives of great men.

Plutarch's Lives—46 biographies of notable Greeks and Romans—had a purpose: to provide role models of men who from small and obscure beginnings became great and powerful through a commitment to virtue—to the good.

THE ROMAN EMPIRE IN 121 A.D.

BRITAIN
ATLANTIC OCEAN
GAUL
SPAIN
Rome
GREECE
BLACK SEA
ASIA MINOR
MEDITERRANEAN SEA
ALEXANDRIA
EXTENT OF THE ROMAN EMPIRE

"One single day acting right should be treasured more than a lifetime of acting wrong."
Cicero
Plutarch

GREEKS		ROMANS
Demosthenes		Cicero
	Eloquent orators	
Aristides		Cato
	Champions of justice	
Alexander the Great		Julius Ceasar
	Brilliant empire builders	

Plutarch said of biography: "Ah, and what greater pleasure can one have? Or what more effective means to moral improvement?"

THE VIRTUES OF THESE GREAT MEN [SERVE] ME AS A SORT OF LOOKING-GLASS, IN WHICH I MAY SEE HOW TO ADJUST AND ADORN MY OWN LIFE...WE... ENTERTAIN EACH SUCCESSIVE GUEST, VIEW THEIR STATURE AND THEIR QUALITIES, AND SELECT FROM THEIR ACTIONS ALL THAT IS NOBLEST AND WORTHIEST TO KNOW.

"My method...is, by the study of history...to receive and retain images of the best and worthiest characters. I thus am enabled to free myself from any ignoble, base, or vicious impressions, contracted from...ill company that I may be unavoidably engaged in, by the remedy of [viewing] these noble examples."

PLUTARCH MY MAN! LAY DOWN THOSE BOOKS AND LET'S PARTY!

SORRY, GUYS, BUT I'M STICKING WITH MY HISTORY. I DON'T WANT TO ENGAGE IN IGNOBLE STUFF.

WAY TO GO PLUTARCH!

THE LAST DAYS OF SOCRATES
BY PLATO

1718—"To return. I continued...employed in my Father's business [making candles and soap] for two years...till I was 12 years old. I disliked the trade."

YUCK!! I THINK I'LL RUN AWAY TO SEA!

"...my father [feared] that if he did not find one for me more agreeable, I should break away and get to sea....[My] bookish inclination at length determined my father to make me a printer."

YOUR BROTHER JAMES IS NOW TWENTY AND HAS HIS OWN PRINT SHOP. YOU'RE SUCH A BOOKISH LAD, YOU SHOULD BECOME HIS APPRENTICE.

I LIKE IT BETTER THAN YOUR TRADE, FATHER, BUT I'D RATHER GO TO SEA. I WANT TO TRAVEL AND SEE THE WORLD.

UPPER CASE
lower case

JAMES FRANKLIN PRINT SHOP

?

"I stood out some time, but at last was persuaded and signed the indentures [contract], when I was but 12 years old. I was to serve as an apprentice till I was 21 years of age...."

BEN, YOU ARE NOW BOUND BY LAW FOR 9 YEARS TO LIVE WITH ME, OBEY ME, AND WORK FOR NO WAGES TILL THE LAST YEAR. IN RETURN, I'LL TEACH YOU THE PRINTER'S TRADE.

OBEY MY BROTHER!? YEAH, RIGHT!

"In a little time I made great proficiency in the business, and became a useful hand to my brother. I now had access to better books....My time for reading was at night...or on Sundays...evading... attendance on public worship, which my Father used to exact of me."

YES, JAMES, I KNOW IT'S MY DUTY TO ATTEND CHURCH. BUT I CAN'T AFFORD THE TIME, THERE'S SO MUCH TO LEARN.

BIBLE

1722—"[At age 16, I read] Xenophon's Memorable Things of Socrates....I was charmed with the Socratic method of dispute, adopted it, dropt my abrupt contradiction, and put on the humble enquirer. I found this method... embarrassing to those against whom I used it, therefore I took a delight in it...and grew... expert in drawing people... into concessions the consequences of which they did not foresee."

I DON'T GET IT. HOW DID I END UP AGREEING WITH HIM?

BEATS ME!

"And now it was that being...made ashamed of my ignorance in figures, which I had twice failed in learning when at school, I took Cocker's [Arithmetic, Being a Plain and Easy Method] and went through the whole by my self with great ease."

BOOK SHOP

FINALLY — AN ARITHMETIC BOOK THAT'S FUN!

I WONDER IF IT HAS CARTOONS?

"About this time I met with an odd volume of the Spectator [a London daily paper published by Joseph Addison and Richard Steele] I thought the writing excellent and wished if possible to imitate it. I [made] short hints of...each sentence, laid them by a few days, and then...tried to complete the papers again.

"By comparing my work with the original, I discovered many faults and amended them; but I sometimes had the pleasure of [improving] the language, and this encouraged me to think I might...in time...come to be a tolerable English writer....

"Intent on improving my language, I [also read] an English grammar...."

NOT BAD.

B.F.'s VERSION

SPECTATOR

Years later Ben said:

PROSE WRITING HAS BEEN OF GREAT USE TO ME IN THE COURSE OF MY LIFE, AND WAS A PRINCIPAL MEANS OF MY ADVANCEMENT. IT SEEMS TO ME THERE IS SCARCE ANY ACCOMPLISHMENT MORE NECESSARY TO A MAN OF SENSE, THAN OF WRITING WELL IN HIS MOTHER TONGUE.

In 1722 Ben tried his new writing skills. "My brother had begun to print a newspaper, The New England Courant. He had some...friends who [wrote] little pieces for this paper. I was excited to try my hand among them. But being still a boy [age 16] and suspecting that my brother would object to printing anything of mine...."
"I contrived to disguise my hand, and, writing an anonymous paper [as Silence Dogood, a country widow], I put it in at night under the door of the printing-house."

QUITE WITTY — LIKE THE SPECTATOR. WHO COULD THIS TALENTED WRITER BE? SURELY AN INGENIOUS MAN OF CHARACTER.

YOU CAN TELL FROM THE PEN NAME, "SILENCE DOGOOD," THAT HE'S READ COTTON MATHER'S ESSAY TO DO GOOD.

James and his friends were surprised and impressed.

Silence Dogood sent a second letter describing her character. Or was it Ben's?

Dear Author of the New England Courant:
...I shall conclude this with my own character.... I am an enemy to vice and a friend to virtue.... a hearty lover of...all good men, and a mortal enemy to arbitrary government and unlimited power.... I have likewise a natural inclination to observe and reprove the faults of others, at which I have an excellent faculty. I speak this by way of warning...for I never intend to wrap my talent in a napkin.
I am courteous, affable, good humored (unless...provoked), handsome, and sometimes witty, but always, your friend and servant,

SILENCE DOGOOD

Silence Dogood was a hit, so Ben wrote 12 more witty, anonymous letters. Some proposed reforms from Defoe's Essay on Projects, such as women's right to education. Most satirized Boston customs and religion, offending political and religious leaders.

SILENCE DOGOOD HAS GONE TOO FAR: SHE SAYS RELIGIOUS HYPOCRITES ARE WORSE THAN NON-BELIEVERS, ESPECIALLY IF THEY SERVE IN GOVERNMENT.

AND WORSE, SHE CLAIMS THAT FREEDOM OF SPEECH GIVES HER THE RIGHT TO SAY THIS!

REV. COTTON MATHER

GOV. SAMUEL SHUTE

Ben finally revealed his secret authorship, and won praise from James' friends. Quite jealous, James complained (with reason) that their praise made Ben vain. This was but one of many master-apprentice conflicts between the brothers.

VAIN?? WHO, ME?

GOOD GRIEF!

"James...had often beat me, which I took extremely amiss. I fancy his harsh and tyrannical treatment of me...[impressed] me with that aversion to arbitrary power that has stuck to me through my whole life."
Ben found an unexpected way to escape.

THE ASSEMBLY ORDERED ME TO STOP PUBLISHING THE COURANT. BUT YOU CAN PUBLISH IT IF I CANCEL YOUR APPRENTICE INDENTURES. OF COURSE, YOU'LL SIGN NEW ONES PRIVATELY.

"I took upon me to assert my freedom, presuming he would not produce the new indentures. It was not fair in me to take this advantage, and this I reckon one of the first errata of my life: but the unfairness of it weighed little with...the...resentment [of] blows....He was otherwise not an ill-natured man; perhaps I was too saucy and provoking."

IF YOU LEAVE, I'LL BLACKBALL YOU WITH EVERY PRINTER IN BOSTON. YOU'LL NEVER GET A JOB.

THEN I'LL RUN AWAY TO NEW YORK. BESIDES, BOSTON LEADERS THINK I'M AN ATHEIST FOR MAKING FUN OF HYPOCRISY.

1723—"So I sold some of my books to raise a little money, [and secretly, with a friend's help] was taken on board [a ship], and...in three days I found my self in New York near 300 miles from home...." Ben asked a New York printer for a job.

I'M ONLY 17, BUT I DO HAVE A TRADE. I'M AN EXPERT PRINTER, AND I OFFER YOU MY SERVICE.

BRADFORD'S PRINT SHOP New York City

I DON'T NEED A PRINTER, BUT MY SON IN PHILADELPHIA DOES. WHY NOT GO THERE?

"Philadelphia was 100 miles farther...[and] I set out in a boat. A drunken Dutchman...fell overboard; I reached through the water and drew him up. [He took] out of his pocket a book, which he desired I would dry for him."

WELL! IT'S MY OLD FAVORITE, PILGRIM'S PROGRESS. THIS IS A GOOD OMEN FOR MY NEW LIFE IN PHILADELPHIA! I WONDER WHAT ADVENTURES AWAIT ME THERE.

PILGRIM'S PROGRESS

1723: PHILADELPHIA—On a September Sunday morning, Ben arrived in Philadelphia, a bustling port of 10,000 on the Delaware River. This city of ethnic diversity and religious tolerance would become his beloved hometown for life.

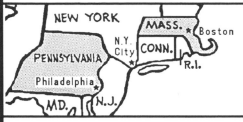

Arriving in rags at age 17, Ben would build a publishing empire and be rich enough at age 42 to retire to scientific pursuits, inventions, and public service.
HOW DID HE DO IT?

"I have been the more particular in [describing]...my first entry into that city that you may in your mind compare such unlikely beginnings with the figure I have since made there. I was in my working dress...dirty from my journey; my pockets were stuffed out with shirts and stockings; I knew no soul, nor where to look for lodging. I was fatigued...hungry...[and had only] a Dutch dollar."
Ben bought three huge rolls and walked up Market Street eating his breakfast.

Ben had no money, but he had a trade. (And, as Poor Richard would say, "He who hath a trade hath an estate.") He immediately found a job at Samuel Keimer's print shop as a journeyman, a welcome step up from an apprentice. Then one day, he had a big surprise!

An improbable development: Ben's brother-in-law Robert Holmes, learning Ben was in Philadelphia, had written urging him to come home. Ben's return letter was read by Holmes in the presence of Gov. Keith, who was impressed with Ben and wanted to aid him.

1724: BOSTON—And so after a seven-month absence, Ben returned home to his surprised family. All were glad to see him, except James. Ben said, "I went to see him...better dressed than ever while in his service. He...looked me all over, and turned to his work again."

Josiah denied Ben's request for a loan.

1724: LONDON—Governor Keith turned out to be a con man. Offering to finance Ben, he sent him to England to buy print equipment—then reneged. Stranded, Ben once again relied on his trade. He worked 1½ years in London print shops where, refusing to drink beer for breakfast, he was called the "water-American."

1726: PHILADELPHIA—At age 20, Ben returned from London wiser about human nature. While at sea, he designed a plan for the future conduct of his life. The goal: happiness.

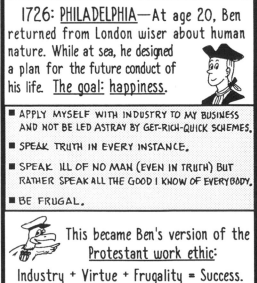

- APPLY MYSELF WITH INDUSTRY TO MY BUSINESS AND NOT BE LED ASTRAY BY GET-RICH-QUICK SCHEMES.
- SPEAK TRUTH IN EVERY INSTANCE.
- SPEAK ILL OF NO MAN (EVEN IN TRUTH) BUT RATHER SPEAK ALL THE GOOD I KNOW OF EVERYBODY.
- BE FRUGAL.

This became Ben's version of the Protestant work ethic:

Industry + Virtue + Frugality = Success.
And it worked!

⊸ BENJAMIN FRANKLIN: PROTESTANT WORK ETHIC ⊸

Benjamin Franklin's version of the Protestant work ethic became one of the strongest influences in American life.

THE PROTESTANT WORK ETHIC: INDUSTRY+VIRTUE+FRUGALITY = SUCCESS

Puritan Version
Industry + Virtue + Frugality = Success / RELIGIOUS WORTH

New England Puritans, unsure whether God had predestined them for salvation (that is, whether God had determined that they would go to heaven), followed John Calvin's advice to glorify God as if they were saved.

HOW MIGHT A PERSON GLORIFY GOD?

1) INDUSTRY—Work hard at your calling.

2) VIRTUE—Be good; obey the 10 Commandments.

3) FRUGALITY—Spend money not on yourself (indulgence diverts you from glorifying God) but on charity and reinvestment in your work.

A PERSON WHO DOES THIS—WORKS HARD, IS HONEST, AND SAVES MONEY—PROBABLY WILL SUCCEED IN MAKING MONEY. WELL, BEFORE LONG WE PURITANS SAW FINANCIAL SUCCESS AS A SIGN OF GOD'S APPROVAL (ALTHOUGH CALVIN DIDN'T SAY SO)—A SIGN THAT A PERSON WAS PREDESTINED FOR SALVATION.

SO TO US PURITANS, SUCCESS BECAME A SYMBOL FOR ONE'S RELIGIOUS WORTH.

INDUSTRY + VIRTUE + FRUGALITY = SUCCESS / RELIGIOUS WORTH.

Benjamin Franklin's Version
Industry + Virtue + Frugality = Success / CHARACTER

Ben secularized the Protestant work ethic by giving it practical rather than religious meaning. He asked not, How one might a person glorify God?—but rather:

HOW MIGHT A PERSON LIVE A USEFUL LIFE?

1) INDUSTRY: "Be industrious and free. If we are industrious we will never starve." "Industry brings comfort, plenty, and respect."

2) VIRTUE—"Sin is not hurtful because it is forbidden, but it is forbidden because it is hurtful." "It [is] in everyone's interest to be virtuous who [wishes] to be happy."

3) FRUGALITY—"Be frugal and free." "Ah, think what you do when you run in debt: you give to another power over your liberty."

TO ME, SUCCESS IS A SYMBOL OF CHARACTER (MORAL WORTH).

INDUSTRY + VIRTUE + FRUGALITY = SUCCESS / CHARACTER

In 1728 Ben, by now a master printer, opened his own print shop and put the Protestant work ethic into practice.

1) INDUSTRY
"In order to secure my credit and character as a tradesman, I took care not only to be in reality industrious and frugal, but to avoid all appearances of the contrary. I dressed plainly; I was seen at no places of idle diversion....And this industry visible to our neighbors began to give us character and credit.

"I mention this industry, though it seems to be talking in my own praise, that those... who read it may know the use of that virtue...."

THAT FRANKLIN IS A GO-GETTER. HE WORKS NIGHT AND DAY, SEVEN DAYS A WEEK.

AND HE PRODUCES QUALITY WORK — ON TIME. HE'S GOT MY BUSINESS.

FRANKLIN'S PRINT SHOP

2) FRUGALITY
By spending little and saving much, Ben soon paid the debts on his shop. He reinvested by starting a newspaper, the Pennsylvania Gazette.

HURRAH! I DON'T LIKE OWING MONEY BECAUSE THE BORROWER IS SLAVE TO THE LENDER.

MORTGAGE PAID IN FULL

3) VIRTUE
"About this time I conceived the bold plan of arriving at moral perfection. I wished to live without committing any fault at any time...."

BUT I SOON FOUND OUT I HAD UNDERTAKEN A DIFFICULT TASK. WHILE GUARDING AGAINST ONE FAULT, I WAS OFTEN SURPRISED BY ANOTHER. HABIT AND INCLINATION WERE TOO STRONG FOR REASON.

VICES ←

VIRTUES →

So Ben designed a way to break bad habits and acquire good ones. He made a list of 13 virtues and practiced each for a week, giving himself a mark for every offense. He repeated the course every 13 weeks, 4 times per year, aiming for a clean slate.

I WAS SURPRISED TO FIND MYSELF FULLER OF FAULTS THAN I IMAGINED, BUT I HAD THE SATISFACTION OF SEEING THEM DIMINISH. HOW ABOUT YOU? READ ON FOR YOUR OWN COPY OF THE 13 VIRTUES CHECK SHEET

TEMPERANCE
SILENCE
ORDER
RESOLUTION
FRUGALITY
INDUSTRY
SINCERITY

"Let no pleasure tempt thee, no profit allure thee, no ambition corrupt thee, no example sway thee, no persuasion move thee, to do any thing which thou knowest to be evil; so shalt thou always live jollily; for a good conscience is a continual Christmas." —Poor Richard's Almanac

		Sun.	Mon.	Tues.	Wed.	Thurs.	Fri.	Sat.
1. TEMPERANCE:	Eat not to dullness. Drink not to elevation.							
2. SILENCE:	Speak not but what may benefit others or yourself. Avoid trifling conversation.							
3. ORDER:	Let all your things have their places. Let each part of your business have its time.							
4. RESOLUTION:	Resolve to perform what you ought. Perform without fail what you resolve.							
5. FRUGALITY:	Make no expense but to do good to others or yourself; i.e., waste nothing.							
6. INDUSTRY:	Lose no time. Be always employed in something useful. Cut off all unnecessary actions.							
7. SINCERITY:	Use no hurtful deceit. Think innocently and justly; if you speak, speak accordingly.							
8. JUSTICE:	Wrong none by doing injuries or omitting the benefits that are your duty.							
9. MODERATION:	Avoid extremes. Forbear resenting injuries so much as you think they deserve.							
10. CLEANLINESS:	Tolerate no uncleanliness in body, clothes, or habitation.							
11. TRANQUILITY:	Be not disturbed at trifles or at accidents common or unavoidable.							
12. CHASTITY:	Rarely use venery but for health or offspring— never to dullness, weakness, or the injury of your own or another's peace or reputation.							
13. HUMILITY:	Imitate Jesus and Socrates.							

"[Pride is] the last vice the good man gets rid of."—Benjamin Franklin

"ORDER gave me the most trouble. The precept of order requiring that every part of my business...have its alloted time, [I designed] the following scheme for the day."

The morning question / What good shall I do this day?	Hour	
	5	Rise, wash, address Powerful Goodness; contrive day's business and take the resolution of the day; prosecute the present study; and breakfast.
	6	
	7	
	8	
	9	
	10	Work.
	11	
	12	Read or overlook my accounts, and dine.
	1	
	2	
	3	Work.
	4	
	5	
	6	Put things in their places, supper, music, or diversion, or conversation; examination of the day.
	7	
Evening question: / What good have I done today?	8	
	9	
	10	Sleep

"...in truth I was incorrigible about order. I was almost ready to content myself with a faulty character in that respect....For something that pretended to be reason was suggesting that....a perfect character might be..envied and hated and that a...man should allow a few faults in himself to keep his friends...."

NOW, WHERE IS MY VIRTUE LIST? OH, WELL — NOBODY'S PERFECT.

"My list of virtues contained at first but twelve. But a Quaker friend kindly informed me that I was generally thought proud, that my pride showed itself frequently in conversation."

THE SPECKLED AX—"[I was] like the man who in buying an ax of smith...,desired to have...the surface as bright as the edge; the smith consented to grind it bright...if he would turn the wheel. He turned while the smith pressed the ax hard...on the stone, which made the turning of it very fatiguing. The man at length would take his ax as it was."

DON'T QUIT NOW —YOUR AX ISN'T BRIGHT YET. IT'S STILL SPECKLED.

GASP! YES, BUT I THINK I LIKE A SPECKLED AX BEST.

BLACKSMITH SHOP

BEN, THEE ARE TOO GOOD TO BE TRUE!

YOU'RE RIGHT! I'LL ADD HUMILITY TO MY LIST.

THE LIST

NOW HE'LL TAKE PRIDE IN THAT!

HUMILITY: "I made it a rule to:

1) "Forbear all direct contradiction of others' opinions and all positive assertion of my own":

2) "Forbid myself every word that imported a fixed opinion, such as 'certainly,' 'undoubtedly.'"

3) "Adopt instead of them, 'I conceive' or 'I imagine' a thing to be so, or 'It so appears to me at present.'"

4) "Deny myself the pleasure of showing... some absurdity in [another's] proposition."

5) "Observe that in some cases...his opinion might be right, but in the present case there 'appeared' or 'seemed to me' some difference."

"This mode [humility] I put on with some violence to my natural inclination, became at length...easy and habitual. I soon found the advantage in this change in my manners....My opinions [had] a readier reception...had less mortification when I was found to be in the wrong, and I more easily prevailed with others to...join me when I happened to be in the right."

THESE PAST FIFTY YEARS NO ONE HAS EVER HEARD A DOGMATICAL EXPRESSION ESCAPE ME. AND TO THIS HABIT (AFTER MY CHARACTER OF INTEGRITY) I THINK IT OWING THAT I HAD SO MUCH WEIGHT WHEN I PROPOSED NEW INSTITUTIONS... AND SO MUCH INFLUENCE IN PUBLIC COUNCILS. FOR I WAS BUT A BAD SPEAKER, NEVER ELOQUENT, SUBJECT TO MUCH HESITATION IN MY CHOICE OF WORDS, HARDLY CORRECT IN LANGUAGE, AND YET I GENERALLY CARRIED MY POINT.

[BUT] YOU WILL SEE [PRIDE] PERHAPS... IN THIS HISTORY. FOR EVEN IF I [THOUGHT] I HAD...OVERCOME IT, I SHOULD PROBABLY BE PROUD OF MY HUMILITY.

WHAT'D I TELL YOU?

-=- BENJAMIN FRANKLIN: THE JUNTO, A DO-GOOD CLUB -=-

"For my own part, when I am...serving others, I do not look upon my self as conferring favors, but as paying debts."—Benjamin Franklin

1727: THE JUNTO—Meanwhile, inspired by Daniel Defoe and Cotton Mather, Ben turned private virtue into public virtue by organizing a self-improvement and public service club called the Junto (Latin for "together"). Also called The Leather Apron Club, it was composed of a dozen fellow tradesmen who were "ingenious friends" and "lovers of reading."

The Friday night meetings were sociable—Ben said, "I love company, chat, a laugh, a glass, and even a song."—and purposeful:

1. Members would each raise one question about morals, politics, or science—to be discussed at the next meeting after everyone had read up on it. Once a quarter each person would write and read an essay on any subject.

2. Discussions would be in the spirit of finding truth, without disputes or desire of victory. Dogmatic statements were penalized by a fee.

Junto membership required a pledge.

1. DO YOU SINCERELY LOVE MANKIND IN GENERAL, OF ANY PROFESSION OR RELIGION WHATSOEVER?

2. DO YOU LOVE TRUTH FOR TRUTH'S SAKE, AND WILL YOU ENDEAVOR TO FIND IT IN YOURSELF AND COMMUNICATE IT TO OTHERS?

WE DO!!

Friday night discussions began with this question:

DO YOU THINK OF ANYTHING IN WHICH THE JUNTO MAY BE SERVICEABLE TO MANKIND, TO THEIR COUNTRY, TO THEIR FRIENDS, OR TO THEMSELVES?

JUNTO IN SESSION

FOR SEVERAL DECADES FRANKLIN LED THE JUNTO IN PROMOTING COMMUNITY PROJECTS THAT TRANSFORMED PHILADELPHIA INTO A MODEL CITY.

THIS PHILADELPHIA TOUR FEATURES BEN FRANKLIN'S CONTRIBUTIONS TO OUR CITY.

I HEAR THE LIBRARY HAS MADE READING QUITE FASHIONABLE HERE.

STREET MANAGEMENT
• PAVING
• LIGHTING
• CLEANING

LIBRARY

AMERICAN PHILOSOPHICAL SOCIETY
FOR PROMOTING USEFUL KNOWLEDGE AMONG THE COLONIES

UNIVERSITY OF PENNSYLVANIA

TOUR GUIDE

I ♥ PHILLY

VOLUNTEER FIRE COMPANY

Ben envisioned an international Junto, THE SOCIETY OF THE FREE AND EASY, uniting virtuous men of all nations for the good of mankind. By practicing the 13 virtues, members would become free from the dominion of vice, and by practicing industry and frugality, free from the slavery of debt. Life then would be easy.

Ben said if villains knew the advantages of being virtuous, they'd switch over immediately!

THERE MUST BE AN EASIER LIFE.

MAYBE WE SHOULD TRY BEN FRANKLIN'S VIRTUES COURSE.

LOOT

PIRATES, INC.

"MY WORK KEPT ME FROM ORGANIZING THE SOCIETY OF THE FREE AND EASY, BUT I NEVER GAVE UP THE IDEA, FOR I HAVE ALWAYS THOUGHT THAT ONE MAN OF TOLERABLE ABILITIES MAY WORK GREAT CHANGES, AND ACCOMPLISH GREAT AFFAIRS AMONG MANKIND, IF HE FORMS A GOOD PLAN AND EXECUTES IT WITH INDUSTRY.

IT MAY BE WELL TO LET YOU KNOW MY RELIGIOUS PRINCIPLES, THAT YOU MAY SEE HOW THOSE INFLUENCED MY LIFE. REVELATION HAD LITTLE WEIGHT WITH ME AS SUCH, BUT I WAS NEVER WITHOUT SOME RELIGIOUS PRINCIPLES.

At age 25 Ben wrote down his own religious creed—arrived at through observing what seemed reasonable.

- There is one God who made all things.
- He governs the world by his providence.
- The most acceptable service to God is doing good to man.
- The soul is immortal.
- God will reward virtue and punish vice either here or hereafter.

"Though I seldom attended any public worship, I had still an opinion of its propriety...when rightly conducted, and I paid my annual subscription for the support of the Presbyterian minister....Had he been... a good preacher...I might have [attended church]....

HIS SERMONS WERE DRY AND UNEDIFYING, SINCE NOT A SINGLE MORAL PRINCIPAL WAS INCULCATED, THEIR AIM SEEMING TO BE RATHER TO MAKE US GOOD PRESBYTERIANS THAN GOOD CITIZENS.

"I had some years before composed a form of prayer...[And] I returned to this and went no more to [church]. My conduct might be blameable, but I leave it without attempting...to excuse it, my purpose being to relate facts, and not to make apologies for them."

Josiah worried about Ben's independent religious ideas and in 1738 wrote his 32-year-old son a letter of concern.

Ben's reply explains his approach to religion.

Honored Father,

You seem concerned lest I have imbibed some erroneous opinions. Doubtless I have my share; and...I imagine a man must have a good deal of vanity who believes...that all the doctrines he holds are true....I am sorry you have uneasiness on my account; and if it were a thing possible for one to alter his opinions in order to please another, I know of none whom I ought more willingly oblige than...yourself. But, since it is no more in man's power to think than to look like another, methinks all that should be expected from me is to keep my mind open to conviction, to hear patiently, and examine attentively whatever is offered me for that end; and if I continue in those same errors, I believe your usual charity will induce you to rather pity and excuse than to blame me.

I think vital religion has always suffered when orthodoxy is more regarded than virtue; and the scriptures assure me that at the last day we shall not be examined what we thought, but what we did; and our recommendation will not be that we said, "Lord, Lord!" but that we did good to our fellow creatures. See Matthew XXV.

I am your dutiful son,
Ben

Ben's practical approach to religion can be seen in an incident with his friend George Whitefield, the famous preacher of the Great Awakening revivals.

IF YOU MADE THIS KIND OFFER OF LODGING FOR CHRIST'S SAKE, YOU SHALL NOT MISS YOUR REWARD.

DON'T LET ME BE MISTAKEN; IT WAS NOT FOR CHRIST'S SAKE, BUT FOR YOURS.

Ben believed that you served God by doing good to his children. He was a friend to all religious sects, feeling there was some truth in all of them.

According to John Adams:

CATHOLICS THINK FRANKLIN ALMOST A CATHOLIC, THE CHURCH OF ENGLAND THINKS OF HIM AS AN ANGLICAN, AND THE QUAKERS CONSIDER HIM A QUAKER.

B. FRANKLIN
PRINTER
CATHOLIC
ANGLICAN
QUAKER
PRESBYTERIAN

JOHN ADAMS

1730—At age 24, Ben married Deborah Read—the girl who had laughed at him when he first arrived in Philadelphia. It was a common-law marriage, for Deborah's first husband had disappeared. Deborah's mind was no match for Ben's, and she had a bad temper. But Ben said, "She was a good and faithful helpmeet, assisted me much in the shop, [and] we throve together."

They reared two children to adulthood: <u>William</u>, Ben's son born by an unknown woman about the time of the marriage, and <u>Sarah</u>, born in 1742. Francis, a son born in 1732, died in 1736.

Because of Ben's prosperity, the children enjoyed advantages Ben had not known as a boy—in the case of William, a fine law education and an aristocratic social life.

In 1762 William won a royal appointment as governor of New Jersey. He remained loyal to the king during the Revolutionary War, an act Ben considered treasonous and hard to forgive.

Between 1732 and 1757 Ben annually published <u>Poor Richard's Almanac</u>, a book combining a calendar with weather and astrological data and sprinkled with proverbs.

"Poor Richard" was a fictitious character who personified Ben's wit and wisdom in a down-home way. For 25 years the almanac was a best-seller. Read in Europe as well as all the colonies, it gained Ben international fame.

Ben published <u>Poor Richard's Almanac</u> as a way to inform the common people, most of whom owned two books, a Bible and an almanac, and few others. He filled it with proverbs showing hard work and frugality "as the means of procuring wealth and thereby securing virtue—it being more difficult for a man in want to act always honestly, as 'It is hard for an empty sack to stand upright.'"

These proverbs contained the wisdom of many ages and nations.
To assemble them. Ben taught himself French, Spanish, Italian, German, and Latin.

Wisdom through humor became Ben's tool for improving the world. He thought a good laugh more effective than a sermon for doing so.

1748-57—At age 42 Ben retired to pursue his major interests: <u>invention</u> and <u>science</u>.
He wanted to improve the physical as well as the moral world.
The items below are a few of his inventions.
He refused to patent any of his inventions, explaining:
"As we enjoy great advantages from the inventions of others, we should be glad of an
opportunity to serve others by an invention of ours; and this we should do freely and generously."

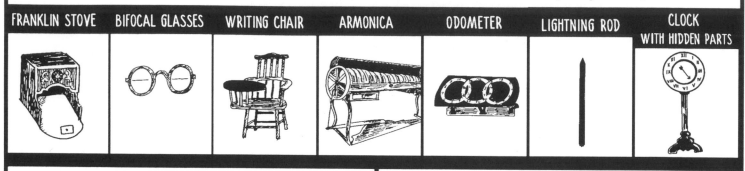

FRANKLIN STOVE	BIFOCAL GLASSES	WRITING CHAIR	ARMONICA	ODOMETER	LIGHTNING ROD	CLOCK WITH HIDDEN PARTS

1752—Ben's major contribution to science was his proof that lightning and electricity were identical.

For this historic discovery Ben won honorary doctorate degrees from Harvard, Yale, and Oxford Universities, as well as membership in the Royal Society of London. He became famous throughout Europe, a great advantage to the American cause when he served as minister to France from 1776 to 1785.

But Ben didn't take himself too seriously. After nearly electrocuting himself at a picnic by trying to cook a turkey with an electric shock from a Leyden jar, he said:

Between 1757 and his death in 1790, age 51 to 84, Ben gave himself to public service, some of which you will read about in later pages. Here is overview of his activities:

1. Colonial postmaster
2. Colonial agent in England
3. Delegate to Albany Congress
4. Delegate to First and Second Continental Congresses
5. Member of Declaration of Independence Committee
6. Minister to France
7. President of Pennsylvania
8. Delegate to Constitutional Convention

The life of Benjamin Franklin now merges with that of the colonies, as events lead toward the American Revolution.

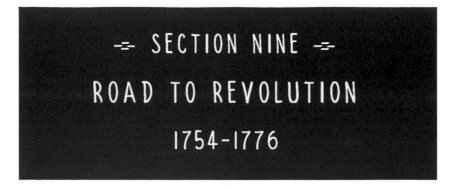
1492   1754-76   2000

"I think the Parliament of Great Britain hath no more right to put their hands into my pocket, without my consent, than I have to put my hands into yours for money...."
—George Washington

"Under the law of nature, all men are born free...."
—Thomas Jefferson

"When a certain great king, whose initial is 6,
Shall force stamps upon paper, and folks to drink tea;
When these folks burn his tea and stamp paper, like stubble,
You may guess that this king is then coming to trouble."—Philip Freneau

POLITICAL CAUSES FOR BREAKING WITH BRITAIN.

1. England's neglect of the colonies

2. Taxation without representation

3. Limitation of Individual rights

ECONOMIC CAUSES FOR BREAKING WITH BRITAIN

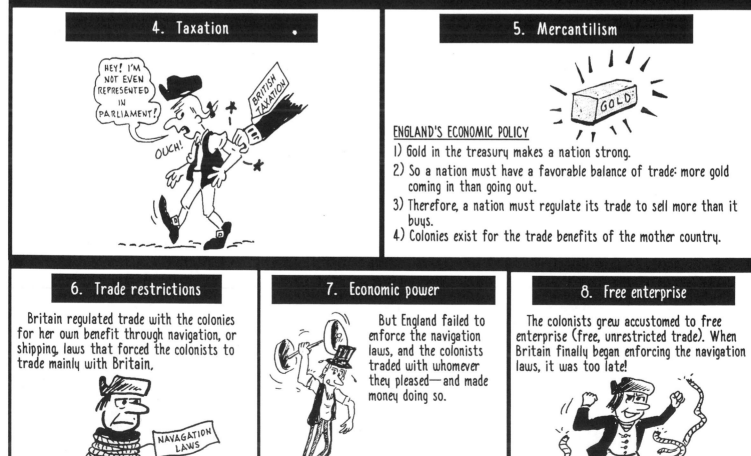

4. Taxation

5. Mercantilism

ENGLAND'S ECONOMIC POLICY
1) Gold in the treasury makes a nation strong.
2) So a nation must have a favorable balance of trade: more gold coming in than going out.
3) Therefore, a nation must regulate its trade to sell more than it buys.
4) Colonies exist for the trade benefits of the mother country.

6. Trade restrictions

Britain regulated trade with the colonies for her own benefit through navigation, or shipping, laws that forced the colonists to trade mainly with Britain.

7. Economic power

But England failed to enforce the navigation laws, and the colonists traded with whomever they pleased—and made money doing so.

8. Free enterprise

The colonists grew accustomed to free enterprise (free, unrestricted trade). When Britain finally began enforcing the navigation laws, it was too late!

1492 ——————————————— 1754-63 ——————————————— 2000

Remember the 3-way race for North America among Spain, France, and England? One contestant, France, now loses.

North America in 1754

Between 1689 and 1763
England and France fought four wars to win control of the eastern half of North America and extend their global empires. They battled in Europe and India and America, engaging various allies.—

HUMAN BEINGS SURE ARE BELLIGERENT CRITTERS!

KING WILLIAM'S WAR, 1689-97
QUEEN ANNE'S WAR, 1702-13
KING GEORGE'S WAR, 1744-48
FRENCH & INDIAN WAR, 1754-63

YEP.

The French and Indian War
erupted in 1754 over disputed claims by England and France to the Ohio River Valley. France built forts there to protect her fur trade—and her claims. Most Indian tribes, except the Iroquois, sided with the French.

In 1754 the Virginia governor sent <u>George Washington,</u> a 22-year-old lieutenant colonel in the Virginia militia, to western Pennsylvania with 150 militiamen to force French withdrawal from land Virginia claimed from her 1609 charter.

OKAY — START PACKING, YOU GUYS!

FORT DUQUESNE.

The French attacked and defeated them near Fort Duquesne (present-day Pittsburgh) in the first battle of the French and Indian War.

Meanwhile, in Albany, New York, delegates from seven colonies discussed colonial defense and <u>Benjamin Franklin's Albany Plan</u> for uniting the colonies under a royally appointed president general and an elected council. Despite his cartoon advice, the colonies said, "No." (And so did the British.)

JOIN, or DIE

1755—British General Edward Braddock, accompanied by George Washington, led British troops against the French at Fort Duquesne. Defeated, he lost half his troops and his life by fighting in column formation (against Washington's advice), instead of behind trees as the French and Indians did. Washington rallied the troops and emerged a hero.

YEA!
RAH! HOORAY!
WAY TO GO!
YO, WASHINGTON!
YAHOO!

GOOD NEWS, DEAR. WE'VE WON THE WAR.

GOOD. NOW THE FRENCH WON'T BLOCK OUR WESTWARD EXPANSION.

BRITISH DEFEAT FRENCH

1763—BRITISH VICTORY!—
Quebec's fall in 1759 led to Britain's victory in 1763. France lost not only the war but also her race for North America.

The <u>1763 Peace Treaty</u> changed the map of North America.

PEACE TREATY SAYS (1) <u>FRANCE GIVES TO ENGLAND:</u> CANADA AND ALL LAND EAST OF MISSISSIPPI RIVER, EXCEPT NEW ORLEANS. (2) <u>FRANCE GIVES TO SPAIN</u> (HER ALLY): FRENCH LAND WEST OF THE MISSISSIPPI RIVER, PLUS NEW ORLEANS. (3) <u>SPAIN GIVES TO ENGLAND:</u> FLORIDA.

CAN THEY DO THAT?

TREATY OF PARIS 1763

North America in 1763

"What do we mean by the Revolution? The war? That was no part of the Revolution: it was only an effect and consequence of it. The Revolution was in the minds and hearts of the people, and this was effected from 1760 to 1775, in the course of fifteen years, before a drop of blood was shed...."—John Adams

1492   1763-74   2000

THE FRENCH AND INDIAN WAR CHANGED EVERYTHING.

<u>Until 1763</u> Britain had paid little attention to her colonies, 3,000 miles distant. Taking advantage of this salutary (beneficial) neglect, the colonists had exercised the liberties of Englishmen and become increasingly autonomous (self-governing), while remaining proud, loyal British subjects.

<u>After 1763</u> victorious Britain tightened control of her vast North American empire (almost doubled in size) in a series of actions that seemed fair to Britain, unfair to the colonists, and that led directly to the American Revolution.

As you read what happened, analyze the cause and effect relationships in the sequence of events, and then decide what you would have done 1) as a colonial leader and 2) as a member of Parliament.

In 1760 George III (age 22) became king of Great Britain. Although not a tyrant, he took his mother's advice to <u>rule</u> as well as <u>reign</u> (unlike easy-going George I and George II).

BE A KING, GEORGE!

LONDON NIGHT LIFE

Insecure, vain, headstrong, and eventually insane, George III and his King's Friends faction in Parliament were ill-equipped to deal with British-American problems following the French & Indian War.

GENTLEMEN - WE HAVE PROBLEMS THROUGHOUT THE EMPIRE: FOR EXAMPLE, PONTIAC'S INDIAN REBELLION WEST OF THE APPALACHIANS.

PSST — WHERE ARE THE APPALACHIANS?

SEARCH ME.

PROBLEM #1: FRONTIER DEFENSE—How could England keep peace along the colonial frontier with Americans raring to cross it and settle Indian lands? In 1763 Chief Pontiac led Indians in the Great Lakes area in a year-long war against such land-hungry colonists.

BRITISH ACTION | AMERICAN REACTION

1. <u>PROCLAMATION LINE OF 1763</u>: would bar westward settlement on Indian lands and, in turn, protect the colonists from invading Indians;

2. <u>10, 000 BRITISH TROOPS</u>: would protect this frontier line, with the colonists to pay one-third of the $1,000,000 annual cost.

"UNFAIR! Our original charters included land west of that line. And we don't want a <u>standing army</u> during peace time!"

DON'T FENCE US IN!

DO NOT PROCEED BEYOND THIS PROCLAMATION LINE.

13 colonies

THIS MEANS <u>YOU</u>! Sincerely GEORGE III

I DON'T RECKON THAT'LL KEEP US OUT, EH DANIEL?

NOPE! WE'RE KENTUCKY BOUND

DANIEL BOONE

PROBLEM #2: TAXES...and then one thing led to another!

BRITISH ACTION	AMERICAN REACTION

1767—TOWNSHEND ACTS

1. Revenue duties on tea, glass, lead, paper, paints
2. Strict customs enforcement, including <u>Writs of Assistance</u> (non-specific search warants)—

Charles Townshend, Chancellor of the Exchequer (Treasury), boasted he could raise revenue through duties, because Americans accepted these <u>external taxes to regulate trade as legal.</u>

"Letters from a Farmer in Pennsylvania," by <u>John Dickinson</u>, a lawyer from Pennsylvania, argued that <u>external taxes to regulate trade were illegal</u> if used to raise revenue. This influential pamphlet urged repeal of the Townshend Acts.

> Those who are taxed without their consent... are slaves.

<u>Sam Adams</u> and fellow radicals in the Massachusetts legislature circulated letters to all the colonies, urging them to <u>boycott</u> (refuse to buy) British goods.

> SORRY, I'M **NOT** BUYING.

Colonists revived <u>James Otis'</u> 1761 claim that <u>Writs of Assistance</u> violated their English rights to sanctity of the home: not to have their homes searched without a warrant.

> HEY! I THOUGHT A MAN'S HOME WAS HIS CASTLE!

1768—BRITISH TROOPS

(4,000) were assigned to Boston to ensure orderly customs collections.

1770: THE BOSTON MASSACRE

Bostonians resented the British troops and often taunted them.
On March 5 a rowdy gang of men and boys threw snowballs and rocks at a British soldier guarding the Boston customshouse across from the Statehouse. Captain Thomas Preston and a few soldiers came to his aid. An unknown person shouted "Fire!"—and the soldiers did, killing 5 colonists including <u>Crispus Attucks,</u> an African-American. Attucks, a former slave, was the first person to die for the nation's liberty.

> WHAT HAPPENED?

> ALL I KNOW IS WE WERE THROWING BRICKS AND SNOWBALLS — THEN THOSE LOBSTER BACKS BEGAN SHOOTING.

1770—TOWNSHEND DUTIES
repealed—on all items <u>except</u> <u>tea</u>

On March 5 (the same day as the Boston Massacre) Lord Frederick North, the new Prime Minister, recommended this action because of pressure from British merchants who had suffered a 38 percent cut in exports from the colonial boycott.

The <u>tea duty</u> was retained to show that Parliament and King George III were still boss.

Two Boston Sons of Liberty used the shooting incident as propaganda to stir revolutionary fervor: 1) <u>Sam Adams</u>, by publicizing it as a massacre of innocent victims, and 2) <u>Paul Revere,</u> with his engraving of British soldiers firing on unarmed men and women, entitled "The Bloody Massacre." Prints were sent to all the colonies.

> MASSACRE

> DID YOU READ THIS?

> NO, BUT I'VE SEEN REVERE'S DRAWING.

Boston lawyer <u>John Adams</u> (Sam Adams' cousin) courageously defended Preston and his men in their murder trial, for he believed they fired in self defense. (John Adams later became the second president of the U.S.) All were acquitted except two who were convicted of manslaughter, branded on the thumb, and released.

> OUCH !! IT HURTS

> YES, BUT THIS IS BETTER THAN A STRETCHED NECK.

BRITISH ACTION	AMERICAN REACTION

1772 — COMMITTEES OF CORRESPONDENCE

1770-73—A calm period as King George III and Lord North avoided further provocation of the colonists

Meanwhile, patriot <u>Sam Adams</u> helped Boston and 80 other Massachusetts towns organize <u>Committees of Correspondence</u> to spread word of any new British aggression. Other colonies followed suit, and by 1774 an intercolonial information network existed that would unite the colonies in fighting for their liberties. If trouble arose—and it soon did—they would be ready.

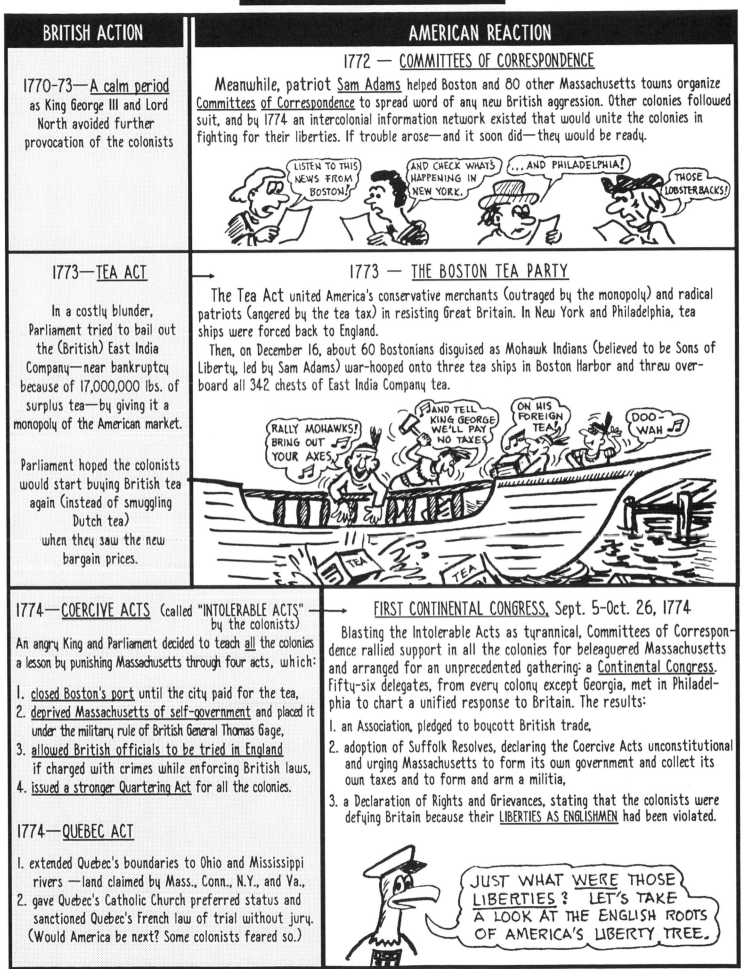

LISTEN TO THIS NEWS FROM BOSTON!

AND CHECK WHAT'S HAPPENING IN NEW YORK.

...AND PHILADELPHIA!

THOSE LOBSTERBACKS!

1773—TEA ACT

In a costly blunder, Parliament tried to bail out the (British) East India Company—near bankruptcy because of 17,000,000 lbs. of surplus tea—by giving it a monopoly of the American market.

Parliament hoped the colonists would start buying British tea again (instead of smuggling Dutch tea) when they saw the new bargain prices.

1773 — THE BOSTON TEA PARTY

The Tea Act united America's conservative merchants (outraged by the monopoly) and radical patriots (angered by the tea tax) in resisting Great Britain. In New York and Philadelphia, tea ships were forced back to England.

Then, on December 16, about 60 Bostonians disguised as Mohawk Indians (believed to be Sons of Liberty, led by Sam Adams) war-hooped onto three tea ships in Boston Harbor and threw overboard all 342 chests of East India Company tea.

RALLY MOHAWKS! BRING OUT YOUR AXES

AND TELL KING GEORGE WE'LL PAY NO TAXES

ON HIS FOREIGN TEA!

DOO-WAH

TEA

1774—COERCIVE ACTS (called "INTOLERABLE ACTS" by the colonists)

An angry King and Parliament decided to teach <u>all</u> the colonies a lesson by punishing Massachusetts through four acts, which:

1. <u>closed Boston's port</u> until the city paid for the tea,
2. <u>deprived Massachusetts of self-government</u> and placed it under the military rule of British General Thomas Gage,
3. <u>allowed British officials to be tried in England</u> if charged with crimes while enforcing British laws,
4. <u>issued a stronger Quartering Act</u> for all the colonies.

1774—QUEBEC ACT

1. extended Quebec's boundaries to Ohio and Mississippi rivers —land claimed by Mass., Conn., N.Y., and Va.,
2. gave Quebec's Catholic Church preferred status and sanctioned Quebec's French law of trial without jury. (Would America be next? Some colonists feared so.)

FIRST CONTINENTAL CONGRESS, Sept. 5-Oct. 26, 1774

Blasting the Intolerable Acts as tyrannical, Committees of Correspondence rallied support in all the colonies for beleaguered Massachusetts and arranged for an unprecedented gathering: a <u>Continental Congress</u>. Fifty-six delegates, from every colony except Georgia, met in Philadelphia to chart a unified response to Britain. The results:

1. an Association, pledged to boycott British trade,
2. adoption of Suffolk Resolves, declaring the Coercive Acts unconstitutional and urging Massachusetts to form its own government and collect its own taxes and to form and arm a militia,
3. a Declaration of Rights and Grievances, stating that the colonists were defying Britain because their <u>LIBERTIES AS ENGLISHMEN</u> had been violated.

JUST WHAT <u>WERE</u> THOSE <u>LIBERTIES</u>? LET'S TAKE A LOOK AT THE ENGLISH ROOTS OF AMERICA'S LIBERTY TREE.

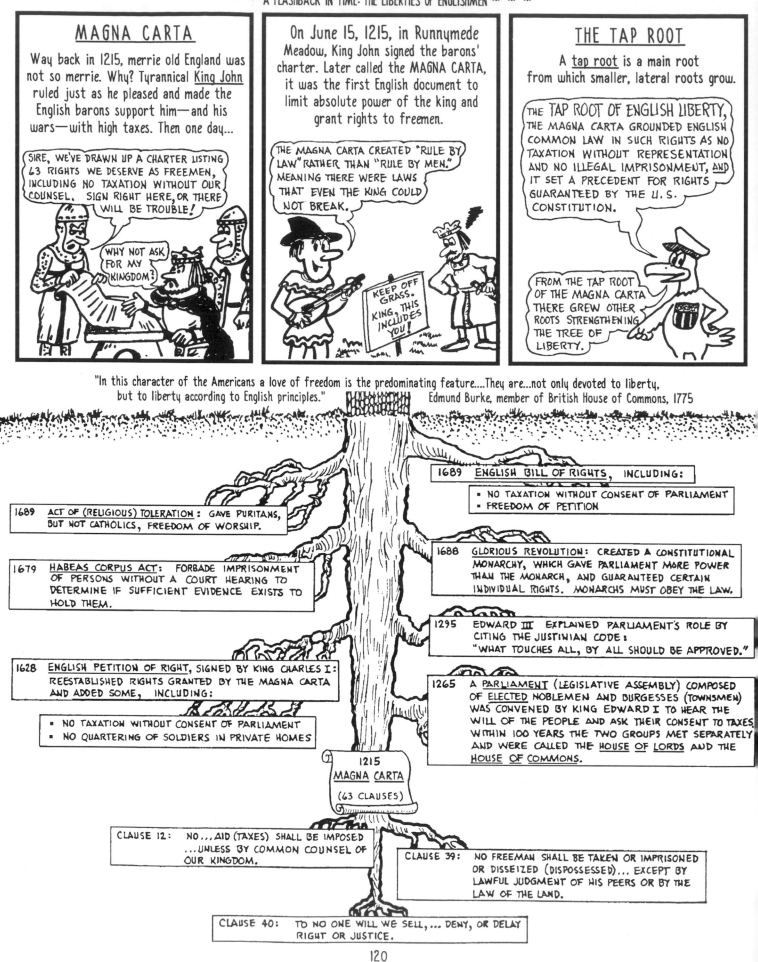

Now, back to Congress in Philadelphia.

On October 26, 1774, the Continental Congress adjourned, agreeing to reconvene May 10, 1775, if King George did not respond to their grievances.

Congressman Charles Thomson wrote to Benjamin Franklin in London:

EVEN YET THE WOUND MAY BE HEALED AND PEACE AND LOVE RESTORED. BUT WE ARE ON THE BRINK OF A PRECIPICE.

The Continental Congressmen did not seek war or independence, only their rights as Englishmen, which they felt Parliament had violated.

PARLIAMENT HAS NO RIGHT TO LEGISLATE FOR US AT ALL, BECAUSE WE HAVE NO ELECTED REPRESENTATIVES IN PARLIAMENT.

JOHN ADAMS

In Parliament, William Pitt and Edmund Burke agreed with the colonists' view of their liberties as Englishmen. They argued for repealing the Coercive Acts.

English merchants suffering from the boycott also urged repeal.

I'M GOING TO LOBBY FOR REPEAL OF THE COERCIVE ACTS – BECAUSE I BELIEVE IN LIBERTY.

PLUS, YOUR SALES ARE WAY DOWN... RIGHT?

But King George III, Lord North, and the "kings' friends" faction refused to yield. In November 1774 the king declared:

THE NEW ENGLAND GOVERNMENTS ARE IN A STATE OF REBELLION. BLOWS MUST DECIDE WHETHER THEY ARE TO BE SUBJECT TO THIS COUNTRY OR INDEPENDENT.

Blows seemed not too distant. General Gage and his British troops were fortifying Boston, while Massachusetts colonists formed a provisional government under John Hancock and signed up men for the militia.

BY GOLLY, I'M READY!

Minutemen were militiamen trained for action at a minute's notice.

Meanwhile, fiery orator Patrick Henry urged the Virginia House of Burgesses to act.

Let us not... deceive ourselves longer. We have done everything that could be done, to avert the storm which is now coming on. We have petitioned; we have remonstrated; we have supplicated; we have prostrated ourselves before the throne.... Our petitions have been slighted...and we have been spurned.

GENTLEMEN, WE MAY CRY PEACE, PEACE — BUT THERE IS NO PEACE. THE WAR IS ACTUALLY BEGUN! THE NEXT GALE THAT SWEEPS FROM THE NORTH WILL BRING TO OUR EARS THE CLASH OF RESOUNDING ARMS! OUR BRETHREN ARE ALREADY IN THE FIELD! WHY STAND WE HERE IDLE?.... IS LIFE SO DEAR, OR PEACE SO SWEET, AS TO BE PURCHASED AT THE PRICE OF CHAINS AND SLAVERY? FORBID IT, ALMIGHTY GOD! I KNOW NOT WHAT COURSE OTHERS MAY TAKE, BUT AS FOR ME, GIVE ME LIBERTY, OR GIVE ME DEATH!

A WAR FOR LIBERTY? PERHAPS —IF THEIR RIGHTS WERE NOT RESTORED. A WAR FOR INDEPENDENCE? FEW HAD ANY DESIRE TO SEPARATE FROM THE MOTHER COUNTRY, ANY MORE THAN YOU OR I WOULD WANT TO SEPARATE FROM OUR COUNTRY. MOST WERE STILL PROUD TO BE SUBJECTS OF THE MIGHTY BRITISH EMPIRE. IT WAS A FAMILY QUARREL — OR WAS IT?

"By the rude bridge that arched the flood, Their flag to April's breeze unfurled,
Here once the embattled farmers stood, And fired the shot heard round the world."—Ralph Waldo Emerson

1492 ————————————————————— 1775 ————————————————————— 2000

April 18, 1775: BOSTON—British General Gage never intended a war—only a raid to seize the gunpowder patriots were stashing away in Concord, Massachusetts.

AND MAJOR PITCAIRN, WHEN YOU PASS THROUGH LEXINGTON, ARREST THOSE REBELS, SAM ADAMS AND JOHN HANCOCK. SAY, YOU GUYS ARE KEEPING THIS MISSION A SECRET, AREN'T YOU?

10 p.m. April 18—Lieutenant Colonel Francis Smith and Major John Pitcairn signaled 700 British soldiers to begin their secret mission. Marching confidently to Concord (about 20 miles from Boston) in the bright red uniforms of the British army—mightiest army in the world, the redcoats sang a song ridiculing their backward frontier cousins, the American Yankees.

CONCORD / LEXINGTON / CHARLES RIVER / CAMBRIDGE / BOSTON
○○○ BRITISH FORCES
••• PAUL REVERE

THOSE YANKEES ARE COUNTRY BUMPKINS —THEY CAN'T FIGHT.

YANKEE DOODLE WENT TO TOWN...♪

"Listen my children, and you shall hear of the midnight ride of Paul Revere."
—Henry W. Longfellow

Silversmith Paul Revere, a member of the Sons of Liberty, and William Dawes galloped by separate routes from Boston to Lexington to warn the patriots.

THE BRITISH ARE COMING!!

WHAT'S THE BIG DEAL? SOME OF MY BEST FRIENDS ARE BRITISH.

Dawn, April 19, 1775: LEXINGTON—Warned by Paul Revere, 70 brave Minutemen, under Captain John Parker, met the British redcoats on Lexington green at sunrise. A shot rang out, then a volley. No one knows who fired first, but the redcoats counted eight Americans dead and ten wounded before marching on to Concord. Sam Adams and John Hancock, both at Lexington, escaped capture—thanks to Paul Revere.

STAND YOUR GROUND! DON'T FIRE UNLESS FIRED UPON; BUT IF THEY MEAN TO HAVE A WAR, LET IT BEGIN HERE!

DISPERSE, YE REBELS! LAY DOWN YOUR ARMS!

Afternoon, April 19: TO CONCORD AND BACK— Dazed by a skirmish with Minutemen at Concord's North Bridge, the British fled back to Boston—via Lexington—through a gantlet of 4,000 angry militiamen (farmers, artisans, teachers, ministers) shooting Indian-style from behind trees and rocks. The Yankees taunted the redcoats with a familiar tune, having adopted "Yankee Doodle" as their own. This song became the American theme song of the Revolution.

♪ YANKEE DOODLE, KEEP IT UP...

YANKEE DOODLE, DANDY, ♪

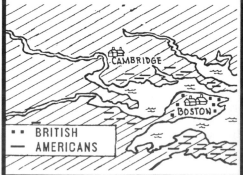

News of the British rout spread throughout the colonies. Soon 16,000 New England militiamen surrounded Boston, trapping General Gage's redcoats in an eleven-month seige, from April 1775 to March 1776.

CAMBRIDGE / BOSTON
•• BRITISH
— AMERICANS

May 1775—Realizing the patriots meant business, England sent three new generals to help General Gage and the beseiged redcoats in Boston. They soon took action.

LET'S GIVE GENERAL GAGE AN "ASSIST."

RIGHT. LET'S END THIS REBELLION!

SHOULDN'T TAKE MORE THAN A WEEK.

GEN. WM. HOWE

GEN. JOHN BURGOYNE

GEN. HENRY CLINTON

June 17, 1775—<u>BATTLE OF BUNKER HILL</u>
General Howe led 2,400 British troops (each with 100 pounds of equipment) in a frontal attack on 1,600 Americans defending Breed's Hill (near Bunker Hill), overlooking Boston.

(PUFF PUFF) THIS BUNKER HILL CAMPAIGN IS A DRAG. WHY CAN'T WE ATTACK SOME REBELS DOWNHILL?

YEAH - AND ON A COOLER DAY!

WELL AT LEAST WE ARE LINED UP IN NEAT ROWS.

Israel Putnam, a farmer/officer, had the patriots hold their fire until the redcoats were 20 yards away. Then they fired, reloaded and fired again—killing or wounding 1,000 men (40% of Howe's troops and 12% of all British officers who would fight in the war). Out of ammunition, they retreated.

FIRE LOW.... EVERY ONE OF YOU CAN KILL A SQUIRREL AT A HUNDRED YARDS.... PICK OFF THE OFFICERS. AND REMEMBER: DON'T FIRE UNTIL YOU SEE THE WHITES OF THEIR EYES.

The Americans lost the battle (with fewer than 500 casualties), but won a strategic victory of confidence and pride. The British never again underestimated the patriots' bravery and marksmanship.

WELL, WE WON BUNKER HILL. AS GENERAL CLINTON PUT IT, ANOTHER SUCH VICTORY WILL RUIN US.

And General Howe never seemed to recover his confidence. Throughout the war he avoided frontal attacks, as well as final pursuit of the enemy.

BOOK SHOP

GOT ANY BOOKS ON CONFIDENCE-BUILDING?

SELF-IMPROVEMENT

May 10, 1775—Meanwhile, the Second Continental Congress met <u>as scheduled</u> at the Philadelphia Statehouse and began to deal with the <u>unscheduled war</u>—while continuing to seek peace. (All states except Georgia sent delegates.)

MAINE (MASS.)

NEW YORK N.H.

MASS.

PENNSYLVANIA CONN.

RHODE ISLAND

MD.

VIRGINIA DELAWARE

NORTH CAROLINA

SOUTH CAROLINA

GEORGIA

☆ Philadelphia Statehouse

June 15, 1775—Congress adopted the New England militia as the new Continental Army. John Adams, seeking colonial unity with a Virginia leader, nominated <u>George Washington</u> commander in chief of the armed forces of the United Colonies.

YOUR PROVEN HEROISM AND HIGH CHARACTER MAKE YOU THE MAN FOR THE JOB.

I ACCEPT, AND I WILL SERVE WITHOUT PAY.

ON JULY 8, 1775, CONGRESS DREW UP THE "OLIVE BRANCH PETITION," ONE LAST ATTEMPT TO GET GEORGE III TO RESTORE ENGLISH LIBERTIES IN AMERICA....

THE PETITION SAID THE COLONIES LOVED THEIR KING TOO MUCH TO REALLY WANT INDEPENDENCE.

ARE YOU GUYS GOING TO READ ALL DAY?

U.S. HISTORY

U.S. HISTORY

August 1775—King George III responded by declaring the colonies to be in a state of rebellion. He said:

I WISH NOTHING BUT GOOD. THEREFORE, WHOEVER DOESN'T AGREE WITH ME IS A TRAITOR AND A SCOUNDREL. SO OBSERVE: THIS IS WHAT I THINK OF THEIR "OLIVE BRANCH PETITION."

RI-I-P

RIGHT, SIRE!

"I hope I shall always possess firmness and virtue enough to maintain (what I consider the most enviable of all titles) the character of an honest man."—George Washington

1492   1775-76   2000

General George Washington (1732-99), a giant of a man in physique and character, held the Continental Army together for eight years through sheer force of character. He became the symbol of the American cause. Patriots trusted and followed him because of his honesty, courage, dignity, and spirited sense of duty.

Thomas Jefferson said of him in 1814: "His integrity was most pure, his justice was the most inflexible I have ever known, no motives of interest, of friendships, or hate, being able to bias his decision. He was, indeed...a wise, a good, and a great man."

Like Columbus in 1492, George Washington, in June 1775, prepared to venture into the unknown —as commander in chief of the Continental Army. Did he think of Columbus as he wrote his brother John?

> I AM EMBARKED ON A WIDE OCEAN, BOUNDLESS IN ITS PROSPECT, AND FROM WHENCE PERHAPS, NO SAFE HARBOR IS TO BE FOUND.

June 1775—As Washington journeyed to Massachusetts to take command of the Continental Army (which still held the British redcoats trapped in Boston), we can imagine that he reflected on his life...

> OH, NO — NOW WE'RE GOING TO GET GEORGE'S LIFE STORY!

BOSTON →
← PHILADELPHIA

"My great grandfather John Washington, an English sailor, came to Virginia in 1657—with no money. Within twenty years, he owned 5,000 acres, including the land that became my plantation, Mount Vernon.

> A GUY NAMED JOHN WASHINGTON JUST TOOK OVER THE WHOLE VALLEY.

> CAN HE DO THAT?

"I was born in 1732 in Westmoreland County, Virginia, into a family of 12 children. Four were my half-siblings. In 1738 we moved to the 260-acre Ferry Farm near Fredericksburg to be near my father's ironworks.

"To develop my character, I copied rules of behavior on pages my mother sewed into a notebook. I still live by them.

RULES OF CIVILITY

"I went to school seven years in Fredericksburg but did not go to college, to my regret. Excelling in geometry (though a poor speller), I became a land surveyor at age 16. I learned about the frontier wilderness by surveying it for settlers.

"I loved to fish and fox hunt, ride horses, and go to plantation parties (where I became an expert dancer).

"My father died when I was 11. At age 21, I inherited Ferry Farm and twenty slaves from him.

"At age 28 (1760), I inherited Mount Vernon from my brother Lawrence. By 1773 I had acquired 40,000 acres of land. I enjoy the land and my life as a planter."

MOUNT VERNON

Potomac River

"At age 21, I joined the Virginia militia for five years (1753-58). Fighting with the British during the French and Indian War gave me a knowledge of British war tactics that should come in handy with my new job.

FRENCH AND INDIANS — HERE WE COME!

"In 1759 I married Martha Custis, a wealthy Virginia widow, and Mount Vernon became our plantation home. I adopted and loved her two children, Jack and Patsy. We had none of our own.

YOU ARE SO GRACEFUL AND LOVELY, MY DEAR.

OH GEORGE, I'M JUST AN OLD-FASHIONED HOUSEKEEPER—STEADY AS A CLOCK, BUSY AS A BEE, AND CHEERFUL AS A CRICKET.

"In 1760 my friend George Mercer described me at age 28 as:

'straight as an Indian,...6 feet 2 inches...175 pounds...[with] A large and straight... nose; blue-gray penetrating eyes....a clear though rather colorless pale skin which burns with the sun....His mouth is large and generally firmly closed, but which from time to time discloses some defective teeth.... His movements and gestures are graceful, his walk majestic, and he is a splendid horseman.'

"I served in the Virginia legislature 15 years (1758-73). There I learned the process of representative government and became friends with Thomas Jefferson, Patrick Henry, James Madison, and other outstanding Virginia leaders.

MR. MADISON, JUST WHAT IS A REPUBLIC?

IT MEANS GOVERNMENT IS A "PUBLIC THING", SIR, WHICH MEANS THE PEOPLE ARE IN CONTROL, MR. WASHINGTON.

"As a Virginia delegate to the First and Second Continental Congresses, I called for action to maintain the liberty that we have derived from our ancestors."

AND NOW, AT AGE 43, HERE I AM ABOUT TO LEAD THAT ACTION. I DO NOT THINK MYSELF EQUAL TO THE COMMAND I AM HONORED WITH.

OH GEORGE, YOU CAN DO IT.

CAMBRIDGE 7 MILES
BOSTON 10 MILES

On July 3, 1775, Washington arrived in Cambridge, Massachusetts, and took command of the Continental Army (about 15,000 men, encamped at Harvard College) still laying siege to the British army trapped in Boston.

Harvard C.
CAMBRIDGE

BOSTON

•• BRITISH
— AMERICANS

Dorchester Heights

Dismayed at the "imperfect obedience" of troops who couldn't even march in step, Washington set stern measures, including 20 lashes for swearing, to make soldiers of them and develop their character.

GET THIS — THE GENERAL EXPECTS US TO KEEP IN STEP.

AND WHAT'S MORE, HE WON'T ALLOW SWEARING AND DRINKING. HEY WATCH IT... ER ... BY SAN FERNANDO!

Success came eight months later on March 17, 1776, when Washington's soldiers positioned cannon on Dorchester Heights and forced General Howe, who had replaced General Gage, to evacuate Boston.

I KNOW! NOW HUSH AND HELP ME PACK.

SIR, THE REBELS ARE SHELLING THE CITY.

GEN. HOWE

The British sailed to Nova Scotia to plan their next move. They took 1,000 loyalists with them. (Eventually 100,000 loyalists left America.)

In April 1776, Washington marched his army to New York City, guessing that Howe would soon attack New York.

CAN YOU DIRECT ME TO NEW YORK CITY?

SURE! WANT TO BUY SOME THEATRE TICKETS?

"The cause of America is in a great measure the cause of mankind."—Thomas Paine

1492   1776   2000

Meanwhile, in January 1776, COMMON SENSE, Thomas Paine's radical pamphlet questioning monarchy, tipped the scales of public opinion toward independence.

TOM PAINE SAYS: IT'S KING GEORGE, NOT PARLIAMENT, THAT ABUSES OUR FREEDOM; HE IS A TYRANT, A ROYAL BRUTE! WHY SHOULD A KING RULE OTHER MEN? BESIDES, DOES IT MAKE SENSE FOR AN ISLAND TO RULE A CONTINENT?

TOM'S RIGHT... INDEPENDENCE NOW!

"O ye that love mankind! Ye that dare oppose not only the tyranny but the tyrant, stand forth! Freedom hath been hunted round the globe. Asia and Africa have long expelled her. Europe regards her like a stranger, and England hath given her warning to depart. O receive the fugitive [freedom], and prepare in time an asylum for mankind!"

Soon the Second Continental Congress, meeting at the Philadelphia Statehouse, was swamped with colonists' demands for independence.

Delegate John Adams wrote his wife:

Dear Abigail, Every Post and every Day rolls in upon us Independence like a Torrent. On May 15 Congress advised the colonies to establish independent state governments.

On June 7, 1776, Richard Henry Lee of Virginia introduced a daring resolution to Congress:

I MOVE THAT THESE UNITED COLONIES ARE, AND OF RIGHT OUGHT TO BE, FREE AND INDEPENDENT STATES.

Deferring a vote for three weeks, Congress appointed a committee of five to write a declaration, "setting forth the causes which impelled us to take this mighty resolution."

ROBERT LIVINGSTON
ROGER SHERMAN
THOMAS JEFFERSON
JOHN ADAMS
BEN FRANKLIN

When asked to write the Declaration, Jefferson said Adams should do it—but Adams explained why Jefferson should.

MR. JEFFERSON, YOU MUST WRITE THE DECLARATION....YOU'RE A VIRGINIAN, YOU ARE POPULAR, AND YOU WRITE TEN TIMES BETTER THAN I.

ALL RIGHT, IF YOU INSIST, MR. ADAMS!

A great choice! Tall, red-haired Thomas Jefferson (age 33 in 1776), gentleman farmer of Monticello near Charlottesville, Virginia, was a genius of the 1st order: lawyer, legislator, scholar, scientist, architect, musician, linguist. Later he served as Virginia governor and U.S. president. Like John Locke, he believed mankind had the ability to reason and the natural rights to freedom, property, and self-government.

HE WAS LIKED AND RESPECTED FOR HIS INTELLIGENCE, ELOQUENCE, AND GOOD WILL.

HE PLAYED THE VIOLIN—AND KNEW GREEK, LATIN, FRENCH AND ITALIAN.

AND HE SURE LOVED TO LEARN. HE'D STUDY 15 HOURS A DAY AT WILLIAM AND MARY COLLEGE IN WILLIAMSBURG—THEN JOG A MILE.

HE'D READ ABOUT ANCIENT AND MODERN GOVERNMENTS, SO HE KNEW THE HISTORY OF FREEDOM VERSUS TYRANNY. AND HE WAS ESPECIALLY AGAINST "EVERY FORM OF TYRANNY."

YEP. HE WAS THE RIGHT MAN TO WRITE AMERICA'S DECLARATION OF INDEPENDENCE!

"I hope and firmly believe that the whole world will, sooner or later, feel benefit from...our assertion of the rights of man."—Thomas Jefferson

"The history of the King of Great Britain is a history of repeated injuries and usurpations, all having in direct object the establishment of an absolute tyranny over these States. To prove this, let facts be submitted to a candid world:"

JEFFERSON INCLUDED ONE IMPORTANT GRIEVANCE WHICH FEW RECALL, BECAUSE—UNFORTUNATELY—CONGRESS REJECTED IT: A PROTEST OF KING GEORGE'S SUPPORT OF THE SLAVE TRADE AND A CALL FOR ITS END.

* Jefferson listed 27 grievances.

Citing repeated petitions for redress, met by repeated injury—Jefferson concluded:

"We, Therefore, the Representatives of the United States of America... solemnly publish and declare that these United Colonies are, and of right ought to be Free and Independent States...."

"And for the support of this declaration, with a firm reliance on the protection of Divine Providence, we mutually pledge to each other our lives, our fortunes, and our sacred honor."

<u>July 4, 1776</u>
The Declaration of Independence was unanimously adopted by the Second Continental Congress—two days after it approved Richard Henry Lee's resolution for Independence.

By August 2, 1776, 56 courageous men, led by <u>John Hancock</u>, president of Congress, had signed "The Unanimous Declaration of the Thirteen United States of America."

William Ellery of Rhode Island positioned himself "to see how my fellow delegates looked as they signed what might be their death warrants.... Undaunted resolution was displayed on every countenance." Only old Stephen Hopkins' hand shook—with palsy. He explained:

MY HAND TREMBLES, BUT MY HEART DOES NOT.

Who were these 56 brave men, many of whom lost lives and fortunes in the War of Independence?

<u>NATIONALITY</u>: 48 American born; 8 Great Britain born
<u>AGE</u>: 26 to 70; most in 30 s and 40 s
<u>OCCUPATION</u>: 23 lawyers; 12 merchants; 6 planters; 4 landowners; 4 doctors; 2 farmers; 2 manufactuers; 1 minister; 1 printer; 1 politician
<u>EDUCATION</u>: 32, college; 9, tutors at home; 8, self-taught; 6, common schools; 1, no information
<u>RELIGION</u>: 55 Protestants; 1 Catholic

The Declaration of Independence launched America—and the world—on the greatest adventure since Columbus:
THE ADVENTURE OF FREEDOM FOR MANKIND!

But Jefferson warned, "eternal vigilance is the price of liberty."

Will you pledge your life, fortune and sacred honor toward this great adventure?

"I cannot say that I think you have been very generous to the Ladies, for whilst you are proclaiming peace and good will to Men, Emancipating all Nations, you insist upon retaining an absolute power over Wives."—Abigail Adams to John Adams, May 7, 1776

"A woman as soon as she is married, is called <u>covert</u>, that is <u>veiled</u>...clouded and overshadowed....her new self is her superior, her companion, her master.... By marriage, the husband and wife are one person under the law...the very being or legal existence of the wife is suspended...incorporated into that of her husband...under whose cover she performs everything."—William Blackstone, <u>Commentaries on the Laws of England</u>, common legal reference in America.

Meanwhile, <u>Abigail Adams</u> of Massachusetts thought the Founding Fathers should emancipate women from their centuries-old subordinate status to men.

Considered intellectually inferior to men, women were expected to obey their husbands and legally were subject to physical punishment as if they were children. They were denied access to higher education and, with some exceptions, they could not vote, hold office, serve on juries, bear witness, sue or be sued. Married women, generally, could not own property.

On March 31, 1776, Abigail wrote her husband John Adams, serving in the Second Continental Congress in Philadelphia with the other Founding Fathers.

REMEMBER THE LADIES 1776 —

TREE OF LIBERTY

DEAR JOHN,

I LONG TO HEAR THAT YOU HAVE DECLARED AN INDEPENDANCY AND BY THE WAY IN THE NEW CODE OF LAWS WHICH I SUPPOSE IT WILL BE NECESSARY FOR YOU TO MAKE I DESIRE YOU WOULD REMEMBER THE LADIES, AND BE MORE GENEROUS AND FAVOURABLE TO THEM THAN YOUR ANCESTORS. DO NOT PUT SUCH UNLIMITED POWER INTO THE HANDS OF THE HUSBANDS. REMEMBER ALL MEN WOULD BE TYRANTS IF THEY COULD. IF PARTICULIAR CARE AND ATTENTION IS NOT PAID TO THE LADIES WE ARE DETERMINED TO FOMENT A REBELION, AND WILL NOT HOLD OURSELVES BOUND BY LAWS IN WHICH WE HAVE NO VOICE, OR REPRESENTATION.

YEAH, SHE SAYS, "IN THIS NEW CODE OF LAWS YOU ARE WRITING, I PRAY YOU WILL REMEMBER THE LADIES. DO NOT PUT UNLIMITED POWER IN THE HANDS OF MEN FOR YOU KNOW ALL MEN WOULD BE TYRANTS IF THEY COULD. LOVE, ABIGAIL"

SOUNDS REVOLUTIONARY TO ME.

DEAR ABIGAIL,

AS TO YOUR EXTRAORDINARY CODE OF LAWS, I CANNOT BUT LAUGH. WE HAVE BEEN TOLD THAT OUR STRUGGLE HAS LOOSENED THE BANDS OF GOVERNMENT EVERY WHERE. THAT CHILDREN AND APPRENTICES WERE DISOBEDIENT— THAT SCHOOLS AND COLLEDGES WERE GROWN TURBULENT —THAT INDIANS SLIGHTED THEIR GUARDIANS AND NEGROES GREW INSOLENT TO THEIR MASTERS. BUT YOUR LETTER WAS THE FIRST INTIMATION THAT ANOTHER TRIBE MORE NUMEROUS AND POWERFULL THAN ALL THE REST WERE GROWN DISCONTENTED. —THIS IS RATHER TOO COARSE A COMPLIMENT BUT YOU ARE SAUCY, I WON'T BLOT IT OUT. DEPEND UPON IT, WE KNOW BETTER THAN TO REPEAL OUR MASCULINE SYSTEMS.

Abigail's prophecy came true. In 1848 the Woman's Rights Movement began in Seneca Falls, New York. It lasted 72 years, ending in 1920 with passage of the 19th Amendment to the U.S. Constitution giving women the right to vote. You'll read of it in a later chapter.

WOMAN'S RIGHTS MOVEMENT

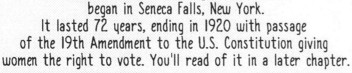

1776   1848   1920   1976

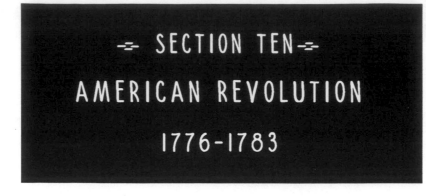

SECTION TEN

AMERICAN REVOLUTION

1776-1783

1492   1776-83   2000

"We fight not to enslave, but to set a country free, and to make room upon the earth for honest men to live in."

Thomas Paine, 1776

56 ꞊ THE REVOLUTIONARY WAR: AN OVERVIEW, 1776–1783 ꞊

revolution: the complete overthrow of a political system

1492   1776–83   2000

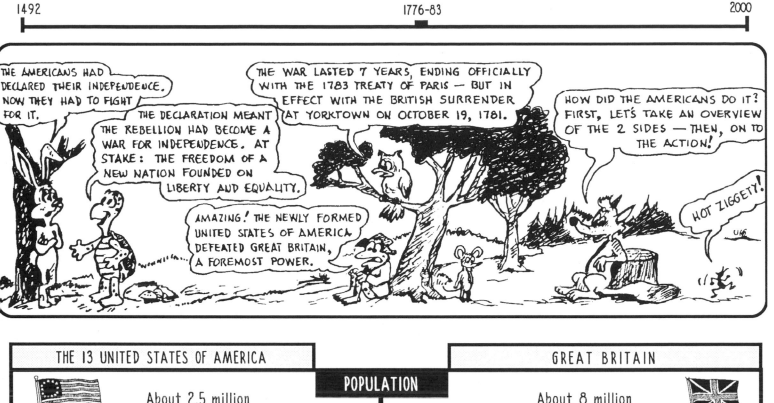

THE 13 UNITED STATES OF AMERICA		GREAT BRITAIN
POPULATION		
About 2.5 million		About 8 million

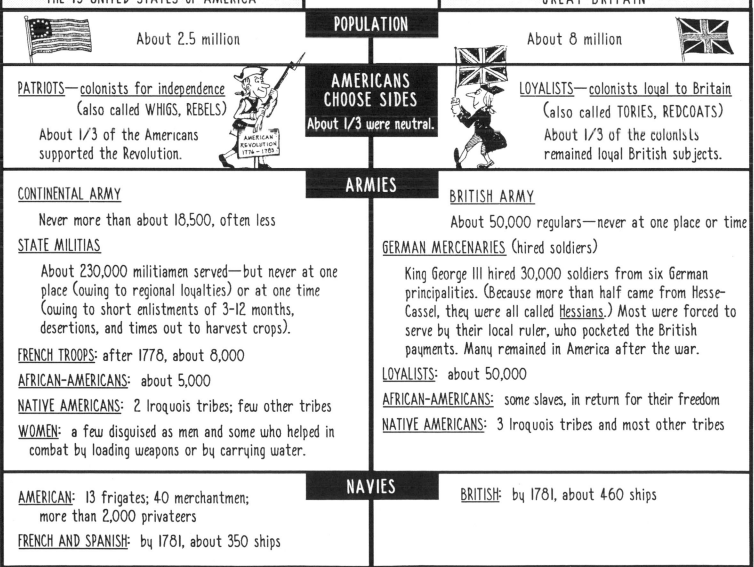

THE 13 UNITED STATES OF AMERICA

POPULATION

About 2.5 million

AMERICANS CHOOSE SIDES
About 1/3 were neutral.

PATRIOTS—colonists for independence
(also called WHIGS, REBELS)

About 1/3 of the Americans supported the Revolution.

ARMIES

CONTINENTAL ARMY

   Never more than about 18,500, often less

STATE MILITIAS

   About 230,000 militiamen served—but never at one place (owing to regional loyalties) or at one time (owing to short enlistments of 3–12 months, desertions, and times out to harvest crops).

FRENCH TROOPS: after 1778, about 8,000

AFRICAN-AMERICANS: about 5,000

NATIVE AMERICANS: 2 Iroquois tribes; few other tribes

WOMEN: a few disguised as men and some who helped in combat by loading weapons or by carrying water.

NAVIES

AMERICAN: 13 frigates; 40 merchantmen; more than 2,000 privateers

FRENCH AND SPANISH: by 1781, about 350 ships

GREAT BRITAIN

About 8 million

LOYALISTS—colonists loyal to Britain
(also called TORIES, REDCOATS)

About 1/3 of the colonists remained loyal British subjects.

BRITISH ARMY

   About 50,000 regulars—never at one place or time

GERMAN MERCENARIES (hired soldiers)

   King George III hired 30,000 soldiers from six German principalities. (Because more than half came from Hesse-Cassel, they were all called Hessians.) Most were forced to serve by their local ruler, who pocketed the British payments. Many remained in America after the war.

LOYALISTS: about 50,000

AFRICAN-AMERICANS: some slaves, in return for their freedom

NATIVE AMERICANS: 3 Iroquois tribes and most other tribes

BRITISH: by 1781, about 460 ships

THE 13 UNITED STATES OF AMERICA

MILITARY LEADERS

GENERAL GEORGE WASHINGTON, 1732-99
Commander in chief, 1775-83

General Benedict Arnold, 1741-1801
(turned traitor in 1779)
General Horatio Gates, 1728-1806
General Nathanael Greene, 1742-86
General Henry Knox, 1750-1806
General Charles Lee, 1731-82
General Benjamin Lincoln, 1733-1810
Commodore Esek Hopkins

FRENCH ALLIES

Lieutenant General Comte de Rochambeau, 1750-1813
Vice-Admiral Comte d'Estaing
Admiral Comte de Grasse

FOREIGN VOLUNTEERS

General Marie Joseph Marquis de Lafayette (French), 1757-1834
General Baron Johan de Kalb (German), 1721-80
Colonel Thaddeus Kosciusko (Polish), 1746-1817
General Count Casimir Pulaski (Polish), 1749-79
General Baron Friedrich von Steuben (Prussian), 1730-94

GREAT BRITAIN

GENERAL WILLIAM HOWE, 1729-1814
Commander in chief, 1775-78
GENERAL HENRY CLINTON, 1738-95
Commander in chief, 1778-83

General Charles Cornwallis, 1738-1805
General John Gentleman Johnny Burgoyne, 1722-92
Admiral Richard Howe, 1726-99
(brother of General William Howe)
Admiral George Rodney, 1719-92

GERMANS HIRED BY THE BRITISH

General Frederick von Riedesal
Colonel Johann Rall

ADVANTAGES

The 13 United States of America

1. <u>Outstanding leadership</u> of General George Washington, a man of high character and inspiring courage
2. <u>Strong motivation</u>—Americans were fighting to become free: free to think for themselves, choose their own laws, and govern themselves.
3. <u>Fighting on home ground</u>—knew the territory
4. <u>Experienced officers</u>—including Washington—who had fought in the French and Indian War
5. <u>Superiority of the American rifle</u> (German-made)—in range and accuracy—over the British smoothbore musket
6. <u>Sharp-shooters</u>—because of frontier experiences

Great Britain

1. <u>Military power</u>—strongest army and navy in the world; well equipped, trained, and disciplined
2. <u>Superior numbers</u>—outnumbering the American patriots in most battles
3. <u>Indian support</u>—from many Native Americans fearful of losing even more land to white settlers
4. <u>Loyalist cooperation</u>—from about one-third of the Americans, who wanted to remain British
5. <u>Hefty war chest</u>, with enough money to hire 30,000 German soldiers (Hessians)
6. <u>Bright red uniforms</u>—took pride in appearance

DISADVANTAGES

The 13 United States of America

1. <u>Inexperienced army and militia</u> (most militiamen were farmers)—untrained and undisciplined
2. <u>Short enlistments</u>—often only 3 to 12 months
3. <u>Brand new navy</u>—few ships to defend coastline
4. <u>Constant shortages</u>: money, arms, food, clothing, medicine
5. <u>Near-bankrupt treasury</u>—Congress printed continental paper money that lost its value because of no hard money (gold/silver), called specie, backing it.
6. <u>Loyalist warfare</u>—often neighbor against neighbor

Great Britain

1. <u>Weak motivation</u>—not fighting for a cause
2. <u>Unaggressive officers</u>—failed to press advantages
3. <u>3,000 miles from British home base</u>—resulting in poor communications and a long supply line
4. <u>1,500-mile enemy coastline</u>—hard to blockade
5. <u>Vast land</u>—could conquer but not hold territory
6. <u>Easy targets</u>—because of red uniforms and classic military tactic of fighting in closed ranks
7. <u>European aid to Americans</u>; fighting European enemies

⇒ THE REVOLUTIONARY WAR: AN OVERVIEW, 1776-1783 ⇐

"...the possession of our Towns, while we have an army in the field, will avail them little....It is our arms they have to subdue."—George Washington

	THE 13 UNITED STATES OF AMERICA	GREAT BRITAIN
GOALS	Preserve the Continental army; and wear down British troops until they give up and go home	Force the Continental army to surrender; restore British control of the 13 colonies
STRATEGIES	Hit and run! Avoid battles; avoid capture. The only victory necessary: the last one	Capture seaports. Then, divide and conquer. How? By Isolating and seizing: 1) New England, 2) the middle states, and 3) the South.
TACTICS	Guerrilla tactics learned from the Indians (surprise raids, fighting from behind trees), as well as conventional 18th century war tactics	Conventional 18th century war tactics: frontal attacks in close ranks

MAJOR BATTLES

"I am well aware of the Toil and Blood and Treasure that it will cost Us to maintain this Declaration, and defend these states."—John Adams

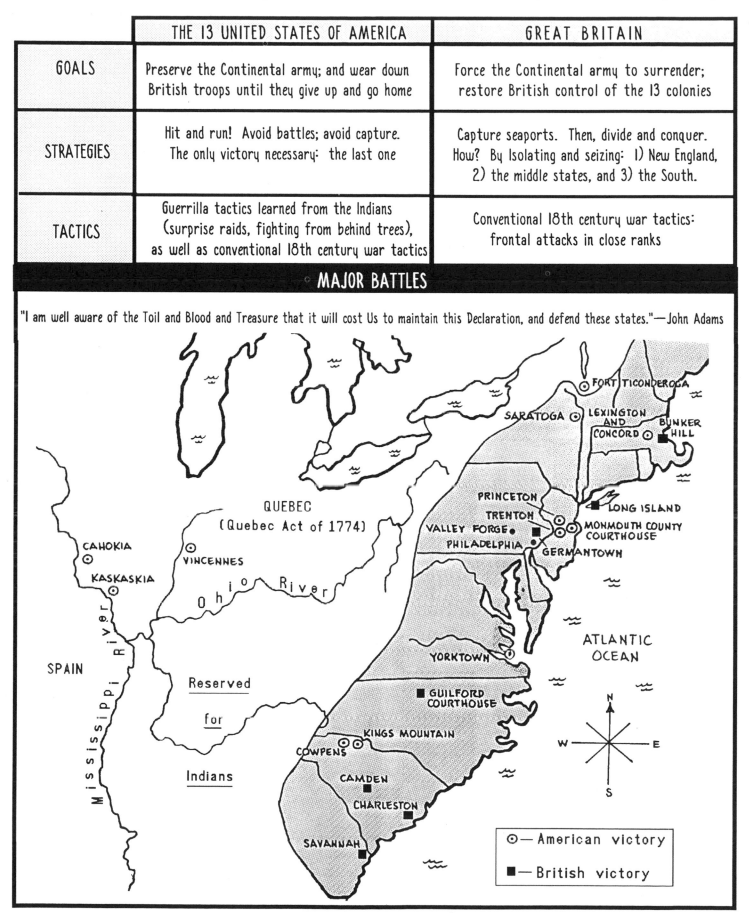

1492   1776   2000

And now back to our story of General Washington and the Continental Army, who in April had forced the British troops to evacuate Boston.

July 2, 1776—Washington had guessed correctly: the British were headed for New York.

Gen. William Howe, hoping to divide the colonies by taking New York, landed 10,000 British soldiers on Staten Island on July 2, the same day Congress voted for independence.

Soon a fleet of 200 ships, led by General Howe's brother Admiral Richard Howe, brought more British redcoats to New York, for a total of 34,000.

July 9—Headquartered in New York City on Manhattan Island, Washington responded to the British threat by having the Declaration of Independence read to his 19,000 troops.

NOW WE HAVE A FRESH INCENTIVE — SOMETHING TO FIGHT _FOR_, AS WELL AS AGAINST.

8:30 a.m., Aug. 27—Washington expected a British attack on Long Island. He told his soldiers:

I HAVE 2 LOADED PISTOLS AND WILL SHOOT ANY MAN WHO TURNS HIS BACK IN BATTLE. EVERYTHING WORTH LIVING FOR IS AT STAKE HERE. I WILL NOT ASK ANY MAN TO GO FURTHER THAN I DO. I WILL FIGHT AS LONG AS I HAVE LEG OR AN ARM.

(GULP) I FEEL MOTIVATED, DON'T YOU, BOYS?

WE S-SURE D-DO!!

The **BATTLE OF LONG ISLAND** began thirty minutes later as the British, aided by fierce Hessians, attacked the patriot army. Outfoxing Washington, Howe's redcoats soundly defeated the Americans.

The patriots' crushing defeat _might_ have signaled the _last_ day of American independence— EXCEPT THAT...

During a heavy fog, Washington made a daring escape by ferrying 9,500 troops from Long Island to Manhattan. Manning the boats were John Glover's fishermen/soldiers from Marblehead, Massachusetts.

OUCH!

OOPS!

ALL RIGHT, MEN.. _UNFIX_ BAYONETS...

But General Howe's redcoats soon had Washington's army on the run.

Fancying a jolly fox hunt, the British chased the Americans out of New York, through New Jersey, and into Pennsylvania. Howe infuriated Washington with the bugle call "Gone to Earth," signifying the fox running for his hole.

Surprisingly, Howe did not move in for the kill (a persistent trait, perhaps a result of his Bunker Hill losses). He returned to New York City, which the British occupied until the end of the war, to set up winter headquarters.

THE HESSIANS ARE IN NEW JERSEY, GUARDING TRENTON AND PRINCETON, SO _WE_ CAN PARTY _ALL WINTER_!

AND WILL YOU APPOINT A SOCIAL DIRECTOR, SIR?

December 1776: A GLOOMY CRISIS— Washington's demoralized troops, down to 3,000, were near desertion. From Pennsylvania, he wrote his brother John.

I THINK THE GAME IS PRETTY NEAR UP.... NO MAN ...EVER HAD A GREATER CHOICE OF DIFFICULTIES AND LESS MEANS TO EX- TRICATE HIMSELF FROM THEM.

COME ON GEORGE, YOU CAN DO IT!

1492   1776   2000

Panel 1:

THE TIDE TURNED WHEN WASHINGTON ASKED THOMAS PAINE, AUTHOR OF "COMMON SENSE" AND NOW A SOLDIER IN THE RETREATING ARMY, TO READ HIS SPIRITED NEW ESSAY, "THE AMERICAN CRISIS" TO THE DEJECTED TROOPS.

Panel 2:

The American Crisis

These are the times that try men's souls. The summer soldier and the sunshine patriot will, in this crisis, shrink from the service of his country. But he that stands it now, deserves the love and thanks of man and woman.

Panel 3:

The soldiers' spirits revived. It was a morale victory, but Washington needed a military victory as well. He had a brilliant idea.

Christmas night we'll surprise-attack the Hessian troops at Trenton, N.J. Get ready to recross the Delaware!

Delaware R. • Princeton / Americans / Trenton

Panel 4:

So on Christmas night, 1776, through a blinding sleet storm, John Glover's fishermen/sailors ferried Washington's 2,400 troops across the ice-clogged Delaware River toward Trenton.

WE MAY CATCH OUR DEATH OF COLD!

REMEMBER THE COUNTERSIGN — "VICTORY OR DEATH."

TRENTON OR BUST

Panel 5:

The freezing troops then marched nine miles to Trenton. Their bare feet wrapped in rags left bloody footprints on the snow, but none complained.

PRESS ON, BOYS, PRESS ON! REMEMBER THE GLORIOUS CAUSE WE ARE FIGHTING FOR.

ALL I CAN REMEMBER IS A WARM STABLE...

Panel 6:

9:00 a.m., December 26, 1776—TRENTON In a smashing victory the patriots surprised the over-celebrated, sleepy Hessians and took Trenton in 45 minutes.

VHAT'S ALL THAT CLATTER?

COULD BE SAINT NICHOLAS, JA?

Capturing 1,000 prisoners, the Americans shouted to the Hessians: "These are the times that try men's souls!" And they danced in the streets.

Panel 7:

January 2, 1777—British General Cornwallis marched south to retake Trenton. Exhausted, he refused advice to attack Washington the night he arrived.

I HAVE THE OLD FOX TRAPPED NOW. I'LL BAG HIM IN THE MORNING

HO HO HUM

Meanwhile:

WE'RE OUTA HERE TONIGHT! BUT LEAVE CAMP FIRES BURNING TO FOOL CORNWALLIS.

Panel 8:

January 3—PRINCETON, NEW JERSEY Washington led a victorious attack on Cornwallis' rearguard at Princeton. Ignoring danger, he charged and cried out:

IT'S A FINE FOX CHASE, MY BOYS!

LOOK AT 'EM SCAMPER

Panel 9:

Washington's brilliant victories reclaimed New Jersey for the patriots, and he now wintered his troops at Morristown. His reputation for courage restored, the nation cheered him as a hero—all except his mother.

When neighbors congratulated Mary Washington in Fredericksburg, she said the news reports of her son's genius were too flattering, but they wouldn't go to his head.

"George will not forget the lessons I have taught him," she said.

1492   1776-83   2000

ABIGAIL ADAMS, 1744-1818

While General Washington winters at Morristown, let me tell you about some other people involved in the Revolution, lest you think only white men fought for American liberty.

<u>I am Abigail Adams</u>. You've met me as the wife of John Adams. I'm also the mother of John Quincy Adams. Both men are future United States presidents.

Patriots, those Americans who supported Independence, were of every nationality and faith, demonstrating the love of freedom that brought us all to this country.

Some groups—such as African-Americans, Native Americans, and all women—were excluded from some or all of the rights we were fighting for in the Revolution; nevertheless, many of us put our shoulders to the wheel, hoping our time would come.

As you remember, I wrote John asking him to remember the ladies in the new code of freedom he and the other Founding Fathers were writing. He laughed at my request, for like most men of his time, he believes women have restricted roles. Let's see for ourselves how some women and African-Americans participated in the War.

And for starters, you might like to read the very first history of the American Revolution. It was written by a woman, my friend Mercy Otis Warren of Plymouth, Massachusetts. (<u>History of the Rise, Progress, and Termination of the American Revolution</u>) This was an unusual feat for a woman, for women in our day were excluded from college and intellectual activities. Mercy became educated through listening to the tutor of her patriot brother, James Otis.

<u>Deborah Sampson</u> yearned to be a soldier, unthinkable for a woman. Brave, imaginative Deborah became the first woman in the American army, serving two years disguised as a man.

<u>Molly Pitcher</u> was the name given to many women who, like Molly Corbin and Mary Hays McCauley, brought water and aid to the soldiers and even manned the cannon when needed.

<u>Phyllis Wheatley</u> displayed such a brilliant mind as a young slave that her Boston owners encouraged her gifts as a poet. Her poem to General George Washington, published in the <u>Pennsylvaia Magazine</u> in 1776, caught the General's attention, and he invited Phyllis for a visit at his Cambridge headquarters.

<u>Peter Salem</u> and other African-Americans fought at Lexington and Bunker Hill. Salem heard Major Pitcairn's "Disperse, ye rebels!" at Lexington and was credited with killing Pitcairn at Bunker Hill. Salem's bravery won the attention and admiration of General Washington, who asked to meet him.

Of 5,000 African-Americans in the Continental Army, most were freedmen. About fifty served in each battalion. There were two all-black regiments—from Rhode Island and Massachusetts. The 400-strong R.I. regiment won fame in the battle of Sullivan, S.C., by withstanding three fierce assaults from 1,500 Hessians.

Now, on to Saratoga, New York. Victory is at hand!

British strategy for 1777 focused on isolating New England with a three-pronged attack. General John Burgoyne was in charge.

General Howe, my troops will march south from Canada and meet yours marching north from New York. Colonel Barry St. Leger will move east.

Oct. 17, 1777—BATTLE OF SARATOGA (N.Y.)

But General Howe, deciding to capture Philadelphia instead, was a "no show," and Burgoyne suffered a disastrous defeat at Saratoga. He surrendered 5,000 men, including seven generals.

The American victory at Saratoga was a turning point. France and Spain realized the colonists could win the war and decided to aid them in defeating Britain, their old enemy. The motivation: revenge and hope of regaining land lost to Britain: Canada in the case of France and Gibraltar in the case of Spain.

1778—A FRENCH-AMERICAN ALLIANCE, negotiated by Benjamin Franklin, was crucial to America's victory in 1783. Britain responded by declaring war on France in 1778.

NOW THAT WE'VE SIGNED THE TREATY—LET'S SWAP A FEW JOKES, MES AMIS.

VERY WELL, DID YOU HEAR THE ONE ABOUT..

1779—SPAIN declared war on Britain and aided the patriots without a formal alliance. Bernardo de Galvez, Spanish governor of Louisiana, aided the patriots by capturing Pensacola, Florida, from Britain. This kept the British from attacking the U.S. from the southwest. Galveston, Texas is named for the heroic Galvez.

VALLEY FORGE—News of the French Alliance cheered Washington's troops as they wintered in bitter cold Valley Forge, Pennsylvania.

Baron Friedrich von Steuben, a Prussian volunteer who spoke no English, drilled the soldiers all winter, frustrated that they couldn't understand his German swearing. He turned them into professionals, and his drill book became standard in the army.

Meanwhile, the British replaced Howe with Clinton as commander in chief and opened a campaign in the south. With loyalist support, they won major victories.

But then, in Yorktown, Virginia, British General Cornwallis fell into a trap laid by Washington.

Williamsburg ★   ★ Yorktown
★ Jamestown

October 19, 1781—BATTLE OF YORKTOWN

With brilliant strategy, Washington had the French fleet block Cornwallis by sea, while the American and French armies surrounded the British by land.

Cornwallis surrendered, effectively ending the war. Pleading illness, he sent General Charles O'Hara to offer his sword. The British troops, marching between lines of French and American troops to lay down their arms, refused to look at the Americans. General Lafayette told the American band to strike up Yankee Doodle, and British heads swung around sharply!

ACTUALLY, THE SURRENDER WOULDN'T BE SO BAD IF THOSE YANKS WOULD STOP PLAYING THAT AWFUL MUSIC.

May 1782—Army officers, angered by Congress' inability to pay them, asked Washington to become king in a monarchy set up by the army. In one of his most important acts, Washington refused this military dictatorship.

AN ABHORRENT IDEA! BANISH THESE THOUGHTS FROM YOUR MIND.

1783—The TREATY OF PARIS gave the United States generous terms:
1. recognition of independence,
2. land stretching west to the Mississippi River (plus navigation rights on the river) and north to the 45th parallel and the Great Lakes (Britain did not want her rival France to have this land.),
3. fishing rights off the Canadian coast.

The United States agreed to urge states to restore loyalist property and pay debts to British merchants.

Britain gave Florida to Spain.

1783: UNITED STATES OF AMERICA

RUSSIAN
UNEXPLORED
CLAIMED BY RUSSIA, SPAIN, BRITAIN
BRITISH
CLAIMED BY BRITAIN AND U.S.
UNITED STATES
ATLANTIC OCEAN
CLAIMED BY SPAIN AND U.S.
SPANISH
PACIFIC OCEAN
GULF OF MEXICO
FRENCH
BRITISH
SPANISH

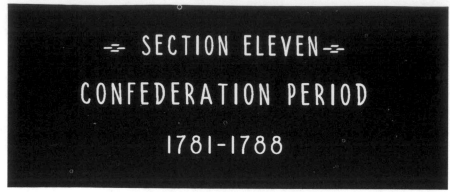

SECTION ELEVEN

CONFEDERATION PERIOD

1781-1788

"If we are not a happy people, it will be our own fault."—John Jay at the signing of the 1783 Peace Treaty.

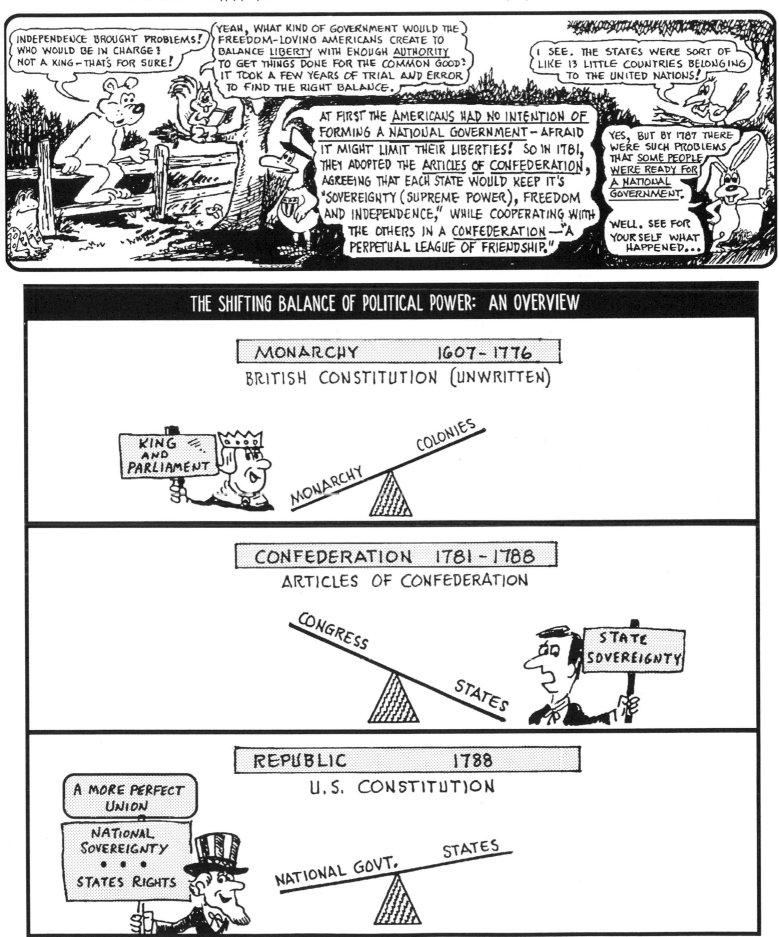

INDEPENDENCE BROUGHT PROBLEMS! WHO WOULD BE IN CHARGE? NOT A KING—THAT'S FOR SURE!

YEAH, WHAT KIND OF GOVERNMENT WOULD THE FREEDOM-LOVING AMERICANS CREATE TO BALANCE LIBERTY WITH ENOUGH AUTHORITY TO GET THINGS DONE FOR THE COMMON GOOD? IT TOOK A FEW YEARS OF TRIAL AND ERROR TO FIND THE RIGHT BALANCE.

I SEE. THE STATES WERE SORT OF LIKE 13 LITTLE COUNTRIES BELONGING TO THE UNITED NATIONS!

AT FIRST THE AMERICANS HAD NO INTENTION OF FORMING A NATIONAL GOVERNMENT—AFRAID IT MIGHT LIMIT THEIR LIBERTIES! SO IN 1781, THEY ADOPTED THE ARTICLES OF CONFEDERATION, AGREEING THAT EACH STATE WOULD KEEP IT'S "SOVEREIGNTY (SUPREME POWER), FREEDOM AND INDEPENDENCE," WHILE COOPERATING WITH THE OTHERS IN A CONFEDERATION—"A PERPETUAL LEAGUE OF FRIENDSHIP."

YES, BUT BY 1787 THERE WERE SUCH PROBLEMS THAT SOME PEOPLE WERE READY FOR A NATIONAL GOVERNMENT.

WELL, SEE FOR YOURSELF WHAT HAPPENED...

THE SHIFTING BALANCE OF POLITICAL POWER: AN OVERVIEW

MONARCHY   1607-1776
BRITISH CONSTITUTION (UNWRITTEN)

KING AND PARLIAMENT

COLONIES

MONARCHY

CONFEDERATION   1781-1788
ARTICLES OF CONFEDERATION

CONGRESS

STATES

STATE SOVEREIGNTY

REPUBLIC   1788
U.S. CONSTITUTION

A MORE PERFECT UNION

NATIONAL SOVEREIGNTY
• • •
STATES RIGHTS

NATIONAL GOVT.

STATES

1492   1781-89   2000

The Confederation Government under the Articles of Confederation

YOU WOULDN'T HAVE RECOGNIZED THE CONFEDERATION GOVERNMENT OF 1781-1789. IT HAD ONLY ONE BRANCH—THE LEGISLATIVE, CALLED CONGRESS.

JUDICIAL (COURTS)   LEGISLATIVE (CONGRESS)   EXECUTIVE (PRESIDENT)

There were no judicial or executive branches.

The single-house Congress was composed of 2 to 7 delegates from each state who voted as a unit. No matter how large a state in population, it only had one vote in Congress.

Votes of two-thirds of the states were required to pass laws, and amendments to the Articles required a unanimous vote.

Congress, designed to be weak, had only these powers:

1. Declare war
2. Make treaties
3. Manage Indian affairs
4. Maintain an army and navy
5. Coin and borrow money
6. Regulate weights and measures
7. Establish a postal service

CAN YOU FIGURE OUT TWO BIG POWERS CONGRESS LACKED?

CONGRESS WAS CRIPPLED BECAUSE IT HAD NO POWER TO RAISE TAXES OR REGULATE COMMERCE.

IT'S THE GOLDEN RULE -- "HE WHO HAS THE GOLD MAKES THE RULES."

The thirteen sovereign states followed this golden rule. Each controlled its own purse strings, holding the powers to:

1. tax, and

TAX Collector

2. regulate trade.

TARIFF WALL

State constitutions were written during the Revolution by every state except Rhode Island and Connecticut (which simply had revised their charters).

They shared these features:
1. three branches of government—with a weak governor, a bicameral legislature (except for unicameral legislatures in PA and NH), and a tenured judiciary,
2. property qualifications for voting and holding office,
3. a Bill of Rights (to guarantee personal liberty).

The Confederation Congress, despite its limitations, passed two important laws stating how America's western lands would be divided and governed.

OH BOY! HERE COME THE SETTLERS!

I RECKON THEY'RE GOING TO SURVEY THIS TERRITORY AND GOVERN US, TOO.

WHOOPEE

NORTHWEST TERRITORY

The Land Ordinance of 1785 allowed the new NORTHWEST TERRITORY to be surveyed and divided into townships 6 miles square and subdivided into 36 sections 1 mile square (640 acres). The sections would be sold at public auction for a minimum of $1.00 per acre. Section 16 of each town would be used to support public education—a priceless gift.

NORTHWEST TERRITORY

MISSISSIPPI RIVER

OHIO RIVER

survey started here

320
80   160
40

1 mile square section = 640 acres

6 mile square township

6	5	4	3	2	1
7	8	9	10	11	12
18	17	16	15	14	13
19	20	21	22	23	24
30	29	28	27	26	25
31	32	33	34	35	36

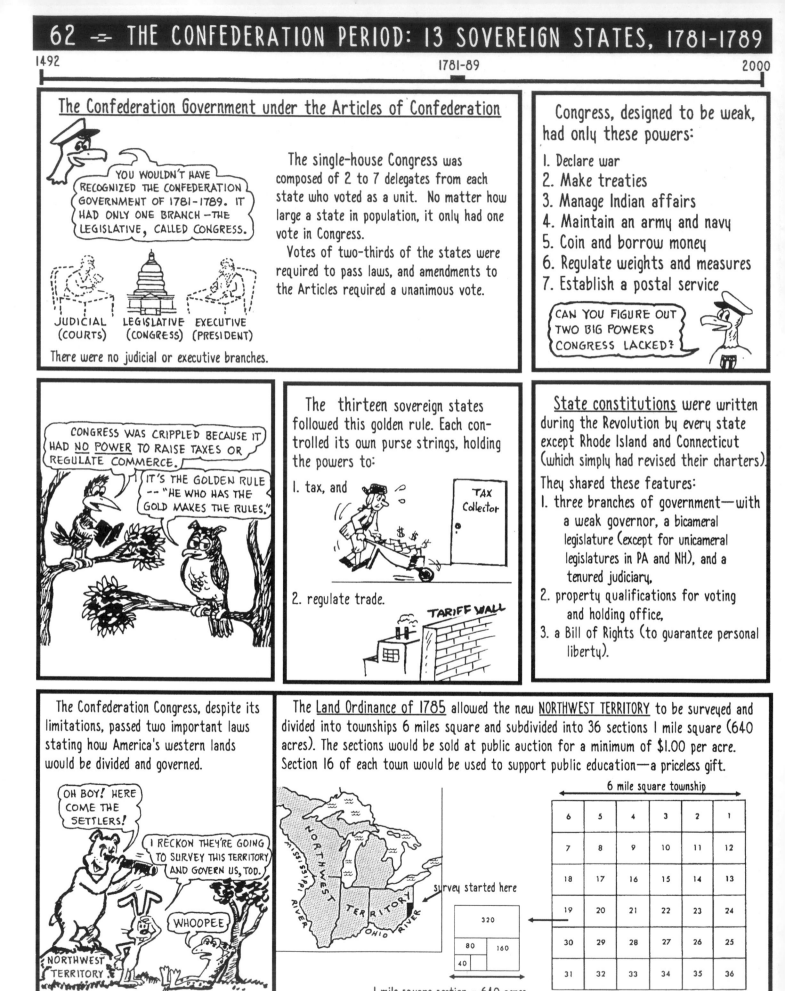

The Northwest Ordinance of 1787

forbade slavery in the Northwest Territory and allowed it to divide politically into not less than three, not more than five territories.

This plan applied to all subsequent territories. The federal government helped territories make rivers navigable, control floods with river levees, and build roads.

TERRITORIAL GOVERNMENT WOULD DEVELOP IN THREE STAGES:

1. a Congressionally appointed governor and 3 judges at the first stage,

2. an elected legislature and a non-voting delegate to Congress when the population reached 5,000 free, white males,

3. a state constitution and admission to statehood when the above population reached 60,000.

The Northwest Ordinance set an important land policy by incorporating new western lands as <u>equal states</u> rather than subordinate colonies—a democratic policy rare in history.

THE CONFEDERATION LASTED ONLY EIGHT YEARS: 1781-89. WHAT WERE THE PROBLEMS?

How would you have solved the Confederation's problems? How did the Constitution solve them?

1. <u>NO TAXING POWER</u>—<u>NO MONEY</u>

The national government gradually went broke. WHY? The Confederation government could request money from the states, but it could not require them to pay taxes. So few did.

They said they gave at the office!

2. <u>INFLATION</u>

The Continental Congress had issued paper money to pay its $40,000,000 war debt. These continental dollars were not backed by gold or silver, so their value was inflated: 40 paper dollars to 1 silver dollar. Creditors avoided debtors trying to pay them with this worthless paper money, and hostility developed between the two groups.

A BUSHEL OF MONEY, BUT NOT WORTH A CONTINENTAL.

Yoo-Hoo!

3. <u>TARIFF WARS</u>—Each state, exercising its sovereignty, charged rival states a tariff (a tax on imported goods).

WHY'D I HAVE TO PAY $10 FOR THESE POTATOES WHEN THEY'RE ONLY $9 IN YOUR STATE?

THAT'S SIMPLE. THE $1⁰⁰ DIFFERENCE IS THE INTERSTATE TARIFF (TAX) NEW YORK HAS ON POTATOES.

NEW JERSEY / N.J. / N.Y. / NEW YORK

4. <u>JEALOUSY AND QUARRELING AMONG THE STATES</u>

Might warfare break out between the sovereign states, as it did frequently in Europe among sovereign nations?

MARYLAND / VIRGINIA / POTOMAC RIVER

WHAT WERE THE PROBLEMS?

5. FOREIGN AFFAIRS IN SHAMBLES

Each state had different trade regulations, a maddening situation for foreign governments and businessmen.

Furthermore, foreign countries distrusted the Confederation because it had no power of the purse to back its agreements.

> BUT MR. ADAMS — WE CAN'T DO BUSINESS WITH 13 SEPARATE COUNTRIES.

6. DISRESPECT FROM OTHER COUNTRIES

Monarchical nations, such as England and Spain, gleefully waited for the Confederation to fall apart. They were certain that the foolish idea of self-government would never work.

> THEY'LL SOON BE BEGGING KING GEORGE TO TAKE THEM BACK INTO THE BRITISH EMPIRE.

LONDON TIMES

7. DEBTOR—CREDITOR CONFLICTS: SHAYS' REBELLION, 1787

In Massachusetts, debt-ridden farmers hurt by inflation couldn't meet payments on their farm mortgages. Rather than go to debtors' prison and/or lose their farms to creditors suing them in court to foreclose (claim the property as payment of the debt), a groups of farmers, led by Daniel Shays, took up arms against the courts.

> WHAT'S GOING ON?
> THE BACKWOODS FOLKS ARE REVOLTING.
> THEY SURE ARE.
> YOW! BAM! POW!!

> NOW JUDGE, YOU DON'T REALLY WANT TO HOLD COURT TODAY, DO YOU?
> ER—NO, I THINK I'LL GO HOME AND READ MY LAW BOOKS.

> FORTUNATELY, THE MASSACHUSETTS MILITIA PUT DOWN SHAYS' REBELLION, FOR THE CONFEDERATION GOVERNMENT WAS TOO WEAK TO ACT IF NEEDED.

THE NATION WAS ALARMED TO SEE ARMED REBELLION AGAINST HONEST DEBTS. CREDITORS—AND ALL PROPERTY OWNERS—FEARED THAT LAW AND ORDER WOULD GIVE WAY TO MOB VIOLENCE WITHOUT A STRONG CENTRAL GOVERNMENT.

George Washington, considering the Confederation's problems, feared the worst. In 1784 he had written:

> I PREDICT THE WORST CONSEQUENCES FROM A HALF-STARVED, LIMPING GOVERNMENT, ALWAYS MOVING ON CRUTCHES AND TOTTERING AT EVERY STEP.

> OH GEORGE, DON'T BE SUCH A PESSIMIST...

In 1787, hearing of Shays' Rebellion, Washington wrote,

"There must be lodged somewhere a supreme power [a national government], without which the union cannot be of long duration."

> What would the Americans do?

Washington's <u>nationalist</u> view—that only a <u>strong, national government</u> could save the states from political and financial ruin—was shared by other American leaders, including his young friends <u>James Madison</u>, a fellow Virginian, and <u>Alexander Hamilton</u> of New York, his chief military aide during the Revolutionary War and a brave war hero.

Madison and Hamilton had become friends as members of the Continental Congress in 1782, when both attempted—in vain—to strengthen the Confederation government.

The three friends shared views personally and through correspondence throughout the 1780's. Individually and together they guided events toward a peaceful overthrow of the Articles of Confederation and the creation of a new constitution that achieved "a more perfect union," which we still enjoy today, 200 years later.

> Here's an idea: Instead of a <u>confederation</u> government—a league of sovereign states, what about a <u>federal</u> government—a union that divides powers between a strong national government and the states? Baron de Montesquieu, the French philosopher, said that concentration of power results in tyranny and that the division and balance of power results in freedom.

> A liberal and energetic constitution, well guarded, might restore us to respectability.

> There may have been some excuse for setting up a weak Confederation, but there is no excuse for continuing it. We must think continentally, as <u>nationalists</u>.

WASHINGTON   MADISON   HAMILTON

1785—MOUNT VERNON CONFERENCE

<u>George Washington</u> helped solve an immediate problem of the Confederation by hosting a meeting of Virginia and Maryland delegates to settle the two states' navigation rights on the Potomac River.

> STOP BICKERING, GENTLEMEN. JOIN ME AT MOUNT VERNON AND WE'LL NEGOTIATE OUR DIFFERENCES.

MARYLAND
VIRGINIA
POTOMAC

1786—ANNAPOLIS CONFERENCE

<u>James Madison</u>, encouraged by Washington's success, got the Virginia legislature to call a meeting of all 13 states to discuss interstate commerce. But delegates from only five states showed up, including Alexander Hamilton.

> COME ON, JEMMY. DON'T WORRY ABOUT THE REST. WE'LL DEAL YOU IN A HAND OF WHIST.

PROPOSAL: A 1787 CONVENTION

<u>Alexander Hamilton</u> snatched victory from defeat by writing a bold proposal for the group, asking Congress to convene all the states in Philadelphia in May 1787 to devise ways "to make the Constitution of the federal government adequate to the exigencies of the Union.

> THEN IT'S AGREED, GENTLEMEN. WE'RE ASKING CONGRESS TO CALL A CONVENTION OF <u>ALL</u> THE STATES TO DISCUSS STRENGTHENING THE ARTICLES OF CONFEDERATION.

> AGREED.

> RIGHT ON, ALEX!

> AGREED.

HAMILTON

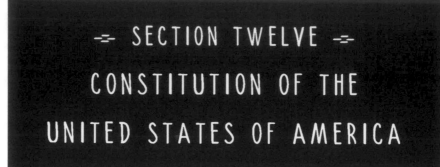

SECTION TWELVE

CONSTITUTION OF THE

UNITED STATES OF AMERICA

1492   1787   2000

"The most wonderful work ever struck off at a given time by the brain and purpose of man."—William E. Gladstone

"Let virtue, honor, the love of liberty...be...the soul of this constitution,
and it will become the source of great and extensive happiness to this and future generations.
Vice, ignorance, and want of vigilance, will be the only enemies able to destroy it."—John Jay

"In New England every citizen...is taught...his religion, the history of his country,
and the leading features of its Constitution.
...it is extremely rare to find a man imperfectly acquinted with all these things,
and a person wholly ignorant of them is a phenonomenon."—Alexis de Tocqueville, 1830

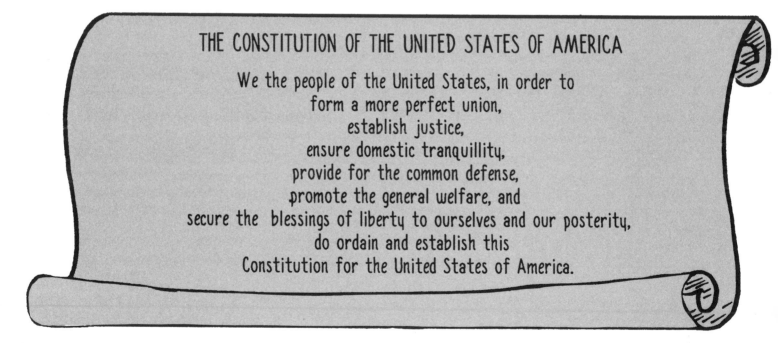

THE CONSTITUTION OF THE UNITED STATES OF AMERICA

We the people of the United States, in order to
form a more perfect union,
establish justice,
ensure domestic tranquillity,
provide for the common defense,
promote the general welfare, and
secure the blessings of liberty to ourselves and our posterity,
do ordain and establish this
Constitution for the United States of America.

"If all the delegates named for this Convention at Philadelphia are present, we will never have seen, even in Europe, an assembly more respectable for the talents, knowledge, disinterestedness, and patriotism of those who compose it."—G.K. Otto, French Charge d'Affaires, Philadelphia, 1787

1492 —————————————————————— 1787 —————————————————————— 2000

Congress, meeting in New York City, reluctantly agreed to the Annapolis proposal. It called for a Federal Convention in Philadelphia on May 14, 1787—but carefully stated that the meeting was "for the sole...purpose of revising the Articles of Confederation."

Now—would the states agree to send delegates? Those undecided did so when they learned that George Washington would be a delegate, for the whole country trusted the beloved Revolutionary War hero. The <u>Pennsylvania Herald</u> wrote: "If the plan is not a good one, it is impossible that either General Washington or Dr. Franklin would have recommended it." So it seemed to all the states except Rhode Island, which—protective of its state's rights—refused to participate.

And so, 12 states sent <u>55 delegates</u> to meet at Philadelphia's State House, now called Independence Hall, where eleven years earlier, in 1776, the Declaration of Independence had been adopted. Disregarding Congress' mandate to preserve the old, they "brought forth on this continent, a new nation, conceived in liberty, and dedicated to the proposition that all men are created equal." (Abraham Lincoln) They emerged, after four months, with the framework for a federal republic of, by, and for the people: <u>39 of the Framers</u> signed the Constitution of the United States "to secure the blessings of liberty to ourselves and our Posterity."

WHO WERE THESE FRAMERS—THESE EXTRAORDINARY MEN OF REASON AND CREATIVITY?

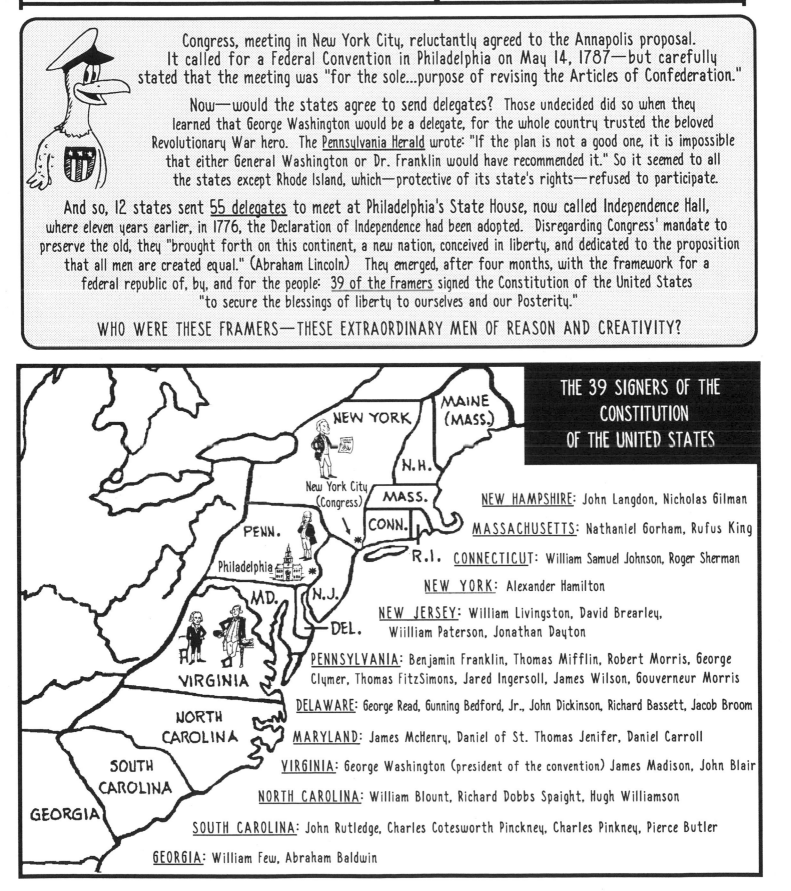

THE 39 SIGNERS OF THE CONSTITUTION OF THE UNITED STATES

NEW HAMPSHIRE: John Langdon, Nicholas Gilman

MASSACHUSETTS: Nathaniel Gorham, Rufus King

CONNECTICUT: William Samuel Johnson, Roger Sherman

NEW YORK: Alexander Hamilton

NEW JERSEY: William Livingston, David Brearley, Wiilliam Paterson, Jonathan Dayton

PENNSYLVANIA: Benjamin Franklin, Thomas Mifflin, Robert Morris, George Clymer, Thomas FitzSimons, Jared Ingersoll, James Wilson, Gouverneur Morris

DELAWARE: George Read, Gunning Bedford, Jr., John Dickinson, Richard Bassett, Jacob Broom

MARYLAND: James McHenry, Daniel of St. Thomas Jenifer, Daniel Carroll

VIRGINIA: George Washington (president of the convention) James Madison, John Blair

NORTH CAROLINA: William Blount, Richard Dobbs Spaight, Hugh Williamson

SOUTH CAROLINA: John Rutledge, Charles Cotesworth Pinckney, Charles Pinckney, Pierce Butler

GEORGIA: William Few, Abraham Baldwin

"Knowledge will forever govern ignorance; and a people who mean to be their own governors must arm themselves with the power which knowledge gives."
— James Madison

1492　　　　　　　　　　　　　　　　　1751　　　　　1836　　　　　　　　　　　　　　2000

Virginia delegate James Jemmy Madison

arrived at the convention eleven days early, armed with a plan of action.
Madison—a 36-year-old bachelor, shy, short (5'6"), soft-spoken, frail, and scholarly—
was a man among men. Described by a contemporary as "no bigger than half a piece of soap,"
he nevertheless would emerge the clear leader of the 1787 Constitutional Convention,
earning the title, Father of the United States Constitution.

Born in 1751 in Port Conway, Virginia, the eldest of 12 children, Madison
grew up near Orange on his family's beautiful Virginia plantation Montpelier, which he
later inherited. He studied at home with tutors, earned a degree in philosophy at Princeton in 1771,
and then became a life-long statesman. He represented Virginia in the state assembly (1776-77)—
where he and Thomas Jefferson began a 50-year friendship—the Confederation Congress
(1780-83), and the U.S. Congress (1790-94). He served his country as secretary of state
(1801-09) and president (1809-17). No wonder Dolley Madison, the vivacious
Philadelphian he married in 1794, called him "the great little Madison."

Madison had spent a year studying for the 1787 Convention, motivated by a burning question:

"How could the country have a strong national government without taking freedom from the people?"

He read more than 200 books on history and philosophy (Aristotle, Voltaire, Montesquieu, Locke, Hume), many sent from France by his close friend Thomas Jefferson, who served as Minister to France from 1785 to 1789.

WOW! THE BOOKS I ORDERED ARE HERE!

YES SIR! A WHOLE WAGONLOAD!

After analyzing ancient and modern governments, Madison outlined their keys to success and failure in a 41-page booklet.

OVER 2,000 YEARS AGO, DEMOCRACY REIGNED IN THE GREEK CITY STATES AND THE ROMAN REPUBLIC. MADISON TRIED TO UNDERSTAND WHAT THESE GOVERNMENTS DID RIGHT...

...AND WHAT WENT WRONG!

Finally, Madison created a 15-point plan of government. Arriving early in Philadelphia, he presented it to the other Virginia delegates, including Governor Edmund Randolph and George Washington, for their suggestions and endorsement.

HERE'S THE IDEA: INSTEAD OF A CONFEDERATION GOVERNMENT — A LEAGUE OF SOVEREIGN STATES, WHAT ABOUT A FEDERAL GOVERNMENT — A UNION THAT DIVIDES POWERS BETWEEN A STRONG NATIONAL GOVERNMENT AND THE STATES?

HMM...

MAKES SENSE.

MIGHT WORK.

The 15-point "Virginia Plan" would provide the agenda for the entire proceedings of the Convention and, modified by important compromises, become the blueprint for the United States Constitution.

WHO'S THAT?

A MAN WITH A PLAN!

TO STATE HOUSE

Most of the 55 white male delegates knew and respected one another through shared adventures:

3—had been in the Stamp Act Congress, 1765.
8—had signed the Declaration of Independence; 2, the Articles of Confederation
42—had served in the First and/or Second Continental Congresses, 1774-1781 and/or the Confederation Congress, 1781-87.
30—were Revolutionary War veterans.
2—would be U.S. presidents (George Washington and James Madison); 1, a vice-president (Elbridge Gerry).
7—had been governors; 9 would be governors.
8—were judges; 2 would be chief justices of the Supreme Court.
2—were college presidents (Princeton and Columbia); 29 were college-educated.
34—had practiced law; 20 had helped write their state constitutions.
18—had worked or studied abroad; many were fluent in Latin, French, and other languages.
8—were born outside the U.S. but all within the British Empire.

Most were prosperous lawyers, businessmen, or plantation owners.
And they were young: average age, 42. Most were in their 30s: Madison was 36; Hamilton, 32.
Washington was 55; Benjamin Franklin, 81, was said to have the mind of a 25 year-old.

And so they slowly gathered—for the CONSTITUTIONAL CONVENTION in Philadelphia, Pennsylvania, May 1787,
at the STATE HOUSE, now called INDEPENDENCE HALL,
scene of 2nd Continental Congress (signing of Declaration of Independence), 1775-81; and Confederation Congress, 1781-85.

"This example of changing the constitution by assembling the wise men of the state, instead of assembling armies, will be worth as much to the world as the former examples we have given it."—Thomas Jefferson

1492   1787   2000

Madison's Virginia Plan had to wait a few days, because spring rains and muddy roads delayed many delegates.

MAYBE THE ARTICLES OF CONFEDERATION AREN'T SO BAD...

TO PHILA-DELPHIA →

The Convention officially began 2 weeks late on Friday, May 25, 1787, with a quorum of 7 states.

During its hot, 4-month schedule of 6-hour meetings, 6 days a week, 13 of the 55 delegates withdrew for personal or policy reasons. The Convention rarely drew more than 30 to 35 delegates at a time.

The first day: George Washington, unanimously elected president of the Convention, took his presiding chair, saying...

LET US RAISE A STANDARD TO WHICH THE WISE AND HONEST CAN REPAIR .... THE EVENT IS IN THE HANDS OF GOD.

On Monday, May 28, 1787, the delegates got down to business. Luckily for us, James Madison decided to sit up front and record for posterity every word said.

His journal, Notes of Debates in the Federal Convention of 1787 (not published until 1840, 4 years after his death), offers you a ringside seat at the Convention—next to him.

IN THIS FAVORABLE POSITION FOR HEARING ALL THAT PASSED, I NOTED....WHAT WAS READ,...OR SPOKEN BY THE MEMBERS. I WAS NOT ABSENT A SINGLE DAY, NOR MORE THAN A FRACTION OF AN HOUR IN ANY DAY.... IT NEARLY KILLED ME!

1492   1787   2000

RULES OF PROCEDURE were adopted by the delegates (who were old hands at running an effective meeting).

1. SECRECY: Delegates could not tell anyone about the procedings until the Convention ended. This allowed them to speak freely and experiment with ideas.

YOU DIDN'T GET A STORY ON THE CONVENTION?

SORRY CHIEF! THEY EVEN LOCKED THE WINDOWS.

PRESS

EDITOR

Amazingly there were no leaks—perhaps because of an early scolding by Washington, when he discovered a delegate's lost notes.

I MUST ENTREAT GENTLEMEN TO BE MORE CAREFUL, LEST OUR TRANSACTIONS GET INTO THE NEWSPAPERS AND DISTURB THE PUBLIC REPOSE BY PREMATURE SPECULATIONS.

He threw the notes on a table, saying, "Let him who owns it take it," and stalked out. No one moved to recover the notes—to this day!

NOT MY NOTES.

NOR MINE.

I DON'T EVEN TAKE NOTES.

2. FLEXIBILITY: No votes were final until the last day, so delegates could change their minds freely. Every issue could be re-voted if anyone wished. Over 569 votes were eventually taken.

YESTERDAY I VOTED FOR A STRONG CENTRAL GOVERNMENT, BUT TODAY I'M IN A "STATES-RIGHTS" MOOD.

3. COURTESY: "Every member, rising to speak, shall address the President; and whilst he shall be speaking, none shall pass between them, or hold discourse or read a book, pamphlet, or paper...."

DOES THIS MEAN I CAN'T BRING MY KNITTING?

After the convention a member would remark in amazement:

SCARCELY AN OFFENSIVE EXPRESSION ESCAPED DURING THE WHOLE SESSION.

YOU MEAN YOU SLEPT THROUGH IT?

Yet, quite often the convention debates grew fierce and tempers short.

Of course, who _would_ misbehave with the dignified, respected Washington seated on the platform, influencing the delegates with his slightest expression of pain or pleasure?

As John Adams once said of the regal Virginian:

"Next to Washington, a king would look like a valet."

Well, jovial <u>Gouverneur Morris</u> boasted one night that he was not intimidated by Washington. He bet Alexander Hamilton and other friends that he would dare greet Washington with a slap on the back.

The next day, more sober, he merely put his hand on Washington's shoulder, then regretted that!

THE GREAT MAN TURNED AND LOOKED AT ME, AND I WISHED THE EARTH HAD YAWNED AND SWALLOWED ME UP.

VIRGINIA PLAN

On Tuesday, May 29, Virginia Governor Edmund Randolph presented the bold, 15-point <u>Virginia Plan</u>, outlining a national republican government with 3 branches:
1) executive; 2) judiciary; and 3) two-house legislature,
with population determining the number of members in both houses of the legislature.

The Virginia Plan caused shock waves!

Most delegates favored strengthening the central government by giving it powers to tax and control commerce. But they were divided between large-state "<u>nationalists</u>," who wanted even greater central powers, and small-state "<u>states' righters</u>," who wanted only to strengthen the Confederation— not overthrow it.

HEY! I THOUGHT WE WERE JUST GOING TO FIX THE ROOF!

ARTICLES OF CONFEDERATION

NATIONALIST WRECKING COMPANY

NEW JERSEY PLAN

So William Paterson of New Jersey presented the small states' <u>New Jersey Plan</u>, which called for merely strengthening the Articles of Confederation, thus <u>retaining state sovereignty</u>.

Gunning Bedford of Delaware challenged the large-state delegates:

I DO NOT, GENTLEMEN, TRUST YOU. WILL YOU CRUSH THE SMALL STATES?

ALEXANDER HAMILTON'S PLAN

Then, out of the blue, Alexander Hamilton of New York presented a <u>3rd plan</u> that—to everyone's surprise—was modeled on the British government, which he admired.

THE PRESIDENT AND SENATORS SHOULD BE <u>ELECTED FOR LIFE.</u>

SOUNDS LIKE A MONARCHY! DOES HAMILTON WANT AN AMERICAN KING?

HAMILTON'S PLAN GIVES SO MUCH POWER TO THE FEDERAL GOVERNMENT, IT MAKES THE VIRGINIA PLAN SEEM MILD BY COMPARISON.

LATER, HAMILTON WAS OFTEN ACCUSED OF WANTING A MONARCHY, BUT HE DENIED IT.

AFTER MY 6-HOUR SPEECH THEY POLITELY IGNORED MY PLAN!

I WOULDN'T HAVE BEEN SO POLITE.

I WOULD HAVE BEEN ASLEEP!

The delegates listened politely to Hamilton for 6 hours, then without comment began to debate the Virginia and New Jersey Plans.

NATIONAL VS. STATE SOVEREIGNTY

Virginia Plan vs. New Jersey Plan

The delegates voted 7-3 for the Virginia Plan. They realized that this meant a revolutionary overthrow of the Confederation and state sovereignty.

WHAT HAPPENED?

THEY JUST VOTED FOR REVOLUTION— 7 TO 3!

The small states, however, objected to the Virginia Plan's population-based legislature. They argued that the large states would have more people, thus more members and votes in Congress, thus more power than the small states.

HI, LITTLE NEIGHBOR!

NOW, DON'T START PICKING ON ME!

PENNSYLVANIA!

DELAWARE

Things were at a stalemate. Ben Franklin urged the two sides to compromise, each giving in a little.

SEEMS THERE WAS THIS CARPENTER— HE WAS ABLE TO JOIN TWO ILL-FITTING BOARDS BY SHAVING A LITTLE OFF EACH . . .

OH, BEN, WE'VE ALL HEARD THAT ONE!

LARGE-STATE—SMALL-STATE COMPROMISE

Roger Sherman of Connecticut offered a compromise.

WE COULD BASE MEMBERSHIP IN THE HOUSE OF REPRESENTATIVES ON POPULATION AND IN THE SENATE ON EQUALITY, WITH EACH STATE ALLOWED 2 SENATORS. TINY DELAWARE WOULD HAVE SENATE VOTES EQUAL TO BIG PENNSYLVANIA.

HEY, THAT'S A GREAT COMPROMISE, ROGER!

This Connecticut Compromise (including the House of Representatives' power to originate money bills), along with the North—South compromises described below, passed 5-4 as THE GREAT COMPROMISE.

Here's how Sherman's plan would work in the case of Pennsylvania (pop. 434,373) and Delaware (pop. 59,096):

☆ Senator
✳ Congressman

PENNSYLVANIA

DELAWARE

By compromising—each side "shaving" some demands in order to reach agreement—the Convention was saved: a valuable lesson!

Solution to this conflict raised a new one—between Northern and Southern states: how to count the slave population in apportioning members of the House of Representatives.

ESTIMATED U.S. POPULATION✳

Whites 81%

Blacks 19%

Others 10%

Slaves in the South 90%

(✳These figures are from the 1790 U.S. census, which shows 757,181 African-Americans in a total population of 3,929,625.)

NORTH—SOUTH COMPROMISES

Southern delegates wanted slaves to count as people so as to have more congressmen representing their states.

Northern delegates called this 1) unfair and 2) inconsistent because slaves were considered property.

Gouverneur Morris voiced a moral protest:

SLAVERY IS THE CURSE OF HEAVEN. ARE THEY MEN? THEN MAKE THEM CITIZENS AND LET THEM VOTE!

1. Three-fifths Compromise

The delegates compromised in a strange way: a slave would count as 3/5 person in determining House representation and direct taxes (taxes owed by states to the federal government).

2. Slave Trade Compromise

Prohibition of slave imports would be delayed for 20 years, but until then (1807) slaveholders could be taxed up to $10.00 per imported slave.

Thus, the Constitution implicitly recognized slavery.✳ However, in 1807 Congress abolished slave importation, and in 1865 the 13th Amendment to the Constitution abolished slavery. (✳The word "slave" is never used in the Constitution. Instead, phrases such as "other persons" and "such persons" refer to slaves.)

AN IRONY: Several of the delegates were against slavery (including Washington, Madison, Hamilton, Franklin, and Mason). But they had to choose between having a constitution and ending slavery. Why? South Carolina and Georgia would not join the new nation without slavery.

As Abraham Lincoln said seven decades later, the word slavery was "hid away in the Constitution, just as an afflicted man hides away a ...cancer, which he dares not cut out at once, lest he bleed to death."

THE DELEGATES CHOSE TO HAVE AN IMPERFECT CONSTITUTION RATHER THAN NONE AT ALL. WHAT WOULD YOU HAVE DONE?

If avoiding the slavery question allowed for a constitution, it also threatened to destroy the constitution 70 years later with the Civil War. <u>George Mason</u>, author of the Virginia Bill of Rights, warned:

THIS INFERNAL SLAVE TRAFFIC WILL BRING THE JUDGMENT OF HEAVEN ON A COUNTRY. PROVIDENCE PUNISHES NATIONAL SINS WITH NATIONAL CALAMITIES.

LEGISLATIVE COMPROMISE

Who should elect the legislators?

NOT THE PEOPLE! THEY CAN BE DUPED BY DEMAGOGUES! THE EVILS WE EXPERIENCE FLOW FROM THE EXCESS OF DEMOCRACY. HAMILTON, SHERMAN, AND G. MORRIS AGREE.

ELBRIDGE GERRY

I DISAGREE. A FREE GOVERNMENT MUST HAVE LEGISLATORS ELECTED <u>BY</u> THE PEOPLE AND ACCOUNTABLE TO THE PEOPLE. GEORGE MASON AND OTHERS THINK SO, TOO.

JAMES MADISON

THE COMPROMISE:
THE HOUSE OF REPRESENTATIVES WOULD BE ELECTED DIRECTLY BY THE PEOPLE.

THE SENATE WOULD BE ELECTED BY THE STATE LEGISLATORS.

(IN 1913 THE 17TH AMENDMENT PROVIDED FOR DIRECT ELECTION OF SENATORS BY THE PEOPLE.)

EXECUTIVE COMPROMISE

DECIDING TO HAVE A STRONG PRESIDENT WAS HARD FOR AMERICANS, WHO WERE FED UP WITH DESPOTIC KINGS. BUT EVERYONE KNEW WASHINGTON WOULD LIKELY BE THE FIRST PRESIDENT.

...AND GEORGE WOULD NEVER TRY TO BE A KING! BUT <u>AFTER</u> GEORGE, WHAT THEN?

Who should elect the president?

THE PEOPLE SHOULD VOTE FOR THE PRESIDENT.

NO. TOO MANY PEOPLE ARE UNEDUCATED. THIS WOULD BE AS UNNATURAL AS ASKING A BLIND MAN TO CHOOSE COLORS. PASSION AND DEMAGOGUERY WOULD PREVAIL OVER REASON!

JAMES WILSON

GEORGE MASON

HAS HE BEEN WATCHING THE T.V. DEBATES?

It took 60 ballots to decide who should elect the president.

The <u>compromise</u>:
The president would be elected <u>indirectly</u> by the people through an <u>Electoral College</u> made up of electors chosen by each state, the number being equal to the number of its congressmen.

The candidate with most votes would be president; the one with the next highest votes would be vice president.

(This was changed in 1804 by the 12th Amendment, which stated that the vice president would be elected on a separate ballot.)

SHOULD THERE BE RELIGIOUS TESTS (REQUIREMENTS) FOR PUBLIC OFFICE? — NO

"Among the most inestimable of our blessings is that...of liberty to worship our Creator in the way we think most agreeable in His will; a liberty deemed in other countries incompatible with good government and yet proved by our experience to be its best support.... The rights of conscience we never submitted [to government] We are answerable for them to our God." —Thomas Jefferson

Eleven states did have religious requirements for public office:

Massachusetts and Maine----------------must be a Christian
NH, NJ, NC, SC, and Georgia-----must be a Protestant Christian
Pennsylvania-------------must believe in God and the Bible
Delaware------------must believe in the Christian Trinity

This meant that the 2,000 Jews and 25,000 Catholics in America—plus people of other faiths or of non-faith—did not qualify for public office in most states.

The delegates rejected the states' practice. Determined that government must not violate people's freedom to believe as they choose, they voted unanimously for Charles Pinckney's proposal:

NO RELIGIOUS TEST SHALL EVER BE REQUIRED AS A QUALIFICATION TO ANY OFFICE OR PUBLIC TRUST UNDER THE AUTHORITY OF THE UNITED STATES.

IT IS IMPOSSIBLE TO MAKE LAWS FOR THE HUMAN MIND. AS JEFFERSON SAID: ALMIGHTY GOD HATH CREATED THE MIND FREE.

Charles Pinckney

James Madison

WHO SHOULD DECLARE WAR? — CONGRESS

THE PRESIDENT, OF COURSE. HE WILL NOT MAKE WAR WITHOUT THE NATION'S SUPPORT.

WHAT! I NEVER EXPECTED TO HEAR IN A REPUBLIC A MOTION TO EMPOWER THE EXECUTIVE ALONE TO DECLARE WAR.

I AM AGAINST GIVING THE POWER OF WAR TO THE EXECUTIVE, BECAUSE HE IS NOT SAFELY TO BE TRUSTED WITH IT.... I AM FOR CLOGGING RATHER THAN FACILITATING WAR.

PIERCE BUTLER

ELBRIDGE GERRY

GEORGE MASON

THE COMPROMISE: CONGRESS HAS THE POWER TO DECLARE WAR; THE PRESIDENT HAS THE POWER TO REPEL SUDDEN ATTACKS.

U.S. CONSTITUTION

SHOULD THERE BE A STANDING ARMY IN PEACETIME? — YES

"If we desire to secure peace,...it must be known that we are at all times ready for war." — George Washington

Americans were suspicious of standing armies in peacetime. They remembered Britain's "peacetime" army that had fired upon them at Lexington.

But Washington's aside comment in response to Elbridge Gerry gave another perspective:

AN ARMY IS DANGEROUS IN PEACETIME. I PROPOSE NO MORE THAN 3,000 TROOPS IN PEACETIME.

THEN I PROPOSE THAT NO ARMY INVADE THE U.S. WITH MORE THAN 3,000 TROOPS!

GEORGE WASHINGTON

THE COMPROMISE: THERE WOULD BE A STANDING ARMY BUT WITH A CIVILIAN —THE PRESIDENT— AS COMMANDER IN CHIEF AND WITH CONGRESS VOTING THE FUNDS.

U.S. CONSTITUTION

July 24-August 7

The delegates took a 10-day break while a 5-man <u>Committee of Detail</u> drafted a report of the Convention's resolves.

THINK I'LL GO FISHING.

The <u>Committee of Detail</u> consulted important documents on government, including the Magna Carta; colonial charters; the Albany Plan of Union; state constitutions; the Articles of Confederation; and a Native American document: THE GREAT LAW OF PEACE, the Iroquois Confederacy's 200-year-old constitution.

Committee Chairman <u>John Rutledge</u> began the meeting by reading from the Iroquois Confederacy's constitution, which both he and Benjamin Franklin admired.

GENTLEMEN, THE IROQUOIS INDIANS' CONSTITUTION HAS ACHIEVED PEACE THROUGH UNION FOR OVER 200 YEARS BY ALLOWING TO EACH OF THE SIX IROQUOIS NATIONS SELF-GOVERNMENT IN INTERNAL AFFAIRS, WHILE UNITING THEM FOR EXTERNAL AFFAIRS. IT BEGINS: "WE, THE PEOPLE, TO FORM A UNION, TO ESTABLISH PEACE, EQUITY AND ORDER...."

GREAT LAW OF PEACE

HEY! WE'RE BEING PLAGIARIZED!

IS THAT BAD?

August 7 — The Committee of Detail submitted its report, organized into twenty-three articles. Then the delegates spent five weeks debating and revising it.

HOW LONG HAVE YOU BEEN HANGING AROUND HERE?

ALL SUMMER..... WAITING FOR THESE GUYS TO FINISH.

INDEPENDENCE HALL

September 8-12 — Gouverneur Morris led a 5-man <u>Committee of Style</u> (including Madison and Hamilton) in writing the final draft of the constitution.

Morris, a masterful writer steeped in the cadences of Shakespeare, distilled twenty-three rambling articles into seven—each clear, concise and eloquent.

Proud of his work, Gouverneur Morris commented:

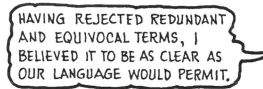

HAVING REJECTED REDUNDANT AND EQUIVOCAL TERMS, I BELIEVED IT TO BE AS CLEAR AS OUR LANGUAGE WOULD PERMIT.

Later, Caleb Strong (delegate from Massachusetts) said, "For my part, I think the whole of it is expressed in the plain, common language of mankind."

September 12-17 — The delegates fine-tuned the final draft, still voting on issues until the last day. <u>George Mason</u> had a last-minute idea, but the delegates unanimously rejected it. Tired and eager to go home, most agreed with <u>Roger Sherman</u>.

I THINK THE CONSTITUTION SHOULD HAVE A BILL OF RIGHTS. I CAN WRITE ONE IN NO TIME. REMEMBER, I WROTE THE ONE FOR VIRGINIA.

A BILL OF RIGHTS IS NOT NECESSARY, BECAUSE ALL POWERS NOT GRANTED TO THE GOVERNMENT ARE RESERVED FOR THE PEOPLE. BESIDES, 8 STATE CONSTITUTIONS ALREADY CONTAIN BILLS OF RIGHTS.

THIS ALMOST FATAL ERROR LATER WOULD CAUSE NEAR-REJECTION OF THE CONSTITUTION IN THE RATIFYING PROCESS. ONLY A PROMISE TO ADD A BILL OF RIGHTS, BY AMENDMENT, RESCUED THE CONSTITUTION. 1791 THE PROMISE WOULD BE FULFILLED WITH THE FIRST TEN AMENDMENTS TO THE U.S. CONSTITUTION — THE BILL OF RIGHTS.

On September 17th, the delegates gathered for a final vote on the constitution. Would it pass?
Benjamin Franklin rose with a speech in his hand. Too weak to stand, he asked James Wilson to read it for him.

Mr. President:

I confess that there are several parts of this Constitution which I do not at present
approve, but I am not sure I shall never approve them. For having lived long, I
have experienced many instances of being obliged by better information, or
fuller consideration, to change opinions even on important subjects,
which I once thought right, but found to be otherwise.

It is therefore that the older I grow, the more apt I am to doubt my own judgment, and to pay more respect to the
judgment of others. Most men indeed, as well as most sects in religion, think themselves in possession of
all truth, and that wherever others differ from them it is so far error....But though many persons
think almost as highly of their own infallibility as of that of their sect, few express it so
naturally as a certain French lady who in a dispute with her sister said,

"I don't know how it happens, Sister, but I meet with nobody but myself that's always in the right."

In these sentiments, Sir, I agree to this Constitution with all its faults, if they are such....I doubt too whether any
other Convention we can obtain, may be able to make a better Constitution. For when you assemble a
number of men to have the advantage of their joint wisdom, you inevitably assemble with those
men all their prejudices, their passions, their errors of opinion, their local interest, and
their selfish views. From such an assembly can a perfect production be expected?

It therefore astonishes me, Sir, to find this system approaching so near to perfection as it does, and I think it will
astonish our enemies who are waiting...to hear that our councils are confounded like those of the Builders of Babel....

Thus I consent, Sir, to this Constitution because I expect no better, and because I am not sure, that it is not the
best....On the whole, Sir, I cannot help expressing a wish that every member of the Convention who may still
have objections to it, would with me, on this occasion doubt a little of his own infallibility, and to
make manifest our unanimity, put his name to this instrument.

Washington then held the vote.

Each state had one vote. Every
state voted "Aye," approving the
Constitution by "the unanimous
consent of the States present..."

Of the 42 delegates present,
thirty-nine signed the
document. Three chose not to:
Mason, because it had no Bill of
Rights; Randolph and Gerry, because
they feared that not enough states
would ratify it and the result might
be "confusion," if not "civil war."

(Later, Randolph supported the
Constitution's ratification, and Gerry
served under the Constitution
as vice president.)

As the delegates came forward, one by one, to sign the Constitution,
Benjamin Franklin looked at the sun on the president's chair and said:

I HAVE OFTEN GLANCED AT THIS SUN, WONDERING IF IT WERE RISING OR SETTING. NOW... I HAVE THE HAPPINESS TO KNOW THAT IT IS A RISING SUN.

"It appears to me, then, little short of a miracle, that the Delegates from so many different States, [different] in their manners, circumstances, and prejudices, should unite in forming a system of national government, so little liable to well founded objections."
—George Washington

republic—a nation in which the supreme power rests in the people entitled to vote and is exercised by representatives elected directly or indirectly by them and responsible to them

federalism—a system of shared power between the states and the national government

The delegates finished their work, emerging with the ultimate compromise: a federal system balancing dual citizenship in both state and national governments, each with its separate sphere and powers.

As the delegates adjourned from the Constitutional Convention, a Philadelphia woman asked Ben Franklin:

WELL BEN, WHAT HAVE WE GOT—A REPUBLIC OR A MONARCHY?

A REPUBLIC, IF YOU CAN KEEP IT.

ALWAYS REMEMBER — IN A REPUBLIC THE GOVERNMENT IS CONDUCTED ONLY BY CONSENT OF THE PEOPLE. THE RULERS ARE SERVANTS, AND THE PEOPLE ARE THEIR SUPERIORS AND SOVEREIGNS.

ratify—to approve by voting
constitution—the fundamental law providing a framework for government

1492   1787–88   2000

Article VII of the Constitution states:

"The ratification of the Conventions of nine states shall be sufficient for the establishment of this Constitution between the states so ratifying the same."

The miracle at Philadelphia would prove unreal unless framers of the Constitution could convince people to approve the Constitution. So take it to the people they did—bypassing the Confederation Congress and state legislatures in favor of state ratifying conventions with elected delegates.

On September 18, 1787, the Constitution was sent to the Confederation Congress in New York, which agreed to send copies to the thirteen states for ratification. On June 21, 1788, New Hampshire became the ninth state to ratify the Constitution, making it the supreme law of the land—by the supreme authority of the people themselves.

The nine-month struggle for ratification pitted supporters of the Constitution, called <u>Federalists</u>, against opponents, called <u>Antifederalists</u>.

THE FEDERALIST PAPERS

Three articulate Federalists—<u>Alexander Hamilton</u>, <u>James Madison</u>, and <u>John Jay</u>—turned the tide with a series of 85 convincing newspaper essays, published under the pseudonym Publius. The essays are the best commentaries ever written on the United States government.

Ratification of the Constitution, as you can see, was a close call. Success came only with the Federalists' promise to amend the Constitution with a Bill of Rights.

June 21, 1788 → New Hampshire, the ninth state to approve, cast the deciding vote for ratification.

STATE	DATE RATIFIED	FOR—AG.
Delaware	Dec. 7, 1787	unanimous
Pennsylvania	Dec. 12, 1787	46—23
New Jersey	Dec. 18, 1787	unanimous
Georgia	Jan. 2, 1788	unanimous
Connecticut	Jan. 9, 1788	128—40
Massachusetts	Feb. 6, 1788	187—168
Maryland	Apr. 26, 1788	63—11
South Carolina	May 23, 1788	149—73
New Hampshire	June 21, 1788	57—47
Virginia	June 25, 1788	89—79
New York	July 26, 1788	30—27
North Carolina	Nov. 21, 1789	195—77
Rhode Island	May 29, 1790	34—32

Just what did the Americans ratify June 21, 1788, as the supreme law of the land?

READ ON FOR YOUR OWN TOUR OF THE CONSTITUTION OF THE UNITED STATES OF AMERICA.

The national government is located in Washington, District of Columbia—a site chosen and surveyed by President George Washington in 1790.

1492   1789   2000

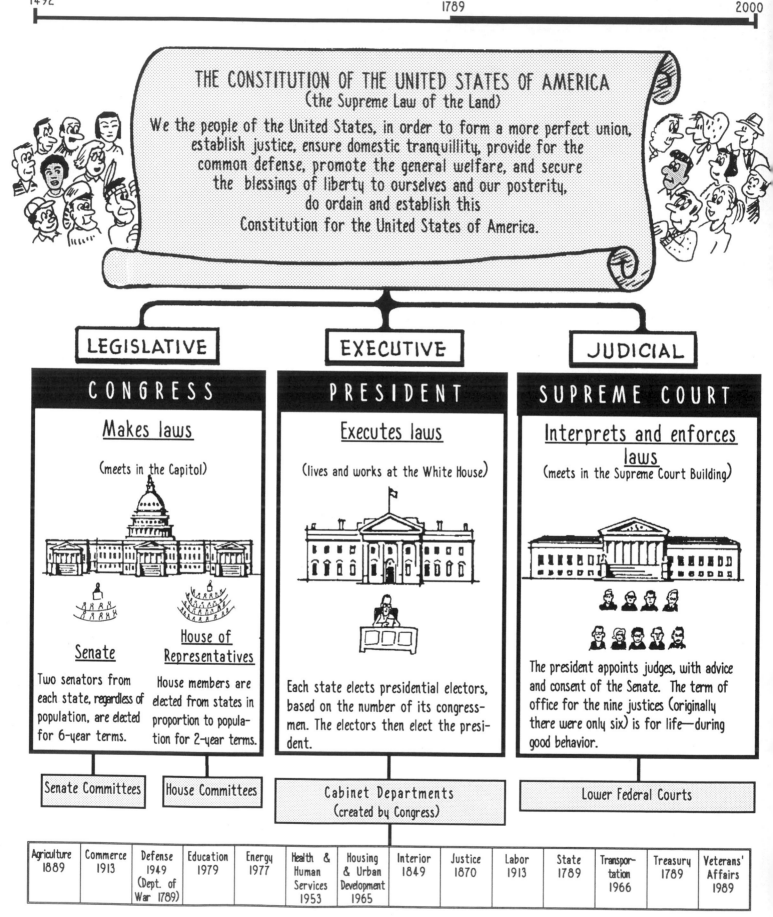

THE CONSTITUTION OF THE UNITED STATES OF AMERICA
(the Supreme Law of the Land)

We the people of the United States, in order to form a more perfect union, establish justice, ensure domestic tranquillity, provide for the common defense, promote the general welfare, and secure the blessings of liberty to ourselves and our posterity, do ordain and establish this Constitution for the United States of America.

LEGISLATIVE   EXECUTIVE   JUDICIAL

CONGRESS

Makes laws

(meets in the Capitol)

Senate

Two senators from each state, regardless of population, are elected for 6-year terms.

House of Representatives

House members are elected from states in proportion to population for 2-year terms.

Senate Committees   House Committees

PRESIDENT

Executes laws

(lives and works at the White House)

Each state elects presidential electors, based on the number of its congressmen. The electors then elect the president.

Cabinet Departments
(created by Congress)

SUPREME COURT

Interprets and enforces laws

(meets in the Supreme Court Building)

The president appoints judges, with advice and consent of the Senate. The term of office for the nine justices (originally there were only six) is for life—during good behavior.

Lower Federal Courts

Agriculture 1889	Commerce 1913	Defense 1949 (Dept. of War 1789)	Education 1979	Energy 1977	Health & Human Services 1953	Housing & Urban Development 1965	Interior 1849	Justice 1870	Labor 1913	State 1789	Transportation 1966	Treasury 1789	Veterans' Affairs 1989

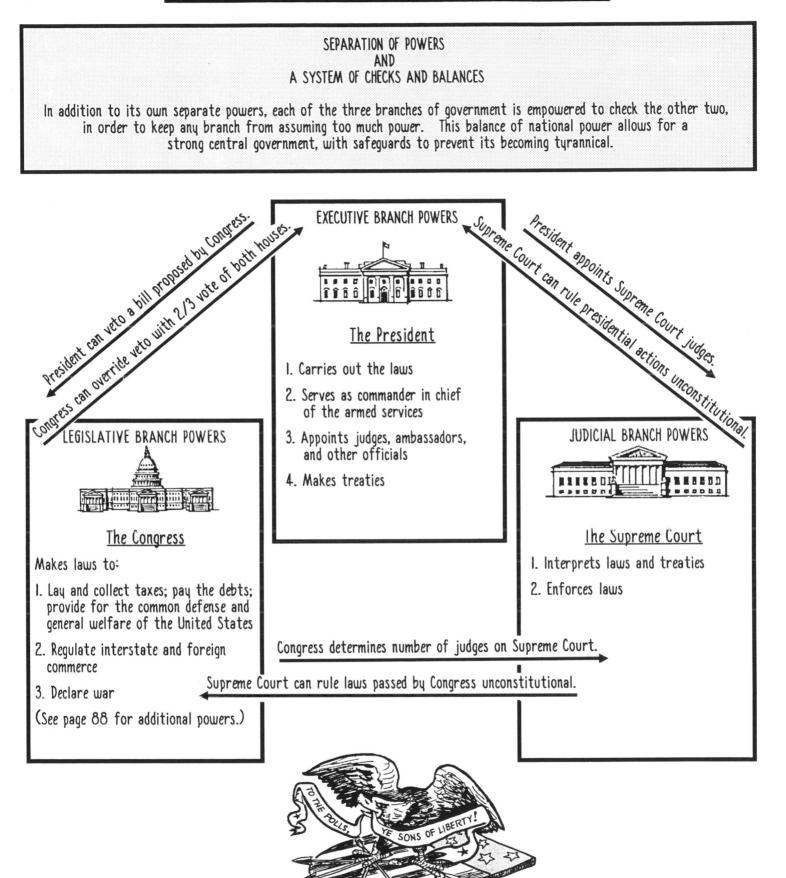

THE NATIONAL GOVERNMENT OF THE UNITED STATES OF AMERICA

SEPARATION OF POWERS
AND
A SYSTEM OF CHECKS AND BALANCES

In addition to its own separate powers, each of the three branches of government is empowered to check the other two, in order to keep any branch from assuming too much power. This balance of national power allows for a strong central government, with safeguards to prevent its becoming tyrannical.

EXECUTIVE BRANCH POWERS

The President

1. Carries out the laws

2. Serves as commander in chief of the armed services

3. Appoints judges, ambassadors, and other officials

4. Makes treaties

President can veto a bill proposed by Congress.

Congress can override veto with 2/3 vote of both houses.

President appoints Supreme Court judges.

Supreme Court can rule presidential actions unconstitutional.

LEGISLATIVE BRANCH POWERS

The Congress

Makes laws to:

1. Lay and collect taxes; pay the debts; provide for the common defense and general welfare of the United States

2. Regulate interstate and foreign commerce

3. Declare war

(See page 88 for additional powers.)

JUDICIAL BRANCH POWERS

The Supreme Court

1. Interprets laws and treaties

2. Enforces laws

Congress determines number of judges on Supreme Court.

Supreme Court can rule laws passed by Congress unconstitutional.

TO THE POLLS.   YE SONS OF LIBERTY!

THE PEOPLE'S POWER

159

THE FEDERAL SYSTEM: DIVISION OF POWERS BETWEEN THE NATIONAL AND STATE GOVERNMENTS

POWERS OF NATIONAL GOVERNMENT

* Regulate interstate and foreign commerce

* Coin money and regulate its value; fix standard of weights and measurments

* Punish counterfeiting of securities and current coin of the United States

* Set uniform rules of naturalization (process of becoming a U.S. citizen) and of bankruptcy (process of relieving debtors of debts they cannot pay)

* Establish post offices

* Promote science and useful arts with patents and copyrights

* Punish piracies and felonies on the high seas

* Declare war

* Raise and support an army

* Provide and maintain a navy

* Make rules for governing armed forces

* Call out state militias to execute U.S. laws, end rebellions, and repel invasions

* Share governance of militias with states

* Govern the national seat of government, a district separate from the states, not to exceed ten square miles (Washington D. C.)

* Govern territories and admit new states

* Make all laws which shall be necessary and proper for carrying into execution the foregoing powers

CONCURRENT POWERS OF NATIONAL AND STATE GOVERNMENTS

* Lay and collect taxes; pay debts

* Borrow money

* Provide for the general welfare

* Establish courts

* Enforce laws

* Punish lawbreakers

* Charter banks

* Make bankruptcy laws

* Build roads

POWERS RESERVED FOR THE STATES

* Establish local governments

* Conduct elections

* Regulate commerce within a state

* Establish and maintain schools

* Make marriage and divorce laws

* Provide for public safety

* Make laws regarding contracts, corporations, wills

* Raise and support a militia

OH YES — ONE THING MORE: THE 10TH AMENDMENT GAVE TO THE STATES "RESERVE POWER." THAT MEANS THE STATES OR THE PEOPLE HAVE ALL POWERS NOT GIVEN TO THE FEDERAL GOVERNMENT OR PROHIBITED TO THE STATES.

To make sure the new national government could not violate individual rights of the people—some dating back to the Magna Carta, Americans insisted that the U.S. Constitution be amended to include a bill (or listing) of these rights, thus guaranteeing them. Several states made this a condition for ratification. So in 1789 Congressman James Madison led the House of Representatives in recommending such amendments to the states for ratification. In 1791 the states ratified the first ten amendments to the Constitution—the Bill of Rights.

1st AMENDMENT:

CONGRESS SHALL MAKE NO LAW RESPECTING AN ESTABLISHMENT OF RELIGION, OR PROHIBITING THE FREE EXERCISE THEREOF; OR ABRIDGING THE FREEDOM OF SPEECH, OR OF THE PRESS; OR OF THE RIGHT OF THE PEOPLE PEACEABLY TO ASSEMBLE, AND TO PETITION THE GOVERNMENT FOR A REDRESS OF GRIEVANCES.

THIS IS THE LONGEST AND MOST IMPORTANT AMENDMENT. NOW LOOK AT WHAT EACH OF ITS 5 PARTS MEANS.

Freedom of Religion

IT'S YOUR CHOICE
CATHOLIC
PROTESTANT
JEWISH
OTHERS
NONE

THE GOVERNMENT CANNOT ESTABLISH AN OFFICIAL RELIGION. THIS MEANS YOU CAN'T BE FORCED TO ATTEND, OR SUPPORT WITH TAXES, ANY RELIGIOUS INSTITUTION.

ESTABLISHMENT CLAUSE

Freedom of Speech

AND FURTHERMORE...

WHAT A LOT OF BUNK! I TOTALLY DISAGREE WITH HIM!

YES, BUT REMEMBER HE HAS A RIGHT TO SAY WHAT HE THINKS!

SOAP

Freedom of the Press

HOLD ON, UNCLE SAM! I KNOW YOU'RE STEAMED, BUT THE GOVERNMENT CANNOT CONTROL THE MEDIA!

DAILY NEWS

Freedom of Assembly

HOW ABOUT IT CHIEF? SHALL I GO BREAK UP THAT CROWD OF DEMONSTRATORS?

NO, NO! THEY'RE A NUISANCE, BUT THEY HAVE A RIGHT TO HOLD A PEACEFUL ASSEMBLY.

Freedom of Petition

UNITED STATES CONGRESS

HEY, GET A LOAD OF ALL THE SIGNATURES!

YEAH - HE'S EXERCISING HIS RIGHT OF PETITION.

A <u>bill</u> is a proposal for a new law.
To become a law, a bill must pass both houses of Congress (the House of Representatives and the Senate) and be signed by the president.
The idea for a law can come from anyone—individuals, interest groups, the president of the United States—
but only a member of the House of Representatives or Senate can sponsor a bill and guide it through the required steps.

<u>ORIGIN</u>—Most bills may originate (be introduced) in either house of Congress or in both houses at the same time. But <u>money</u> bills must originate in the House of Representatives.

<u>COMMITTEES</u>—About 10,000 bills per year are introduced. Each is given a number and assigned to a standing, or permanent, committee—such as agriculture, energy or labor. There are 22 committees in the House of Representatives and 15 in the Senate; each has several sub-committees. A bill might be 1,000 pages long and involve 200 people on 15 subcommittees.

<u>HEARINGS</u>—Subcommittees hold hearings at which experts and interested parties speak for or against the bill. The sub-committee then makes recommendations about the bill to the full committee.

<u>COMMITTEE ACTION</u>—The full committee may: 1) approve, 2) rewrite and approve, 3) amend (change) and approve, 4) reject the bill. (Only about 1,000 of 10,000 bills considered per year become laws; most die in committee.) If approved, the bill goes to the house of origin for debate.

<u>CONGRESSIONAL ACTION</u>—Back in its house of origin the bill is debated, perhaps amended, and voted on. If passed, it goes to the other house for the same action. If both houses approve the final bill, it goes to the president.

<u>EXECUTIVE ACTION</u>—The president may:

1) veto the bill;

2) sign the bill, making it a law;

3) hold the bill without signing. Unsigned, it becomes a law in 10 days if Congress is in session; it dies if Congress adjourns before 10 days (a pocket veto).

If the president vetoes a bill, Congress may override the veto, and the bill becomes a law without the president's approval.

<u>JUDICIAL ACTION</u>—If a law does not conform to the United States Constitution, the Supreme Court has the power to declare the law unconstitutional.

1492   1789   1877   2000

adventure—the exploring of new and unknown worlds; a bold undertaking in which hazards are to be met, and the issue hangs upon unforeseen events

```
1492                                    1789        1877              2000
├──────────────────────────────────────┼══════════┼──────────────────┤
```

WOULD THE CONSTITUTION OF THE UNITED STATES WORK?

No one knew for sure, but in 1789 the new republic ventured into the unknown with superb leadership: an enlightened group of statesmen committed to the idea that free human beings were capable of self-government.

The new nation "conceived in liberty" made great progress between 1789-1877, extending the democratic experiment westward to the Pacific coast. But by mid-19th century, the hazards of excluding women and African-Americans from citizenship led to two unforeseen events: the beginning of a 72-year woman's rights movement (1848-1920) and a traumatic, four-year civil war (1861-65). The result: female and black emancipation, albeit slow, incomplete, and accompanied by protest.

How did it all happen, and where would it lead? Read on for 80 years of unmatched drama, as the United States expanded westward—tripling its size—in a remarkable adventure of self-government.

THE UNITED STATES: 1789-1877

OREGON COUNTRY 1846

BRITISH CESSION 1818

BRITISH CESSION 1842

MEXICAN CESSION 1848

LOUISIANA PURCHASE 1803

THE UNITED STATES IN 1783

ORIGINAL THIRTEEN STATES

VIRGINIA 1607

TEXAS ANNEXATION 1845

GADSDEN PURCHASE 1853

W. FLORIDA 1810-13

E. FLORIDA 1819

ALASKA 1867

SECTION THIRTEEN
FEDERALIST ERA, 1789-1800

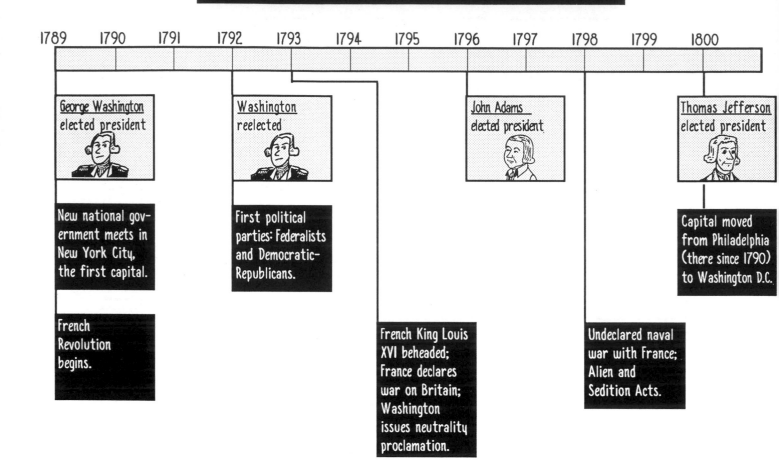

1789 | 1790 | 1791 | 1792 | 1793 | 1794 | 1795 | 1796 | 1797 | 1798 | 1799 | 1800

George Washington elected president

Washington reelected

John Adams elected president

Thomas Jefferson elected president

New national government meets in New York City, the first capital.

First political parties: Federalists and Democratic-Republicans.

Capital moved from Philadelphia (there since 1790) to Washington D.C.

French Revolution begins.

French King Louis XVI beheaded; France declares war on Britain; Washington issues neutrality proclamation.

Undeclared naval war with France; Alien and Sedition Acts.

WASHINGTON'S INAUGURATION
* * 1789 * *

"My station is new; and if I may use the expression, I walk on untrodden ground."—President George Washington
"We are in a wilderness without a single footstep to guide us."—Congressman James Madison

1492   1789   2000

THE FEDERALISTS IN POWER

On March 4, 1789, the first Congress under the U.S. Constitution met in Federal Hall in New York City, the temporary capital.

Most of the 81 congressmen (22 senators and 59 representatives, elected on Feb. 4) were Federalists; 54 had served at either the Constitutional Convention or a state ratifying convention, and all but 7 had approved ratification of the Constitution. The new government was in friendly hands.

ON APRIL 6 THE SENATE COUNTED BALLOTS CAST EARLIER BY THE PRESIDENTIAL ELECTORS. GEORGE WASHINGTON WAS UNANIMOUSLY ELECTED PRESIDENT. JOHN ADAMS WAS ELECTED VICE-PRESIDENT.

THERE WERE NO POLITICAL PARTIES THEN, AND NO ONE EXPECTED THERE TO BE.

April 30, 1789—INAUGURATION DAY

I DO SOLEMNLY SWEAR THAT I WILL FAITHFULLY EXECUTE THE OFFICE OF PRESIDENT OF THE UNITED STATES AND WILL, TO THE BEST OF MY ABILITY, PRESERVE, PROTECT, AND DEFEND THE CONSTITUTION OF THE UNITED STATES, SO HELP ME GOD.

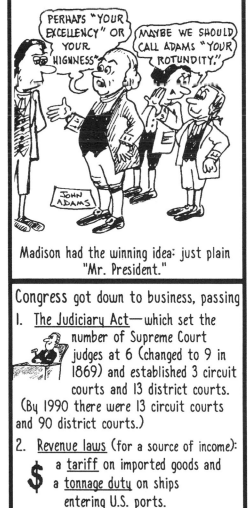

TITLES? Accustomed to a monarchy, no one knew exactly how to act in a republic; there were no precedents. What should the president be called?

PERHAPS "YOUR EXCELLENCY" OR YOUR HIGHNESS"

MAYBE WE SHOULD CALL ADAMS "YOUR ROTUNDITY."

JOHN ADAMS

Madison had the winning idea: just plain "Mr. President."

Congress got down to business, passing

1. The Judiciary Act—which set the number of Supreme Court judges at 6 (changed to 9 in 1869) and established 3 circuit courts and 13 district courts. (By 1990 there were 13 circuit courts and 90 district courts.)

2. Revenue laws (for a source of income): a tariff on imported goods and a tonnage duty on ships entering U.S. ports.

THE CABINET

Washington appointed talented men of divergent views to head the executive departments. These officials soon became known as the Cabinet. Washington, a consensus leader who wanted to hear all points of view, met frequently with them to seek their counsel on vital issues. He set the precedent for present-day cabinet meetings.

LITTLE DID I KNOW THAT FIREWORKS WOULD START BETWEEN HAMILTON AND JEFFERSON, RESULTING IN POLITICAL PARTIES BEFORE THE END OF MY ADMINISTRATION! WELL, HERE'S HOW IT HAPPENED....

the BOSS

SECRETARY OF TREASURY: Alexander Hamilton

SECRETARY OF STATE: Thomas Jefferson

SECRETARY OF WAR: Henry Knox

ATTORNEY GENERAL: Edmund Randolph

Hamilton "...had...the breadth of mind to grapple with the machine of government as a whole..."—Henry Adams

1492   1755   1804   2000

"The Little Lion," they called the aggressive Lieutenant Colonel Hamilton during the Revolutionary War. Now, at age 35, the 5'7" Hamilton was Secretary of the Treasury, and his roar would bring order, efficiency, and financial stability to the new republic. An aristocratic, handsome man, he had a brilliant mind and abrasive ways.

Born in 1755 in the British West Indies—of an English/French mother and Scottish father who never married—Hamilton grew up reading Plutarch's Lives of the ancient Greeks and Romans and idolizing Julius Caesar. At age 16, he arrived in New York to study math and political science at King's College (Columbia). He became a lawyer and married wealthy Elizabeth Schuyler; they had seven children. He served heroically in the Revolutionary War and at age 22 became chief aide to General Washington—who, some said, loved him as a son.

From 1789 to 1795, the Little Lion's financial prowess gave the nearly bankrupt new nation a sound economy, readying it for the industrial growth he envisioned but never witnessed. In 1804 Aaron Burr, a political opponent, killed Hamilton in a duel.

FINANCIAL REPORT

1790—The Nation's First Crisis: THE DEFICIT

Congress asked Hamilton to figure out what to do about the staggering Revolutionary War debt it inherited from the Confederation.

NATIONAL DEBT $42,414,000

FOREIGN DEBT $11,710,000

STATE DEBT $21,339,000

HAMILTON'S FINANCIAL PROGRAM

Hamilton knew that the nation—like a person—had to pay its debts in order to establish credit (the ability to borrow money when needed) and to earn respect from the wealthy class, whose support it needed.

To do this, Hamilton proposed and executed a bold 4-point plan—all designed to strengthen the central government. The opposition his plan aroused led to the creation of political parties.

1. FUND FULL PAYMENT OF FOREIGN AND NATIONAL DEBT

—by selling new U.S. bonds to investors.

FOREIGN AND DOMESTIC DEBT

Madison and others opposed payment of the national debt at face value because speculators had bought many of the depreciated war bonds at discount prices. But Congress passed the measure.

2. ASSUMPTION OF STATE DEBT —to bind creditors (lenders) to the national governemnt.

SURE! JUST TOSS IT ON, SON!

FOREIGN AND DOMESTIC DEBT

STATE DEBT

Southern states (except S.C.) objected because they had paid most of their debt and did not want to subsidize that of the North.

A Capital Compromise

Hamilton worked out a deal with Jefferson and Madison to trade southern votes for assumption—in exchange for northern votes for a southern national capital, located on the Potomac River.

MARYLAND

District of Columbia (Capitol: 1800—)

Washington

Mount Vernon

VIRGINIA

NEW JERSEY

DELAWARE

ATLANTIC OCEAN

Chesapeake Bay

Potomac R.

3. AN EXCISE TAX ON WHISKEY

—for a source of income to pay the debt.

In 1794 Pennsylvania farmers, who took their corn to market more cheaply by turning it into whiskey, rebelled against the tax.

Washington and Hamilton accompanied a militia of 15,000, led by Gen. Henry Lee, to crush the Whiskey Rebellion and assert the government's power to collect taxes voted on by a representative Congress.

4. A FEDERALLY CHARTERED BANK OF THE UNITED STATES

Hamilton displayed his financial genius with a bold proposal for a national bank, jointly owned and directed by the government (20%) and private investors (80%).

Ten million dollars worth of shares would be sold (at $400 per share) to capitalize the Bank of the U.S. Shareholders would receive dividends from interest on the bank's loans.

Although modeled on the century-old Bank of England, the proposal seemed hazardous to a nation with few banks of any kind and only three state banks.

THE BANK OF THE UNITED STATES would:

1) be the depository for federal funds, and 2) receive tax funds paid by the people, thus collecting the nation's financial resources into one giant pool, from which it could then:

3) loan money to the government and to businessmen, thus aiding the development of roads, bridges, factories, etc.,

4) issue sound paper money, backed by its hard coin deposits.

I'M BACKING YOU, BUDDY.

TAX Collector

Congress approved the Bank bill, despite fierce opposition led by Madison and Jefferson. The two men then prepared their case for urging Washington to veto the Bank bill.

THE BANK FAVORS THE RICH MAN, ABLE TO SPEND $400 A SHARE. THE RICH THEN GET RICHER ON DIVIDENDS FROM TAXPAYERS' DEPOSITS!

HAMILTON FAVORS GOVERNMENT BY THE "RICH AND WELL-BORN."

BESIDES IT'S UNCONSTITUTIONAL!

Washington, concerned about the constitutionality of the bank, asked Jefferson and Hamilton each to give their opinions on the issue.

JEFFERSON
presented a strict, narrow construction of the Constitution.

THE CONSTITUTION SAYS WHAT IT MEANS AND MEANS WHAT IT SAYS. NOWHERE DOES IT MENTION CREATING A BANK. IF WE START READING BETWEEN THE LINES, THE FEDERAL GOVERNMENT WILL USURP MORE AND MORE POWER.

HAMILTON
presented a loose, broad construction of the Constitution.

ARTICLE I, SECTION 8 OF THE CONSTITUTION ALLOWS CONGRESS TO "MAKE ALL LAWS WHICH SHALL BE NECESSARY AND PROPER FOR CARRYING INTO EXECUTION" ITS STATED POWERS AND TO "PROVIDE FOR ... THE GENERAL WELFARE." NOW, THE POWER TO TAX IMPLIES THE POWER TO CREATE A BANK TO HOLD THE TAX FUNDS — CLEARLY A "NECESSARY AND PROPER" ACT.

Hamilton won the day: Washington signed the Bank bill. Political parties began to form around Jefferson's and Hamilton's views of the Constitution.

"Jefferson said, 'the many!' Hamilton said, 'the few!' Like opposite sides of a penny were those exalted two.
If Jefferson said, 'It's black, sir!' Hamilton cried, 'it's white!' But, 'twixt the two, our Constitution started working right."
—Stephan Vincent Benet

FEDERALIST PARTY

B A S E D O N

ALEXANDER HAMILTON'S VIEWS

By the election year of 1792, Hamilton and Jefferson headed rival political parties to enact their views.

Both parties had the same goal, a free republic, but differed in means to attain it.

The political party system (continuing since 1792 to the present), at first feared divisive, has proved vital for democracy.

Why?

Parties provide for dissent and choice, the lifeblood of freedom.

REPUBLICAN PARTY*

(not the same as today's Republican party)
*also called Democratic-Republican

B A S E D O N

THOMAS JEFFERSON'S VIEWS

SOCIAL

PESSIMISTIC VIEW OF HUMAN NATURE

Hamilton believed people are basically selfish—thus need the restraint of strong government.

OPTIMISTIC VIEW OF HUMAN NATURE

Jefferson believed people are basically good—thus capable of self-government.

POLITICAL: Who Should Govern?

Both Hamilton and Jefferson believed that an aristocracy should rule—but differed as to what kind:

Hamilton favored:

a rich and well-born aristocracy, based on birth, wealth, and status.

He agreed with John Jay that, "Those who own the country ought to govern it." They had more at stake, so they would be more responsible.

BIRTH WEALTH STATUS

TALENT VIRTUE

THE 5 PILLARS OF ARISTOCRACY
(as described by John Adams)

Jefferson favored:

a natural aristocracy, based on talent and virtue.

He advocated rule by educated men of property, but he promoted widespread access to both education and property.

WELL, MY DEAR — AS ONE OF THE ELITE, I MUST GO HELP RUN THE GOVERNMENT. "DUTY CALLS."

A LIKELY STORY...

VOTE FOR GREENE

BUT GREENE IS JUST AN ORDINARY FELLOW...

TRUE, BUT HE'S A MAN OF PROVEN ABILITY.

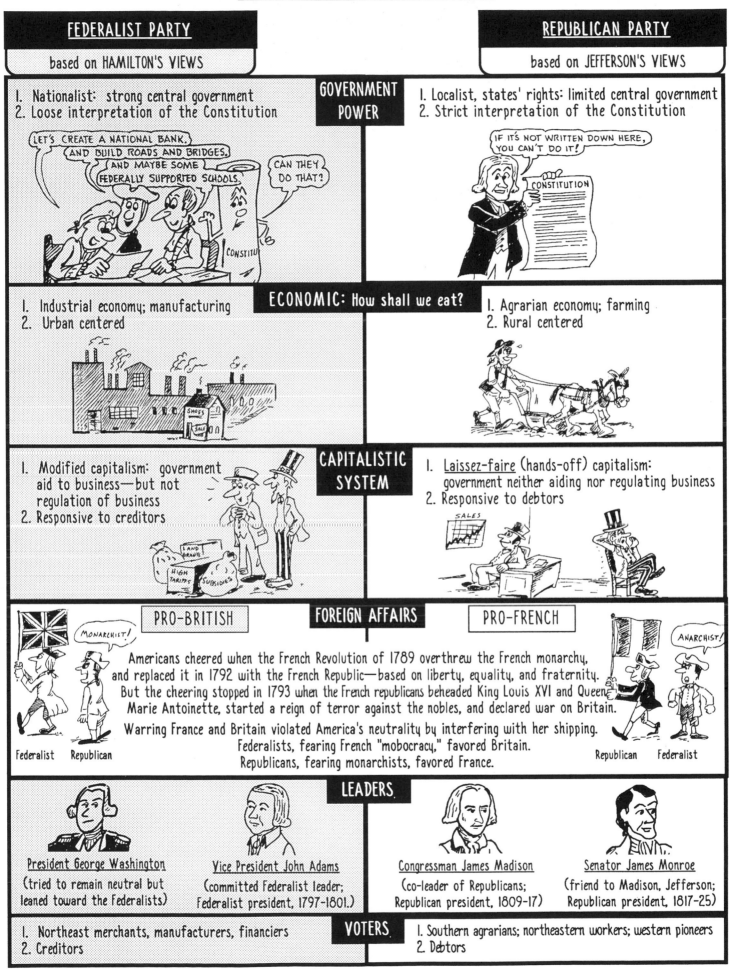

FEDERALISTS VS. REPUBLICANS

FEDERALIST PARTY
based on HAMILTON'S VIEWS

REPUBLICAN PARTY
based on JEFFERSON'S VIEWS

GOVERNMENT POWER

Federalist:
1. Nationalist: strong central government
2. Loose interpretation of the Constitution

LET'S CREATE A NATIONAL BANK, AND BUILD ROADS AND BRIDGES, AND MAYBE SOME FEDERALLY SUPPORTED SCHOOLS.
CAN THEY DO THAT?
CONSTITU...

Republican:
1. Localist, states' rights: limited central government
2. Strict interpretation of the Constitution

IF IT'S NOT WRITTEN DOWN HERE, YOU CAN'T DO IT!
CONSTITUTION

ECONOMIC: How shall we eat?

Federalist:
1. Industrial economy; manufacturing
2. Urban centered

SHOES SALE

Republican:
1. Agrarian economy; farming
2. Rural centered

CAPITALISTIC SYSTEM

Federalist:
1. Modified capitalism: government aid to business—but not regulation of business
2. Responsive to creditors

LAND GRANTS
HIGH TARIFFS SUBSIDIES

Republican:
1. Laissez-faire (hands-off) capitalism: government neither aiding nor regulating business
2. Responsive to debtors

SALES

FOREIGN AFFAIRS

PRO-BRITISH

MONARCHIST!

PRO-FRENCH

ANARCHIST!

Americans cheered when the French Revolution of 1789 overthrew the French monarchy, and replaced it in 1792 with the French Republic—based on liberty, equality, and fraternity.
But the cheering stopped in 1793 when the French republicans beheaded King Louis XVI and Queen Marie Antoinette, started a reign of terror against the nobles, and declared war on Britain.

Warring France and Britain violated America's neutrality by interfering with her shipping.
Federalists, fearing French "mobocracy," favored Britain.
Republicans, fearing monarchists, favored France.

Federalist Republican

Republican Federalist

LEADERS

President George Washington
(tried to remain neutral but leaned toward the Federalists)

Vice President John Adams
(committed Federalist leader; Federalist president, 1797-1801.)

Congressman James Madison
(co-leader of Republicans; Republican president, 1809-17)

Senator James Monroe
(friend to Madison, Jefferson; Republican president, 1817-25)

VOTERS

Federalist:
1. Northeast merchants, manufacturers, financiers
2. Creditors

Republican:
1. Southern agrarians; northeastern workers; western pioneers
2. Debtors

171

78 -:- AMERICAN POLITICAL PARTIES AND PRESIDENTS, 1789-1881 -:-

"A zeal for different opinions concerning religion...government...and many other points, or an attachment to different leaders have...divided mankind into parties....But the most common source of factions has been the various and unequal distribution of property. Those who hold, and those who are without property, have ever formed distinct interests in society....A landed interest, a manufacturing interest, a mercantile interest, a moneyed interest, with many lesser interests, always appear in civilized nations and divide them into different classes, motivated by different sentiments and views.

"The regulation of these various interests forms the principal task of modern legislation, and involves the spirit of party and faction in the ordinary operations of government."
—James Madison, The Federalist, Number 10

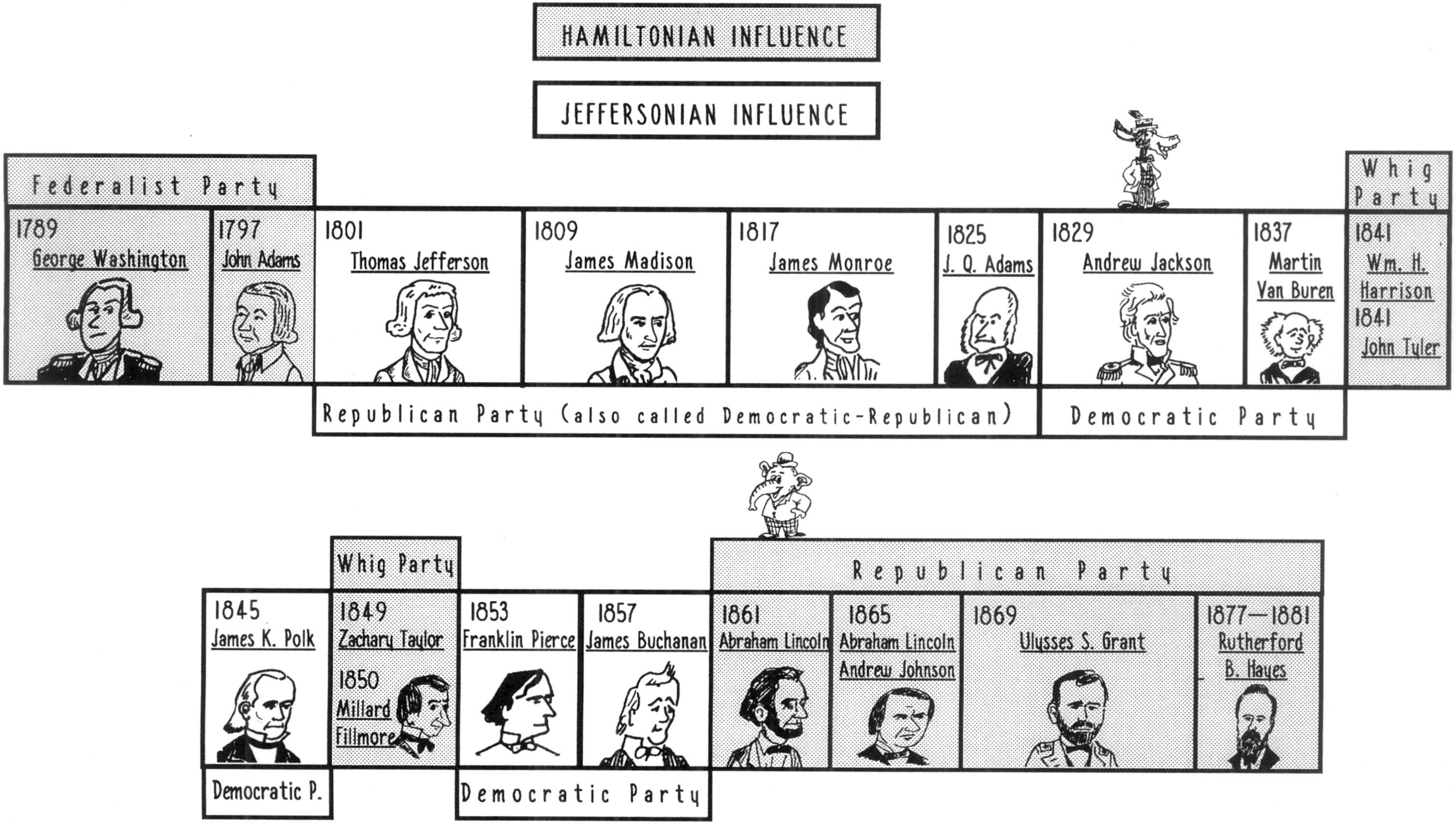

HAMILTONIAN INFLUENCE

JEFFERSONIAN INFLUENCE

Federalist Party

1789 George Washington	1797 John Adams

Whig Party

1841 Wm. H. Harrison	1841 John Tyler

1801 Thomas Jefferson	1809 James Madison	1817 James Monroe	1825 J. Q. Adams

Republican Party (also called Democratic-Republican)

1829 Andrew Jackson	1837 Martin Van Buren

Democratic Party

Republican Party

1861 Abraham Lincoln	1865 Abraham Lincoln / Andrew Johnson	1869 Ulysses S. Grant	1877—1881 Rutherford B. Hayes

Whig Party

1849 Zachary Taylor	1850 Millard Fillmore

1853 Franklin Pierce	1857 James Buchanan

Democratic Party

1845 James K. Polk

Democratic P.

1492   1793-1801   2000

Great Britain and France waged war from 1793 to 1802 and again from 1803 to 1815. The United States, dependent on trade with each, tried valiantly to maintain neutrality. After veering toward war with Britain in 1794 and with France in 1798, the new nation fought Britain in the War of 1812 and—in what might be called a second war of independence—finally gained freedom from Europe's entangling alliances.

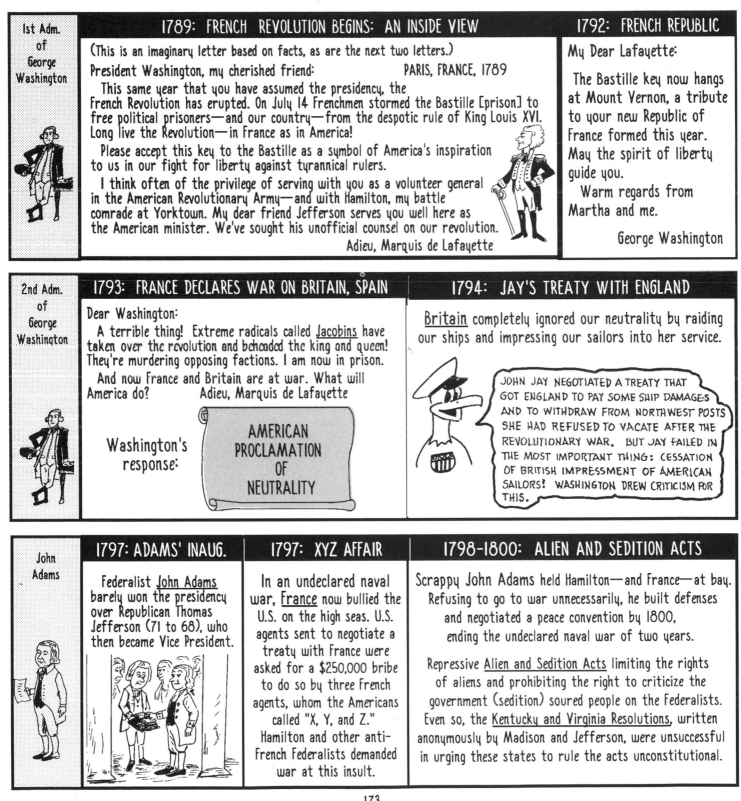

1st Adm. of George Washington

1789: FRENCH REVOLUTION BEGINS: AN INSIDE VIEW

(This is an imaginary letter based on facts, as are the next two letters.)

President Washington, my cherished friend: PARIS, FRANCE, 1789

This same year that you have assumed the presidency, the French Revolution has erupted. On July 14 Frenchmen stormed the Bastille [prison] to free political prisoners—and our country—from the despotic rule of King Louis XVI. Long live the Revolution—in France as in America!

Please accept this key to the Bastille as a symbol of America's inspiration to us in our fight for liberty against tyrannical rulers.

I think often of the privilege of serving with you as a volunteer general in the American Revolutionary Army—and with Hamilton, my battle comrade at Yorktown. My dear friend Jefferson serves you well here as the American minister. We've sought his unofficial counsel on our revolution.

Adieu, Marquis de Lafayette

1792: FRENCH REPUBLIC

My Dear Lafayette:

The Bastille key now hangs at Mount Vernon, a tribute to your new Republic of France formed this year. May the spirit of liberty guide you.

Warm regards from Martha and me.

George Washington

2nd Adm. of George Washington

1793: FRANCE DECLARES WAR ON BRITAIN, SPAIN

Dear Washington:

A terrible thing! Extreme radicals called <u>Jacobins</u> have taken over the revolution and beheaded the king and queen! They're murdering opposing factions. I am now in prison.

And now France and Britain are at war. What will America do?   Adieu, Marquis de Lafayette

Washington's response:

AMERICAN PROCLAMATION OF NEUTRALITY

1794: JAY'S TREATY WITH ENGLAND

<u>Britain</u> completely ignored our neutrality by raiding our ships and impressing our sailors into her service.

JOHN JAY NEGOTIATED A TREATY THAT GOT ENGLAND TO PAY SOME SHIP DAMAGES AND TO WITHDRAW FROM NORTHWEST POSTS SHE HAD REFUSED TO VACATE AFTER THE REVOLUTIONARY WAR. BUT JAY FAILED IN THE MOST IMPORTANT THING: CESSATION OF BRITISH IMPRESSMENT OF AMERICAN SAILORS! WASHINGTON DREW CRITICISM FOR THIS.

John Adams

1797: ADAMS' INAUG.

Federalist <u>John Adams</u> barely won the presidency over Republican Thomas Jefferson (71 to 68), who then became Vice President.

1797: XYZ AFFAIR

In an undeclared naval war, <u>France</u> now bullied the U.S. on the high seas. U.S. agents sent to negotiate a treaty with France were asked for a $250,000 bribe to do so by three French agents, whom the Americans called "X, Y, and Z." Hamilton and other anti-French Federalists demanded war at this insult.

1798-1800: ALIEN AND SEDITION ACTS

Scrappy John Adams held Hamilton—and France—at bay. Refusing to go to war unnecessarily, he built defenses and negotiated a peace convention by 1800, ending the undeclared naval war of two years.

Repressive <u>Alien and Sedition Acts</u> limiting the rights of aliens and prohibiting the right to criticize the government (sedition) soured people on the Federalists. Even so, the <u>Kentucky and Virginia Resolutions</u>, written anonymously by Madison and Jefferson, were unsuccessful in urging these states to rule the acts unconstitutional.

"...the plan should be drawn on such a scale as to leave room for the aggrandizement and embellishment which the increased wealth of the nation will permit it to pursue at a period however remote."—Pierre L'Enfant, 1791

1492   1800   2000

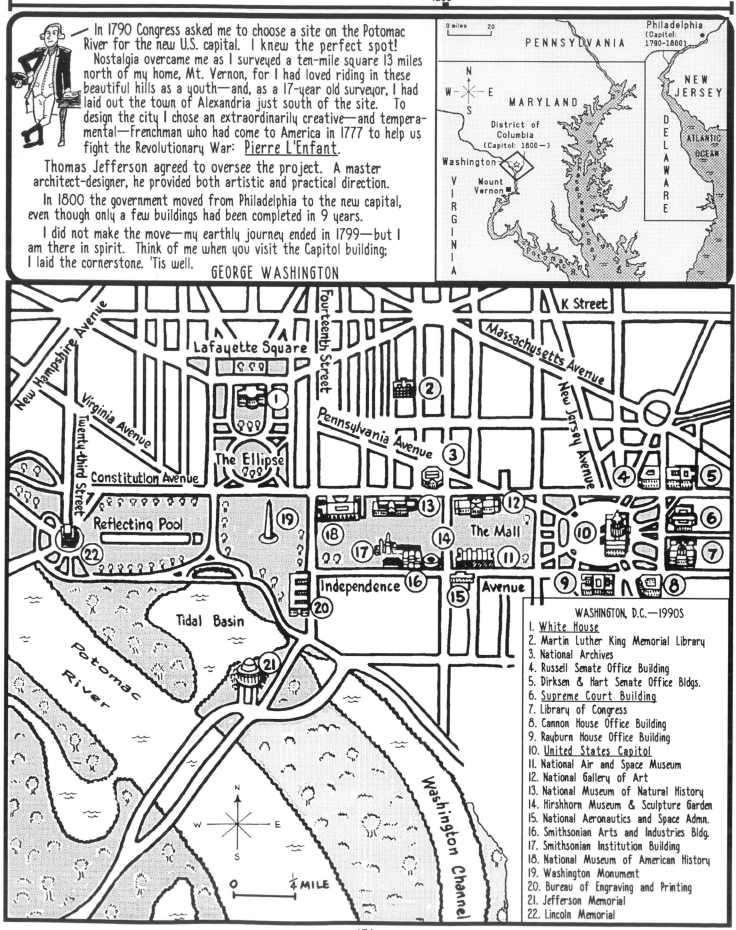

In 1790 Congress asked me to choose a site on the Potomac River for the new U.S. capital. I knew the perfect spot!

Nostalgia overcame me as I surveyed a ten-mile square 13 miles north of my home, Mt. Vernon, for I had loved riding in these beautiful hills as a youth—and, as a 17-year old surveyor, I had laid out the town of Alexandria just south of the site. To design the city I chose an extraordinarily creative—and temperamental—Frenchman who had come to America in 1777 to help us fight the Revolutionary War: <u>Pierre L'Enfant</u>.

Thomas Jefferson agreed to oversee the project. A master architect-designer, he provided both artistic and practical direction.

In 1800 the government moved from Philadelphia to the new capital, even though only a few buildings had been completed in 9 years.

I did not make the move—my earthly journey ended in 1799—but I am there in spirit. Think of me when you visit the Capitol building; I laid the cornerstone. 'Tis well.

GEORGE WASHINGTON

WASHINGTON, D.C.—1990S

1. <u>White House</u>
2. Martin Luther King Memorial Library
3. National Archives
4. Russell Senate Office Building
5. Dirksen & Hart Senate Office Bldgs.
6. <u>Supreme Court Building</u>
7. Library of Congress
8. Cannon House Office Building
9. Rayburn House Office Building
10. <u>United States Capitol</u>
11. National Air and Space Museum
12. National Gallery of Art
13. National Museum of Natural History
14. Hirshhorn Museum & Sculpture Garden
15. National Aeronautics and Space Admn.
16. Smithsonian Arts and Industries Bldg.
17. Smithsonian Institution Building
18. National Museum of American History
19. Washington Monument
20. Bureau of Engraving and Printing
21. Jefferson Memorial
22. Lincoln Memorial

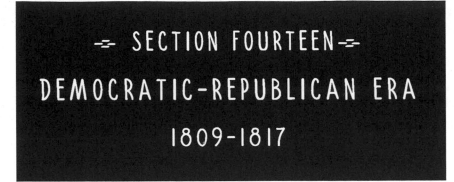

1492   1801   1817   2000

"That government governs best which governs least."
"The freedom and happiness of man...are the sole objects of all legitimate government."—Thomas Jefferson

1492   1801-09   2000

1800—In a bitterly contested election, the Republicans ousted the Federalists, who had been in power for ten years. Republican Thomas Jefferson became the first president to be inaugurated in the new capital Washington, D.C. He intended to redirect government power from central to state and local levels, away from the aristocratic few toward the competent many.

Could the nation withstand the transfer of power from one political party to another? Yes, thanks to Jefferson. In one of the finest inaugural addresses of any American president, he challenged the American people to seek the essentials of democracy: TOLERANCE OF DISSENT, CONCILIATION OF DIFFERENCES, and UNITY AMIDST DIVERSITY.

Thomas Jefferson: Inaugural Address, March 4, 1801 (excerpts)

"Friends and Fellow-Citizens: ....During the contest of opinion through which we have passed, the animation of discussions...has sometimes worn an aspect which might impose on strangers unused to think freely and to speak and to write what they think; but this being now decided by the voice of the nation...all will, of course, arrange themselves under the will of the law, and unite in common efforts for the common good.

"All, too will bear in mind this sacred principle, that though the will of the majority is in all cases to prevail, that will to be rightful must be reasonable; that the minority possess their equal rights, which equal law must protect, and to violate would be oppression.

"Let us, then, fellow-citizens, unite with one heart and one mind. Let us restore to social intercourse that harmony and affection without which liberty and even life itself are but dreary things. And let us reflect that, having banished from our land that religious intolerance under which mankind so long bled and suffered, we have yet gained little if we countenance a political intolerance as despotic, as wicked, and capable of as bitter and bloody persecutions....

"But every difference of opinion is not a difference of principle. We have called by different names brethren of the same principle. We are all Republicans, we are all Federalists. If there be any among us who would wish to dissolve this Union or to change its republican form, let them stand undisturbed as monuments of the safety with which error of opinion may be tolerated where reason is left free to combat it.

"I know, indeed, that some honest men fear that a republican government can not be strong....I believe this, on the contrary, the strongest government on earth....Sometimes it is said that man can not be trusted with the government of himself. Can he then, be trusted with the government of others? Or have we found angels in the forms of kings to govern him? Let history answer this question.

"Let us, then, with courage and confidence pursue our own Federal and Republican principles, our attachment to union and representative government....Still one thing more...[is needed]—a wise and frugal government, which shall restrain men from injuring one another, shall leave them otherwise free to regulate their own pursuits of industry and improvement, and shall not take from the mouth of labor the bread it has earned...."

FRUGAL AND LIMITED GOVERNMENT—Jefferson's principle of governing was exercised by Secretary of the Treasury Albert Gallatin and Congress by reducing 1) taxes, 2) defense expenditures, and 3) the national debt (from 83 to 57 million dollars).

JUDICIAL REVIEW—The Supreme Court, however, gained power from Federalist Chief Justice John Marshall's 1803 decision in Marbury vs. Madison: the power to declare acts of Congress unconstitutional through the right of judicial review.

1492   1803   2000

1803—As president, Thomas Jefferson's greatestest accomplishment was purchase of the vast Louisiana Territory from France. More than doubling the size of the United States, the acquisition made continental expansion inevitable. Soon the country would stretch from sea to sea.

You remember the "musical chairs" way Arkansas changed owners—belonging first to the mighty Spanish empire, then the mightier French empire, then the Spanish again. Well, the music wasn't over.

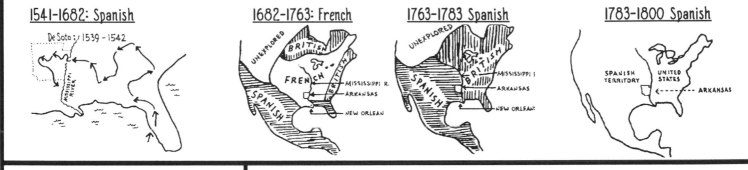

1541-1682: Spanish   1682-1763: French   1763-1783 Spanish   1783-1800 Spanish

In 1800 Napoleon Bonaparte, the new military dictator of France who aspired to be master of the world, forced Spain to cede Louisiana back to France.

Jefferson feared that France would close the Mississippi River to U.S. commerce. The action would affect thousands of Americans who had settled west of the Appalachian mountains since Daniel Boone first carved the Wilderness Road in 1775. These western farmers floated their crops to market on the Mississippi River.

As protection, Jefferson had Congress authorize a $2,000,000 offer to buy the port city of New Orleans from France. To everyone's amazement Napoleon offered to sell <u>all</u> of Louisiana—and for only $15,000,000! French foreign minister Talleyrand explained why.

Overjoyed at the spectacular deal, Jefferson realized the Constitution did not provide for such a purchase, so he suggested an amendment. Congress warned there was no time, so he reluctantly adopted a Hamiltonian loose construction position, arguing for implied powers. Congress quickly voted approval. But not everyone agreed with the purchase.

"Honored parents, I now take this opportunity to let you know where I am and what I am doing. I am on an expedition to the westward with Captain Lewis and Captain Clark, who are appointed by the President of the United States to go through the interior parts of North America. We shall ascend the Missouri River and then go by land to the Western Ocean. I do not know when I can write to you again."—John Ordway

1492　　　　　　　　　　　　　　　　　　　　　　1804-06　　　　　　　　　　　　　　　　　　　　　2000

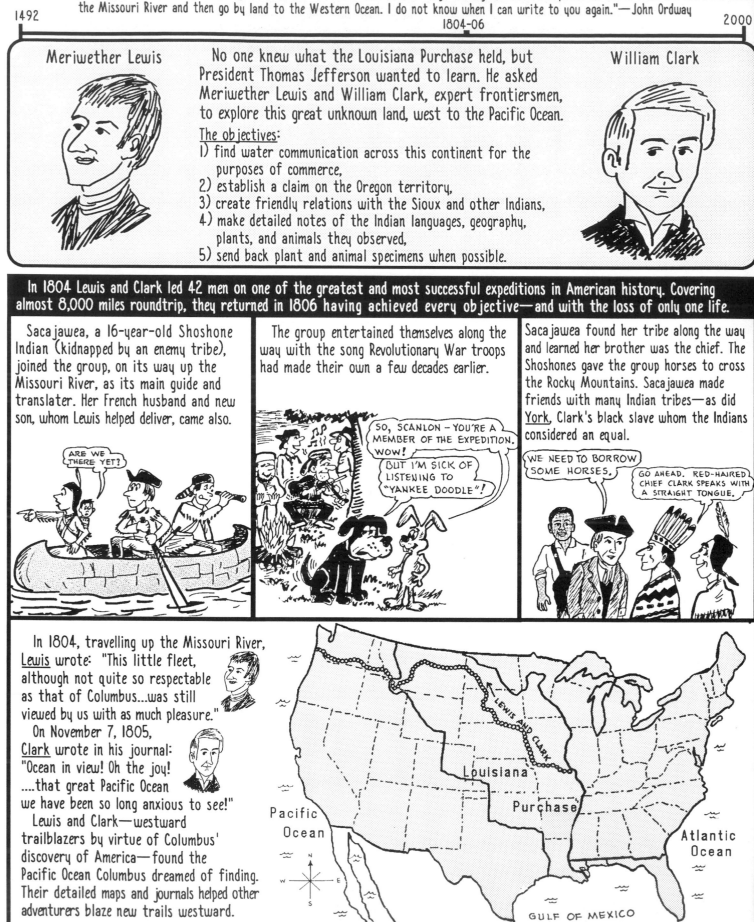

Meriwether Lewis

No one knew what the Louisiana Purchase held, but President Thomas Jefferson wanted to learn. He asked Meriwether Lewis and William Clark, expert frontiersmen, to explore this great unknown land, west to the Pacific Ocean.

The objectives:
1) find water communication across this continent for the purposes of commerce,
2) establish a claim on the Oregon territory,
3) create friendly relations with the Sioux and other Indians,
4) make detailed notes of the Indian languages, geography, plants, and animals they observed,
5) send back plant and animal specimens when possible.

William Clark

In 1804 Lewis and Clark led 42 men on one of the greatest and most successful expeditions in American history. Covering almost 8,000 miles roundtrip, they returned in 1806 having achieved every objective—and with the loss of only one life.

Sacajawea, a 16-year-old Shoshone Indian (kidnapped by an enemy tribe), joined the group, on its way up the Missouri River, as its main guide and translater. Her French husband and new son, whom Lewis helped deliver, came also.

ARE WE THERE YET?

The group entertained themselves along the way with the song Revolutionary War troops had made their own a few decades earlier.

SO, SCANLON - YOU'RE A MEMBER OF THE EXPEDITION. WOW!

BUT I'M SICK OF LISTENING TO "YANKEE DOODLE"!

Sacajawea found her tribe along the way and learned her brother was the chief. The Shoshones gave the group horses to cross the Rocky Mountains. Sacajawea made friends with many Indian tribes—as did York, Clark's black slave whom the Indians considered an equal.

WE NEED TO BORROW SOME HORSES.

GO AHEAD. RED-HAIRED CHIEF CLARK SPEAKS WITH A STRAIGHT TONGUE.

In 1804, travelling up the Missouri River, Lewis wrote: "This little fleet, although not quite so respectable as that of Columbus...was still viewed by us with as much pleasure."

On November 7, 1805, Clark wrote in his journal: "Ocean in view! Oh the joy! ....that great Pacific Ocean we have been so long anxious to see!"

Lewis and Clark—westward trailblazers by virtue of Columbus' discovery of America—found the Pacific Ocean Columbus dreamed of finding. Their detailed maps and journals helped other adventurers blaze new trails westward.

Pacific Ocean

LEWIS AND CLARK

Louisiana Purchase

Atlantic Ocean

GULF OF MEXICO

In May 1803, two weeks after selling Louisiana to the U.S., Napoleon declared war on Great Britian—a war that would last 12 years, until the defeat of France at Waterloo in 1815.
Like Federalist presidents George Washington and John Adams in the 1790s,
Republican presidents Thomas Jefferson (1801-09) and James Madison (1809-17)
found neutrality difficult, for France and Britain each blockaded the
other's coast and seized neutral ships attempting to trade with the other.
Americans—after losing more than 500 ships to France and 900 to England—finally had enough!
In what might be called a "Second War of Independence," the United States declared war on Great Britain in 1812,
emerged with a settled peace in 1815, and remained free of entangling European alliances for the next 100 years.

FOREIGN ACTION

FRANCE

1803: FRANCE DECLARED WAR ON GREAT BRITAIN

1806-07: CONTINENTAL SYSTEM
1) blockade of British ports (Berlin Decree),
2) confiscation of neutral ships bound for Britain (Milan Decree).

GREAT BRITAIN

1805: ESSEX CASE—British court ruled against shipping goods from the French West Indies to France via the U.S. (500 U.S. ships were seized under this ruling.)

1807: ORDERS IN COUNCIL (series)
1) blockade of French ports,
2) confiscation of neutral ships bound for French ports.

1803-12: BRITISH IMPRESSMENT OF AMERICAN SAILORS

Chesapeake-Leopard Affair
(1807)—The British ship Leopard fired upon the American ship Chesapeake just off the U.S. coast. Then the British captain impressed (captured for service) four of the U.S. sailors.
Americans called for war!

ONCE AN ENGLISHMAN, ALWAYS AN ENGLISHMAN!

1803-1812: BRITISH INCITEMENT OF INDIANS IN NORTHWEST TERR.

HERE YOU ARE, BOYS!

WOW! BRITISH-MADE RIFLES!

WHO ARE WE SUPPOSED TO FIGHT?

Rifles

1811: Battle of Tippecanoe William H. Harrison destroyed the Shawnee town of British-aided Chief Tecumseh and his brother the Prophet, who organized northwest Indians against the whites.

AMERICAN REACTION

2nd Adm. of Thomas Jefferson

1807: EMBARGO ACT
Seeking to retaliate short of war, Jefferson pushed through the Republican Congress an embargo, which forbade U.S. trade with all foreign ports. This drastic measure hurt New England businessmen, driving them into the Federalist camp, and caused an economic depression. So, just before Jefferson left office, the Republicans passed the Non-Intercourse Act.

1809: NON-INTERCOURSE ACT
1) repealed the Embargo Act,
2) opened trade with all ports except French and British,
3) provided for resumption of trade with France or Britain if either ceased violating U.S. neutral rights.

1st Adm. of James Madison

1810: MACON'S BILL NO. 2
1) opened trade with France and Britain,
2) provided that if either France or Britain ceased violating U.S. neutral rights, U.S. would restore non-intercourse with the other.

1810: WAR HAWKS, such as Henry Clay (Kentucky) and John C. Calhoun (South Carolina), were a group of new, nationalistic congressmen from the agrarian, land-hungry West and South, who pressured President Madison to declare war against Britain, for these reasons:
1) preserve national honor,
2) restore farm prices depressed by trade restrictions,
3) annex Canada to end British incitement of Indians,
4) annex Spanish West Florida,

AMERICA GOES TO WAR: A TRAGIC IRONY

JUNE 1, 1812: Madison asked Congress to declare war on Britain.
JUNE 16, 1812: Britain, unaware of the U.S. action, yielded to the pressure of her merchants and repealed the Orders in Council.
JUNE 18, 1812: Congress, unaware U.S. sanctions had worked, declared war on Britain—the war that need not have been!

1492   1812-15   2000

The War of 1812 was a stalemate; each side's disadvantages counterbalanced the other's. It ended in a truce and return to the status quo. Yet the war had important results: European nations finally recognized U.S. independence, freeing the U.S. to pursue domestic rather than foreign concerns.

UNITED STATES OF AMERICA

DISADVANTAGES

1. The U.S. was unprepared for war.
   a. Small, poorly trained and equipped army; never more than 35,000
   b. Old generals, left over from Revolutionary War; average age, 60 yrs.
   c. Raw militias, many of which refused to fight outside own states
   d. Small navy: 20 frigates and sloops, 170 small gunboats
2. Lack of a national bank limited financial resources.
   The Bank of the U.S. charter was not renewed by the Republican Congress in 1811.
3. New England and New York opposed "Mr. Madison's War,"
   as they called it, for—unlike the agrarian West and South—the commercial Northeast suffered from the war's curtailment of trade.

GREAT BRITAIN

1. Britain did not want war with the U.S.
   The Napoleonic wars had cost Britain four billion dollars and a 33 percent cut in exports by 1811. Britain needed the U.S. trade, worth 60 million dollars per year.
2. Second-string resources used for U.S. war.
   Britain's main resources and efforts were used in the war with France.
3. Treasury depleted by 1814.

MAJOR BATTLES AND EVENTS

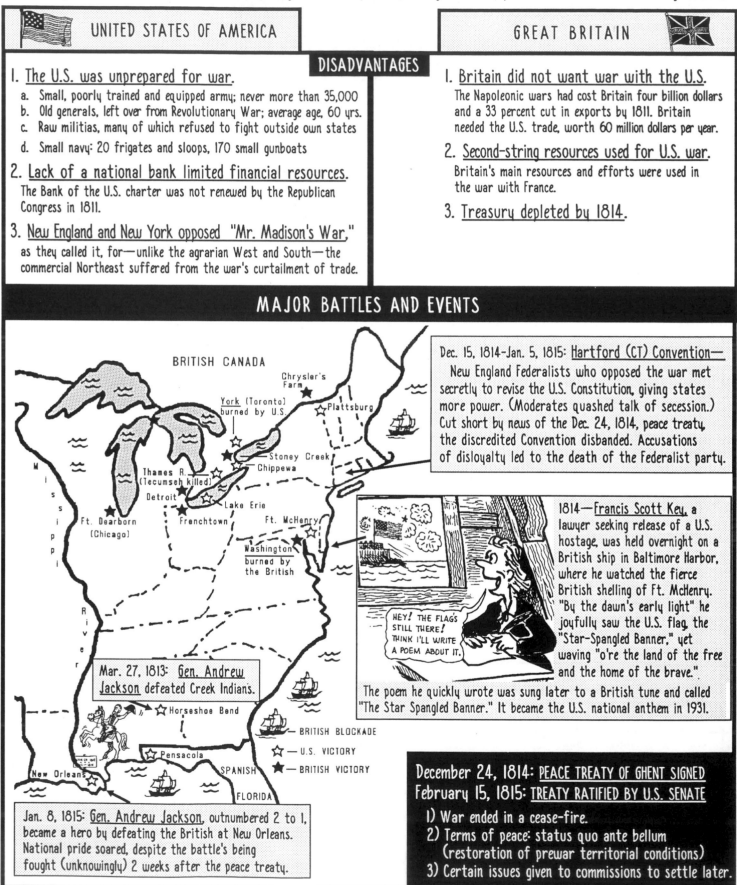

Dec. 15, 1814–Jan. 5, 1815: Hartford (CT) Convention—New England Federalists who opposed the war met secretly to revise the U.S. Constitution, giving states more power. (Moderates quashed talk of secession.) Cut short by news of the Dec. 24, 1814, peace treaty, the discredited Convention disbanded. Accusations of disloyalty led to the death of the Federalist party.

1814—Francis Scott Key, a lawyer seeking release of a U.S. hostage, was held overnight on a British ship in Baltimore Harbor, where he watched the fierce British shelling of Ft. McHenry. "By the dawn's early light" he joyfully saw the U.S. flag, the "Star-Spangled Banner," yet waving "o're the land of the free and the home of the brave."

HEY! THE FLAG'S STILL THERE! THINK I'LL WRITE A POEM ABOUT IT.

The poem he quickly wrote was sung later to a British tune and called "The Star Spangled Banner." It became the U.S. national anthem in 1931.

BRITISH CANADA

Chrysler's Farm
York (Toronto) burned by U.S.
Plattsburg
Stoney Creek
Chippewa
Thames R. (Tecumseh killed)
Detroit
Lake Erie
Ft. Dearborn (Chicago)
Frenchtown
Ft. McHenry
Washington burned by the British
Mississippi River

Mar. 27, 1813: Gen. Andrew Jackson defeated Creek Indians.

Horseshoe Bend
Pensacola
New Orleans
SPANISH FLORIDA

— BRITISH BLOCKADE
☆ — U.S. VICTORY
★ — BRITISH VICTORY

Jan. 8, 1815: Gen. Andrew Jackson, outnumbered 2 to 1, became a hero by defeating the British at New Orleans. National pride soared, despite the battle's being fought (unknowingly) 2 weeks after the peace treaty.

December 24, 1814: PEACE TREATY OF GHENT SIGNED
February 15, 1815: TREATY RATIFIED BY U.S. SENATE
1) War ended in a cease-fire.
2) Terms of peace: status quo ante bellum (restoration of prewar territorial conditions)
3) Certain issues given to commissions to settle later.

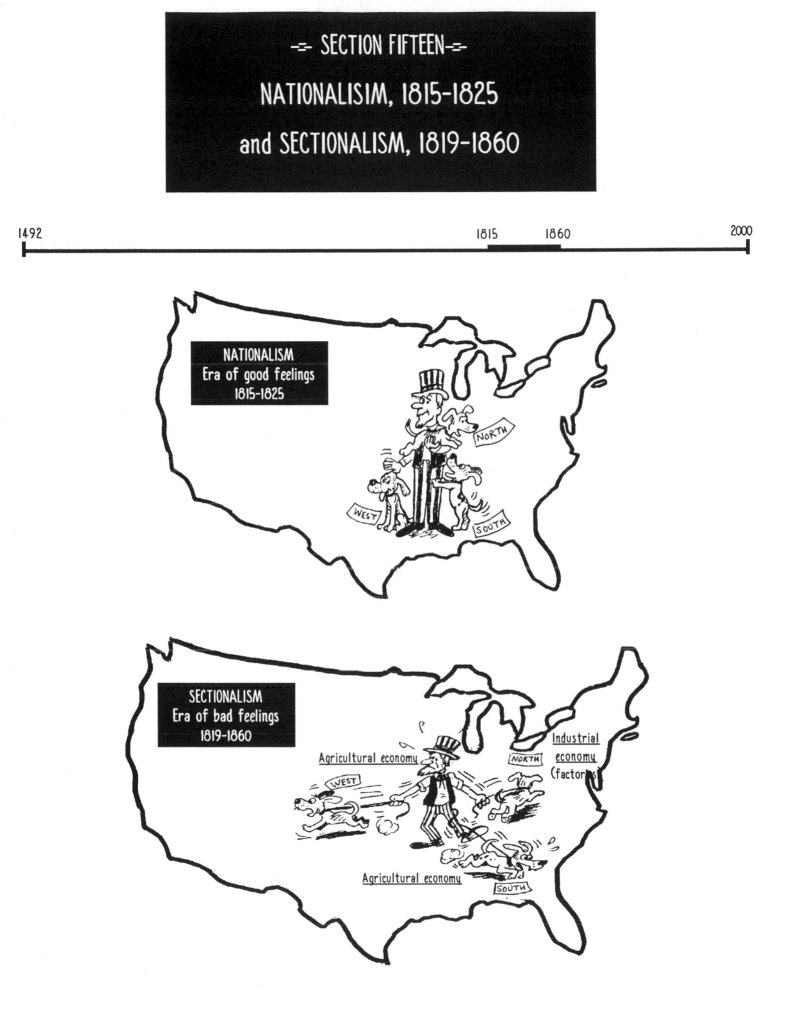

-=- SECTION FIFTEEN -=-

NATIONALISIM, 1815-1825

and SECTIONALISM, 1819-1860

1492   1815   1860   2000

NATIONALISM
Era of good feelings
1815-1825

NORTH

WEST

SOUTH

SECTIONALISM
Era of bad feelings
1819-1860

Agricultural economy

Industrial economy (factories)

WEST

NORTH

Agricultural economy

SOUTH

nationalism—national unity; a sense of pride and interest in one's country; a strengthening of the national government

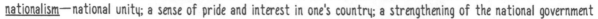

1492   1815-25   2000

We Americans were proud of ourselves for standing up to the mighty British Empire a second time. We seemed to have their respect—and Europe's—and our own for the first time. All sections of the U.S.—<u>north</u>, <u>south</u>, and <u>west</u>—began pulling together, cooperating to build our nation.

NORTH

WEST

SOUTH

The <u>Era of Good Feelings</u> describes the reign of Republicans as the single party in a unified nation.

Remember, the Federalists Party died in 1815. No need for parties now; we Republicans represent the whole country. We feel we are not a party; we are the whole!

<u>James Monroe</u>
Republican President,
1817-25

REPUBLICANS ACQUIRE HAMILTONIAN VIEWS.

A new generation of Republicans began shifting from Jeffersonian to <u>Hamiltonian</u> positions. Why? The war showed them that <u>a strong central government</u> and <u>industrialization</u> were essential for national security. They were sometimes called "Federalists without elitism."

INSTEAD OF:	THEY ADVOCATED:
1) Agrarianism	1) Industrialism
2) Narrow construction of the Constitution	2) Broad construction of the Constitution
3) States' rights (state sovereignty)	3) Nationalism (national sovereignty)

1816—THREE LAWS STRENGTHEN THE NATIONAL GOVERNMENT.

In 1816 Republicans enacted three laws that increased the central government's powers. Hamilton would have been pleased, Jefferson displeased.

1. <u>TARIFF OF 1816</u>—first tariff high enough to protect American industry
2. <u>BANK OF THE UNITED STATES</u> re-chartered
3. <u>MILITARY EXPANSION</u>
   a) enlargement of West Point Military Academy
   b) standing army of 10,000; enlarged navy

1824—THE AMERICAN SYSTEM

<u>Congressman Henry Clay</u> of Kentucky proposed a plan, called the American System, calling for <u>federal aid for internal improvements</u> (roads, canals, bridges) financed by
1) the protective tariff, and
2) the Bank of the U.S.

All sections win: aided by the tariff, <u>northern</u> industry will create markets for <u>western</u> and <u>southern</u> raw products, which can be shipped on roads and canals financed by the tariff, Bank, and federal funds.

JOHN MARSHALL STRENGTHENS THE CAPITALIST ECONOMIC SYSTEM.

<u>John Marshal</u> (a Federalist), Supreme Court Chief Justice from 1801 to 1835, increased the national government's power to promote a free market economy by strengthening the <u>capitalist system</u>: the rights to 1) <u>private property</u>, 2) <u>free enterprise</u> (work), and 3) <u>profit</u>. He did so through several Supreme Court decisions, setting forth these principles:

1. Broad construction of the Constitution
2. Supremacy of federal power over the states
3. Supremacy of federal over state courts
4. Freedom of American business from government restraint ("The power to tax is the power to destroy.")
5. Supremacy of capitalism as America's economic system

industrial revolution—a vast economic reorganization, with machines and factories replacing hand tools and craft shops

THE INDUSTRIAL REVOLUTION burst forth in America in 1815, favored by Republican policies during the War of 1812. But it had begun earlier through the ingenuity of two men.

1790: <u>Samuel Slater</u>, a British textile worker, memorized textile machine blueprints, secretly brought them to America, and started at Pawtucket, R.I. the first factory in the U.S.

A PENNY FOR YOUR THOUGHTS, MR. SLATER.

1798: <u>Eli Whitney</u>, a Connecticut school teacher, created the technique of interchangeable parts, which made possible mass-production industry.

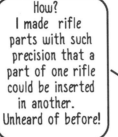

How? I made rifle parts with such precision that a part of one rifle could be inserted in another. Unheard of before!

AN IRONY

1793: While on a tutoring job in South Carolina, Eli Whitney rescued the dying cotton business by inventing the cotton gin, thus making slavery a vital institution for the south.

Ironically, Whitney's contribution to industrialization helped the North defeat the South in the Civil War (1865), an event that ended slavery.

INDUSTRIAL AND TRANSPORTATION REVOLUTIONS 1815—

A TRANSPORTATION REVOLUTION,

aided by the industrial revolution and Clay's American System, enabled the U.S. to develop a national market economy.

The steamboat (1807), Cumberland National Road (1811-18), Erie Canal (1825), and railroad (1830)

were important beginnings in lowering transportation costs and speeding communication.

ERIE CANAL

NATIONAL ROAD

BOONESBOROUGH

WILDERNESS ROAD

ARE WE THERE YET?

DIET COLA

A National Language and Education: The Power of a School Teacher

Noah Webster, while teaching school in Connecticut, (1758-1843) saw the need to create a national, "Americanized" language as a bond of national union. Why? 1) to discourage sectionalism, and 2) to discourage immigrants' "blind imitation" of their native language and customs, a practice that—"once laudable"—limited their national identity as Americans.

Banking on the power of <u>textbooks</u>, Webster wrote numerous dictionaries (incorporating many Indian words), blue-backed spellers, and other textbooks that highlighted American speech, customs, and values.

American Dictionary

British spelling:	American spelling:
colour	color
theatre	theater
gaol	jail

More than 60,000,000 copies of Webster's <u>American Spelling Book</u> (1783), used well into the 20th century, shaped the national character of several generations of Americans.

1820: THE MISSOURI COMPROMISE settled a slavery dispute and avoided a threat to national unity.

In 1818 Missouri petitioned for statehood as a slave state, an event that threatened to upset the balance of power: there were 11 free states and 11 slave states. New York Congressman James Tallmadge introduced an amendment to the statehood bill, prohibiting further importation of slaves into Missouri and freeing the children (at age 25) of slaves already there. Although the Tallmadge Amendment failed to pass, it stirred the first national debate on slavery.

Congress solved the immediate problem with the MISSOURI COMPROMISE OF 1820 which:

1) allowed Missouri to enter the Union as a slave state—but prohibited slavery in the rest of the Louisiana Purchase (excluding Missouri) north of 36 degrees and 30 minutes north latitude, a line called the Missouri Compromise Line (forming the border between Missouri and Arkansas); and

2) provided for Maine to enter the Union as a free state, balancing the number of slave and free states in the Union, with 12 each.

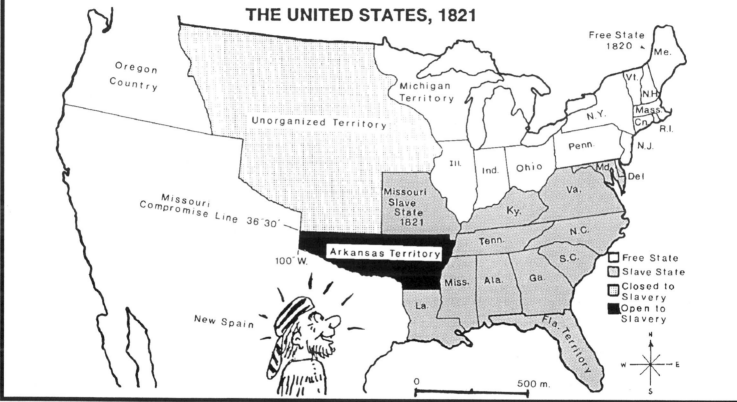

THE UNITED STATES, 1821

1823: THE MONROE DOCTRINE was the ultimate expression of nationalism.

In 1821 the U.S. gladly recognized the recently won independence of Spain's Latin American colonies and, along with Britain, welcomed trade with them.

Meanwhile, Europe's monarchical nations—France, Austria, Prussia, and Russia—planned to help Spain's king regain the colonies, lest the revolutionary spirit spread.

In 1823 Britain, fearful that trade would be disrupted, proposed a joint British-U.S. statement warning Europe against interfering with Latin American independence. The U.S., wanting no entangling alliance with Britain, decided to issue an independent warning.

President James Monroe boldly proclaimed
the western hemisphere closed
to European colonization.
If Europe observed this,
the U.S. would not intervene
in Europe's affairs.

sectionalism: conflict among geographic sections of the nation; loyalty to one's sectional interests

1492   1819   1860   2000

By 1819 sections of the U.S. began pulling apart. Why? New developments, such as
1) westward expansion,
2) the rise of King Cotton in the South, and
3) an economic depression that created conflicting economic and political interests in the North, South, and West.

Agricultural economy (small farms) WEST
NORTH
Industrial economy (factories)
Agricultural economy (small/large cotton farms; slave labor) SOUTH

Each section wanted national laws favoring its economy. Conflicts arose because a law benefiting one section might harm another.

By inference you can see the logical consequences: Conflicting economic interests led to political rivalry, as each section wanted strong congressional representation to carry the vote for its economic interests.

Forty years of sectional rivalry led to the Civil War (1861-65).
To unravel the causes of the War, let's tune in to what each section wanted.

TODAY I AM INTERVIEWING 3 KEY PERSONS ON SECTIONAL ISSUES. WITH ME IN THE STUDIO ARE A WESTERN FARMER, A SOUTHERN PLANTER, AND A NORTHERN INDUSTRIALIST. THEY WILL EXPLAIN THEIR PREFERENCES ON EACH ISSUE BELOW.

ISSUES	WESTERN FARMER	SOUTHERN PLANTER	NORTHERN INDUSTRIALIST
WESTERN LAND	LOW PRICES—to aid settlement by small farmers	LOW PRICES—1) to encourage westward expansion of slavery; 2) to expand cotton farming by replacing worn-out farm land	HIGH PRICES—to discourage westward migration of northeastern labor force
LABOR	FREE LABOR (no slaves)—to avoid job competition on farms from cheap slave labor	SLAVE LABOR—to do the hard, non-wage work of producing cotton, the south's "white gold"	FREE LABOR (no slaves)—to provide a skilled work force for business

185

SECTIONALISM: ISSUES THREATENING NATIONAL UNITY, 1819-1860

ISSUES	WESTERN FARMER	SOUTHERN PLANTER	NORTHERN INDUSTRIALIST
TARIFF (a tax on imports)	<u>HIGH TARIFF</u>—with revenue used to build roads, bridges, and canals for shipping western farm products to eastern markets	<u>LOW TARIFF</u>— 1) to export raw farm products on favorable terms, and 2) to keep down cost of buying manufactured goods	<u>HIGH TARIFF</u>—to protect manufactured goods from being undersold by foreign competitors
INTERNAL IMPROVEMENTS	<u>FOR</u> INTERNAL IMPROVEMENTS (roads, bridges, canals)— to create eastern market for farm goods. "THIS IMPROVED ROAD SURE HELPS GETTING MY PRODUCE TO MARKET."	<u>AGAINST</u> INTERNAL IMPROVEMENTS— to avoid large government expenditures which might require a higher tariff to refill the treasury. "WHY SPEND TAX MONEY ON ROADS WHEN WE CAN USE THESE STREAMS?"	<u>FOR</u> INTERNAL IMPROVEMENTS— to create a western market for manufactured goods. "THAT NEW ROAD WILL HELP ME MARKET MY MANUFACTURED ITEMS."
MONEY	<u>SOFT (OR "CHEAP") MONEY</u>—paper money not backed by specie (gold), thus in large supply, of less worth, and easier for debtor farmers to obtain. "WITH THESE INFLATED DOLLARS WE CAN PAY OFF OUR MORTGAGE."	<u>SOFT MONEY</u>—Farmers (agrarians) often were in debt because crop markets were unpredictable. They liked paying their debts with cheap, inflated dollars, but their creditors didn't like it. Through inference, can you figure out why? "Yoo HOO!!"	<u>HARD MONEY</u>—paper money backed by specie—Northern businessmen often were creditors (lenders). To get their dollars's worth, they wanted debts repaid them in hard, sound money (backed by gold)—not soft, cheap, inflated money.

Tally the bottom line of these <u>sectional economic views</u>, and you quickly see that the <u>North</u> and <u>South</u> differed on all five issues. This caused a <u>political power struggle</u> between the <u>free labor states of the North</u> and the <u>slave labor states of the South.</u> The section controlling the federal government would set economic policies, such as tariffs, that would affect the very livelihood of the other. <u>Political power, then, became crucial to economic interests.</u>

By 1861 the political power struggle between North and South would lead to the Civil War.

1492   1824-28   2000

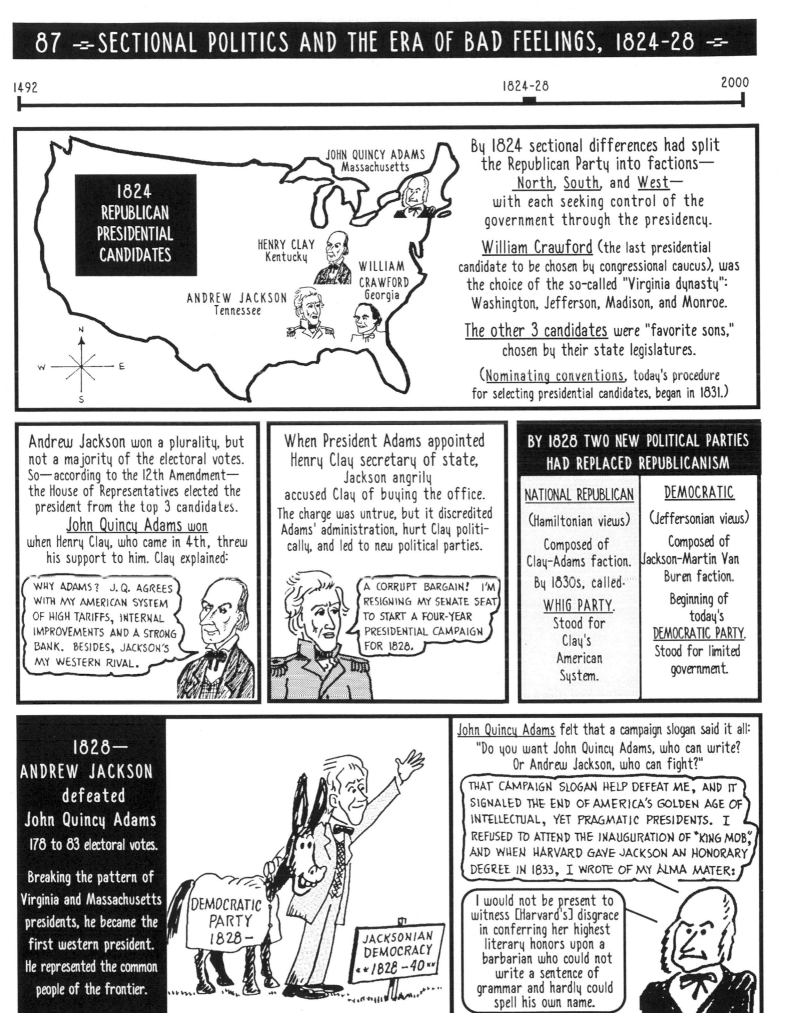

1824 REPUBLICAN PRESIDENTIAL CANDIDATES

JOHN QUINCY ADAMS
Massachusetts

HENRY CLAY
Kentucky

ANDREW JACKSON
Tennessee

WILLIAM CRAWFORD
Georgia

By 1824 sectional differences had split the Republican Party into factions— North, South, and West— with each seeking control of the government through the presidency.

William Crawford (the last presidential candidate to be chosen by congressional caucus), was the choice of the so-called "Virginia dynasty": Washington, Jefferson, Madison, and Monroe.

The other 3 candidates were "favorite sons," chosen by their state legislatures.

(Nominating conventions, today's procedure for selecting presidential candidates, began in 1831.)

Andrew Jackson won a plurality, but not a majority of the electoral votes. So—according to the 12th Amendment— the House of Representatives elected the president from the top 3 candidates.

John Quincy Adams won when Henry Clay, who came in 4th, threw his support to him. Clay explained:

WHY ADAMS? J. Q. AGREES WITH MY AMERICAN SYSTEM OF HIGH TARIFFS, INTERNAL IMPROVEMENTS AND A STRONG BANK. BESIDES, JACKSON'S MY WESTERN RIVAL.

When President Adams appointed Henry Clay secretary of state, Jackson angrily accused Clay of buying the office.

The charge was untrue, but it discredited Adams' administration, hurt Clay politically, and led to new political parties.

A CORRUPT BARGAIN! I'M RESIGNING MY SENATE SEAT TO START A FOUR-YEAR PRESIDENTIAL CAMPAIGN FOR 1828.

BY 1828 TWO NEW POLITICAL PARTIES HAD REPLACED REPUBLICANISM

NATIONAL REPUBLICAN	DEMOCRATIC
(Hamiltonian views)	(Jeffersonian views)
Composed of Clay-Adams faction. By 1830s, called: **WHIG PARTY.** Stood for Clay's American System.	Composed of Jackson-Martin Van Buren faction. Beginning of today's **DEMOCRATIC PARTY.** Stood for limited government.

1828— ANDREW JACKSON defeated John Quincy Adams 178 to 83 electoral votes.

Breaking the pattern of Virginia and Massachusetts presidents, he became the first western president. He represented the common people of the frontier.

DEMOCRATIC PARTY 1828-

JACKSONIAN DEMOCRACY ** 1828-40 **

John Quincy Adams felt that a campaign slogan said it all: "Do you want John Quincy Adams, who can write? Or Andrew Jackson, who can fight?"

THAT CAMPAIGN SLOGAN HELP DEFEAT ME, AND IT SIGNALED THE END OF AMERICA'S GOLDEN AGE OF INTELLECTUAL, YET PRAGMATIC PRESIDENTS. I REFUSED TO ATTEND THE INAUGURATION OF "KING MOB," AND WHEN HARVARD GAVE JACKSON AN HONORARY DEGREE IN 1833, I WROTE OF MY ALMA MATER:

I would not be present to witness [Harvard's] disgrace in conferring her highest literary honors upon a barbarian who could not write a sentence of grammar and hardly could spell his own name.

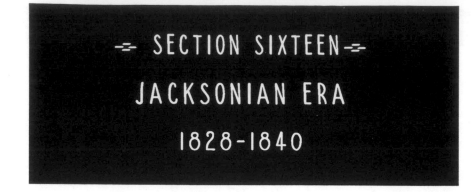
1492   1828   1840   2000

<u>democracy</u>—rule by the people
"Let the people rule."—Andrew Jacksonn

"I was born for a storm. Calm does not suit me."—Andrew Jackson

1492   1828   1840   2000

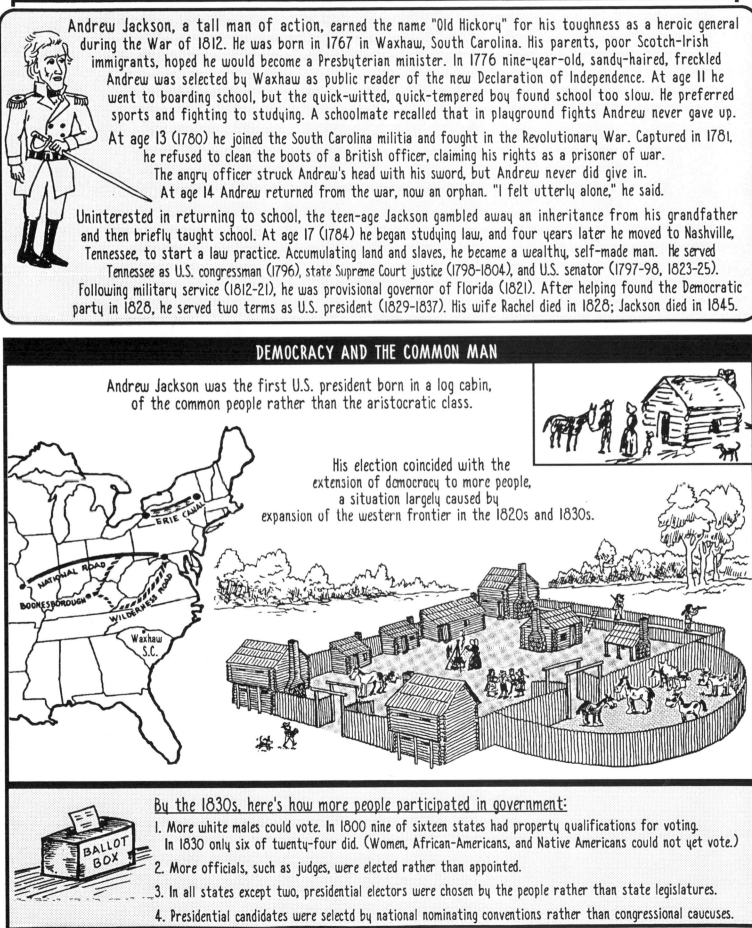

Andrew Jackson, a tall man of action, earned the name "Old Hickory" for his toughness as a heroic general during the War of 1812. He was born in 1767 in Waxhaw, South Carolina. His parents, poor Scotch-Irish immigrants, hoped he would become a Presbyterian minister. In 1776 nine-year-old, sandy-haired, freckled Andrew was selected by Waxhaw as public reader of the new Declaration of Independence. At age 11 he went to boarding school, but the quick-witted, quick-tempered boy found school too slow. He preferred sports and fighting to studying. A schoolmate recalled that in playground fights Andrew never gave up.

At age 13 (1780) he joined the South Carolina militia and fought in the Revolutionary War. Captured in 1781, he refused to clean the boots of a British officer, claiming his rights as a prisoner of war. The angry officer struck Andrew's head with his sword, but Andrew never did give in. At age 14 Andrew returned from the war, now an orphan. "I felt utterly alone," he said.

Uninterested in returning to school, the teen-age Jackson gambled away an inheritance from his grandfather and then briefly taught school. At age 17 (1784) he began studying law, and four years later he moved to Nashville, Tennessee, to start a law practice. Accumulating land and slaves, he became a wealthy, self-made man. He served Tennessee as U.S. congressman (1796), state Supreme Court justice (1798-1804), and U.S. senator (1797-98, 1823-25). Following military service (1812-21), he was provisional governor of Florida (1821). After helping found the Democratic party in 1828, he served two terms as U.S. president (1829-1837). His wife Rachel died in 1828; Jackson died in 1845.

DEMOCRACY AND THE COMMON MAN

Andrew Jackson was the first U.S. president born in a log cabin, of the common people rather than the aristocratic class.

His election coincided with the extension of democracy to more people, a situation largely caused by expansion of the western frontier in the 1820s and 1830s.

ERIE CANAL

NATIONAL ROAD

BOONESBOROUGH

WILDERNESS ROAD

Waxhaw S.C.

By the 1830s, here's how more people participated in government:

1. More white males could vote. In 1800 nine of sixteen states had property qualifications for voting. In 1830 only six of twenty-four did. (Women, African-Americans, and Native Americans could not yet vote.)

2. More officials, such as judges, were elected rather than appointed.

3. In all states except two, presidential electors were chosen by the people rather than state legislatures.

4. Presidential candidates were selectd by national nominating conventions rather than congressional caucuses.

BALLOT BOX

189

As U.S. president, Jackson exerted strong leadership. He believed the executive alone represented all the people. He emphasized 1) political democracy, 2) economic democracy (in terms of opportunity), and 3) national rather than state sovereignty.

SPOILS SYSTEM

Jackson believed the common man could hold office without experience, so he advocated

1) rotation in office, and
2) the spoils system: rewarding political supporters with public office.

IT MEANS THAT EVEN WE MIGHT GET A GOVERNMENT JOB, LUKE!

WHAT'S THIS "SPOILS SYSTEM"?

1832—BANK WAR

Jackson vetoed (rejected) a bill to re-charter the Second Bank of the U.S., arguing that the bank favored the rich and denied common people equal economic opportunity. (Would Jefferson have approved?)

Jackson transferred government deposits to selected state banks (called "pet banks" by Jackson's opponents).

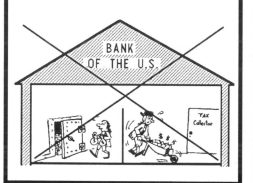

BANK OF THE U.S.

TAX Collector

1828-32—TARIFF PROBLEMS

Could South Carolina nullify (declare invalid) a federal law it considered unconstitutional?

"ABSOLUTELY!" said John C. Calhoun of South Carolina in his 1828 "South Carolina Exposition and Protest." This document protested the high 1828 "Tariff Of Abominations" on the basis of states' rights—meaning

TARIFF WALL

that a state has a right to judge whether a law passed by Congress is constitutional.

Calhoun (vice president 1825-32) thus challenged the Union with a doctrine of states' rights, that is, state sovereignty.

TROUBLE LIES AHEAD!

January, 1830—WEBSTER-HAYNE DEBATE

In Congress Senators Daniel Webster of Massachusetts and Robert Hayne of South Carolina debated whether sovereignty (supreme power) belonged to the Federal Union or the states. Jackson agreed with Webster's strong defense of national sovereignty.

LIBERTY AND UNION, NOW AND FOREVER, ONE AND INSEPARABLE!

DANIEL WEBSTER

April, 1830—A CLASH OF TOASTS

At a Jefferson Day Dinner tempers flared as Jackson gave a toast to national sovereignty—and a veiled warning to Calhoun.

Eyes flashing, Calhoun, toasted state sovereignty in return.

With South Carolina claiming the rights of nullification and secession, might there be a civil war in the 1830s? It seemed possible.

OUR UNION: IT MUST BE PRESERVED!

THE UNION: NEXT TO OUR LIBERTY, MOST DEAR!

ANDREW JACKSON

JOHN C. CALHOUN

1832-33—NULLIFICATION CRISIS

South Carolina nullified the Tariffs of 1828 and 1832 and threatened to secede (officially withdraw) from the Union if challenged.

Congress quickly passed the Force Bill, authorizing military action to enforce the tariff. Jackson threatened to lead the army against South Carolina and hang John C. Calhoun.

South Carolina avoided civil war by accepting the 1833 Compromise Tariff but turned right around and nullifed the Force Bill!

GRRR...

GRRR...

JACKSON

CALHOUN

Both sides claimed victory and saved face.

"If suddenly we tear our hearts from the homes around which they are twined, our heart-strings will snap."—a Seminole Indian

1830: INDIAN REMOVAL ACT—In response to land-hungry white settlers, beginning in 1817 Presidents Monroe, Adams, and Jackson had advocated the removal of Native Americans to public lands west of the Mississippi River—land then perceived as The Great American Desert. In 1830, upon Jackson's urging, Congress passed the Indian Removal Act, allowing the federal government to do so if the Indians were given compensation.

GEORGIA AND THE CHEROKEE INDIANS—Meanwhile, in 1828 gold was discovered on Cherokee land in Georgia, land guaranteed the Cherokees by federal treaty in 1791. In 1830 Georgia tried to force Cherokee removal by claiming ownership of this land. The Cherokees sued, and Supreme Court Chief Justice John Marshall ruled in the Cherokees' favor.

A STATE CANNOT OVERRULE A FEDERAL TREATY. THEREFORE GEORGIA CANNOT FORCE THE CHEROKEE NATION TO LEAVE THE LAND GUARANTEED IT BY A U.S. TREATY.

CHIEF JUSTICE JOHN MARSHALL

PRESIDENTIAL DEFIANCE—It's the president's duty to enforce the laws. But Jackson refused to enforce Marshall's ruling, and Georgia took over the Cherokee land. The Cherokees ceded their land rights to the United States for $5,000,000 and, in 1838, moved to Indian Territory.

JOHN MARSHALL HAS MADE HIS DECISION. NOW LET HIM ENFORCE IT!

1830s-40s—INDIAN REMOVAL AND THE TRAIL OF TEARS

Under the Indian Removal Act most of the 125,000 Native Americans east of the Mississippi River were pressured to cede their ancestral lands to the United States and move to Indian Territory (present-day Oklahoma and Kansas). The Black Hawk War in Illinois and the Seminole War in Florida were futile resistance attempts.

Jackson's Indian removal policy culminated in 1838 when federal troops marched 15,000 Cherokee Indians to Indian Territory, about 4,000 Cherokees died on this sorrowful trail, called the Trail of Tears.

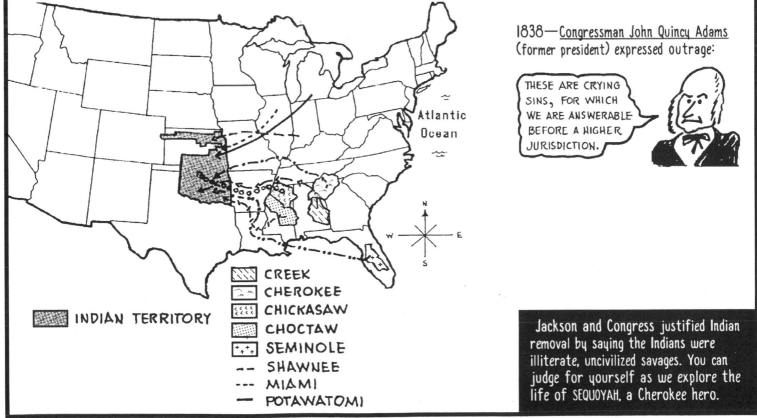

1838—Congressman John Quincy Adams (former president) expressed outrage:

THESE ARE CRYING SINS, FOR WHICH WE ARE ANSWERABLE BEFORE A HIGHER JURISDICTION.

Atlantic Ocean

INDIAN TERRITORY

CREEK
CHEROKEE
CHICKASAW
CHOCTAW
SEMINOLE
SHAWNEE
MIAMI
POTAWATOMI

Jackson and Congress justified Indian removal by saying the Indians were illiterate, uncivilized savages. You can judge for yourself as we explore the life of SEQUOYAH, a Cherokee hero.

"My fellow chiefs and I are interested in finding some sculptor who can carve a head of an Indian Chief who was killed many years ago. [We] would like the White man to know that the Red man had great heroes too."—Henry Standing Bear, Sioux, 1939

1492　　　　　　　　　　　　　　　　　　　　　　1770　　1843　　　　　　　　　　2000

Most Europeans who colonized North America considered Native Americans savages— sometimes brutal, sometimes noble savages but in any case inferior.

A major reason for this judgment: North Americans Indians were illiterate; none had a written language.

Today In the United States Capitol there stands a statue of SEQUOYAH, a Cherokee Indian who achieved a heroic feat in 1821: he invented a writing system for the Cherokee language.

The Cherokees became the first North American Indians to have a written language, and Sequoyah became the only man in history to singlehandedly create a written language.

-=- CHEROKEE SYLLABARY -=-

The Cherokee Nation originally covered parts of eight present-day states, much of it in the Appalachian Mountains. Cherokee Indians believed the Great Spirit gave them this beautiful land.

Pacific Ocean
Atlantic Ocean
WV VA KY NC TN SC AL GA
Gulf of Mexico
0　　500 miles

Sequoyah was born about 1770 in Taskigi, Tennessee, to a Cherokee woman named Wu Teh and a white trader named George Gist. Gist deserted Wu Teh at the time of her son's birth. Sequoyah, also named George Gist, grew up as a Cherokee. He chose never to learn English or adopt the new ways of the white man.

PROFESSOR JONES
ENGLISH LESSONS

Sequoyah liked to hear stories from the village storytellers, the medicine men, who were the Cherokees' "living books." They remembered their stories through the pictorial designs of wampum (shell) belts, similar to those of the Iroquois.

GREAT STORIES! HOW DO YOU REMEMBER THEM ALL?
WAMPUM POWER
WAMPUM BELTS

Sequoyah had a new experience with stories one day when he and a friend met three white hunters: one of the men read aloud from a book. The book was better than wampum belts: it held more! It was made of thin leaves of paper with markings like crows' tracks, and it seemed that the leaves talked to the reader. Sequoyah bought the "talking leaves" for two deer skins, a high price.

WOW!!

<u>syllable</u>—a character or set of characters representing one sound
<u>syllabary</u>—a list of syllables

<u>phon</u>—sound
<u>phonics</u>—learning to read by sounding out words and decoding the sounds into letter-symbols or syllable-symbols
<u>literacy</u>—the state of being able to read and write

1821—In Arkansas, near present-day Russellville, Sequoyah completed his work. He had reduced the Cherokee language to 86 syllables, each with a single sound. The result: a <u>SYLLABARY</u>, a list of 86 syllables represented by 86 symbols. The syllabary was similar to the English alphabet, made up of 26 letters each with several sounds. Although longer than the alphabet, the syllabary proved easier to use in learning to read because each syllable had only one sound.

Using Sequoyah's syllabary, many Arkansas Cherokees learned to read within a few days. The secret to their quick literacy? <u>Phonics</u>: using the <u>sounds</u> of syllables as keys to decode words and as building blocks to form words.

(Phonics also can help anyone easily learn to read in English. How? by learning the <u>sounds</u> of the 26 letters in the alphabet and using the sounds as decoders and building blocks of words.)

CHEROKEE SYLLABARY
Ꭰa Ꭱe Ꭲi Ꭳo Ꭴu Ꭵv
Ꭶ Ꭷka Ꭸge Ꭹgi Ꭺgo Ꭻgu Ꭼgv
ha Ꭾhe Ꭿhö Ꮀho Ꮁhu Ꮂhv
Ꮄle Ꮅli Ꮆlo Ꮇlu Ꮈlv
Ꮉma Ꮋmi Ꮌmo Ꮍmu
Ꮎna Ꮒni Ꮓno Ꮔnu Ꮕnv
Ꮏhna Ꮐnah
Ꮖqwa Ꮗwa Ꮘqwi Ꮙqwo Ꮚqwu Ꮛqwv
Ꮝs Ꮜsa Ꮞse Ꮟsi Ꮠso Ꮡsu Ꮢsv
Ꮣda Ꮥde Ꮧdi Ꮩdo Ꮪdu Ꮫdv
Ꮤta Ꮦte Ꮨti
Ꮬhla Ꮭtla Ꮮtle Ꮯtli Ꮰtlo Ꮱtlu Ꮲtlu
Ꮳtsa Ꮴtse Ꮵtsi Ꮶtso Ꮷtsu Ꮸtsv
Ꮹwa Ꮺwe Ꮻwi Ꮼwo Ꮽwu Ꮾwv
Ꮿya Ᏸye Ᏹyi Ᏺyo Ᏻyu Ᏼyv

At the Arkansas Cherokees' urging, Sequoyah journeyed to New Echota, Georgia, to show his syllabary to the eastern Cherokees—specifically, to Chief John Ross and the Cherokee National Council.

SEQUOYAH, HOW DO WE KNOW THIS ISN'T A TRICK? YOU COULD HAVE MADE UP THIS LETTER!

THE ARKANSAS CHEROKEES WROTE YOU THIS LETTER USING MY SYLLABARY. THIS SHOULD PROVE IT WORKS.

Sequoyah introduced his daughter Ayokeh, who had learned to read in one week with the syllabary. Chief John Ross said he would believe Sequoyah if Ayokeh could read a letter he privately would dictate to Sequoyah.

WAY TO GO, AYOKEH.

IT WORKS! READING AND WRITING IN CHEROKEE! A WONDERFUL GIFT. NOW, HOW FAST CAN CHEROKEES LEARN TO READ?

Tribal leaders selected bright young Cherokees, and Sequoyah taught them to read in three days. The children then taught their parents and grandparents. Within a year literacy had spread like wildfire among the eastern Cherokees.

SEE, MOTHER, IT'S AS EASY AS DA RE TI.

COME, GRANDFATHER. THE CHILDREN SAY WE MUST ALL DO OUR HOMEWORK. HA, HA!

1828—The Cherokees in New Echota, Georgia, bought a printing press for Sequoyah's syllabary and began publishing the Cherokee Phoenix, a newspaper written in Cherokee and English. They also published the Bible and their 1828 Constitution, modeled on the U.S. Constitution.

IS THERE A KIDS' SECTION?

1838—THE TRAIL OF TEARS

When Congress passed the 1830 Indian Removal Act, the Cherokee Indians thought they would be exempt. Surely Sequoyah's syllabary and the rapid spread of literacy among the Cherokee nation would demonstrate that they were civilized people. Already successful farmers with a democratic government, now they could read and write.

But gold had been discovered on their land, and Georgians determined to have their land, regardless of Chief Justice John Marshall's ruling. And so the Cherokees journeyed westward on the Trail of Tears.

Sequoyah accompanied the Arkansas Cherokees to Indian Territory. He soon left for Mexico to seek a lost tribe and was heard from no more. But his spirit lingers in the giant Sequoyah tree named for him and in Cherokee literature.

Pacific Ocean

Atlantic Ocean

N W E S

Cherokee Land
Indian Territory

1492   1830   1860   2000

The Jacksonian's emphasis on the common man stimulated organized efforts to reform society, thereby releasing the natural goodness within each person.
Chief among these efforts (which included school, prison, and hospital reform, as well as temperance crusades), were

THE ABOLITION CRUSADE to end slavery, and

THE FEMINIST CRUSADE to end women's subjection to men.

"In thinking of America, I sometimes find myself admiring her bright blue sky—her grand old woods—her fertile fields—her beautiful rivers—her mighty lakes and star-crowned mountains. But my rapture is soon checked. When I remember that all is cursed with the infernal spirit of slaveholding and wrong...I am filled with unutterable loathing." —Frederick Douglass

EARLY EFFORTS TO END SLAVERY

1688—German Friends in Germantown, Pennsylvania, declared slavery contrary to Christianity.

1775—Quakers in Pennsylvania organized the first antislavery society in the U.S.

1783—A judicial decision interpreted the Massachusetts Constitution of 1780 as having abolished slavery with the phrase, all men are born free and equal.

1780-86—Legislation gradually to abolish slavery was enacted in Penn., Conn., R.I., N.Y., N.J.

1785-92—Emancipation societies were formed in states from Massachusetts to Virginia.

1787—Slavery was prohibited in the Northwest Territory.

1807—Importation of slaves was prohibited, according to a provision in the U.S. Constitution.

1817—The American Colonization Society was formed by southerners to encourage emancipation and to send free blacks to Africa. By 1860, 15,000 blacks had been sent to the Society's African colony, Liberia. Heading the Society at various times were James Madison, James Monroe, and John Marshall. Supporters included Thomas Jefferson and Abraham Lincoln.

1831—The Abolition Crusade

differed from earlier antislavery efforts by emphasizing racial equality and a quick end to slavery.

William Lloyd Garrison started abolitionism in Boston in 1831 when he founded The Liberator, a newspaper demanding the immediate abolition of slavery.

Abolition societies quickly sprang up throughout the North, numbering 2,000 chapters by 1840.

1831—The Nat Turner slave rebellion

occurred in Virginia the same year The Liberator first appeared. Consequently, southerners blamed abolitionists for the rebellion.

Nat Turner led 70 other slaves in killing their white masters and their families. After a manhunt in which about 100 blacks were killed, Turner and 19 other slaves were executed.

The Underground Railroad

was a secret network of routes leading fugitive slaves to Canada and freedom. Black abolitionist Harriet Tubman, an escaped slave, was one of its most famous conductors. She made 19 trips to lead 300 slaves to freedom. Pointing her pistol at those who hesitated, she would warn, "Live free or die."

Frederick Douglass, an escaped slave inspired by The Liberator, became one of the most effective abolitionists. In 1841 Garrison called him a "more eloquent champion of liberty than Patrick Henry."

During the Civil War, Douglass was encouraged by President Abraham Lincoln's 1863 Emancipation Proclamation, which freed slaves in all areas not controlled by the Union. He visited Lincoln to protest discrimination against black Union soldiers. Lincoln replied:

THE MERE EXISTENCE OF BLACK SOLDIERS IS A GAIN.

Douglass campaigned for extension of the vote for blacks and for women. You will read more of him in the next chapter on women's rights.

LUCRETIA MOTT

The abolitionist crusade of the 1830s accidentally sparked a woman's rights crusade that radically changed American society. HOW DID THIS HAPPEN?

Women abolitionists met opposition to their <u>right to speak in public</u>, based on society's centuries-old perceptions of: 1) female intellectual inferiority, and 2) female subordination to males, supported by Biblical references to female obedience, submission, and silence.

Rejected as equals by male abolitionists and barred from their organizations, women formed female abolition societies and began to speak for their own rights as well as those of blacks. It all started in 1833 when <u>Lucretia Mott</u>, a Quaker minister related to Benjamin Franklin, founded the Philadelphia Female Anti-Slavery Society

---

1833—<u>The Philadelphia Female Anti-Slavery Society</u> gave women their first exposure to organizations. Restricted by the idea that "Woman's place is in the home," women did not belong to groups or have experience in the "unfeminine" act of speaking in public. Ignorant of how to conduct a meeting, Lucretia Mott asked a black freedman to preside.

> I'LL PRESIDE THIS TIME, BUT YOU NEED TO LEARN THE PARLIAMENTARY RULES OF ORDER.

> RULES OF ORDER? WHAT'S THAT?

PHILADELPHIA FEMALE ANTI-SLAVERY SOCIETY

1837—Competence replaced ignorance as women abolitionists throughout the Northeast learned to chair meetings, prepare agendas, and conduct petition campaigns. When abolitionist Theodore Weld offered to preside at the 1837 <u>National Female Anti-Slavery Society Convention</u> in New York (81 delegates from 12 states), the reply came:

> THIS GENTLEMAN HAS A MESSAGE FROM ABOLITIONIST THEODORE WELD OFFERING TO CHAIR OUR MEETING.

> TELL MR. WELD THAT WHEN THE WOMEN GOT TOGETHER THEY FOUND THEY HAD MINDS OF THEIR OWN, AND COULD TRANSACT THEIR BUSINESS WITHOUT HIS DIRECTION.

1837—Women abolitionists drew criticism for speaking in public, a violation of scripture according to some. In 1837 Massachusetts Congregationalist ministers publicly chastised them with a <u>Pastoral Letter</u> issued by the church's General Association.

> "We invite your attention to the dangers which...threaten the female character with wide-spread and permanent injury....The appropriate duties and influence of women are clearly stated in the New Testament. Those duties and that influence are unobtrusive and private, but the source of mighty power....The power of woman is her dependence, flowing from the consciousness of that weakness which God has given her for her protection.... But when she assumes the place and power and tone of a man as a public reformer...she yields the power which God has given her for protection, and her character becomes unnatural."

1838—Abolitionist Sarah Grimke, in <u>Letters on the Equality of the Sexes and the Condition of Woman</u>, refuted the ministers' claim that female subjection to men was the will of God.

> "No one can desire more earnestly than I do, that woman may move exactly in the sphere which her Creator has assigned her....
>
> The Lord Jesus defines the duties of his followers in the Sermon on the Mount. He lays down grand principles by which they should be governed, without any reference to [gender]...I...find him giving the same directions to women as to men, never...referring to the distinction now so strenuously insisted upon between masculine and feminine virtues: this is one of the anti-Christian 'traditions of men'...instead of the 'commandments of God.' Men and women were CREATED EQUAL; they are both moral and accountable beings, and whatever is <u>right</u> for man to do is <u>right</u> for woman."

feminist—a person (male or female) who advocates equal rights for women
"We women have good cause to be grateful to the slave." "In striving to strike his irons off, we found...that we were manacled ourselves."
—Abby Kelley

In response to attacks on their right to speak in public, <u>Sara Grimke</u>, her sister <u>Angelina Grimke</u>, and <u>Lucretia Mott</u> became feminist leaders, advocating the rights of women as well as those of blacks. Angelina Grimke explained why.

WOMAN'S RIGHTS? THIS IS RIDICULOUS!

BETTER GET USED TO IT HENRY, TIMES ARE CHANGING.

REGIONAL WOMAN'S RIGHTS CONFERENCE FEATURING

WE ARE PLACED UNEXPECTEDLY IN A VERY TRYING SITUATION, IN THE FOREFRONT OF AN ENTIRELY NEW CONTEST—A CONTEST FOR THE RIGHTS OF WOMAN AS A MORAL, INTELLIGENT AND RESPONSIBLE HUMAN BEING.

ANGELINA GRIMKE (1805-76)

SARAH GRIMKE (1792-1873)

LUCRETIA MOTT (1793-1880)

Four other women abolitionists became outstanding feminist leaders.

THERE IS A GREAT STIR ABOUT COLORED MEN GETTING THEIR RIGHTS, BUT NOT A WORD ABOUT COLORED WOMEN; AND IF COLORED MEN GET THEIR RIGHTS, AND NOT COLORED WOMEN THEIRS... THE COLORED MEN WILL BE MASTERS OVER THE WOMEN, AND IT WILL BE JUST AS BAD AS BEFORE.

SOJOURNER TRUTH (c. 1797-1883) was born a slave named Isabella. Freed when New York abolished slavery in 1827, she changed her name to reflect a new mission: <u>travelling</u> about telling the <u>truth</u> about slavery and women. Illiterate, she wrote her autobiography through dictation and became a powerful orator in the abolition and feminist movements.

DISFRANCHISEMENT SAYS TO ALL WOMEN: YOUR JUDGMENT IS NOT SOUND; YOUR OPINIONS ARE NOT WORTHY OF BEING COUNTED. THE MOST IGNORANT AND DEGRADED MAN WHO WALKS TO THE POLLS FEELS HIMSELF SUPERIOR TO THE MOST INTELLIGENT WOMAN.

<u>SUSAN B. ANTHONY</u> (1820-1906), a Quaker teacher reared in Rochester, New York, teamed with Elizabeth Cady Stanton from 1851 to 1902 to mastermind the feminist crusade. A superb organizer, she was called "the Napoleon of the woman's movement."

...THE BATTLE IS NOT WHOLLY FOUGHT UNTIL WE STAND EQUAL IN THE CHURCH, THE WORLD OF WORK, AND HAVE AN EQUAL CODE OF MORALS FOR BOTH SEXES.

ELIZABETH CADY STANTON (1815-1902) grew up in Johnstown, New York, observing her lawyer father advise women of their inferior legal status. She organized the woman's movement in 1848 and, with Anthony, led it for more than 50 years. Intelligent, educated, witty, and articulate, she was the movement's philosopher and speechwriter.

<u>LUCY STONE</u> (1818-93) of Massachusetts was nineteen when she heard her minister read the 1837 Pastoral Letter scolding women reformers about speaking in public. Her "indignation blazed" and she decided: "If ever I have anything to say in public, I shall say it...." And she did, becoming one of the most eloquent speakers for the causes of abolition and women's rights.
Lucy Stone was among the first women in America to attend college.

Would you have been a feminist if you had lived in the 1800s?

Imagine your response as we read next of Lucy Stone's experiences at Oberlin College, the first college to admit women as students.

1492   1843-47   2000

THE MYTH OF THE MINDLESS WOMAN

American men have had access to higher education since 1636, with the opening of Harvard College.

But American women were denied this privilege for 201 years, until 1837 when Oberlin College in Ohio became the first college to admit women.

The reasons? For centuries people have believed in:

1) <u>Female intellectual inferiority</u>—Beginning with Aristotle 2,400 years ago, people have mistakenly believed that women's brains were inferior to men's; therefore female education was wasteful.

2) <u>Female subordination</u>—The Biblical injuction for wives to obey their husbands would be undermined by educated women trained to think for themselves, logically and analytically.

OBERLIN COLLEGE

<u>Lucy Stone</u> broke new ground in becoming one of the first coeds at Oberlin College in 1843. She would graduate with honors four years later, Massachusetts' first woman college graduate. Meanwhile, her studies in Greek and Hebrew convinced her that Biblical passages about female submission had been misinterpreted by male scholars.

Lucy found that even Oberlin held traditional views about women's subordinate role.

Oberlin officials referred to male students as the "leading sex" and expected female students to fulfill their feminine role, as Lucy said, "by washing the men's clothing, caring for their rooms, serving them at table, listening to their orations, but, themselves remaining respectfully silent in public assemblages...."

THIS IS COLLEGE? WASHING THE MEN'S CLOTHES? CLEANING THEIR ROOMS? SERVING THEIR MEALS?

CO-ED COLLEGES ARE REALLY GREAT. I'M GLAD OBERLIN LED THE WAY.

OBERLIN UNIVERSITY LAUNDRY

Oberlin allowed women to take debate classes, but forbade the unfeminine activity of actually debating. Lucy took action.

SORRY YOU GIRLS CAN'T TAKE PART IN THE DEBATES. SPEAKING IN PUBLIC IS VERY UNFEMININE, YOU KNOW.

COME ON, WE'RE GOING TO FORM OUR OWN SECRET SOCIETY — IN THE WOODS.

In 1847 Lucy's class chose her as an outstanding graduate who would write and read an essay for commencement. As a woman, however, she'd have to sit silently while a professor read it. She refused. (In 1877 Lucy was an honored speaker at Oberlin's Jubilee.)

CONGRATULATIONS ON A WONDERFUL ESSAY. OF COURSE I'LL HAVE TO READ IT FOR YOU AT COMMENCEMENT.

NO WAY!

In 1855 Lucy Stone married abolitionist Henry Blackwell. Desiring equality, they omitted the word "obey" from her vows. And she kept her own name, saying, "A wife should no more take her husband's name than he should hers."

Since then, married women who keep their name often are called "Lucy Stoners."

WHAT DO YOU MEAN, YOU WANT TO BE A LUCY STONER?

"When I first heard from from the lips of Lucretia Mott that I had the same right to think for myself that Luther, Calvin, and John Knox had, and the right to be guided by my own convictions, and would no doubt live a happier life than if guided by theirs, I felt at once a new-born sense of dignity and freedom..."—Elizabeth Cady Stanton

1492   1840   2000

Elizabeth Cady Stanton first conceived the idea of a woman's rights organization in 1840 while attending the World Anti-Slavery Convention in London with her abolitionist husband Henry Stanton. Although not a delegate herself, Stanton reacted strongly to the Convention's discrimination against the United States' eight women delegates, among whom was **Lucretia Mott**.

Stanton, a young bride of 25, and Mott, married and 46, became fast friends on the trip. Their response to the events below has affected every woman in America—and every man.

ENGLAND
London

1840: **WORLD ANTI-SLAVERY CONVENTION**—Clergy delegates led a move to reject the eight U.S. female delegates, insisting that women occupy a subordinate position to men, as divinely decreed by Eve's creation from Adam's rib. Despite protests by Henry Stanton and Wendell Phillips, the women were admitted only as guests and seated behind a half-curtain.

THIS WAY LADIES. REMEMBER WHAT ST. PAUL SAID IN THE NEW TESTAMENT: "LET YOUR WOMEN KEEP SILENCE IN THE CHURCH." THAT GOES FOR MEETINGS, TOO.

NON-SPEAKING SECTION

Wendell Phillips, misjudging the significance of the matter, responded graciously to rejection of the women delegates. This reaction of a man who had championed their cause disappointed the women.

I HAVE NO DOUBT THE WOMEN WILL SIT WITH AS MUCH INTEREST AS GUESTS AS IF THEY HAD BEEN DELEGATES.

IT IS ALMOST IMPOSSIBLE FOR THE MOST LIBERAL OF MEN TO UNDERSTAND WHAT LIBERTY MEANS FOR WOMEN.

HE JUST DOESN'T GET IT!

WENDELL PHILLIPS U.S.A.

NON-SPEAKING SECTION

William Lloyd Garrison, keynote speaker and the most prominent figure in the abolition movement, demonstrated his support of the women's cause in a way that made him a hero in their eyes. He refused to give his speech, declined his seat as a delegate, and sat with the women throughout the 10-day meeting.

AFTER BATTLING MANY LONG YEARS FOR THE LIBERTIES OF AFRICAN SLAVES, I CAN TAKE NO PART IN A CONVENTION THAT STRIKES DOWN THE MOST SACRED RIGHTS OF ALL WOMEN.

WHAT A MAN!

NON-SPEAKING SECTION

Stanton later recalled in her autobiography that the remark was heard on all sides, It is about time some demand was made for new liberties for women. She and Lucretia Mott resolved to hold a woman's rights convention when they returned home. After an eight-year delay, they would do so.

LUCRETIA, WE CAN'T HELP FREE THE SLAVES UNTIL WE GAIN FREEDOM. WHEN WE GET HOME, LETS FORM A WOMEN'S RIGHTS SOCIETY.

YOU'RE RIGHT, ELIZABETH!

LONDON SOUVENIRS

1492   1848   2000

In 1848 Elizabeth Cady Stanton and Lucretia Mott launched the woman's rights movement with the following notice in the Seneca County Courier:

"WOMAN'S RIGHTS CONVENTION—
A convention to discuss the social, civil, and religious rights of woman will be held in the Wesleyan Chapel, Seneca Falls, New York...the 19th and 20th of July current [1848]."

More than 300 people,—including 40 men—from a 50-mile radius attended the meeting. They were young (average age 35), white, and middle class; many were reformers associated with abolitionism, temperance, and freesoil political parties.

DECLARATION OF SENTIMENTS—Delegates discussed and voted on this radical document written by Stanton. It paraphrased the DECLARATION OF INDEPENDENCE: After the preamble came a listing of 18 grievances against not King George but "men." There followed 12 resolutions for action.

DECLARATION OF SENTIMENTS — WE HOLD THESE TRUTHS TO BE SELF-EVIDENT THAT ALL MEN AND WOMEN ARE CREATED EQUAL....

All 12 resolutions passed. Four of the most radical were:

RESOLVED, That all laws which prevent woman from occupying such a station in society as her conscience shall dictate, or which place her in a position inferior to that of man, are contrary to the great precept of nature, and therefore of no force or authority.

RESOLVED, That woman is man's equal—was intended to be so by the Creator, and the highest good of the race demands that she should be recognized as such.

RESOLVED, That woman has too long rested satisfied in the circumscribed limits which corrupt customs and perverted application of the Scriptures have marked out for her, and that it is time she should move in the enlarged sphere which her great Creator has assigned her.

RESOLVED, That the speedy success of our cause depends upon the zealous and untiring efforts of both men and women, for the overthrow of the monopoly of the pulpit, and for the securing to women an equal participation with men in the various trades, professions, and commerce.

The ninth resolution at first was considered too radical to pass. Even Lucretia Mott told Stanton so. Henry Stanton was so embarrassed by it, he left town, and Stanton's father thought her insane. The resolution stated:
RESOLVED, That it is the duty of the women of this country to secure to themselves the sacred right to the elective franchise.

Delegate Frederick Douglass saved the resolution. The only man who favored it, he stood by Stanton's side and spoke of its importance. It carried by a narrow margin. Douglass later said he was prouder of this act than any other in his public life.

THE POWER TO VOTE IS ESSENTIAL TO OBTAINING ALL OTHER RIGHTS.

The 72-year Woman's Rights Movement officially began as 100 delegates, 68 women and 32 men, signed the Declaration of Sentiments. It ended in 1920 with passage of the 19th Amendment granting female suffrage.
  By 1900 participants in this feminist crusade (which always included men) numbered 2,000,000.

WOMAN'S RIGHTS MOVEMENT

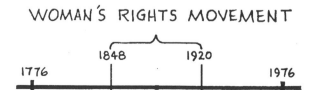

1776   1848   1920   1976

Despite criticism from press, pulpit, and much of society, courageous feminist reformers won rights for women in four areas: physical, intellectual, spiritual, and social.
  Read on to compare women's status, as described in the Declaration of Sentiments, with these reforms.

☆ DECLARATION OF SENTIMENTS ☆

DECLARATION OF SENTIMENTS — WE HOLD THESE TRUTHS TO BE SELF-EVIDENT THAT ALL MEN AND **WOMEN** ARE CREATED EQUAL....

THE HISTORY OF MANKIND is a history of repeated injuries and usurpations on the part of man toward woman, having in direct object the establishment of an absolute tyranny over her. To prove this, let facts be submitted to a candid world.

■ He has never permitted her to exercise her inalienable right to the elective franchise.

■ He has compelled her to submit to laws, in the formation of which she had no voice.

■ He has withheld from her rights which are given to the most ignorant and degraded men—both natives and foreigners.

■ Having deprived her of this first right of a citizen, the elective franchise, thereby leaving her without representation in the halls of legislation, he has oppressed her on all sides.

■ He has made her, if married, in the eye of the law, civilly dead.

■ He has taken from her all right in property, even to the wages she earns.

■ He has made her, morally, an irresponsible being, as she can commit many crimes with impunity, provided they be done in the presence of her husband. In the covenant of marriage, she is compelled to promise obedience to her husband, he becoming, to all intents and purposes, her master—the law giving him power to deprive her of her liberty and to administer chastisement.

■ He has so framed the laws of divorce, as to what shall be the proper causes, and in case of separation, to whom the guardianship of the children shall be given, as to be wholly regardless of the happiness of women—the law, in all cases, going upon a false supposition of the supremacy of man, and giving all power into his hands.

■ After depriving her of all rights as a married woman, if single, and the owner of property, he has taxed her to support a government which recognizes her only when her property can be made profitable to it.

■ He has monopolized nearly all the profitable employments, and from those she is permitted to follow, she receives but a scanty remuneration. He closes against her all the avenues to wealth and distinction which he considers most honorable to himself. As a teacher of theology, medicine, or law, she is not known.

■ He has denied her the facilities for obtaining a thorough education, all colleges being closed against her.

■ He allows her in Church, as well as State, but a subordinate position, claiming Apostolic authority for her exclusion from the ministry, and, with some exceptions, from any public participation in the affairs of the Church.

■ He has created a false public sentiment by giving to the world a different code of morals for men and women, by which moral delinquencies which exclude women from society, are not only tolerated, but deemed of little account in man.

■ He has usurped the prerogative of Jehovah himself, claiming it as his right to assign for her a sphere of action, when that belongs to her conscience and to her God.

■ He has endeavored, in every way that he could, to destroy her confidence in her own powers, to lessen her self-respect, and to make her willing to lead a dependent and abject life.

■ Now in view of this entire disfranchisement of one-half the people of this country, their social and religious degradation-in view of the unjust laws above mentioned, and because women do feel themselves aggrieved, oppressed, and fraudulently deprived of their most sacred rights, we insist that they have immediate admission to all the rights and privileges which belong to them as citizens of the United States.

■ In entering upon the great work before us, we anticipate no small amount of misconceptions, misrepresentations, and ridicule; but we shall use every instrumentality within our power to effect our object. We shall employ agents, circulate tracts, petition the State and National legislatures, and endeavor to enlist the pulpit and press in our behalf. We hope this Convention will be followed by a series of Conventions embracing every part of the country....

RESOLVED, That woman is man's equal—was intended to be so by the creator, and the highest good of the race demands that she should be recognized as such...

RESOLVED, That it is the duty of the women of this country to secure to themselves their sacred right to the elective franchise....

1492   1848   1920   2000

1848—WOMEN'S STATUS   PHYSICAL   1848-1920—FEMINIST REFORMS

D R E S S

MODEST

Respectable women were covered from head to toe. Layers of clothing that weighed 12 to 15 pounds interfered with movement, and corsets exerting up to 80 pounds of pressure caused internal injuries.

PRACTICAL

Dress reform came first. In 1850 Elizabeth Miller, Stanton's cousin, designed a comfortable outfit freeing women from corsets and heavy skirts. It was called the Bloomer after Amelia Bloomer who popularized it.

By 1854 ridicule from the press, accusations of immorality from the pulpit, and pleas from embarrassed children forced feminists to give up the Bloomer in order not to jeopardise reforms such as the vote.

H E A L T H

WEAK

Nineteenth century chivalry idealized female weakness, causing women to cultivate helplessness.

MY DEAR, LET ME HELP YOU!

OH, LESTER — I FEEL FAINT!

SO FEMININE! WOMAN'S WEAKNESS IS HER CHARM...

STRONG— Charlotte Perkins Gilman (1860-1935) reminded women that weakness could be an invitation to male aggression as well as protection. And Sojourner Truth noted the irony of "weaker vessels" working the fields.

THIS ARM HAS WORKED HARD IN THE SLAVE FIELDS FROM SUN-UP TO SUN-DOWN MANY A DAY — AND AIN'T I A WOMAN?

E X E R C I S E

DELICATE

Sports were too dangerous for weak women, and it was feared that calesthenics would masculinize women and give them a "gymnasium face."
Most doctors recommended housework as the only safe exercise for women.

GUESS I'LL LIVE FOREVER!

FIT

Invention of the bicycle proved a breakthrough: finally an activity considered safe for women. But they were encouraged to get a thoracic exam first.

The Washington D.C. Bicycle Society, and others like it, protested women's new mobility, saying it would break up the American home.

B I R T H   C O N T R O L

IGNORANT

Birth control was illegal and knowledge of it considered immoral.

THERE WAS AN OLD WOMAN WHO LIVED IN A SHOE. SHE HAD SO MANY CHILDREN SHE DIDN'T KNOW WHAT TO DO.

INFORMED—Margaret Sanger (1883-1960) worked from 1912 until her death to make birth control legal. She even went to jail briefly for violating a law against sending birth control information through the mail.

THANK YOU MARGARET SANGER

BIRTH CONTROL CLINIC

"A man asks not 'Is she clever?' but 'Is she pretty?'"—anonymous
"A woman...if she have the misfortune of knowing anything, should conceal it as well as she can." Jane Austen, Northanger Abbey

1848—WOMEN'S STATUS | **INTELLECTUAL** | **1848-1920—FEMINIST REFORMS**

S C H O O L

NO COLLEGE; DOMESTIC SUBJECTS—
Intellect was considered a male possession; therefore, "feminine girls" had little interest or need for education. Smart girls learned to conceal their knowledge.

HIGHER EDUCATION—
While Harvard College was built for men only six years after the Puritans arrived in Massachusetts (1636), women were denied access to college for 201 years.

In 1837 Mary Lyon founded Mount Holyoke and Oberlin became the first coeducational college (1837). In the 1830s and 1840s Catharine Beecher crusaded in the Midwest for teacher-training colleges. After the Civil War more women's colleges opened:
1865—Vassar
1875—Smith and Wellesley
1885—Bryn Mawr

By 1900 women had access to 80 % of all institutions of higher learning.

B R A I N

SMALL; INFERIOR CAPACITY—
Doctors warned girls and women against difficult subjects for fear of brain fever.

NORMAL
Women's success in the new colleges offered proof their brains could handle difficult subjects.

In 1915 Bryn Mawr President M. Carey Thomas wrote:

"We did not really know anything about...the intellectual capacity of women when we began to educate them....We were told that their brains were too light, their foreheads too small, their reasoning powers too defective, their emotions too easily worked upon to make good students. None of these things has proved to be true. Women have proved themselves equal to men, even slightly superior."

M A R R I A G E

SUBMISSIVE; OBEDIENT—
It seemed logical for mentally inferior persons, such as women, to be subservient.

INDEPENDENT
Feminists such as Lucy Stone and Elizabeth Cady Stanton took the word "obey" out of their marriage vows. They urged other women to do the same and to think for themselves.

Susan B. Anthony encouraged women to be independent and autonomous (self-governing).

-= SECTION EIGHTEEN =-
AMERICAN LITERATURE
1800-1865

<u>literature</u>—writings marked by beauty of expression, by a universal appeal to intellect and emotion

1492   1800   1865   2000

"In the four quarters of the globe, who reads an American book?"—Sydney Smith, <u>Edinburgh Review</u>, 1820

"The Americans have no national literature, and no learned men....The talents of our transatlantic brethren show themselves chiefly in political pamphlets. The Americans are too young to rival in literature the old nations of Europe. They have neither history, nor romance, nor poetry, nor legends on which to exercise their genius and kindle their imagination."—<u>British Critic</u>, 1819

"I must study politics and war,
that my sons may have liberty to study mathematics and philosophy, geography, natural history...commerce and agriculture,
in order to give their children a right to study painting, poetry, music, architecture, statuary, tapestry and porcelain."—John Adams

As John Adams explained, the arts develop in their own time. In America's third century, excited by nationalism and Jacksonian democracy, Americans cast off their artistic dependence on Europe and produced a great national literature.

"The things I want to know are in books."—Abraham Lincoln

TRENDS IN AMERICAN LITERATURE

1765-1800: CLASSICISM—reason, balance, order.

<u>1800-65:</u> <u>ROMANTICISM</u>—emotion, imagination, intuition, optimism, individualism, nature, democracy, history.

1865-1900: REALISM—commonplace details of everyday life, regional topics with local color.

1900-17: NATURALISM—harsh aspects of life, people victims of circumstances; pessimism, cynicism.

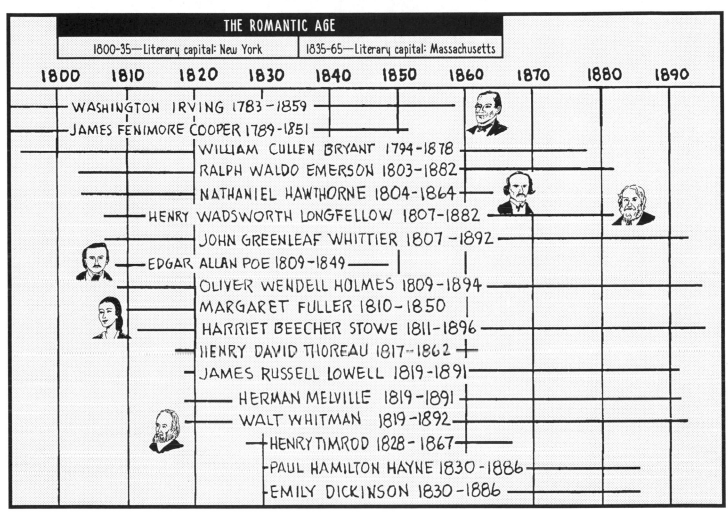

THE ROMANTIC AGE

| 1800-35—Literary capital: New York | 1835-65—Literary capital: Massachusetts |

| 1800 | 1810 | 1820 | 1830 | 1840 | 1850 | 1860 | 1870 | 1880 | 1890 |

WASHINGTON IRVING 1783-1859

JAMES FENIMORE COOPER 1789-1851

WILLIAM CULLEN BRYANT 1794-1878

RALPH WALDO EMERSON 1803-1882

NATHANIEL HAWTHORNE 1804-1864

HENRY WADSWORTH LONGFELLOW 1807-1882

JOHN GREENLEAF WHITTIER 1807-1892

EDGAR ALLAN POE 1809-1849

OLIVER WENDELL HOLMES 1809-1894

MARGARET FULLER 1810-1850

HARRIET BEECHER STOWE 1811-1896

HENRY DAVID THOREAU 1817-1862

JAMES RUSSELL LOWELL 1819-1891

HERMAN MELVILLE 1819-1891

WALT WHITMAN 1819-1892

HENRY TIMROD 1828-1867

PAUL HAMILTON HAYNE 1830-1886

EMILY DICKINSON 1830-1886

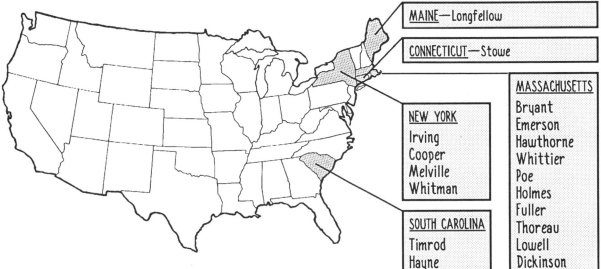

MAINE—Longfellow

CONNECTICUT—Stowe

NEW YORK

Irving
Cooper
Melville
Whitman

SOUTH CAROLINA

Timrod
Hayne

MASSACHUSETTS

Bryant
Emerson
Hawthorne
Whittier
Poe
Holmes
Fuller
Thoreau
Lowell
Dickinson

"Every [romantic] author of note made at least one attempt to use American history in a major literary work."—Russell B. Nye

1492   1800   1865   2000

Washington Irving

Named for George Washington, Irving became the first American fiction writer to gain an international reputation.

In 1809 his Knickerbocker's History of New York, an amusing account of the Dutch in his home state, was well received; instant fame came ten years later with Sketch Book, a collection of Dutch-American tales including "Rip Van Winkle" and "The Legend of Sleepy Hollow." In 1859 he wrote Life of George Washington.

James Fenimore Cooper

Cooper, bored with an English novel, said he could write a better one. His wife challenged him to do so, and he did. The Spy, a tale of the American Revolution, became the first great American novel.

Like Irving he wrote, in Leatherstocking Tales, of American scenes familiar to him: Indians on the New York frontier. High adventure awaits the reader of these five tales, which include "The Last of the Mohicans" (1826).

William Cullen Bryant

"So live, that when thy summons comes to join
The unnumerable caravan which moves
To that mysterious realm, where each shall take
His chamber in the silent halls of death,
Thou go not, like the quarry slave at night,
Scourged to his dungeon, but, sustained and soothed
By an unaltering trust, approach thy grave
Like one who wraps the drapery of his couch
About him, and lies down to pleasant dreams."

Bryant prayed as a child to become a famous poet. Poems like "Thanatopsis" (above), composed at age 17, made him the first major American poet.

TRANSCENDENTALISM   Ralph Waldo Emerson

Nineteenth century romanticism was a reaction to the Enlightenment emphasis on reason in the eighteenth century. In the 1830s romanticism found philosophic expression in Transcendentalism, in the idea that each person can know truth intuitively by transcending—going beyond—reason and the five senses and consulting the spark of the divine, or Oversoul, within us all.

The Transcendental movement originated in Boston with Unitarian ministers Ralph Waldo Emerson and George Ripley, who resigned their pulpits because of the church's "corpse-cold" rationality. In 1836 Emerson and other Boston intellectuals began meeting in the home of George and Sophia Ripley to discuss the difference in intuition and reason. Unlike Puritans and Deists who saw God as a Creator apart from us, they saw God as a creative force flowing through us, making knowledge available intuitively—directly from within. This fostered an optimistic belief in the goodness of man, the chief characteristic of Transcendentalism.

Led by Emerson, the Transcendental movement included the writers below and many others responsible for the literary "flowering of New England," humanitarian reforms, and utopian societies. Their individualism, faith in progress, and egalitarianism had much in common with Jacksonian America.

Emerson became America's favorite philosopher. He shaped the American character through lectures and essays.

"Trust thyself; every heart vibrates to that iron string....
Nothing is at last sacred but the integrity of your own mind....
An institution is the lengthened shadow of one man...
and all history resolves itself...
into the biography of a few stout and earnest persons.
Let a man know his worth."
—from "Self Reliance"

Henry David Thoreau

"If a man does not keep pace with his companions, perhaps it is because he hears a different drummer. Let him step to the music which he hears."

Thoreau was a friend and neighbor of Emerson's in Concord, Massachusetts. His book Walden (1854) describes a two-year experiment in self-reliance while living in the woods near Walden Pond. Opposed to slavery, he was a conductor in the Underground Railroad.

Margaret Fuller

"We would have every barrier thrown down. We would have every path laid open to Woman as freely as to Man."

Also a friend of Emerson's, Fuller was a brilliant scholar who argued for female equality. Her 1845 book Woman in the Nineteenth Century described the inferior status of American women and influenced the feminist movement.

Nathaniel Hawthorne

Born in Salem, Massachusetts, Hawthorne was a descendant of a Salem witch trial judge. The Scarlet Letter (1850), his most famous novel, explores good and evil in a Puritan New England town.

Hawthorne, his friend Herman Melville, and Edgar Allan Poe were unlike most Transcendentalists: they looked on the dark side of life.

⇥ MEET THE AUTHORS ⇤

Henry Wadsworth Longfellow

"Why don't you speak for yourself, John?"
—from "The Courtship of Miles Standish"

Longfellow, the most influential and beloved poet of his era, is the only American honored with a bust in the Poet's Corner of Westminster Abbey. A descendent of John Alden and Priscilla Mullins, about whom he wrote in "The Courtship of Miles Standish," he brought American history to life through this and other narrative poems, including "Evangeline" and "The Midnight Ride of Paul Revere."

John Greenleaf Whittier

"We cross the prairies as of old
The Pilgrims crossed the sea,
To make the West, as they the East,
The homestead of the free!"
—from "The Kansas Emigrants"

An abolitionist Quaker, Whittier wrote this verse encouraging Northern freesoilers to settle in Kansas and make it a non-slave state. In addition to being chief poet of the abolitionist movement, he wrote poems, such as "Snowbound," about the charms of New England country life.

Edgar Allan Poe

"It was many and many a year ago,
In a kingdom by the sea,
That a maiden there lived
whom you may know
By the name of Annabel Lee.
And this maiden she lived
with no other thought
Than to love and be loved by me."
—from "Annabel Lee"

Born in Boston and reared in Richmond, Virginia, Poe was a master of detective and mystery stories, as well as poetry.

Oliver Wendell Holmes

"She has gone, she has left us in passion and pride,
Our stormy-browed sister, so long at our side.
She has torn her own star
from our firmament's glow,
And turned on her Brother the face of a foe!"
—from "Brother Jonathan's Lament for Sister Caroline" (about South Carolina's secession)

Holmes, son of a Congregationalist minister, taught medicine at Harvard for 47 years and wrote novels, witty essays (Autocrat at the Breakfast Table), and poems ("Old Ironsides").

Harriet Beecher Stowe

"So you're the little woman who wrote the book that made this great war," said President Lincoln when he met Stowe in 1862.

Indeed, Stowe's novel Uncle Tom's Cabin (1852), dramatizing the evils of slavery, galvanized support for the Union in the Civil War. Politically, it was the most influential literature since Thomas Paine's Common Sense.

Stowe, daughter of a Congregationalist minister, wrote other novels which dealt with Puritan traits in New England life.

James Russell Lowell

Like Longfellow and Holmes, Lowell was from a distinguished New England family and taught at Harvard. (He followed Longfellow as professor of modern languages.)

A literary critic, poet and abolitionist, Lowell is best known for the Bigelow Papers, satirical verses portraying the Mexican War (1846-48) as an American crime committed in behalf of slavery.

Herman Melville

"...a whale ship was my Yale College and my Harvard."—Herman Melville

Melville, a literary genius, had an ordinary boyhood in New York City and Albany. One of his grandfathers participated in the Boston Tea Party, another in the Revolution. In 1841 Melville went to sea on a whaling ship and returned to write Moby Dick, America's greatest epic novel. A study of human nature, it deals with the problems of free will and fate. Melville dedicated it to his friend Hawthorne. In this and other novels, Melville attacked social injustice.

Walt Whitman

"I celebrate myself to celebrate every man and woman alive."
—from "Song of Myself"

A New York journalist, Whitman became one of America's greatest poets. He loved life, America, democracy, and the common people. He sang joyous praises to all in a shocking new form of poetry using free verse and slang. He published his poems in nine editions of Leaves of Grass. Whitman was a fervent abolitionist.

Emily Dickinson

"To make a prairie it takes a clover and one bee,
and revery.
The revery alone will do
If bees are few."
—from "To Make a Prairie"

A shy recluse in Amherst, Massachusetts, Dickinson published only a few poems in her lifetime. But the 1,800 poems she left, published in 1890, earned her reputation as one of America's finest poets.

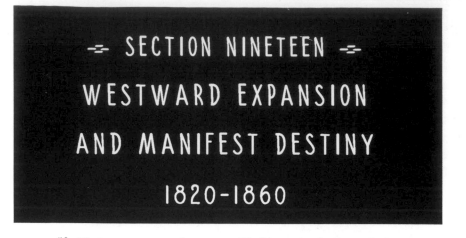

"Go West, young man, and grow up with the country."—Horace Greeley.

1492   1820   1860   2000

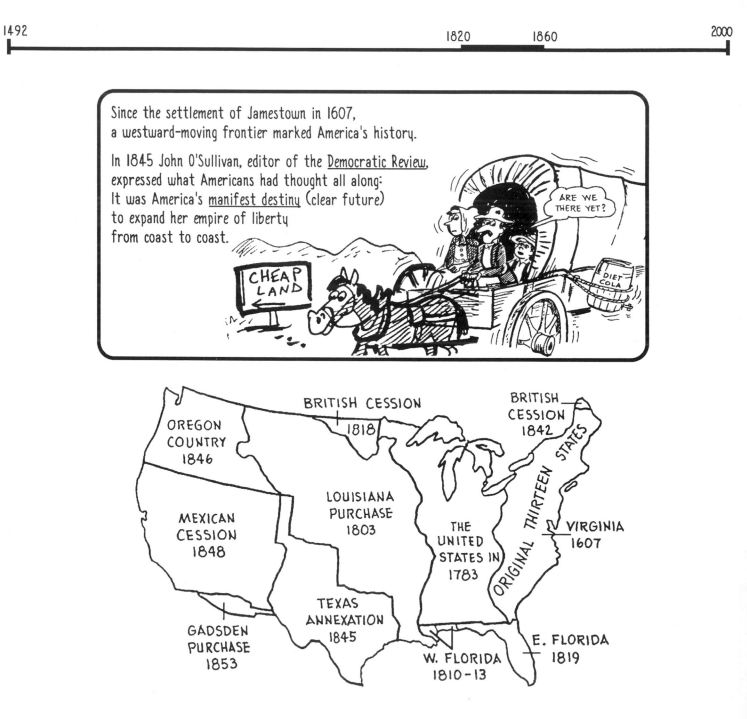

Since the settlement of Jamestown in 1607,
a westward-moving frontier marked America's history.

In 1845 John O'Sullivan, editor of the Democratic Review,
expressed what Americans had thought all along:
It was America's manifest destiny (clear future)
to expand her empire of liberty
from coast to coast.

"I am listening to the tread of unnumbered millions to come."—Henry Clay, putting his ear to the ground on the Wilderness Road

1492 ——————————————————— 1775 ——— 1860 ——————————————————— 2000

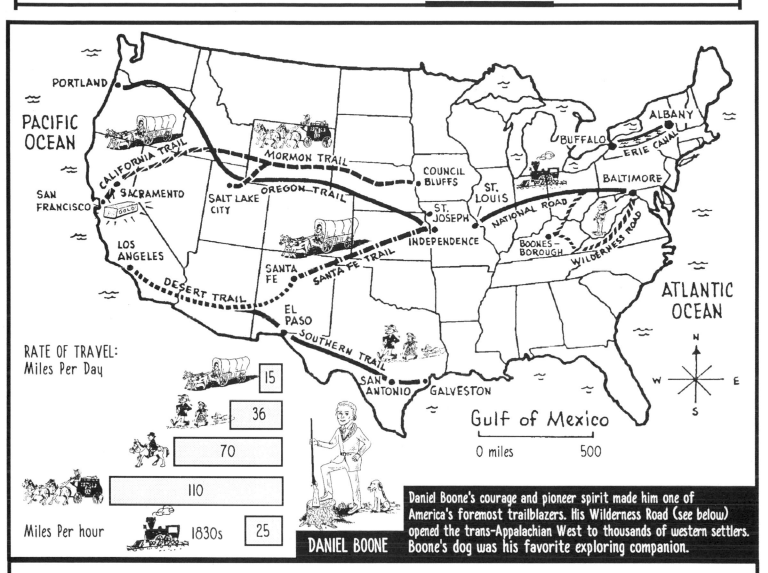

RATE OF TRAVEL:
Miles Per Day

covered wagon	15
pioneers on foot	36
horse rider	70
stagecoach	110

Miles Per hour   train 1830s   25

DANIEL BOONE

Daniel Boone's courage and pioneer spirit made him one of America's foremost trailblazers. His Wilderness Road (see below) opened the trans-Appalachian West to thousands of western settlers. Boone's dog was his favorite exploring companion.

WESTWARD ROUTES

Imagine the United States with thousands of Indian paths but no roads. Early settlers followed these paths—many formed first by buffalo—and gradually widened them for wagons and stagecoaches. Some they lined with stones. Others remained primitive; wagon drivers caught on tree stumps left in the way would exclaim, "I'm stumped."

■ **WILDERNESS TRAIL**—In 1775 Daniel Boone and a crew of "30 guns" hacked the first highway into the West. They followed the ancient Iroquois-Cherokee Warrior Path through the Cumberland Gap into Kentucky.

■ **NATIONAL ROAD**—In 1818 the federal government completed this crushed-stone road. Unlike most trails, it had a scattering of inns.

■ **ERIE CANAL**—In 1825 this spectacular engineering feat opened a trade route from the Great Lakes to the Hudson River and Atlantic Ocean, making New York City the nation's leading commercial center. (Thomas Jefferson, said of the Erie Canal proposal: "Why, sir, you talk of making a canal 350 miles through the wilderness—it is little short of madness....") Canal building continued, in part because Robert Fulton's steamboat (1807) proved water travel could be efficient.

■ **SANTA FE TRAIL**—Santa Fe, founded by the Spanish in 1610, was closed to "Americanos" until 1821 when Mexico won its independence from Spain and opened Santa Fe to American traders. William Bucknell led the first American wagon train into Santa Fe in 1822. Today, on the edge of the city, you can see wagon ruts carved by Bucknell, Kit Carson, and other adventurers.

■ **OREGON TRAIL**—In 1841 settlers lured by fertile land began trekking 2,000 miles to the Oregon country, jointly occupied by the United States and Britain since 1818. In 1843 they established a provisional government and demanded annexation to the U.S.

■ **MORMON TRAIL**—In 1847 Brigham Young led the first of 15,000 Mormons, members of the Church of Jesus Christ of Latter-day Saints, to Utah as a haven from persecution. Utah became a state in 1896, after the Mormons agreed to give up polygamy.

■ **CALIFORNIA TRAIL**—Gold, discovered in 1848 at Sutter's Fort near Sacramento, drew a "goldrush" of people racing across the continent to strike it rich—80,000 by 1849. Called "forty-niners," they soon wrote a state constitution and sought U.S. annexation.

"It may be easily foreseen that if Mexico takes no step to check this change, the province of Texas will soon cease to belong to her."
—Alexis de Tocqueville

1492   1836   2000

STEPHEN F. AUSTIN

SAM HOUSTON

Did the 1803 Louisiana Purchase include Texas? Many Americans, including Henry Clay and John Quincy Adams, thought so. However, in the 1819 Adams-Onis Treaty, the United States bought Florida from Spain and gave up its claim to Texas in return for Spain's giving up its claim to the Oregon country.

Texas—a fertile land watered by many rivers—attracted westward bound United States citizens, even though it was a province of Spain. In 1821 Moses Austin, a Connecticut-born resident of Missouri, obtained a land grant from Spain, with permission to bring United States citizens to settle in Texas. He died shortly thereafter, before carrying out his plan.

Moses' son Stephen F. Austin, born in Virginia and now a judge in Little Rock, Arkansas, obtained Moses' grant. In December 1821 he brought 300 families to Texas. They settled on the Brazos River in southeast Texas, founding the first Anglo-American colony in Texas. Upon arrival the new settlers learned that Mexico had won independence from Spain. In 1824 the provinces of Texas and Coahuila were united to form one state in the republic of Mexico.

As Mexican citizens, Anglo-Texans fell under Mexican laws that threatened their way of life. The law required that they become Catholics and prohibited ownership of slaves. However, they did have local self-government, that is, until 1835 when Mexican President General Santa Anna became dictator and abolished local government. The angry Texans set up a provisional government. On March 2, 1836, they declared their independence from Mexico and prepared to defend it. Defeat seemed certain for them when, on March 6, Santa Anna's troops killed 183 Texas rebels defending the Alamo, an abandoned mission in San Antonio. Rebel leaders included William B. Travis, James Bowie, and Davy Crockett. Then, on March 27 the Mexicans massacred 342 rebels at Goliad.

On April 21 General Sam Houston turned the tide. With 900 Texas rebels crying "Remember the Alamo!" "Remember Goliad!" he defeated Santa Anna's larger army at the Battle of San Jacinto and won Texas' independence from Mexico. Houston became president of the new Republic of Texas and requested annexation by the United States. President Jackson, his close friend, refused. Jackson feared not only war with Mexico but civil war as well, for Texas would enter the Union as a slave state, upsetting the balance of free and slave states. Texas remained an independent republic until finally annexed to the United States in 1845.

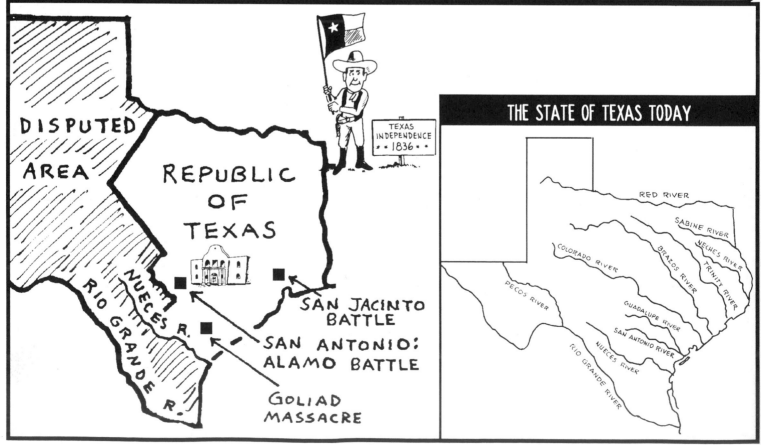

DISPUTED AREA

RIO GRANDE R.

NUECES R.

REPUBLIC OF TEXAS

TEXAS INDEPENDENCE ⋅ 1836 ⋅

SAN JACINTO BATTLE

SAN ANTONIO: ALAMO BATTLE

GOLIAD MASSACRE

THE STATE OF TEXAS TODAY

RED RIVER
SABINE RIVER
NECHES RIVER
TRINITY RIVER
BRAZOS RIVER
COLORADO RIVER
PECOS RIVER
GUADALUPE RIVER
SAN ANTONIO RIVER
NUECES RIVER
RIO GRANDE RIVER

1492   1846-48   2000

1844—James Polk, Tennessee Democrat, won election as president on a platform calling for annexation of Oregon and Texas, with a general understanding that the South would accept Oregon if the West and North would accept Texas, a slave state.

Through a joint resolution in Congress, Texas was admitted to the Union in December 1845, and the Oregon boundary dispute was settled with Britain in June 1846. (Oregon became a state in 1859.)

Time now to settle the dispute with Mexico about Texas' southern boundary. The U.S. claimed the Rio Grande River as the boundary; Mexico claimed the Nueces River.

OREGON COUNTRY 1846 / BRITISH CESSION 1818 / BRITISH CESSION 1842 / MEXICAN CESSION 1848 / LOUISIANA PURCHASE 1803 / THE UNITED STATES IN 1783 / ORIGINAL THIRTEEN STATES / VIRGINIA 1607 / TEXAS ANNEXATION 1845 / GADSDEN PURCHASE 1853 / W. FLORIDA 1810-13 / E. FLORIDA 1819

1845—Polk sent <u>John Slidell</u> to Mexico to offer to buy the disputed land, plus California and New Mexico. But Mexico refused to deal with him.

YANKEE? HEY, I'M FROM THE **SOUTH!**

YANKEE GO HOME!

JOHN SLIDELL

January 1846—Polk sent <u>General Zachary Taylor</u> with troops to the disputed area, a violation of international law.

April 24—Mexicans killed 11 Americans on the Mexican side of the Rio Grande.

April 30—Mexican troops attacked the Americans in the disputed zone.

May 11—Polk asked Congress for (and received) a declaration of war, saying:

Mexico has shed American blood on American soil!

Illinois Congressman Abraham Lincoln opposed the war, questioning whether blood was shed on Mexican or American soil. He asked Polk a pointed question:

SHOW US THE SPOT WHERE AMERICAN BLOOD WAS SHED!

MAP

<u>Most southerners favored the war,</u> thinking that any territory won would be organized into slave states.

<u>Many northerners opposed the war</u> for the same reason.

1848: <u>TREATY OF GUADALUPE HIDALGO</u>

The United States defeated Mexico, in part because of superior commanders: Generals Zachary Taylor, Winfield Scott, and Stephen Kearny and Commodore John Sloat.

<u>The peace treaty provided that:</u>

1. <u>Mexico</u> would accept the Rio Grande River as the Texas border and cede New Mexico and California to the U.S.

2. The <u>United States</u> would assume claims of Americans citizens against Mexico and pay Mexico $15,000,000.

THE BIG QUESTION:
Should the new U.S. territory be slave or free?

"All legislation...is founded upon the principle of mutual concession....Let him who elevates himself above humanity, above its weaknesses, its infinities, its wants, its necessities, say, if he pleases, 'I will never compromise'; but let no one who is not above the frailties of our common nature disdain compromise."—Henry Clay

1492   1850   2000

HENRY CLAY, THE GREAT COMPROMISER

The Mexican War intensified sectional conflicts and made slavery a political issue for the first time since the Compromise of 1820. (Before and after 1820, there had been an unspoken agreement among factions to avoid making slavery a political issue.)

In 1846 Pennsylvania Congressman David Wilmot—representing the antislavery, northeastern segment of the Democratic party—introduced the Wilmot Proviso which proposed banning slavery in territory acquired from Mexico (except Texas).

The Wilmot Proviso twice passed the northern dominated House of Representatives and twice failed in the southern dominated Senate, so it did not become a law. It did, however, stir a bitter four-year debate.

Debate heated up when California, quickly populated after the discovery of gold in 1848, applied for admission as a free state. Admittance would upset the balance of 15 free and 15 slave states.

Senator Henry Clay, now an old man of 73, saved the day. Sponsor of the Compromise of 1820 and the 1833 Compromise Tariff, Clay had learned Benjamin Franklin's technique for helping opposite sides shave a little off each side to make two boards fit.

Clay masterminded the Compromise of 1850. His greatest legislative achievement, it delayed the Civil War for a decade. Can you see how both North and South shaved a little off their sides?

Texas gave up her western boundary claim of the Rio Grande River in return for U.S. assumption of her $10,000,000 debt from days of the Texas Republic. This strip of land was added to the New Mexico Territory.

(Advantage: balanced)

Utah Territory

2. The two territories could vote on whether to permit slavery. (Advantage: South)

New Mexico Territory

1. California admitted as a free state (Adv.: North)

3. **Texas**

4. YOU CAN'T DO THAT!

SLAVE AUCTION Washington, D.C.

COMPROMISE OF **1850**

HENRY CLAY

The slave trade (but not slavery) was abolished in the District of Columbia. (Advantage: North)

5. A strong fugitive slave law was passed to ensure the return of runaway slaves. (Advantage: South)

"'A house divided against itself cannot stand.'
I believe this government cannot endure, permanently half slave and half free.
I do not expect the Union to be dissolved—I do not expect the house to fall—but I do expect it will cease to be divided.
It will become all one thing, or all the other." —Abraham Lincoln, 1858

1850 — Compromise of 1850

1852 — Uncle Tom's Cabin by Harriet B. Stowe

WHAT A HORRIBLY CRUEL SYSTEM! THOSE AWFUL SLAVEHOLDERS!

1854 — Kansas-Nebraska Act
Republican Party forms

1857 — Dred Scott Decision

1858 — Lincoln—Douglas Debates

1859 — Harper's Ferry

1860 — Lincoln elected president
South Carolina secedes

1861 — 11 Southern states form Confederacy
Civil War starts

CIVIL WAR 1861—1865

FAILURE OF THE COMPROMISE OF 1850

The Compromise of 1850 didn't work.

Why?

It could not hold the Union together when, as Lincoln said,
the cancer of slavery—which the Founding Fathers
dared not cut out in 1787 lest the patient die of bleeding—
spread its malignancy throughout the expanding nation.

During a decade of conflict leading to the Civil War,
Abraham Lincoln
emerged as a national leader,
and in 1860 a divided nation elected him
president of the United States.

To better understand the Civil War
read the following MINI-BIOGRAPHY OF ABRAHAM LINCOLN,
the man on whose shoulders it fell to preserve the Union.

(The historical narrative of events leading to the Civil War resumes on page 238.)

"His greatest mission was to accomplish two things:
first, to save his country from dismemberment and ruin;
and, second, to free his country from the great crime of slavery....
infinite wisdom has seldom sent any man into the world better fitted for his mission than Abraham Lincoln."
—Frederick Douglass

Abraham Lincoln, 16th and tallest (6'4") president of the United States (1861-65)
ranks as one of the greatest leaders in American history and one of the world's noblest men.

No one would have anticipated this on February 12, 1809, the day Lincoln was born.
As he himself said of his early life, "It can all be condensed into a single sentence and that
sentence you will find in Gray's Elegy, 'The short and simple annals of the poor.'"

Unlike the aristocratic Founding Fathers,
such as his boyhood heroes George Washington and Thomas Jefferson,
Lincoln was a backwoodsman born in a one-room, dirt-floor log cabin on the Kentucky frontier,
the first U.S. president born outside the 13 original colonies. His formal schooling—acquired,
as he said, "by littles" between ages six and seventeen—amounted to about one year.
All that he learned beyond that year, he taught himself.

And yet, through self-education
he became the most eloquent speaker and the finest writer
of all the presidents. And through his commitment to democracy and freedom, he became
the "Savior of the Union" and the "Great Emancipator" of enslaved African-Americans.

The secret to his success?
His virtuous character—honesty, integrity, love, justice, courage, kindness, perseverance,
humility, humor—and, according to Lincoln, the providence of God.

"The biographer's mission is to perpetuate a man as he was in the days he lived—a spring task of bringing to life again."—Paul Murray Kendall

1810	1815	1820	1825	1830	1835	1840	1845	1850	1855	1860	1865	1870

Born, 1809; birth to age 7, lived on Nolin Creek and Knob Creek farms, Kentucky

Age 7-21
Little Pigeon Creek Farm, Indiana
Farm work, rail splitting

Age 22-28
New Salem, Illinois
Clerk, surveyer, merchant, lawyer

Illinois Legislature

Age 28-36
Springfield, Illinois
Lawyer

Age 36-38
U.S. Congress

Age 38-52
Springfield, Illinois
Lawyer

Age 52-56
U.S. President
CIVIL WAR

April 14, 1865
President Lincoln assassinated

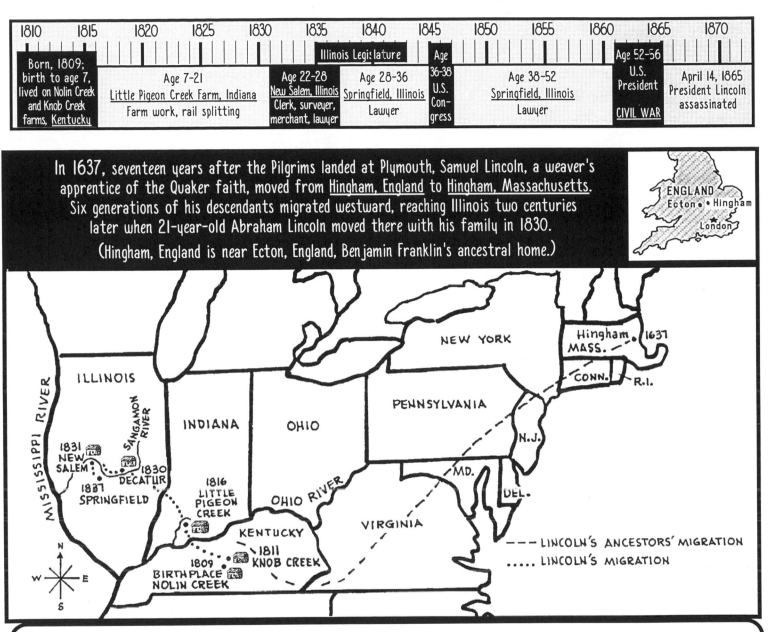

In 1637, seventeen years after the Pilgrims landed at Plymouth, Samuel Lincoln, a weaver's apprentice of the Quaker faith, moved from Hingham, England to Hingham, Massachusetts. Six generations of his descendants migrated westward, reaching Illinois two centuries later when 21-year-old Abraham Lincoln moved there with his family in 1830.

(Hingham, England is near Ecton, England, Benjamin Franklin's ancestral home.)

ENGLAND
Ecton • Hingham
★ London

---- LINCOLN'S ANCESTORS' MIGRATION
..... LINCOLN'S MIGRATION

In 1859 Lincoln wrote an autobiographical sketch, recalling:

"I was born February 12, 1809, in Hardin County, Kentucky. My parents were both born in Virginia of undistinguished families....My mother [Nancy], who died in my tenth year, was of a family of the name of Hanks....My paternal grandfather [also named] Abraham Lincoln emigrated from Rockingham County, Virginia to Kentucky, about 1781—or 2, where, a year or two later, he was killed by Indians, not in battle, but by stealth, when he was laboring to open a farm in the forest. His ancestors, who were Quakers, went to Virginia from Berks County, Pennsylvania....

"My father [Thomas], at the death of his father, was but six years of age; and he grew up, literally without education. He removed from Kentucky to...Indiana, in my eighth year. We reached our new home about the time the state came in the Union [1816]. It was a wild region, with many bears and other wild animals still in the woods. There I grew up.... At twenty-one I came to Illinois....

"If any personal description of me is thought desirable, it may be said, I am, in height, six feet, four inches, nearly; lean in flesh, weighing, on an average, one hundred and eighty pounds; dark complexion, with coarse black hair, and grey eyes...."

In 1806 Thomas Lincoln married Nancy Hanks. They lived briefly on his 230-acre Mill Creek farm and then moved eight miles south to Elizabethtown, Kentucky, where Tom earned enough as a skilled carpenter and cabinet maker to buy two town lots. In 1807 Sarah, the Lincoln's first child, was born in their Elizabethtown log cabin.

The Lincolns were not poor, according to frontier standards. In 1808 Tom paid $200 cash for a second farm of 348 acres, increasing his land holdings to 586 acres, plus the two town lots. The new place, called <u>Sinking Spring Farm</u>, was on <u>Nolin Creek</u>, 14 miles southeast of Elizabethtown, three miles from Hodgen's mill (present-day Hodgenville).

Tom moved his family into a log cabin near the beautiful spring for which the new farm was named.

And here in 1809—in the small (18' by 16'), one-room log cabin—was born Abraham Lincoln.

SINKING SPRING FARM ON NOLIN CREEK

Today, the National Park Service invites you to visit Abraham Lincoln's birthplace.

ABRAHAM LINCOLN BIRTHPLACE
NATIONAL HISTORIC SITE
2995 LINCOLN FARM ROAD
HODGENVILLE, KENTUCKY 42748

KENTUCKY

NOLIN CREEK
BIRTH PLACE 1809

On February 12, 1809, Nancy Hanks Lincoln gave birth to a baby boy. She and Tom named him Abraham, for his grandfather.

The proud father notified Betsy and Thomas Sparrow, Nancy's relatives who lived nearby with their nine-year-old foster son Dennis Hanks, Nancy's cousin.

Dennis was excited to have a new playmate. He and Abraham would be close companions for two decades.

Many years later Dennis Hanks recalled Abraham's birth.

"Babies wasn't as common as blackberries in the woods of Kaintucky. Mother come over an' washed him an'... that's all the nuss'n either of 'em got....Well, now, he looked just like any other baby, at fust—like red cherry pulp squeezed dry. An' he didn't improve none as he growed older. Abe never was much fur looks."

1809-11—Young Abraham lived for two years on the Nolin Creek Sinking Spring Farm. Later he remembered nothing of his birthplace, but we can imagine him and his sister Sarah (two years older) playing in the cool water of the sunken, limestone spring—just downhill from their cabin—which gave Sinking Spring Farm its name. (Today, visitors can see the same clear spring, still running.)

In 1809 Kentucky had been a state for only 17 years. Stores were scattered, and so the Lincolns, like other frontier farmers, learned to live resourcefully off their land.

■ <u>Food</u> came from Tom's farming (mostly corn) and hunting (deer, elk, bear) and from wild berries, apples, cherries, hazel nuts, and walnuts.

■ <u>Shelter</u>, a log cabin, was built from white oak and other hardwood trees.

■ <u>Clothing</u> came from flax and wool and skins. The family wore linsey-woolsey clothing, made of linen and wool fibers spun by Nancy, as well as buckskin. Walnut shells served as buttons and, when boiled, as a brown dye.

KNOB CREEK FARM, KENTUCKY, Age 2-7

In 1811, when Abraham was two, the Lincolns moved 10 miles northeast to a more fertile farm on Knob Creek and stayed five years. Thomas Lincoln, Jr. was born here; he died in infancy. Abraham's earliest recollection was of Knob Creek:
"Our farm was composed of three fields which lay in the valley surrounded by high hills and deep gorges...."
The Louisville-Nashville Cumberland Road passed the Lincoln cabin. It offered Abe
a window to the world as he talked to travellers with interesting tales.
By day the family worked; at night they listened to Nancy tell Bible stories; on Sundays they attended Little Mount Baptist Church.

Today, you can visit Lincoln's Knob Creek home and see the fields he helped plant and a replica of his cabin.

ABRAHAM LINCOLN'S BOYHOOD HOME
U.S. 31 E
HODGENVILLE, KY 42748

INDIANA | OHIO
1816 LITTLE PIGEON CREEK
OHIO RIVER
KENTUCKY
KNOB CREEK 1811
NOLIN CREEK BIRTH PLACE 1809

Frontier life was fun, as well as work. Dennis Hanks, Abraham's cousin, recalled, "Abe was right out in the woods, about as soon's he was weaned, fishin' in the crick...goin' on coon hunts with Tom an' me an' the dogs; follerin' up bees to find bee-trees, an' drappin' corn fur his pappy. Mighty interestin' life fur a boy...."

GIT UN BY, FELLERS

Abraham recalled, "My father suffered greatly for want of an education, and he determined at an early date that I should be well educated." "There were some schools, so called; but no qualification was ever required of a teacher, beyond 'readin, writin, and cipherin'....There was absolutely nothing to excite ambition for education." "I went to school by littles"—a little at ages 6, 7, 11, 14, and 17—totaling about a year. All were subscription (tuition) schools run by individual teachers.

ABE AND SARAH NEED TO GO TO SCHOOL AND GIT SOME EDDICATION. THERE'S USE IN KNOWIN' HOW TO SPELL AS WELL AS SHOOT A TURKEY.

YES, TOM. THEY'VE GOT TO LARN ALL THEY KIN AND GIT TO BE OF SOME ACCOUNT.

1815—Abraham never forgot his first teacher, Zachariah Riney, who ran a log schoolhouse two miles from the Knob Creek farm. Like most schools then, it was a blab school: students said their lessons aloud to 1) learn by repetition, and 2) show they were studying, so as to avoid the hickory switch. Abraham said blabbing helped him learn faster by using two senses—seeing and hearing. He read aloud the rest of his life.

A-B-C, BLAB BLAB
FOUR SCORE AND SEVEN...
BLAB BLAB
A,B,C, D.E...
A,B,C, BLAB BLAB!
A,B,C, D,E,F,G...
ABC DEF
ABC DEF
ABC DEF

INDIANA—In 1816, when Abraham was seven, the Lincolns moved 100 miles northwest to Indiana, a two-week journey through thick forests and across the Ohio River. They moved, Lincoln said, "...chiefly on account of the difficulty in land titles in Kentucky and partly on account of slavery." Unlike Kentucky, Indiana was a free state, having been created from the Northwest Territory where the Northwest Ordinance prohibited slavery.

ANDERSON CREEK
INDIANA
OUR HOMESTEAD IS 16 MILES ON UP THE WAY.
OHIO RIVER
KENTUCKY

LITTLE PIGEON CREEK FARM, INDIANA, Age 7-21

1816—The United States was only 40 years old when the Lincolns settled in Indiana on 160 acres of land near Little Pigeon Creek, a 25 square-mile-community scattered with the log cabins of 27 other pioneer families. To encourage settlement of the wilderness frontier, the U.S. government offered pioneers the right to buy land for $2.00 per acre if they would settle and work the land. Tom acquired his land in this way. (By 1820, 40 families had settled within six square miles of the Lincolns; by 1822, within a one-mile radius lived nine families with 49 children.)

On arrival, the Lincolns lived briefly in a three-sided shelter called a "half-face" camp, Then seven-year-old Abraham helped Tom build a 20' by 18' cabin with one room and a loft.

In 1817 the Sparrows and Dennis Hanks moved nearby.

INDIANA

1816 LITTLE PIGEON CREEK

HOPE THEY DON'T FIND MY HONEY TREE

Today, the National Park Service invites you to visit:

LINCOLN BOYHOOD NATIONAL MEMORIAL
LINCOLN CITY, INDIANA 47552

1818—When Abraham was nine, tragedy struck. Nancy died of <u>milk sickness</u> (as had the Sparrows weeks earlier), caused by poisoned milk from cows that ate white snakeroot plants. In what must have been the saddest day of his life, Abraham helped his father build a coffin and bury his mother.

NANCY LINCOLN 1784-1818

1819—The next year Tom (age 41) went to Kentucky to propose to an acquaintance from Elizabethtown: Sally (Sarah) Johnston (age 31), a widow with three children (ages 5, 7, and 9). She declined because she had some debts. Tom paid the debts, and they married December 2.

I HAVE NO WIFE, AND YOU HAVE NO HUSBAND. I CAME A PURPOSE TO MARRY YOU. I KNOWED YOU FROM A GAL, AND YOU KNOWED ME FROM A BOY. I HAVE NO TIME TO LOSE; AND, IF YOU BE WILLIN', LET IT BE DONE STRAIGHT OFF.

1819—Tom returned home with Sally and her children and introduced Abraham (age 10) and Sarah (age 12) to their new family. Abraham's stepmother was a kind, loving person. She made a wonderful home for Tom, their five children, and Dennis Hanks (who had moved in with the Lincolns). Eight people now lived in the 20' by 18' cabin.

AND WE'RE HER YOUNG-UNS: ELIZABETH, JOHN, AND MATILDA.

THIS HERE'S SALLY, YORE NEW MAMMY.

1827—Abraham and his stepmother Sally laughed and joked together and sometimes played tricks on each other. One day she teased him about growing so tall. At age 16, he was 6 feet.

I KIN WASH FOOT-PRINTS OFF THE FLOOR, BUT KEEP YOUR HEAD CLEAN OR YOU'LL MAKE HEADPRINTS ON THE CEILING.

Mischievous Abe had an idea.

ABE!

Years later Sally recalled: "Abe was fond of fun, sport, wit, and jokes....He never drank whisky...was temperate in all things, too much so, I thought sometimes. He never told me a lie...never evaded, never quarreled ....He never swore...." She added:

ABE WAS A GOOD BOY... NEVER GAVE ME A CROSS WORD OR LOOK... HE WAS KIND TO EVERYBODY AND TO EVERYTHING... HIS MIND AND MINE, WHAT I HAD, SEEMED TO RUN TOGETHER — MOVE IN THE SAME CHANNEL.

ABRAHAM LINCOLN: INDIANA SCHOOLDAYS

"Abe could easily learn and long remember....What he learned and stored away was well defined in his own mind, repeated over and over again and again, till it was...fixed...permanently in his memory."—Sally Lincoln

In Indiana Abraham continued going to school by littles.

1820—At age 11, Abraham went for three months to the log cabin school of Andrew Crawford, who taught (in addition to the 3 R's) manners by having students practice introductions.

1826—At age 17, Abraham walked or rode a horse four miles to Azel Dorsey's school. Here he practiced writing a fine, clear script, patterning his handwriting on George Washington's and Thomas Jefferson's. He wrote essays to read in class, including one on cruelty to animals. (After shooting a turkey at age 11, Abraham had resolved never to kill animals.)

Schoolmaster Dorsey held a spelling match every Friday, which Abraham usually won. Once when his friend and rival Katy Roby stumbled on the word "defied," Abraham couldn't resist helping her.

Abraham was good at arithmetic, too. He said: "We had an old dog-eared arithmetic in our house and father determined that somehow, or else, I should cipher clear through that book." Abraham ciphered on a wooden shovel when he had no paper. And sometimes he got carried away!

Logic was extremely important to Abraham. He thought about things until he could make sense of them.

"I remember how when a mere child, I used to get irritated when anybody talked to me in a way I could not understand....I can remember going to my little bedroom, after hearing the neighbors talk of an evening with my father ...trying to make out what was the exact meaning of some of their, to me, dark sayings."

"I could not sleep, although I tried to, when I got on such a hunt for an idea until I had caught it; and when I thought I had got it, I was not satisfied until I had it in language plain enough, as I thought, for any boy I knew to comprehend. This was a kind of passion with me, and it has stuck by me...."

"The things I want to know are in books. My best friend is the man who'll git me a book I ain't read."—Abraham Lincoln, at about age 13
"When I was a boy in Indiana, I borrowed and read every book I could hear of for thirty miles around."—Abraham Lincoln

Once Abraham learned to read, books and newspapers opened a wide, new world for him, transporting him beyond the Indiana frontier. His family owned few books, but he became so hooked on reading he'd walk miles to borrow one. Some books sparked his imagination, some fed his hunger for knowledge and beauty; some taught him public speaking; some made him laugh.

John Bunyan, The Pilgrim's Progress

Daniel Defoe, Robinson Crusoe

Arabian Nights

A.T. Lowe, Columbian Class Book

When Abraham borrowed this book on world geography and history it expanded his knowledge even beyond the planet: it explained the solar system. He tried sharing this new knowledge with pretty Katy Roby, but his timing seemed off.

William Scott, Lessons in Elocution

Abraham learned how to put his message across from this book. He liked public speaking and practiced on folks who gathered at the Gentryville store by imitating preachers and politicians, such as his hero Henry Clay. People said Abraham was a great mimic.

Plutarch, Noble Lives of Ancient Greeks and Romans

Abraham learned virtues—and gained more speaking practice—by imitating ancient orators he admired in Plutarch's Lives.

J. Quinn, Quinn's Jests

Abraham carried this joke book with him constantly. Humorous stories became an important part of his life. Folks would hang around Abraham for hours, listening to him spin funny yarns—at Gentry's store, at cabin raisings, at corn huskings.

Three books—the Bible, Aesop's Fables, and Shakespeare's Dramatic Works—
became Abraham's favorites and shaped his life more than any others.
As a youth he read them over and over, memorizing much of them, and they remained his constant companions as an adult.
Their literary styles—reflecting parable, fable, metaphor, parallelism, cadence, humor—marked his own speech and writing.
Their moral lessons—of honesty, integrity, love, justice, courage, kindness, humility—
taught him about human nature and profoundly influenced his character.

King James Bible

Young Abraham learned moral values from the Bible.

"...WHAT DOTH THE LORD REQUIRE OF THEE, BUT TO DO JUSTLY, AND TO LOVE MERCY, AND TO WALK HUMBLY WITH THY GOD?" MICAH 6:8

1861-65—As president, Abraham kept a Bible on his desk and read it often for guidance and comfort. All his life he read and quoted the Bible. He once said:

IN REGARD TO THIS GREAT BOOK I HAVE BUT TO SAY, IT IS THE BEST GIFT GOD HAS GIVEN TO MEN. ALL THE GOOD SAVIOUR GAVE TO THE WORLD WAS COMMUNICATED THROUGH THIS BOOK. BUT FOR IT WE COULD NOT KNOW RIGHT FROM WRONG.

Abraham's parents were Baptists, but he never joined a church. He couldn't reconcile the bitter rivalry he saw among religious groups with what he read in the Bible: "God is love." He said:

WHEN I FIND A CHURCH WHOSE MAIN DOCTRINE IS THE GOLDEN RULE, I WILL JOIN THAT CHURCH.

GOLDEN RULE
THOU SHALT LOVE THY NEIGHBOR AS THYSELF.

Aesop's Fables (550 B.C.)

Aesop was born a slave in Phrygia, a country in Asia Minor, during the golden age of ancient Greece. His wisdom and skill in writing won him freedom, and he became a philosopher who taught morals and universal truths through fanciful stories.
Young Abraham learned the value of honesty through the fable "THE SHEPHERD-BOY AND THE WOLF."

A shepherd-boy who tended his flock near a village enjoyed fooling people by calling "Wolf, wolf!" when there was no wolf. Then he laughed at those who came to his aid.

HA, HA! THERE'S NO WOLF. I FOOLED YOU AGAIN!

THERE'S NOT A WOLF WITHIN MILES.

HEE! HEE!

One day he cried "Wolf!" in earnest, but no one came. The wolf ate his sheep.
THE MORAL: He who tells lies is not believed, even when he speaks the truth.

WOLF! WOLF!
I'M SERIOUS, GUYS! THIS IS FOR REAL!

POOR STAN'S A GONER

THERE'S A MORAL IN THIS SOMEWHERE.

HEY, THIS IS NO JOKE!

I'M OUTTA HERE.

William Shakespeare, Dramatic Works

In Shakespeare's plays (read while in Indiana in Lessons in Elocution) Abraham discovered the beauty and imagery of words. The English dramatist became his favorite author and Richard III a favorite play.

"NOW IS THE WINTER OF OUR DISCONTENT MADE GLORIOUS SUMMER BY THIS SUN OF YORK..."

MY DISCONTENT IS WITH THIS SUMMER PLOUGHING.

1861-65—As president, Abraham kept Shakespeare's plays on his desk along with the Bible and read both frequently. He identified with Hamlet's fatalism (that what will be, will be). He once said:

I HAVE FOUND ALL MY LIFE, AS HAMLET SAYS, "THERE IS A DIVINITY THAT SHAPES OUR ENDS, ROUGH-HEW THEM HOW WE WILL."

Shakespeare

PRESIDENT

Through books Abraham met the Founding Fathers, and they became his life-long heroes.

Parson Weems, The Life and Memorable Actions of George Washington, 1809

A biography of George Washington by Parson M.L. Weems captivated Abraham. It became his favorite book and inspired his ambition for public service.

1861—As president-elect, Lincoln described to the New Jersey Senate this book's impact on him.

MAY I BE PARDONED IF, ON THIS OCCASION, I MENTION THAT AWAY BACK IN MY CHILDHOOD, THE EARLIEST DAYS OF MY BEING ABLE TO READ, I GOT HOLD OF A SMALL BOOK ... WEEMS' LIFE OF WASHINGTON. I REMEMBER ALL THE ACCOUNTS THERE GIVEN OF THE BATTLE FIELDS AND STRUGGLES FOR THE LIBERTIES OF THE COUNTRY... AND YOU KNOW, FOR YOU HAVE BEEN BOYS, HOW THESE EARLY IMPRESSIONS LAST LONGER THAN OTHERS. I RECOLLECT THINKING ... THAT THERE MUST HAVE BEEN SOMETHING MORE THAN COMMON THAT THOSE MEN STRUGGLED FOR.

Thomas Jefferson, The Declaration of Independence, 1776

1826—Abraham first read the Declaration of Independence at age 17, the year Thomas Jefferson died.

JEFFERSON WROTE THAT EXACTLY 50 YEARS AGO.

1861—Three decades later, President-elect Lincoln described his feelings at Independence Hall in Philadelphia, birthplace of the Declaration of Independence.

I HAVE NEVER HAD A FEELING, POLITICALLY, THAT DID NOT SPRING FROM SENTIMENTS EMBODIED IN THE DECLARATION OF INDEPENDENCE. I HAVE OFTEN PONDERED OVER THE DANGERS WHICH WERE INCURRED BY THE MEN WHO ASSEMBLED HERE AND FRAMED AND ADOPTED THE DECLARATION... I HAVE OFTEN INQUIRED OF MYSELF WHAT GREAT PRINCIPLE OR IDEA IT WAS THAT KEPT THIS CONFEDERACY SO LONG TOGETHER. IT WAS... THAT SENTIMENT IN THE DECLARATION OF INDEPENDENCE WHICH GAVE... PROMISE THAT IN DUE TIME THE WEIGHTS WOULD BE LIFTED FROM THE SHOULDERS OF ALL MEN, AND THAT ALL SHOULD HAVE AN EQUAL CHANCE.

Benjamin Franklin, Autobiography, 1771-89

Abraham often read this book and probably used Franklin's method of self-improvement: a black mark for each fault committed, with the aim of a clean slate. Abe and Ben were alike in many ways.

VIRTUES LIST
TEMPERANCE
SILENCE
ORDER
RESOLUTION
FRUGALITY
INDUSTRY
SINCERITY

1841—Lincoln gave the advice below first to G.E. Pickett, then often repeated it to others.

ALWAYS REMEMBER: FALSEHOOD IS THE WORST ENEMY A FELLOW CAN HAVE. TRUTH IS YOUR TRUEST FRIEND, NO MATTER WHAT THE CIRCUMSTANCES ARE.

"I was raised to farm work, which I continued till I was twenty two."—Abraham Lincoln

And so, Abraham read and read—early in the morning before work and even in the fields while working. According to Sally, "As a usual thing Mr. Lincoln never made Abraham quit reading if he could avoid it." But sometimes Tom's patience wore thin. He and Dennis Hanks didn't understand Abraham's intellectual curiosity.

I NEVER SEE ABE 'AT HE DON'T HAVE A BOOK SOME'ERS 'ROUND. IT DON'T SEEM NATURAL TO SEE A FELLER READ LIKE THAT. THERE'S SOMPEN' PECULIARSOME ABOUT ABE!

FER A BIG, STRAPPIN' FELLER LIKE ABE TO TAKE TO BOOKS IS UNUSUAL!

Despite his reading, from age 8 to 21 Abraham worked hard physically. When not farming, he usually had an ax or a maul in hand—clearing the forest and splitting logs into rails for fences. (He once earned a pair of trousers by splitting 400 rails.) At 18, Abraham was 6'4" and so strong he could do the work of three men with an ax—and perform the amazing feat of holding his ax straight out by the handle.

Tom sometimes hired Abraham out to neighbors for 25 cents-per-day and kept Abraham's wages. This was a customary practice; until age 21 a child's labor and wages legally belonged to his or her parents. But Abraham didn't like work. He said to neighbor John Romine:

MY FATHER TAUGHT ME TO WORK, BUT NOT TO LOVE IT. I NEVER DID LIKE TO WORK, AND I DON'T DENY IT. I'D RATHER READ, TELL STORIES, CRACK JOKES, TALK, LAUGH!

1828: NEW ORLEANS—Abraham saw his first big city at age 19. James Gentry hired him to help his son Allen pole a flatboat of produce down the Ohio and Mississippi Rivers to sell in New Orleans: a 1,200-mile journey. Abraham saw new sights, including black slave markets with people being sold like cattle. (There were 200 slave traders in New Orleans.) Earning $24 for the three-month job, he gave this to Tom.

WE OUGHTA WRITE A BOOK ABOUT THIS ADVENTURE!

YEAH, ABE. WE COULD CALL IT LIFE ON THE MISSISSIPPI.

1830: ILLINOIS—In search of better land and to avoid a new outbreak of milk sickness, Tom once again moved his family, this time to Decatur, Illinois. (Sarah, Abraham's sister, had died in 1828.) Abraham later recalled having to rescue his dog who couldn't make it across an icy stream.

COME BACK, ABE! YOU'RE WASTIN' TIME—IT'S JEST A DOG!

I'M COMIN' LI'L FELLER!

Abraham, now 21, was no longer legally bound to contribute labor and wages to his parents. But he stayed on a year in Decatur to help Tom build a cabin and plant corn. Finally, at age 22, Abraham struck off on his own, moving to New Salem for six years, then to Springfield.

Before following Abraham Lincoln to Illinois, flash-forward to a poem he composed in 1844 on a visit to the Indiana boyhood home he left in 1830.

"In the fall of 1844...I went into the neighborhood in that state in which I was raised, where my mother and only sister were buried, and from which I had been absent about fifteen years. That part of the country is, within itself as unpoetical as any spot of the earth; but still, seeing it and its objects and inhabitants aroused feelings in me which were certainly poetry; though whether my expression of those feelings is poetry is quite another question."—A. Lincoln

MY CHILDHOOD'S HOME
by Abraham Lincoln, 1844

My childhood's home I see again,
    And sadden with the view;
And still, as memory crowds my brain,
    There's pleasure in it too.

O Memory! thou midway world
    'Twixt earth and paradise,
Where things decayed and loved ones lost
    In dreamy shadows rise,

And, freed from all that's earthly vile,
    Seem hallowed, pure, and bright,
Like scenes in some enchanted isle
    All bathed in liquid light.

As dusky mountains please the eye
    When twilight chases day;
As bugle-notes that, passing by,
    In distance die away;

As leaving some grand waterfall,
    We, lingering, list its roar—
So memory will hallow all
    We've known, but know no more.

Near twenty years have passed away
    Since here I bid farewell
To woods and fields, and scenes of play,
    And playmates loved so well.

Where many were, but few remain
    Of old familiar things;
But seeing them, to mind again
    The lost and absent brings.

The friends I left that parting day,
    How changed, as time has sped!
Young childhood grown, strong manhood gray,
    And half of all are dead.

I hear the loved survivors tell
    How nought from death could save,
Till every sound appears a knell,
    And every spot a grave.

I range the fields with pensive tread,
    And pace the hollow rooms,
And feel (companion of the dead)
    I'm living in the tombs.

And now away to seek some scene
    Less painful than the last—
With less of horror mingled in
    The present and the past.

The very spot where grew the bread
    That formed my bones, I see.
How strange, old field, on thee to tread,
    And feel I'm part of thee!

NEW SALEM, Age 22-28

1831—Free now to make his way in the world, Abraham wondered what he would become.
Perhaps a steamboat captain—Mississippi River life, teeming with frontier traffic, intrigued him; perhaps a blacksmith.
But one thing for sure: not a rail-splitting farmer!

As luck would have it, a businessman named Denton Offutt offered him a job clerking in Offutt's store in New Salem,
a frontier village of about 100 people and 25 cabins on a bluff overlooking the Sangamon River.
Entering New Salem, Illinois in 1831 as a self-described "friendless, uneducated, penniless boy," "a piece of floating driftwood,"
Abraham would leave for Springfield in 1837 as a respected lawyer and member of the Illinois legislature.
These six years in New Salem were the most formative of his adult life.

RUFFIANS—New Salem society had three groups: ruffians, intellectuals, and those in between. Abraham first encountered the ruffians: the Clary's Grove boys, who ruled the village. They respected only physical strength; their leader Jack Armstrong earned his rank by outfighting everyone else. Denton Offutt bragged to Bill Clary about his new store clerk Abe Lincoln.

Abraham didn't want to fight, but he had no choice. On Saturday everyone in New Salem came to watch—and bet, mostly on Jack. Jack fought dirty by stomping Abraham's foot. Abraham lifted him, shook him, and threw him in the dust.

The angry Clary's Grove gang rushed Abraham, but he held them back with a dare.

Jack and the gang respectfully acknowledged Abraham as their new leader. They admired him even after they discovered his "strange" traits: he read books; he didn't drink, smoke, or swear; and he was honest. Before Abraham, they considered these sissy traits, but not after Abraham!

intellectual: "one who has an active life of the mind"—Richard Hofstadter
"The way for a young man to rise is to improve himself every way he can...."—Abraham Lincoln
"The ideal college consists of a log of wood with an instructor on one end and a student on the other."—Horace Mann

INTELLECTUALS—Abraham's gift for spinning funny yarns made him popular with most everyone in New Salem. But it took longer to make friends with the intellectuals, for they linked him with the ruffians.

He joined the intellectuals' New Salem Debate Society and surprised them with the force and logic of his first debate. Dr. John Allen said:

THERE'S MORE IN LINCOLN'S HEAD THAN JOKES. HE'S ALREADY A FINE SPEAKER. ALL HE LACKS IS CULTURE.

AND IN CONCLUSION...

MENTOR GRAHAM—Abraham, aware of his "defective" education (as he later called it), asked Mentor Graham, New Salem's outstanding schoolmaster to teach him grammar. Instead of laughing at a grown man wanting to learn grammar, Graham encouraged Abraham.

MENTOR, I'M IGNORANT ABOUT GRAMMAR. I'D REALLY LIKE TO LEARN IT.

GOOD! THERE IS NOTHING MORE IMPORTANT THAN GRAMMAR TO ENABLE YOU TO THINK. MEN WHO MASTER TWO THINGS: CONSTRUCTIVE THOUGHT AND CONVINCING EXPRESSION OF IT CAN BE PUBLIC MEN WHO MOVE THE HUMAN RACE FORWARD.

Mentor Graham said English Grammar (1828) by Samuel Kirkham was the best textbook, so Abraham walked eight miles to borrow a copy. Sections on parts of speech, punctuation, diagramming, eloquent word order, public speaking, good writing, and provincialisms were interspersed with morals—such as "A good man is a great man." (This exceptional textbook helped several generations of students write and speak well.)

And so 24-year-old Abraham studied with 33-year-old Mentor Graham—on a log in the woods, in the teacher's school with other students (including Abraham's good friend Ann Rutledge), and in Graham's home.

READ ALOUD WHEN YOU ARE ALONE. PUT THE BOOK AWAY AND WRITE OUT YOUR OWN STATEMENT OF WHAT YOU HAVE READ. DID YOU GET ALL OF IT? LOOK BACK AND SEE.

VERB - A WORD WHICH SIGNIFIES TO BE, TO DO, OR TO SUFFER

OR, TO CROAK!

PROVINCIALISMS—Abraham worked hard to rid himself of frontier speech patterns. (However, all his life he said "git" and "thar.")

I BE GOING. - I AM GOING.

TAIN'T NO BETTER THAN HIZZEN. - 'TIS NO BETTER THAN HIS.

IZZENT THAT LINE WRIT WELL? - IS NOT THAT LINE WELL-WRITTEN?

'TIS?

Years later, Graham wrote: "When Lincoln came into our house that first time, he walked straight to my bookshelves and straight to my heart. For about six months he was my scholar and I was his teacher.

"I have taught in my life [4,000] pupils and no one has ever surpassed him in rapidly acquiring the rules of English grammar.

I have known him to study for hours the best way of three to express an idea.

WHY, COME ON IN LINC...?

1861—When Lincoln was inaugurated President of the United States, Mentor Graham sat on the platform. The master teacher must have been proud of his pupil's eloquent speech: moving the human race forward through "constructive thought and convincing expression."

THOUGH PASSION MAY HAVE STRAINED, IT MUST NOT BREAK OUR BONDS OF AFFECTION. THE MYSTIC CHORDS OF MEMORY, STRETCHING FROM EVERY BATTLE-FIELD AND PATRIOT GRAVE TO EVERY LIVING HEART AND HEARTHSTONE, ALL OVER THIS BROAD LAND, WILL YET SWELL THE CHORUS OF THE UNION, WHEN AGAIN TOUCHED, AS SURELY THEY WILL BE, BY THE BETTER ANGELS OF OUR NATURE.

Every man is said to have his peculiar ambition....I have no other so great as that of being truly esteemed of my fellow men."—Abraham Lincoln, 1832 election speech

In March 1832 Abraham decided to run for the Illinois House of Representatives. Why not? Offut's store had failed, and he was out of a job; George Washington's life inspired him toward public service; he kept up with politics through the newspapers; he liked people and people liked him. He based his campaign on Whig party principles, stated in his announcement speech.

Fellow citizens,
I presume you all know who I am. I am humble Abraham Lincoln. I have been solicited by many friends to become a candidate for the legislature. My politics are short and sweet, like the old woman's dance. I am in favor of a national bank, internal improvements, and a high protective tariff. These are my sentiments and political principles. If elected I shall be thankful; if not it will be all the same.

The Black Hawk War interrupted Abraham's campaign. He enlisted for 90 days of militia service in a war against Chief Black Hawk and 500 Sac and Fox Indians, who tried to reclaim the Illinois homeland they had signed away by treaty in 1831. Chief Black Hawk claimed:

LAND CANNOT BE SOLD. NOTHING CAN BE SOLD BUT SUCH THINGS AS CAN BE CARRIED AWAY.

Abraham's company—mostly New Salem men, including the Clary Grove boys—elected him captain by lining up behind him, an honor he said gave him more pleasure than any he ever had. But respect didn't mean obedience.

ALL RIGHT, MEN—LINE UP STRAIGHT AND STAY IN STEP!

GO TO THE DEVIL, SIR!

In his first and only military service, Abe had a lot to learn. One day, marching his men 20-abreast toward a gate, he forgot the command for a single-file column. His quick wit came to the rescue.

THIS COMPANY IS DISMISSED FOR TWO MINUTES, WHEN IT WILL FALL IN AGAIN ON THE OTHER SIDE OF THE GATE.

The capture of Black Hawk brought a quick end to the war. Abraham, having seen only one Indian (whose life he saved) and having battled only mosquitoes, returned home to battle for his legislative candidacy, to no avail.

WELL, ABE LOST THE ELECTION. SPENT TOO MUCH TIME IN THE WAR. DIDN'T CAMPAIGN ENOUGH.

YES, BUT HE DID WELL IN NEW SALEM — 277 OF 300 VOTES!

In 1834 Abraham <u>did win</u> election to the Illinois House of Representatives, as a Whig. He set a high standard for campaigning. After hitching a ride to a political rally with his opponent, he ended his speech by telling the audience:

I AM TOO POOR TO OWN A CARRIAGE, BUT MY FRIEND HAS GENEROUSLY INVITED ME TO RIDE WITH HIM. I WANT YOU TO VOTE FOR ME IF YOU WILL, BUT IF NOT THEN VOTE FOR MY OPPONENT, FOR HE IS A FINE MAN.

AND I HAVE TO LISTEN TO <u>BOTH</u> OF THEM—ALL DAY!

THE LONG NINE—Abraham won reelection in 1836, 1838, and 1840 and served with distinction. In 1836 he became Whig leader in the House and, along with the "Long Nine" legislators (all 6' plus) from Sangamon County, masterminded moving the capital from Vandalia to Springfield. Abraham liked being a politician and was proud to be one.

MR. LINCOLN, MAY I JOIN YOUR FACTION?

WELL, LET'S SEE HOW YOU MEASURE UP.

ILLINOIS LEGISLATURE

"I planted myself upon the truth and the truth only, so far as I knew it, or could be brought to know it."—Abraham Lincoln, 1858

"...some things legally right are not morally right."—Abraham Lincoln, 1848

How did Abraham—a self-educated backwoodsman—become such a successful state politician? As he said in 1832, "I have no wealthy or popular relation to recommend me." William Herndon, his law partner from 1844 to 1865, pointed to his virtues, chief of which was honesty. Abraham developed such a strong reputation for honesty that in the 1860 presidential election he ran as "Honest Abe."

1832: STORE CLERK—Abraham's reputation for honesty began in New Salem. As a clerk in Offutt's store, he once walked six miles to correct an error of a few pennies.

1833: MERCHANT—After the Black Hawk War Abraham bought a store (on credit) in partnership with William Berry. Neither partner had a talent for business. Berry drank up the profits in whiskey, and Abraham read. Within months, Abraham said, the store "winked out."

Berry soon died, leaving Abraham with the store's entire debt: $1,100. Instead of skipping town, a common frontier practice, Abraham asked his creditors for time to pay the debt. As a congressman in 1847, he was still making payments.

1833: POSTMASTER—Fortunately, Abraham found work as a surveyor (Graham helped him learn surveying) and New Salem postmaster. Infrequently a postal agent came to collect the postage money.

In 1837 Abraham moved to Springfield—nearly penniless but with $17 of uncollected postage money. He could have borrowed and repaid this fund; no one would have known. But he did not.

1837: LAWYER—Abraham was ambitious: by 1834 he wanted more than anything to be a lawyer. He feared his lack of education meant he didn't have enough sense to be one. But encouraged by Springfield lawyer John Stuart, he borrowed law books, studied three years on his own, and earned his law license in 1837. A curious incident spurred him on.

Abraham advised honesty in these 1850 notes for a law lecture:

There is a vague popular belief that lawyers are necessarily dishonest....Let no young man choosing the law for a calling for a moment yield to the popular belief—resolve to be honest at all events; and if in your own judgment you cannot be an honest lawyer, resolve to be honest without being a lawyer.

1835-49: POLITICIAN—During eight years as an Illinois legislator and two years as a U.S. congressman, Abraham set a high standard for honesty. After one election he returned $199.25 of the $200 donors had contributed to his campaign.

"I had studied law and removed to Springfield to practice it." —Abraham Lincoln

SPRINGFIELD, ILLINOIS, AGE 28-57

In April 1837 Abraham moved to Springfield to begin his law practice with John Stuart and continue serving in the Illinois legislature. Springfield, population 2,000 (a big city compared to New Salem), was the new capital, owing largely to Abraham's legislative influence.

Abraham rode into Springfield on a borrowed horse with all his belongings in two saddle bags and a total wealth of $7.00.

Unlike his entry into New Salem six years earlier, however, he now had a profession and a direction in life.

For two-and-a-half decades he would successfully practice law—with John Stuart until 1841, Stephen Logan until 1844, and William (Billy) Herndon until 1861.

> SO THIS IS SPRINGFIELD! NOW, WHERE'S THE FEED STORE?

Abraham found lodging with <u>Joshua Speed</u>, a young merchant who liked Abe so much on first meeting, he invited the new arrival to share the quarters above his store. They lived together four years, and Speed became the closest friend Abraham ever had.

> WHY DON'T YOU JUST MOVE IN HERE WITH ME?

Merchants and politicians gathered at Speed's store to spin yarns and argue politics. Lincoln, a Whig favoring a strong central government, argued most with fellow legislator <u>Stephen A. Douglas</u>, a states' rights Democrat. They would be rivals for 20 years.

> SO, LINCOLN— YOU'VE STATED YOUR WHIG VIEWS. NOW LET ME SET YOU STRAIGHT! HERE'S HOW WE DEMOCRATS VIEW THINGS.

Despite new friendships, Abraham was lonely. He missed Ann Rutledge, a New Salem friend whose death in 1835 had saddened him.

ANN RUTLEDGE d. 1835

May, 1837—After a month in Springfield Abraham tried to escape a current romance. In 1836 he had impulsively proposed to Mary Owens, a New Salem visitor from Kentucky. He soon regretted proposing but felt honor bound to keep his word.

Friend Mary,

There is a great deal of flourishing about in carriages here, which it would be your doom to see without sharing in it. You would have to be poor without the means of hiding your poverty. Do you believe you could bear that patiently? What I have said I will positively abide by, provided you wish it. My opinion is you better not do it.

Yours, etc.
Lincoln

Abraham soon wrote again, saying: "If it suits you better not to answer this—farewell—a long life and a merry one attend you." To his surprise Mary <u>did</u> reject him, and Abraham unexpectedly found his pride wounded. He wrote his friend Mrs. O.H. Browning in 1838:

She whom I [believed] nobody else would have, had actually rejected me with all my fancied greatness. And to cap the whole, I then for the first time began to suspect that I was really a little in love with her.... Others have been made fools of by the girls; but this can never with truth be said of me. I most emphatically, made a fool of myself. I have now come to the conclusion never again to think of marrying.

⊰ ABRAHAM LINCOLN: MARY TODD LINCOLN, 1818-1882 ⊱

"I warned Mary that she and Mr. Lincoln were not suitable....they were different in nature, and education and raising. They had no feelings alike. They were so different that they could not live happily as man and wife."—Elizabeth Todd Edwards, sister of Mary Todd

Abraham's resolve not to marry couldn't withstand the blue-eyed charms of saucy, aristocratic, Mary Todd (5'2"), the well-educated granddaughter of Levi Todd, who helped found Kentucky. In 1839, at age 21, Mary moved to Springfield from Lexington, Kentucky, to live with her sister and brother-in-law Elizabeth and Ninian Edwards. Ninian was a respected legislator, and the Edwards were among Springfield's social elite.

1839—Joshua Speed brought Abraham to a party at the Edwards' mansion, and cupid struck.

> I'VE BEEN WANTIN' TO DANCE WITH YOU IN THE WORST WAY.

> AND YOU ARE!

Abraham found that Stephen Douglas—his Democratic political rival, known as the "Little Giant" (5'4")—also was his romantic rival. Whom would Mary choose?

Elizabeth said of her sister: "Mary loved show and power, and was the most ambitious woman I ever knew. She used to contend when a girl, to her friends in Kentucky, that she was destined to marry a president, and in Springfield she repeated the absurd boast."

> MRS. PRESIDENT???

1840—Far-sighted Mary chose Abraham. (In 1858 Douglas would defeat Lincoln in the senate race, but in 1860 Lincoln would defeat Douglas in the presidential race.) Abraham and Mary became engaged, but things did not seem right to Elizabeth, who observed:

"Mary invariably led the conversation. Mr. Lincoln would sit at her side and listen. He scarcely said a word, but gazed on her as if irresistibly drawn towards her by some superior and unseen power."

Abraham soon realized he'd made a mistake. He wrote Mary that he did not love her enough to warrant her marrying him. He asked Speed to deliver the letter, but Speed tossed it in the fire, saying:

> IF YOU HAVE THE COURAGE OF MANHOOD, GO SEE MARY BY YOURSELF. TELL HER THE FACTS: YOU DO NOT LOVE HER AND YOU WILL NOT MARRY HER. BE CAREFUL NOT TO SAY TOO MUCH, AND THEN LEAVE AT YOUR EARLIEST OPPORTUNITY.

Abraham tried to break the engagement, but when he told Mary he didn't love her, she burst into tears. Abraham reported his reaction to Speed.

> TO TELL YOU THE TRUTH, SPEED, IT WAS TOO MUCH FOR ME. I FOUND THE TEARS TRICKLING DOWN MY OWN CHEEKS. I CAUGHT HER IN MY ARMS AND KISSED HER.

> AND THAT'S HOW YOU BROKE YOUR ENGAGEMENT? YOUR CONDUCT AMOUNTS TO A RENEWAL OF THE ENGAGEMENT, AND IN DECENCY YOU CANNOT BACK DOWN NOW

January 1, 1841—

On what Abraham called the "fatal first," he did break his engagement to Mary. He then experienced such a deep depression that friends feared he would take his life.

He recovered and a year later renewed his relationship with Mary.

On November 4, 1842, in a ceremony at the Edwards' home, Abraham Lincoln married Mary Todd.

A week later Lincoln ended a business letter to a client with the news:

"Nothing new here, except my marrying, which to me is a matter of profound wonder."

FAMILY ALBUM—In 1844, after 18 months in a boarding house, Abraham and Mary moved to a nice home at 8th and Jackson Streets and lived there until 1861. They shared a deep love of their children, only one of whom would grow to adulthood. (Willie and Tad would be the first presidential children to live in the White House.) Mary called Abraham "Mr. Lincoln". He called her "Mother."

- **Robert** (1843-1926), a Harvard graduate, became a successful lawyer, statesman (secretary of war, minister to Great Britain) and businessman (president, Pullman Company). In 1875 he had Mary committed to a mental institution, where she stayed for four months.
- **Eddie** (Edward, 1846-50) died at age four in Springfield.
- **Willie** (William, 1850-1862) was the child most like Abraham. His death in the White House at age 11 devastated Abraham and drove Mary to the brink of mental illness.
- **Tad** (Thomas, 1853-1871), a hyperactive child and a slow learner, did not read until age nine. (Abraham urged his tutors not to rush him.) Fun-loving and full of pranks, Tad enjoyed life in the White House perhaps more than any person. He died in Chicago at age 18.

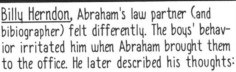

ROBERT · WILLIE · TAD

Both parents indulged the children, and Abraham admitted that they never controlled them. He said:

> IT IS MY PLEASURE THAT MY CHILDREN ARE FREE, HAPPY, AND UNRESTRAINED BY PARENTAL TYRANNY.

Billy Herndon, Abraham's law partner (and bibiographer) felt differently. The boys' behavior irritated him when Abraham brought them to the office. He later described his thoughts:

> I'D LIKE TO WRING THE NECKS OF THOSE BRATS AND PITCH THEM OUT THE WINDOW.

Abraham himself was none too neat at the office, as evidenced by a littered desk and orange seeds sprouting in dusty corners. Absent-minded, he kept up with papers by filing them in his hat, and he had a bundle marked: "When you can't find it anywhere else, look here.

> HEY, BILLY! THAT DEED I LOST? IT WAS RIGHT HERE IN MY HAT!

> GOOD GRIEF!

At home, neither Abraham nor Mary proved easy to live with. Abraham read on the floor—aloud—and answered the door in his socks. Mary had temper tantrums, loud enough for neighbors to hear. When she exploded, Abraham simply would leave the house.

> MR. LINCOLN! WHY ARE YOU SO DISORDERLY?!

> NOW, MOTHER! TEMPER, TEMPER!

> HE ALWAYS DOES.

> HE'LL LEAVE THE HOUSE SOON!

Mary did not mix with her in-laws. Remarkably, neither she nor the children ever met Abraham's parents, who lived 90 miles away in Charleston. (Mary wrote Sally only once, in 1867, saying that Tad was named for Abraham's father.) Abraham visited Tom and Sally alone and infrequently, mostly to see his beloved stepmother. He helped Tom financially but was estranged from him.

In 1851 Tom Lincoln lay dying, but Abraham did not visit him because Mary was ill. He wrote John Johnston, his stepbrother:

> SAY TO MY FATHER THAT IF WE COULD MEET NOW IT IS DOUBTFUL WHETHER IT WOULD NOT BE MORE PAINFUL THAN PLEASANT.

Abe did not attend his father's funeral.

Abraham Lincoln practiced law in Springfield for 24 years. Starting out as a self-taught beginner in 1837, he became one of the most sought-after, respected trial lawyers in Illinois. He was successful, prosperous, and well-liked.

HOW DID HE DO IT?

RESOLUTION: In 1855 Abraham shared his key to success with Isham Reavis, an aspiring young lawyer. In the 1990s his words to Reavis continue to inspire students.

FOR A FIRST YEAR LAW STUDENT, YOU SEEM AWFULLY CHEERFUL.

I REMEMBER LINCOLN'S WORDS: "IF YOU ARE RESOLUTELY DETERMINED TO BE A LAWYER, THE THING IS HALF-DONE. YOUR OWN RESOLUTION TO SUCCEED IS MORE IMPORTANT THAN ANY OTHER THING."

CLASS OF 1997

LAW SCHOOL

SELF-RELIANCE—Abraham told Reavis: "It is but a small matter if you read [law] with anybody or not. I did not read with anyone. Get the books, and read... them til you understand them...that is the main thing.

"It is of no consequence to be in a large town while you are reading. I read at New Salem, which never had 300 people.... The books, and your capacity for understanding them, are just the same in all places."

(SIGH) WONDER WHAT'S ON THE "TUBE"?

CAN'T STUDY LAW THROUGH SOUND BITES. REMEMBER, LINCOLN SAID WE'VE GOT TO READ THESE BOOKS 'TILL WE UNDERSTAND THEM.

CLASS OF 1997

CASES   LAW

HONESTY—When Abraham thought fees collected by his partner were too high, he rejected his half until they had been reduced. This practice attracted grateful clients but irritated a judge who heard about it.

LINCOLN! YOUR CHEAP FEES WILL IMPOVERISH ALL LAWYERS.

TEMPERANCE—Abraham explained to his law partner Billy Herndon, a habitual drinker, why he did not use alcohol.

NO, BILLY. I HATE THE STUFF. IT ENFEEBLES MY MIND.

CLEAR, CONCISE LANGUAGE—Abraham spoke with such logic and clarity that jurors and judges alike—whether uneducated or learned—listened and understood him.

THAT ABE SURE HAS A KNACK FOR PLAIN TALK.

YEP. HE MAKES EVERY POINT CRYSTAL CLEAR.

JOKES AND STORYTELLING— "They say I tell a great many stories," Abraham said; "I reckon I do, but I have found...that common people...are more easily informed through the medium of a broad illustration than in any other way."

A county clerk recalled being fined by Judge David Davis for cracking up over a joke Lincoln whispered to him.

MR. LINCOLN, THIS MUST BE STOPPED. YOU ARE CONSTANTLY DISTURBING THIS COURT WITH YOUR STORIES. I'M FINING THIS LAW CLERK $5.00.

THE STORY'S WORTH THE FINE.

THE JUDGE ALWAYS WANTS TO HEAR THE STORY LATER.

RESPECT FOR THE LAW—Abraham's success was rooted in his firm belief in rule by law. In an 1838 address protesting mob violence, he said:

Let every American, every lover of liberty...swear by the blood of the Revolution, never to violate...the laws of the country; and never to tolerate their violation by others....let every man remember that to violate the law, is to trample on the blood of his father....

Let reverence for the laws...be taught in school...preached from the pulpit, proclaimed in legislative halls, and enforced in courts of justice. And, in short, let it become the political religion of the nation....Let me not be understood as saying there are no bad laws....I mean to say no such thing. But I do mean to say, that, although bad laws...should be repealed as soon as possible, still while they continue in force, for the sake of example, they should be religiously observed.

Washington, D.C.—In 1847 Lincoln won election as a Whig to the U.S. House of Representatives. He served one term.

In Congress Lincoln took an unpopular stance by opposing the Mexican-American War and challenging <u>President James Polk</u> to prove he had not unconstitutionally started the war. Polk ignored him.

> LET PRESIDENT POLK ANSWER WITH FACTS, AND NOT WITH ARGUMENTS. LET HIM REMEMBER HE SITS WHERE WASHINGTON SAT, AND SO REMEMBERING, LET HIM ANSWER, AS WASHINGTON WOULD ANSWER.

Back home in Illinois people who supported the Mexican-American War accused Lincoln of being unpatriotic. Even Billy Herndon did. Abraham wrote Herndon that the Constitution gave war-making powers to Congress—<u>not</u> the president—and for good reasons.

> Dear Billy,
> ...Kings had always been involving and impoverishing their people in wars, pretending...that the good of the people was the object...[The Founding Fathers] resolved to so frame the Constitution that <u>no one man</u> should hold the power of bringing this oppression upon us. But your view destroys the whole matter and places our president where kings have always stood.
>
> A. Lincoln

Billy Herndon

1849—After a disappointing term Lincoln returned home feeling he had accomplished little in Congress, where the dominating issue was extension of slavery into the new western territories acquired by the Mexican-American War.

He had: 1) supported the Wilmot Proviso prohibiting extension of slavery into the new territoris, but it failed to pass;
2) failed to gain support for his proposed bill to prohibit slavery in Washington, D.C.;
3) failed to win recognition in the national Whig party.

1849-54: SPRINGFIELD, ILLINOIS—Convinced he had no future in politics, Lincoln resumed practicing law in Springfield and in the Eighth Judicial District circuit courts, to which he and other lawyers travelled for six months of the year.

> YOU'RE STUDYING EUCLID'S GEOMETRY? WHY ON EARTH, ABE?

> WELL, IT HELPS ME SHARPEN MY LOGIC FOR THE COURT ROOM.

> THAT ABE'S A SMART THINKER. HE OUGHTA BE PRESIDENT.

EIGHTH JUDICIAL DISTRICT, WHERE LINCOLN PRACTISED LAW IN CIRCUIT COURTS

Springfield

In 1854 the KANSAS-NEBRASKA ACT caused Lincoln to reenter national politics, determined to stop the spread of slavery. He was 'thunderstruck" by this act, which legalized slavery in an area protected from slavery since 1820 by the Missouri Compromise.

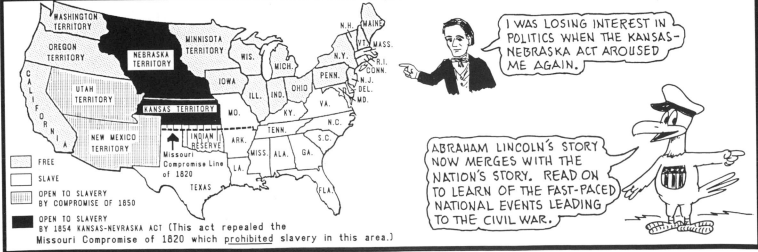

> I WAS LOSING INTEREST IN POLITICS WHEN THE KANSAS-NEBRASKA ACT AROUSED ME AGAIN.

> ABRAHAM LINCOLN'S STORY NOW MERGES WITH THE NATION'S STORY. READ ON TO LEARN OF THE FAST-PACED NATIONAL EVENTS LEADING TO THE CIVIL WAR.

FREE

SLAVE

OPEN TO SLAVERY BY COMPROMISE OF 1850

OPEN TO SLAVERY BY 1854 KANSAS-NEVRASKA ACT (This act repealed the Missouri Compromise of 1820 which <u>prohibited</u> slavery in this area.)

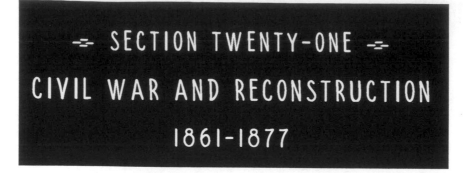

SECTION TWENTY-ONE
CIVIL WAR AND RECONSTRUCTION
1861-1877

"War is a terrible thing."—General William Tecumseh Sherman

1492   1861-77   2000

"...that strange, sad war...."—Walt Whitman

Lincoln's story merges with events leading up to the Civil War. Before exploring those events, here is an overview of the causes of the war, all of which add up to a conflict of interests between the North and South. Ironically, <u>James Madison</u> saw the heart of the problem during the Constitutional Convention. He wrote in 1787:

"It seemed now to be pretty well understood that the real <u>difference of interests</u> lay not between the large and small but between the the Northern and Southern states. The institution of slavery and its consequences formed a line of discrimination."

Sure enough, from 1850 to 1861 the "difference of interests" between the slave-holding South and the free North escalated into tragic consequences: the American Civil War, also called the War Between the States.

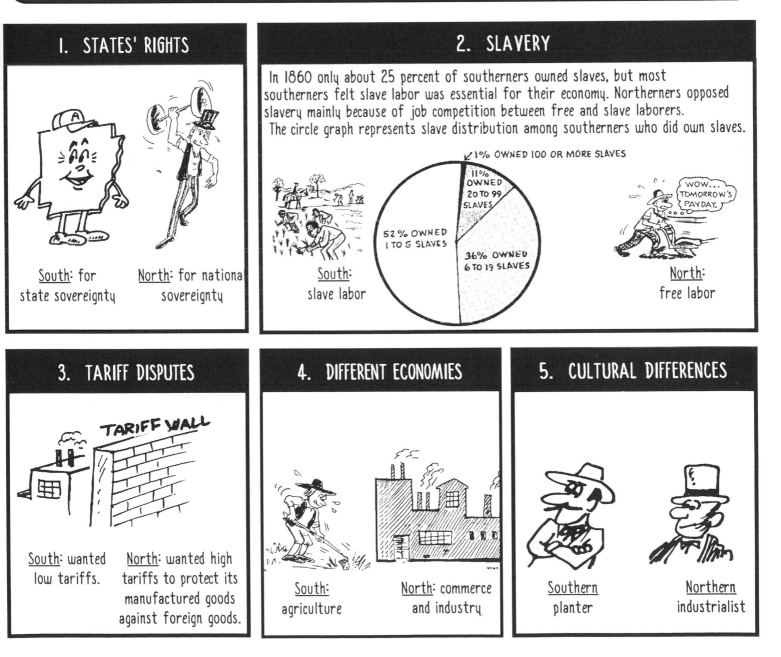

1. STATES' RIGHTS

<u>South</u>: for state sovereignty   <u>North</u>: for national sovereignty

2. SLAVERY

In 1860 only about 25 percent of southerners owned slaves, but most southerners felt slave labor was essential for their economy. Northerners opposed slavery mainly because of job competition between free and slave laborers.
The circle graph represents slave distribution among southerners who did own slaves.

↙1% OWNED 100 OR MORE SLAVES

11% OWNED 20 TO 99 SLAVES

52% OWNED 1 TO 5 SLAVES

36% OWNED 6 TO 19 SLAVES

<u>South</u>: slave labor

WOW... TOMORROW'S PAYDAY.

<u>North</u>: free labor

3. TARIFF DISPUTES

TARIFF WALL

<u>South</u>: wanted low tariffs.   <u>North</u>: wanted high tariffs to protect its manufactured goods against foreign goods.

4. DIFFERENT ECONOMIES

<u>South</u>: agriculture   <u>North</u>: commerce and industry

5. CULTURAL DIFFERENCES

<u>Southern</u> planter   <u>Northern</u> industrialist

1850	1852	1854	1857	1858	1859	1860	1861
Compromise of 1850	Uncle Tom's Cabin by Harriet B. Stowe	Kansas-Nebraska Act	Dred Scott Decision		Harper's Ferry	Lincoln elected president	11 Southern states form Confederacy
		Republican Party forms		Lincoln—Douglas Debates	South Carolina secedes		Civil War starts

As you read the events in this decade of conflict, imagine how you would have handled the "difference of interests" of the North and South. How would you have distinguished between facts and opinions?

1852—UNCLE TOM'S CABIN, Harriet Beecher Stowe's novel dramatizing the cruelties of slavery, touched readers emotionally and created widespread antislavery support among northerners. One of the most influential books ever written, it sold 300,000 copies the the first year. Uncle Tom's Cabin was perceived differently by:

NORTHERNERS

"WHAT A HORRIBLY CRUEL SYSTEM! THOSE AWFUL SLAVEHOLDERS!"

SOUTHERNERS

"WHAT KINDA' YANKEE ABOLITIONIST PROPAGANDA IS THIS?"

1854: KANSAS-NEBRASKA ACT—This act, which so angered Lincoln, was proposed by Illinois Senator Stephen A. Douglas, a northern Democrat courting favor with southern Democrats. It allowed the Kansas and Nebraska territories popular sovereignty (the right to decide for themselves) about slavery. The act pleased southerners but outraged many northerners because it repealed the 1820 Missouri Compromise, which had prohibited slavery in this area by declaring forever free the Louisiana Purchase north of the line 36° 30" (except Missouri).

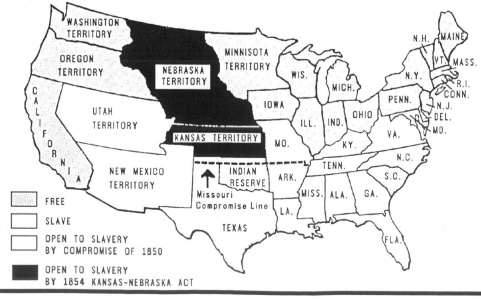

FREE

SLAVE

OPEN TO SLAVERY BY COMPROMISE OF 1850

OPEN TO SLAVERY BY 1854 KANSAS-NEBRASKA ACT

1856: BLEEDING KANSAS—Popular sovereignty caused a small scale civil war in Kansas which lasted four months and caused 200 deaths. Armed combat raged between proslavery settlers, mostly Missouri immigrants, and antislavery settlers, mostly New England immigrants financed by New England abolitionist Eli Thayer's Emigrant Aid Society and led by John Brown. Kansas eventually became a free state (1861).

The Kansas conflict of 1856 proved a dark forecast of things to come.

1856: BIRTH OF THE REPUBLICAN PARTY—(formed locally in 1854)

For the first time, sectional political parties developed as North and South divided over the slavery issue.

■ The Republican party was created by northerners committed to stop expansion of slavery into the territories. It drew antislavery people from several parties, including Whig, Democratic, Free Soil, and American (a secret, anti-Catholic party nicknamed "Know Nothing").

■ The Democratic party split into northern and southern factions.

■ The Whig party died as northern Whigs joined the Republican party, and southern Whigs joined the Democrats.

> IF YOU'RE A 1990s REPUBLICAN, HERE'S WHERE YOU GOT YOUR START!

1856: ABRAHAM LINCOLN JOINS THE REPUBLICAN PARTY—

Lincoln, an outstanding Whig politician in Illinois, reluctantly switched parties to stop the spread of slavery.

> I HEAR LINCOLN'S INSIDE — SWITCHING FROM THE WHIGS TO THE REPUBLICANS.

> YEP – SAYS HE'S "UN-WHIGGING."

ILLINOIS REPUBLICAN PARTY HDQS.

BOSS

1857: DRED SCOTT DECISION—

Dred Scott, a Missouri slave, sued for his freedom after briefly living with his owner on free soil in the North. Shock waves jolted the nation when Supreme Court Chief Justice Roger Taney ruled that:

1) Slaves were not citizens, so they could not bring suit in court.
2) Slaves were property.
3) Because the 5th Amendment protected property, and slaves were property, Congress could not ban slavery from the territories.
4) The Missouri Compromise, which had banned slavery, was unconstitutional.

Southerners were overjoyed at the ruling. Northerners were dismayed and began joining the Republican party in droves.

1858: LINCOLN-DOUGLAS DEBATES—

In the Illinois senate race Republican Abraham Lincoln and Democrat Stephen A. Douglas debated the slavery issue in seven cities. Crowds of 12,000 heard Lincoln describe his position as antislavery but not abolitionist: Slavery was wrong but legal, being protected by the Constitution. Slavery, therefore, could not be abolished where it existed; but it should not be expanded. Douglas won the senate race, but Lincoln won national attention as a rising political star.

• DEBATE SITES

• FREEPORT
• OTTAWA
GALESBURG
☆ SPRINGFIELD
• QUINCY
CHARLESTON
• ALTON
JONESBORO

> WHEN HE INVITES ANY PEOPLE WILLINGLY TO ESTABLISH SLAVERY, HE IS BLOWING OUT THE MORAL LIGHTS AROUND US.

1859: HARPER'S FERRY—

Fanatical abolitionist John Brown and his followers seized the federal arsenal at Harper's Ferry, Virginia. They hoped to stir a slave revolt in Virginia and end slavery.

Captured and executed, Brown became a martyred hero for many northerners.

"At your request, I'll be perfectly frank. The taste [of the presidency] is in my mouth a little."—Abraham Lincoln

242

November 1860: <u>Charleston, South Carolina</u>—Lincoln's election as president convinced South Carolina the North was "abolition-crazed" and would destroy the South's way of life.

THAT DOES IT! WE'RE LEAVING THE UNION!

LINCOLN WINS

SOUTH CAROLINA

December 20, 1860—South Carolina seceded from the Union and urged other southern states to follow.

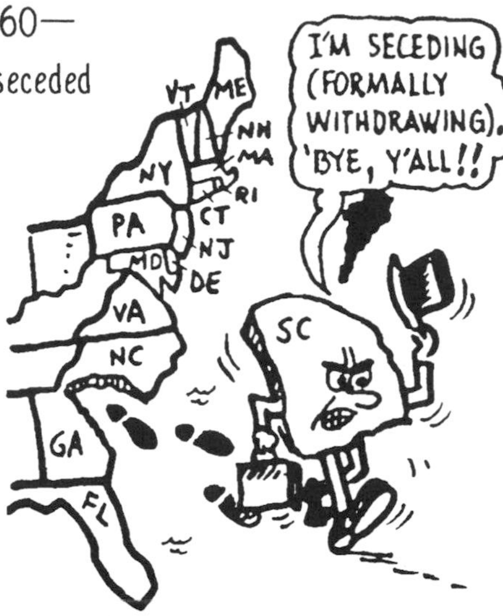

I'M SECEDING (FORMALLY WITHDRAWING). 'BYE, Y'ALL!!

THE CONFEDERATE STATES OF AMERICA

February 4, 1861: <u>Montgomery, Alabama</u>—Six other southern states seceded. Along with South Carolina, they formed a new government under the name CONFEDERATE STATES OF AMERICA. They wrote a constitution and elected officials. <u>Jefferson Davis</u> of Mississippi was elected president. A West Point graduate, he had served the United States as a colonel in the Mexican War, a congressman, and secretary of war.

Constitution of the Confederate States of America

PRESIDENT JEFFERSON DAVIS

The Confederate Constitution was similar to that of the United States but differed in: 1) establishing state sovereignty, 2) protecting slavery in states and territories, 3) banning protective tariffs, and 4) limiting the president to one six-year term.

April 12, 1861—CIVIL WAR began when the new Confederate army fired on Fort Sumter, a federal fort in Charleston, South Carolina. When President Lincoln requested troops from the states, four more southern states seceded.

OL' ABE MUST BE KIDDING.

WE'RE NOT GOING TO FIGHT OUR SISTER STATES.

GOVERNOR

May 29, 1861—Eleven states now formed the Confederacy. After Virginia seceded, the Confederate Congress voted to move its capital to Richmond, Virginia. Had you been a southerner at this time, would you have voted for secession? What factors would have influenced your decision?

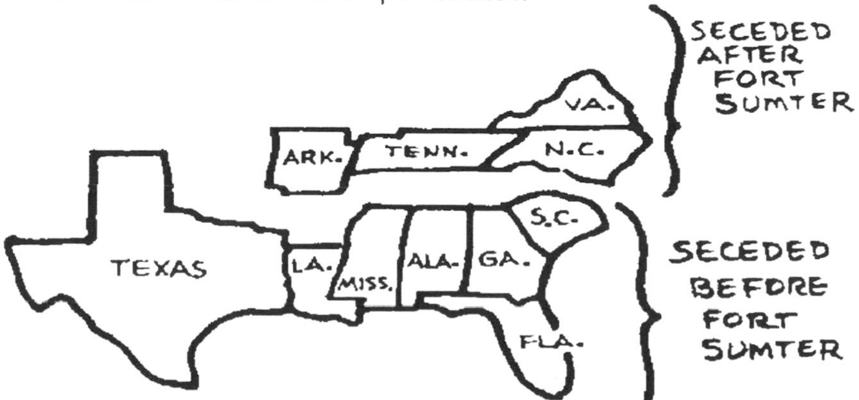

SECEDED AFTER FORT SUMTER

SECEDED BEFORE FORT SUMTER

VA. ARK. TENN. N.C. S.C. TEXAS LA. MISS. ALA. GA. FLA.

"Secession! Peaceable secession! Sir, your eyes and mine are never destined to see that miracle."—Daniel Webster, 1850

March 4, 1861: LINCOLN'S FIRST INAUGURAL—Abraham Lincoln took off his new top hat and searched for a place to put it. Stephen Douglas, his old rival, took the hat and whispered to Mary Lincoln, "If I can't be president, I can at least hold his hat."

Southern secession had created a crisis. Of 34 states formerly in the Union, Lincoln presided over only 27.
What would he do? Declare war? Accept secession and let the Confederacy go in peace? In a memorable address, Lincoln declared:

■ "I have no purpose...to interfere with the institution of slavery in the States where it exists. I believe I have no lawful right to.

■ "...no State, upon its own mere motion, can lawfully get out of the Union....I now consider that...the Union is unbroken; and... I shall take care...that the laws of the Union be faithfully executed in all the States.

■ "In doing this there needs to be no bloodshed or violence.

■ "One section of the country believes slavery is right, and ought to be extended while the other believes it is wrong, and ought not to be extended. This is the only substantial dispute.

■ "In your hands, my dissatisfied countrymen, and not in mine, is the momentous issue of civil war. The government will not assail you. You can have no conflict, without being yourselves the aggressors. You have no oath registered in Heaven to destroy the government, while I shall have the most solemn oath to 'preserve, protect and defend' it.

■ "I am loath to close. We are not enemies, but friends. We must not be enemies." Then these final words:

THOUGH PASSION MAY HAVE STRAINED, IT MUST NOT BREAK OUR BONDS OF AFFECTION. THE MYSTIC CHORDS OF MEMORY, STRETCHING FROM EVERY BATTLE-FIELD AND PATRIOT GRAVE TO EVERY LIVING HEART AND HEARTHSTONE, ALL OVER THIS BROAD LAND, WILL YET SWELL THE CHORUS OF THE UNION, WHEN AGAIN TOUCHED, AS SURELY THEY WILL BE, BY THE BETTER ANGELS OF OUR NATURE.

FORT SUMTER: THE CIVIL WAR BEGINS.

April 12, 1861: Charleston, South Carolina—Fort Sumter, on an island in Charleston Harbor, was in a dangerous situation: federal property on Confederate soil. Lincoln notified Jefferson Davis that he was sending food and supplies to the Fort. With no arms included, this was not a hostile act.

The Confederates thought otherwise. They attacked Fort Sumter April 12 at 4:30 a.m., and the next day Major Robert Anderson surrendered the Fort. With rebel yells and a Confederate victory the Civil War began.
Where would it end?

Fort Sumter

"I feel that I would like to shoot a Yankee, and yet I know that this would not be in harmony with the spirit of Christianity."—William Nugent, Miss.

1492   1861-65   2000

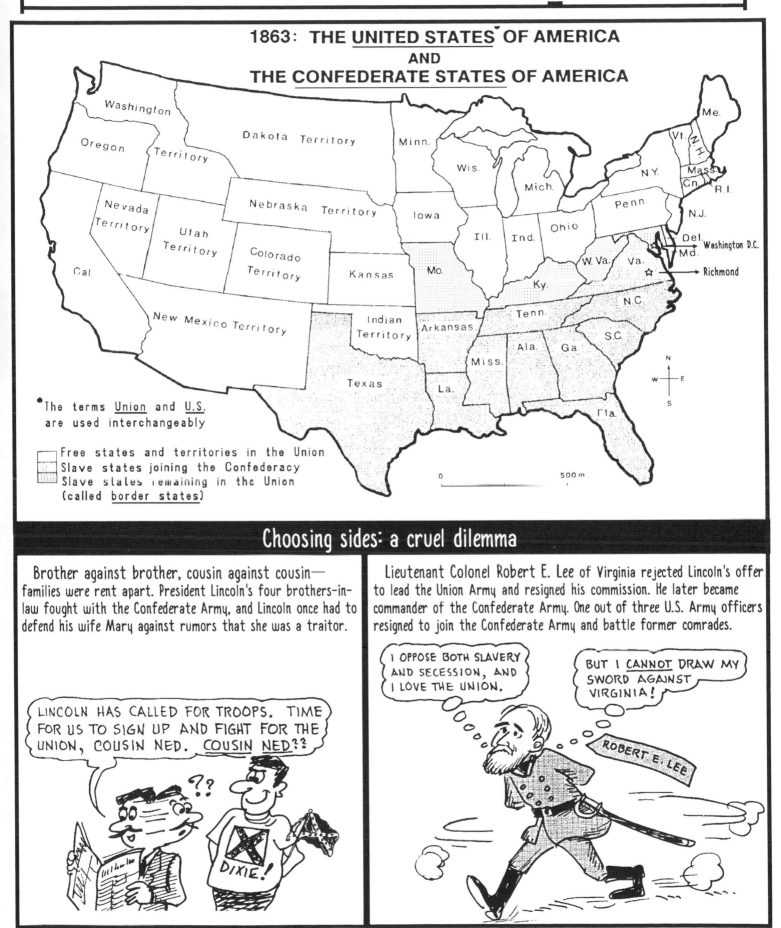

1863: THE <u>UNITED STATES</u>* OF AMERICA
AND
THE <u>CONFEDERATE STATES</u> OF AMERICA

*The terms <u>Union</u> and <u>U.S.</u> are used interchangeably

☐ Free states and territories in the Union
▨ Slave states joining the Confederacy
▦ Slave states remaining in the Union (called <u>border states</u>)

Choosing sides: a cruel dilemma

Brother against brother, cousin against cousin—families were rent apart. President Lincoln's four brothers-in-law fought with the Confederate Army, and Lincoln once had to defend his wife Mary against rumors that she was a traitor.

Lieutenant Colonel Robert E. Lee of Virginia rejected Lincoln's offer to lead the Union Army and resigned his commission. He later became commander of the Confederate Army. One out of three U.S. Army officers resigned to join the Confederate Army and battle former comrades.

245

"...[black soldiers] have proved themselves among the bravest of the brave, performing deeds of daring and shedding their blood with a heroism unsurpassed by any other race." Secretary of War Edwin M. Stanton

1492   1861-65   2000

After reading this chapter, how would you evaluate the strengths and weaknesses of each side? What predictions would you make about the length of the war? What generalization (summary) would you make about the North's eventual victory?

CONFEDERATE STATES OF AMERICA	UNITED STATES OF AMERICA
POPULATION	
▪ 11 states: 9 million people, including 3.5 million slaves	▪ 23 states: 22 million people
ARMIES	
▪ <u>CONFEDERATE ARMY</u>: 600,000 to 1,500,000 total, according to estimates (There are no exact statistics because the Confederate archives in Richmond were destroyed by fire.)	▪ <u>UNION ARMY</u>: 2,128,948 total (In 1861 the entire United States Army consisted of only 16,350 men.)
	▪ <u>AFRICAN-AMERICANS</u>: 178,895 total (134,111 from slave states) 21 Congressional Medal of Honor recipients
	In 1863 the all-black 54th Regiment from Massachusetts performed with great valor at the Battle of Fort Wagner.
	Lincoln defended the use of blacks in the military:
▪ <u>AFRICAN-AMERICANS</u>: Not until March 13, 1865, did the Confederate government open the army to blacks. It was too late; the Confederacy surrendered on April 9, 1865.	"You say you will not fight to free Negroes. Some of them seem willing to fight for you. [After victory] there will be some black men who can remember that, with silent tongue and clenched teeth, and steady eye and well-poised bayonet, they have helped mankind on to this great consummation; while, I fear, there will be some white ones, unable to forget that with malignant heart and deceitful speech, they strove to hinder it."
NAVIES	
▪ The Confederacy had no real navy, only a few cruisers. It relied on privateers to run the Union blockade of the 3,500-mile southern coast.	▪ 42 ships in 1861; 671 ships in 1864
	▪ 84,415 white sailors; 29,00 black sailors

THE CIVIL WAR: AN OVERVIEW

CONFEDERATE STATES OF AMERICA

UNITED STATES OF AMERICA

MILITARY LEADERS

GENERAL ROBERT E. LEE
Commander, Army of Northern Virginia

General Pierre G.T. Beauregard
General Braxton Bragg
General Simon Bolivar Buckner
General Jubal Early
General Nathan Bedford Forrest
General Ambrose P. Hill
General John Bell Hood
General Thomas J. (Stonewall) Jackson
General Albert Sidney Johnston
General Joseph E. Johnston
General James Longstreet
General John C. Pemberton
General J.E.B. (Jeb) Stuart

LIEUTENANT GENERAL ULYSSES S. GRANT
Commander, All Northern Armies

General Don Carlos Buell
General Ambrose E. Burnside
General Benjamin F. Butler
Admiral David G. Farragut
General Henry W. Halleck
General Joseph Hooker
General Irvin McDowell
General George B. McClellan
General George G. Meade
General John Pope
General William S. Rosecrans
General Winfield Scott
General Philip Sheridan
General William Tecumseh Sherman

ADVANTAGES

- Outstanding generals, many of whom had fought in the Mexican War
- Strong military tradition
- Strong motivation—fighting to preserve way of life
- Fighting on home ground—knew the territory
- Skilled with guns and horses because of rural experiences
- Cotton could be exchanged on world market for weapons and manufactured goods.

- Superior leadership of Abraham Lincoln
- Larger population.
- Military power—a five to two advantage in men available to fight
- Industrial power; more manufactured goods
- Greater wealth
- Three-fourths more railroads
- Two-thirds more farm acreage
- Controlled shipping

DISADVANTAGES

- Autocratic leadership of Jefferson Davis
- Inflation: printed paper money that lost its value because of no hard money (gold/silver), called specie, backing it
- Inferior numbers in men, money, and machinery
- State sovereignty yielded to national sovereignty in order to conduct the war.

- Weak motivation—not fighting for a cause.
- Unaggressive officers—failed to press advantages.
- Far from home base—resulting in poor communications and a long supply line
- 3,500-mile enemy coastline—hard to blockade
- Vast land—could conquer but not hold territory
- European aid to Confederacy

IMPROVED TECHNOLOGY MADE THE CIVIL WAR AMERICA'S FIRST MODERN WAR

RAILROADS   WEAPONRY   IRONCLAD SHIPS   CAMERAS   TELEGRAPH   MEDICINE

Clara Barton established a precedent for female nurses in the Union Army. In 1881 she founded the American Red Cross.

"We seek peace—enduring peace. More than an end to war, we want an end to the beginning of all wars—yes, an end to this brutal, inhuman and thoroughly impractical method of settling the differences between governments."—Franklin D. Roosevelt, 1945

CASUALTIES:

THE CIVIL WAR RESULTED IN ALMOST AS MANY DEATHS AS THE TOTAL OF ALL OTHER AMERICAN WARS.

One in every five military men in the Civil War died in service.
Of 620,000 men who died, 340,000 were from the North and about 280,000 from the South.
Of the survivors, the last "Billy Yank," Albert Woolson, died in 1956 at the age of 109;
the last "Johnny Reb," Walter Williams, died in 1959 at age 117.

In 1913 at a fiftieth anniversary reunion at Gettysburg, Union and Confederate veterans
reenacted Pickett's Charge, the South's disasterous attack of Union forces.
Describing the event from the Union side, Philip Meyers wrote:
"We could see not rifles and bayonets but canes and crutches....
At the sound of the Confederates' rebel yell, the Yankees...
burst from behind the stone wall, and flung themselves
upon their former enemies...not in mortal combat,
but reunited in brotherly love and affection."

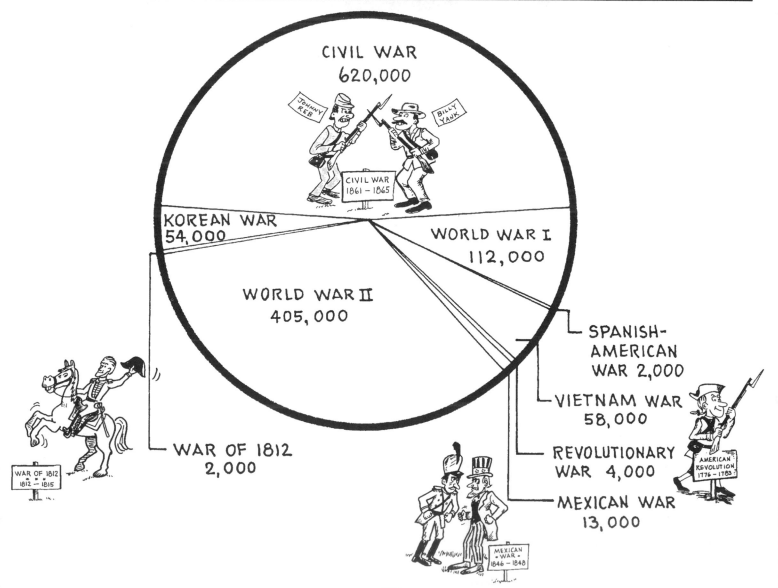

CIVIL WAR
620,000

CIVIL WAR
1861 – 1865

KOREAN WAR
54,000

WORLD WAR I
112,000

WORLD WAR II
405,000

SPANISH-
AMERICAN
WAR 2,000

VIETNAM WAR
58,000

REVOLUTIONARY
WAR 4,000

MEXICAN WAR
13,000

WAR OF 1812
2,000

1492   1861-65   2000

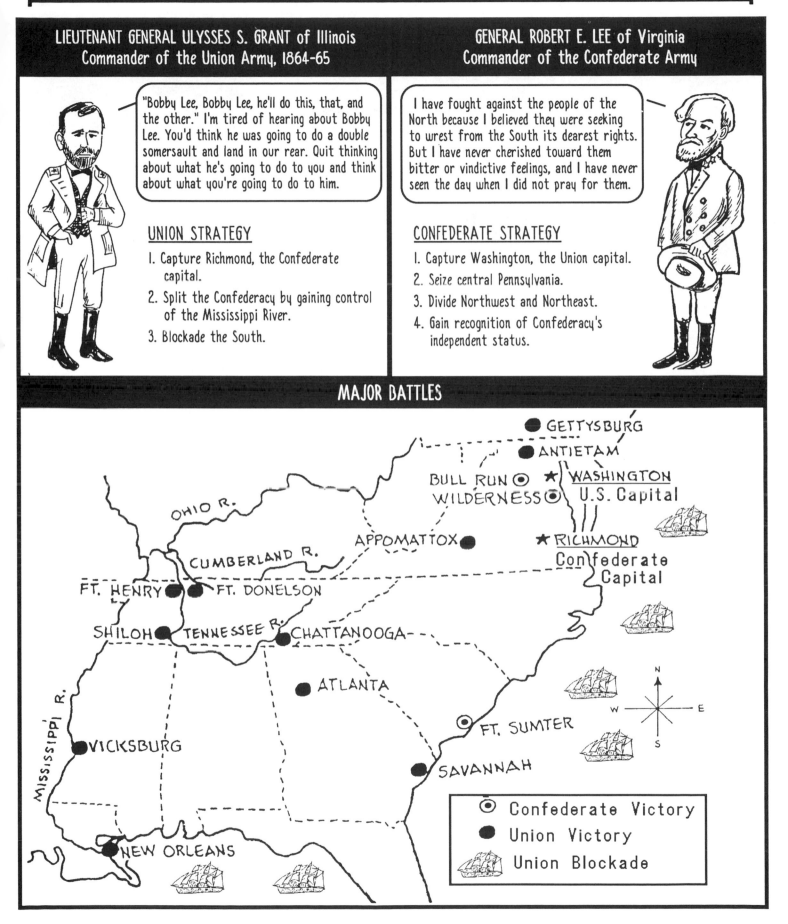

LIEUTENANT GENERAL ULYSSES S. GRANT of Illinois
Commander of the Union Army, 1864-65

"Bobby Lee, Bobby Lee, he'll do this, that, and the other." I'm tired of hearing about Bobby Lee. You'd think he was going to do a double somersault and land in our rear. Quit thinking about what he's going to do to you and think about what you're going to do to him.

UNION STRATEGY

1. Capture Richmond, the Confederate capital.
2. Split the Confederacy by gaining control of the Mississippi River.
3. Blockade the South.

GENERAL ROBERT E. LEE of Virginia
Commander of the Confederate Army

I have fought against the people of the North because I believed they were seeking to wrest from the South its dearest rights. But I have never cherished toward them bitter or vindictive feelings, and I have never seen the day when I did not pray for them.

CONFEDERATE STRATEGY

1. Capture Washington, the Union capital.
2. Seize central Pennsylvania.
3. Divide Northwest and Northeast.
4. Gain recognition of Confederacy's independent status.

MAJOR BATTLES

GETTYSBURG
ANTIETAM
BULL RUN ⊙ ★ WASHINGTON
WILDERNESS ⊙ U.S. Capital
OHIO R.
APPOMATTOX ★ RICHMOND
CUMBERLAND R. Confederate Capital
FT. HENRY · FT. DONELSON
SHILOH TENNESSEE R. CHATTANOOGA
ATLANTA
MISSISSIPPI R.
FT. SUMTER ⊙
VICKSBURG
SAVANNAH
NEW ORLEANS

Legend:
- ⊙ Confederate Victory
- ● Union Victory
- 🚢 Union Blockade

N W E S

"My paramount object in this struggle is to save the union, and is not either to save or to destroy slavery. If I could save the Union without freeing any slave I would do it, and if I could save it by freeing all the slaves I would do it; and if I could save it by freeing some and leaving others alone I would also do that....I intend no modification of my oft-expressed personal wish that all men everywhere could be free."—Abraham Lincoln, 1862

1863—THE EMANCIPATION PROCLAMATION

President Lincoln and Congress agreed on the purpose of the war: it was to restore the Union—not free the slaves.
But pressure built to make the war a crusade against slavery.
In 1863 Lincoln used his authority as commander in chief to strike a blow at the Confederates.
He freed their slaves by the EMANCIPATION PROCLAMATION. This changed the purpose and course of the war.

IMPACT OF THE EMANCIPATION PROCLAMATION

Turned the war into a fight for freedom as well as for union.

Swayed British opinion to the Union side.

Persuaded blacks to enlist in the Union army.

"That speech won't scour. It's a flat failure," said Abraham Lincoln after completing his Gettysburg remarks.
"I should be glad if I could flatter myself that I came as near to the central idea of the occasion, in two hours, as you did in two minutes."
—Edward Everett

1492   1863   2000

July 3, 1863, marked the turning point in the Civil War, as the Union won two great battles:
Gettysburg, Pennsylvania, in the East and Vicksburg, Mississippi, in the West.
On November 19, 1863, a ceremony was held at Gettysburg to dedicate a national cemetery
for those who died there —51,000 Union and Confederate soldiers.
A crowd of 20,000 gathered to hear the great orator Edward Everett speak for two hours.
Following Everett, President Lincoln delivered the few "appropriate remarks" requested of him.
He spoke for two minutes.
In ten sentences Lincoln gave one of the world's great statements on democracy and the purpose in dying—and living—for it.

"Four score and seven years ago our Fathers brought forth on this continent, a new nation, conceived in liberty, and dedicated to the proposition that all men are created equal.

"Now we are engaged in a great civil war, testing whether that nation or any nation so conceived and so dedicated, can long endure. We are met on a great battle-field of that war. We have come to dedicate a portion of that field as a final resting place for those who here gave their lives that that nation might live. It is altogether fitting and proper that we should do this.

"But, in a larger sense, we can not dedicate—we can not consecrate—we can not hallow—this ground. The brave men, living and dead, who struggled here, have consecrated it, far above our poor power to add or detract. The world will little note, nor long remember what we say here, but it can never forget what they did here. It is for us the living, rather, to be dedicated here to the unfinished work which they who fought here have thus far so nobly advanced. It is rather for us to be here dedicated to the great task remaining before us—that from these honored dead we take increased devotion to that cause for which they gave the last full measure of devotion—that we here highly resolve that these dead shall not have died in vain   that this nation, under God, shall have a new birth of freedom—and that government of the people, by the people, and for the people, shall not perish from the earth."

"As to peace...three things are indispensable. 1. The restoration of national authority throughout all the states. 2. No receding...on the slavery question.... 3. No cessation of hostilities short of an end of the war...."—Abraham Lincoln, April 6, 1865

1492   1865   2000

December 8, 1863—LINCOLN'S "TEN PERCENT" RECONSTRUCTION PLAN

Anticipating the war's end, Lincoln announced a lenient plan of reconstructing, or rebuilding, the Union. He said the South had rebelled rather than seceded, therefore he as commander in chief should direct reconstruction. Congress said it should do so because the South <u>had</u> seceded and should be treated as a conquered land. Lincoln's plan reflected his approach: "Let 'em up easy."

THE UNITED STATES HAS BEEN BROKEN UP BY THE SECEDING STATES. NOW THE UNION MUST BE PUT TOGETHER AGAIN.

1) Amnesty: All southerners, except Confederate leaders, could win pardon and regain citizenship by taking an oath to support the Constitution and a proposed 13th Amendment abolishing slavery.

2) When ten percent of a state's registered voters, as of 1860, took the oath, they could re-establish their state government's ties to the Union.

July 1864—Congress disregarded Lincoln's plan and passed the harsher <u>Wade-Davis Bill</u>, which he vetoed.

March 4, 1865—LINCOLN'S SECOND INAUGURAL ADDRESS

After winning reelection in November 1864, Lincoln called for a time of healing.

With malice toward none; with charity toward all; with firmness in the right... let us strive on to finish the work we are in; to bind up the nation's wounds...to do all which may achieve and cherish a just, and a lasting peace.

April 9, 1865—THE WAR ENDED IN A UNION VICTORY as General Lee surrendered his Confederate Army to General Grant at Appomattox Court House, a village in Virginia. Under Lincoln's authority, Grant gave unconditional terms of surrender, along with generous concessions.

<u>Grant's terms of surrender</u>: "Peace being my great desire, there is but one condition I would insist upon...that the men and officers surrendered shall be disqualified for taking up arms again, against the Government of the United States." Grant then added one of the most humane conditions in military history: after signing paroles, the soldiers were not to be disturbed by the United States authority...." There would be no jailing or hanging of traitors. Neither Lincoln nor Grant wanted to punish the South.

Lee and Grant set outstanding examples of reconciliation: Following the surrender, Grant silenced Union celebrations, saying, "The war is over; the rebels are our countrymen again."

Lee swore allegiance to the United States, influencing thousands of his devoted ex-soldiers to do the same. He became president of Washington College in Lexington, Virginia (later named Washington and Lee University), where he told students: "Make your sons Americans." He once warned a professor to stop speaking disrespectfully of Grant, under penalty of being fired.

GENERAL LEE, YOUR MEN WILL NEED THEIR HORSES FOR SPRING PLOWING. THEY MAY KEEP THEM.

THAT'S VERY GENEROUS, GENERAL GRANT. MY MEN WILL BE PLEASED.

<u>**Appomattox**</u> is a short distance from <u>Jamestown</u>, where America's democratic experiment in self-government began. Therein lies the meaning of the Civil War for us: the democratic experiment survived a threat to its very existence, and we are the beneficiaries. It could have gone another way. Had the South successfully seceded, other disgruntled states could follow, gradually undoing the Union.

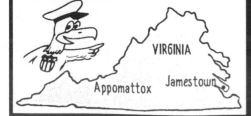

VIRGINIA

Appomattox   Jamestown

April 14, 1865—Five days after the war ended, John Wilkes Booth, a crazed actor seeking vengence for the South, assassinated Lincoln at Ford's Theatre. Walt Whitman expressed the nation's unspeakable grief in his poem "O Captain! My Captain!"

"O Captain! my Captain! our fearful trip is done....
The ship has weather'd every rack, the prize we sought is won....
But O heart! heart! heart!
O the bleeding drops of red,
Where on the deck my Captain lies,
Fallen cold and dead....
The ship is anchor'd safe and sound,
its voyage closed and done,
From fearful trip the victor ship comes in with object won;
Exult O shores, and ring O bells!
But I with mournful tread, walk the deck my Captain lies,
Fallen cold and dead."

DIARY ABRAHAM LINCOLN SLAIN!

1492 ———————————————————————— 1865-77 ———————————————————————— 2000

1865— President Andrew Johnson of Tennessee followed a Reconstruction plan similar to Lincoln's, beginning while Congress was in summer recess. By December, all the southern states except Texas had met Johnson's requirements for readmission to the Union:

1) loyalty oaths in exchange for amnesty for all southerners except Confederate leaders and those whose wealth exceeded $20,000 (Johnson disliked rich people.),

2) ratification of the 13th Amendment,

3) repudiation of Confederate war debts,

4) disavowal of secession ordinances.

1866—Congressional Radical Republicans, led by Congressman Thaddeus Stevens and Senator Charles Sumner, rejected Johnson's moderate plan, refused to admit the southern states, and set up the Joint Committee of Fifteen to direct Reconstruction. Alarmed by southern Black Codes restricting former slaves, they increased the power of the Freedman's Bureau, an agency to help the 4,000,000 freed slaves.

In 1867 Congress passed the First Reconstruction Act, replacing southern governments with five military districts. Readmission to the Union now required:

1) writing state constitutions giving blacks the vote; ratification of the 14th Amendment,

2) later, ratification of the 15th Amendment.

RECONSTRUCTION AMENDMENTS

13TH AMENDMENT: ABOLISHED SLAVERY

Ratified December 18, 1865

14TH AMENDMENT: GRANTED BLACK CITIZENSHIP

Ratified July 28, 1868

15TH AMENDMENT: GAVE BLACK MALES THE VOTE

Ratified March 30, 1870

1868: Impeachment of President Johnson

Radical Republicans impeached (brought to trial) Johnson for firing Secretary of War Edwin Stanton, a Radical Republican, and thus violating the Tenure of Office Act. The Senate vote was one short of the two-thirds needed for conviction. Johnson remained in office but lost power to the Radicals.

1868—Ulysses S. Grant was elected president, with the support of Radical Republicans. Blacks now had the vote (and elective office) in the new southern governments, and Grant received nearly all 700,000 black votes cast. The Ku Klux Klan, a secret white society, intimidated blacks to keep them from voting.

1877—The Compromise of 1877 ended Reconstruction. In the 1876 contested presidential election, Republican Rutherford B. Hayes gained southern support by promising to end military rule in the South. Blacks gradually lost their political and civil rights but began regaining them in the 1960s, based on the Reconstruction Amendments.

And so we close this half of America's story of liberty with Lincoln's words:

"With malice toward none; with charity toward all; with firmness in the right... let us strive on to finish the work we are in...."

"Posterity! You will never know how much it cost the present generation to preserve your freedom.
I hope you will make good use of it."—John Quincy Adams

1492   1607   1877   2000

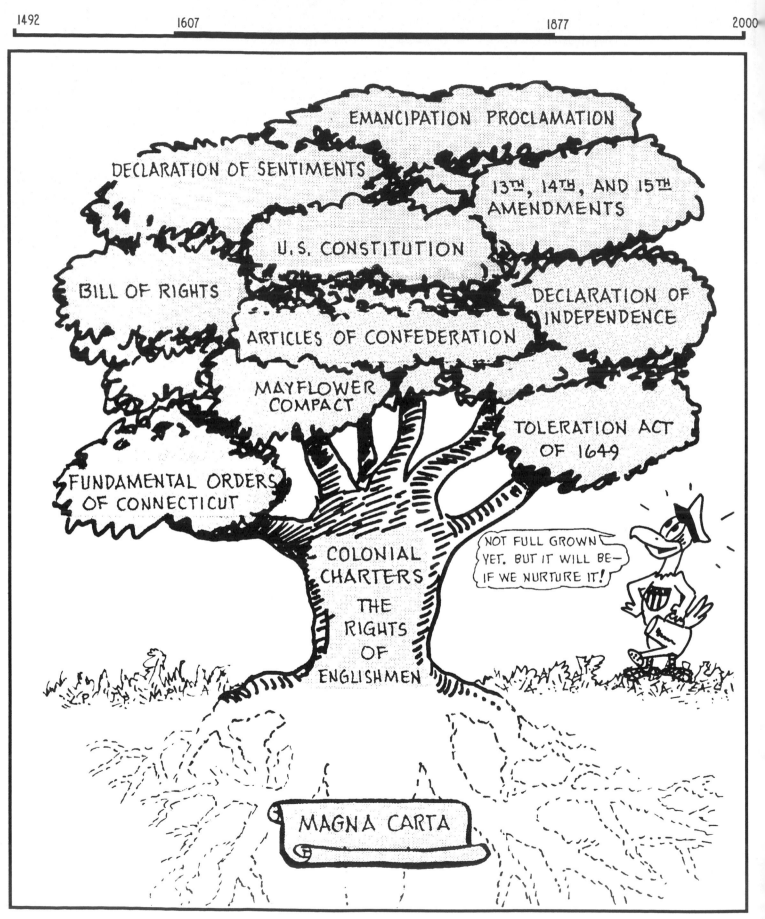

254

The STATUE OF LIBERTY, towering 305 feet above New York Harbor, was a gift from France to the United States in 1886. It honors the 1778 French-American alliance, negotiated by Benjamin Franklin, that helped the United States win independence. It symbolizes the American dream of creating a land of liberty, and it represents the Founding Fathers' goal of inspiring liberty among all nations.

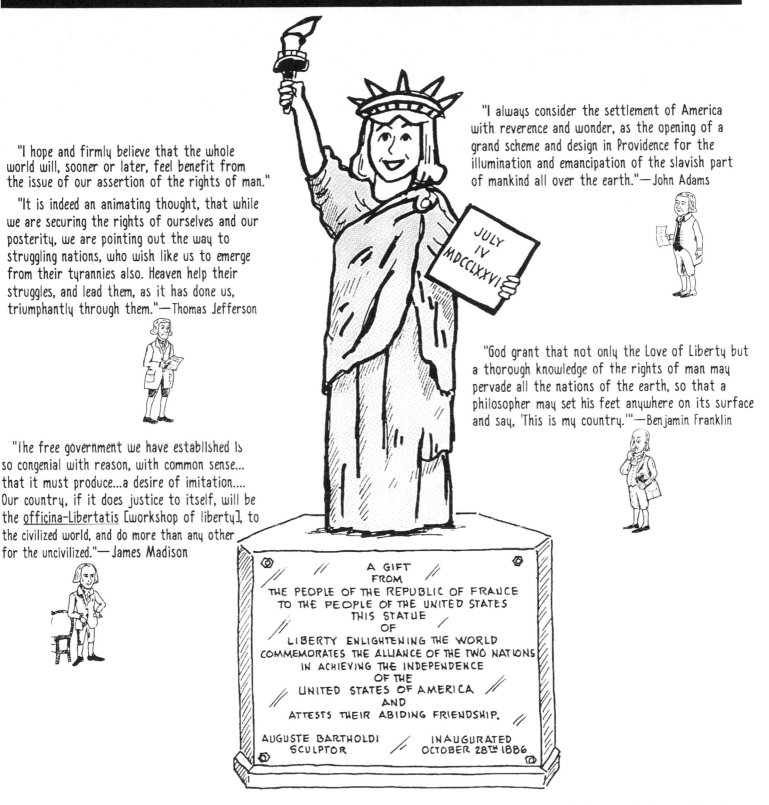

"I hope and firmly believe that the whole world will, sooner or later, feel benefit from the issue of our assertion of the rights of man."

"It is indeed an animating thought, that while we are securing the rights of ourselves and our posterity, we are pointing out the way to struggling nations, who wish like us to emerge from their tyrannies also. Heaven help their struggles, and lead them, as it has done us, triumphantly through them."—Thomas Jefferson

"The free government we have established is so congenial with reason, with common sense... that it must produce...a desire of imitation.... Our country, if it does justice to itself, will be the officina-Libertatis [workshop of liberty], to the civilized world, and do more than any other for the uncivilized."—James Madison

"I always consider the settlement of America with reverence and wonder, as the opening of a grand scheme and design in Providence for the illumination and emancipation of the slavish part of mankind all over the earth."—John Adams

"God grant that not only the Love of Liberty but a thorough knowledge of the rights of man may pervade all the nations of the earth, so that a philosopher may set his feet anywhere on its surface and say, 'This is my country.'"—Benjamin Franklin

A GIFT FROM THE PEOPLE OF THE REPUBLIC OF FRANCE TO THE PEOPLE OF THE UNITED STATES THIS STATUE OF LIBERTY ENLIGHTENING THE WORLD COMMEMORATES THE ALLIANCE OF THE TWO NATIONS IN ACHIEVING THE INDEPENDENCE OF THE UNITED STATES OF AMERICA AND ATTESTS THEIR ABIDING FRIENDSHIP.

AUGUSTE BARTHOLDI SCULPTOR   INAUGURATED OCTOBER 28TH 1886

June 10, 1990—"We live during a remarkable moment in world history, an exhilarating time—the triumph of freedom [in Eastern Europe]. But freedom has a constant companion—challenge. And so I challenge you to make the most of our changing world, to take risks to do something extraordinary. Whatever you do, live a life of adventure and meaning so brilliant that like a Roman candle, it lights up the world. Dazzle us. Astonish us. Be extraordinary!"—George Bush, President of the United States, 1989-1993.

THE DECLARATION OF INDEPENDENCE
In Congress, July 4, 1776
The Unanimous Declaration of the Thirteen United States of America

When in the Course of human events, it becomes necessary for one people to dissolve the political bands which have connected them with another, and to assume among the powers of the earth, the separate and equal station to which the Laws of Nature and of Nature's God entitle them, a decent respect to the opinions of mankind requires that they should declare the causes which impel them to the separation.

We hold these truths to be self-evident, that all men are created equal, that they are endowed by their Creator with certain unalienable Rights, that among these are Life, Liberty and the pursuit of Happiness. That to secure these rights, Governments are instituted among Men, deriving their just powers from the consent of the governed, That whenever any Form of Government becomes destructive of these ends, it is the Right of the People to alter or to abolish it, and to institute new Government, laying its foundation on such principles and organizing its powers in such form, as to them shall seem most likely to effect their Safety and Happiness. Prudence, indeed, will dictate that Governments long established should not be changed for light and transient causes; and accordingly all experience hath shown, that mankind are more disposed to suffer, while evils are sufferable, than to right themselves by abolishing the forms to which they are accustomed. But when a long train of abuses and usurpations, pursuing invariably the same Object evinces a design to reduce them under absolute Despotism, it is their right, it is their duty, to throw off such Government, and to provide new Guards for their future security. Such has been the patient sufferance of these Colonies; and such is now the necessity which constrains them to alter their former Systems of Government. The history of the present King of Great Britain is a history of repeated injuries and usurpations, all having in direct object the establishment of an absolute Tyranny over these States. To prove this, let Facts be submitted to a candid world.

He has refused his Assent to Laws, the most wholesome and necessary for the public good.

He has forbidden his Governors to pass Laws of immediate and pressing importance, unless suspended in their operation till his Assent should be obtained; and when so suspended, he has utterly neglected to attend to them.

He has refused to pass other Laws for the accommodation of large districts of people, unless those people would relinquish the right of Representation in the Legislature, a right inestimable to them and formidable to tyrants only.

He has called together legislative bodies at places unusual, uncomfortable, and distant from the depository of their Public Records, for the sole purpose of fatiguing them into compliance with his measures.

He has dissolved Representative Houses repeatedly, for opposing with manly firmness his invasions on the right of the people.

He has refused for a long time, after such dissolutions, to cause others to be elected; whereby the Legislative powers, incapable of Annihilation, have returned to the People at large for their exercise; the State remaining in the mean time exposed to all the dangers of invasion from without, and convulsions within.

He has endeavoured to prevent the population of these States; for that purpose obstructing the Laws for Naturalization of Foreigners; refusing to pass others to encourage their migrations hither, and raising the conditions of new Appropriations of Lands.

He has obstructed the Administration of Justice, by refusing his Assent to Laws for establishing Judiciary powers.

He has made Judges dependent on his Will alone, for the tenure of their offices, and the amount and payment of their salaries.

He has erected a multitude of New Offices, and sent hither swarms of Officers to harass our people, and eat out their substance.

He has kept among us, in times of peace, Standing Armies without the Consent of our legislatures.

He has affected to render the Military independent of and superior to the Civil power.

THE DECLARATION OF INDEPENDENCE

He has combined with others to subject us to a jurisdiction foreign to our constitution, and unacknowledged by our laws; giving his Assent to their Acts of pretended Legislation:

For quartering large bodies of armed troops among us:

For protecting them, by a mock Trial, from Punishment for any Murders which they should commit on the Inhabitants of these States:

For cutting off our Trade with all parts of the World:

For imposing Taxes on us without our Consent:

For depriving us in many cases, of the benefits of Trial by Jury:

For transporting us beyond Seas to be tried for pretended offences:

For abolishing the free System of English Laws in a neighbouring Province, establishing therein an Arbitrary government, and enlarging its Boundaries so as to render it at once an example and fit instrument for introducing the same absolute rule into these Colonies:

For taking away our Charters, abolishing our most valuable Laws, and altering fundamentally the Forms of our Government:

For suspending our own Legislatures, and declaring themselves invested with Power to legislate for us in all cases whatsoever.

He has abdicated Government here, by declaring us out of his Protection and waging War against us.

He has plundered our seas, ravaged our Coasts, burnt our towns, and destroyed the lives of our people.

He is at this time transporting large Armies of foreign Mercenaries to compleat the works of death, desolation and tyranny, already begun with circumstances of Cruelty and perfidy scarcely paralleled in the most barbarous ages, and totally unworthy the Head of a civilized nation.

He has constrained our fellow Citizens taken Captive on the high Seas to bear Arms against their Country, to become the executioners of their friends and Brethren, or to fall themselves by their Hands.

He has excited domestic insurrections amongst us, and has endeavoured to bring on the inhabitants of our frontiers, the merciless Indian Savages, whose known rule of warfare, is an undistinguished destruction of all ages, sexes and conditions.

In every stage of these Oppressions We have Petitioned for Redress in the most humble terms: Our repeated Petitions have been answered only by repeated injury. A Prince, whose character is thus marked by every act which may define a Tyrant, is unfit to be the ruler of a free people.

Nor have We been wanting in our attentions to our British brethren. We have warned them from time to time of attempts by their legislature to extend an unwarrantable jurisdiction over us. We have reminded them of the circumstances of our emigration and settlement here. We have appealed to their native justice and magnanimity, and we have conjured them by the ties of our common kindred to disavow these usurpations, which, would inevitably interrupt our connections and correspondence. They too have been deaf to the voice of justice and of consanguinity. We must, therefore, acquiesce in the necessity, which denounces our Separation, and hold them, as we hold the rest of mankind, Enemies in War, in Peace Friends.

We, Therefore, the Representatives of the united States of America, in General Congress, Assembled, appealing to the Supreme Judge of the world for the rectitude of our intentions, do, in the Name, and by the Authority of the good People of these Colonies, solemnly publish and declare, That these United Colonies are, and of Right ought to be, Free and Independent States; that they are Absolved from all Allegiance to the British Crown, and that all political connection between them and the State of Great Britain, is and ought to be totally dissolved; and that as Free and Independent States, they have full Power to levy War, conclude Peace, contract Alliances, establish Commerce, and to do all other Acts and Things which Independent States may of right do. And for the support of this Declaration, with a firm reliance on the protection of divine Providence, we mutually pledge to each other our Lives, our Fortunes, and our sacred Honor.

THE CONSTITUTION OF THE UNITED STATES

PREAMBLE

We the People of the United States, in order to form a more perfect Union, establish Justice, insure domestic Tranquility, provide for the common defence, promote the general Welfare, and secure the Blessings of Liberty to ourselves and our Posterity, do ordain and establish this Constitution for the United States of America.

ARTICLE I: THE LEGISLATIVE BRANCH

Section 1. All legislative Powers herein granted shall be vested in a Congress of the United States, which shall consist of a Senate and House of Representatives.

Section 2. The House of Representatives shall be composed of Members chosen every second Year by the People of the several States, and the Electors in each State shall have the Qualifications requisite for Electors of the most numerous Branch of the State Legislature.

No Person shall be Representative who shall not have attained to the Age of twenty-five years, and have been seven Years a Citizen of the United States, and who shall not, when elected, be an Inhabitant of that State in which he shall be chosen.

Representatives and direct Taxes shall be apportioned among the several States which may be included within this Union, according to their respective Numbers, which shall be determined by adding to the whole Number of free Persons, including those bound to Service for a Term of Years, and excluding Indians not taxed, three-fifths of all other Persons. The actual Enumeration shall be made within three Years after the first Meeting of the Congress of the United States, and within every subsequent Term of ten Years, in such Manner as they shall by Law direct. The Number of Representatives shall not exceed one for every thirty Thousand, but each State shall have at Least one Representative; and until such enumeration shall be made, the State of New Hampshire shall be entitled to choose three, Massachusetts eight, Rhode Island and Providence Plantations one, Connecticut five, New York six, New Jersey four, Pennsylvania eight, Delaware one, Maryland six, Virginia ten, North Carolina five, South Carolina five, and Georgia three.

When vacancies happen in the Representation from any State, the Executive Authority thereof shall issue Writs of Election to fill such Vacancies.

The House of Representative shall choose their Speaker and other Officers; and shall have the sole Power of Impeachment.

Section 3. The Senate of the United States shall be composed of two Senators from each State, chosen by the Legislature thereof, for six Years; and each Senator shall have one Vote.

Immediately after they shall be assembled in Consequence of the first Election, they shall be divided as equally as may be into three Classes. The Seats of the Senators of the first Class shall be vacated at the Expiration of the second Year, of the second Class at the expiration of the fourth Year, and of the third Class at the Expiration of the sixth Year, so that one third may be chosen every second Year: and if Vacancies happen by Resignation, or otherwise, during the Recess of the Legislature of any State, the Executive thereof may make temporary Appointments until the next Meeting of the Legislature, which shall then fill such Vacancies.

No Person shall be a Senator who shall not have attained to the Age of thirty Years, and been nine Years a Citizen of the United States, and who shall not, when elected, be an Inhabitant of that State for which he shall be chosen.

The Vice President of the United States shall be President of the Senate, but shall have no Vote, unless they be equally divided.

The Senate shall choose their other Officers, and also a President pro tempore, in the absence of the Vice President, or when he shall exercise the Office of President of the United States.

The Senate shall have the sole Power to try all Impeachments. When sitting for that Purpose, they shall be on Oath or Affirmation. When the President of the United States is tried, the Chief Justice shall preside: And no Person shall be convicted without the Concurrence of two thirds of the Members present.

Judgment in Cases of Impeachment shall not extend further than to removal from Office, and disqualification t o hold and enjoy any Office of Honor, Trust or Profit under the United States: but the Party convicted shall nevertheless be liable and subject to Indictment, Trial, Judgment and Punishment, according to Law.

Section 4. The Times, Places and Manner of holding Elections for Senators and Representatives, shall be prescribed in each State by the Legislature thereof; but the Congress may at any time by Law make or alter such Regulations, except as to the Place of choosing Senators.

The Congress shall assemble at least once in every Year, and such Meeting shall be on the first Monday in December, unless they shall by Law appoint a different Day.

Section 5. Each House shall be the Judge of the Elections, Returns and Qualifications of its own Members, and Majority of each shall constitute a Quorum to do Business; but a smaller number may adjourn from day to day, and may be authorized to compel the Attendance of absent Members, in such Manner, and under such Penalties as each House may provide.

Each House may determine the Rules of its Proceedings, punish its Members for disorderly Behavior, and with the concurrence of two thirds, expel a Member.

Each House shall keep a Journal of its Proceedings, and time to time publish the same, excepting such Parts as may in their Judgment require Secrecy; and the Yeas and Nays of the Members of either House on any question shall, at the Desire of one fifth of those Present, be entered on the Journal.

Neither House during the Session of Congress, shall, without the Consent of the other, adjourn for more than three days, nor to any other Place than that in which the two Houses shall be sitting.

Section 6. The Senators and Representatives shall receive a Compensation for their Services, to be ascertained by Law, and paid out of the Treasury of the United States. They shall in all Cases, except Treason, Felony and Breach of the Peace, be privileged from Arrest during their Attendance at the Session of their respective Houses, and in going to and returning from the same; and for any Speech or Debate in either House, they shall not be questioned in any other Place.

No Senator or Representative shall, during the Time for which he was elected, be appointed to any civil Office under the authority of the United States, which shall have been created, or the Emoluments whereof shall have encreased during such time; and no Person holding any Office under the United States, shall be a Member of either House during his Continuance in Office.

Section 7. All Bills for raising Revenue shall originate in the House of Representatives; but the Senate may propose or concur with Amendments as on other Bills.

Every Bill which shall have passed the House of Representatives and the Senate, shall, before it comes a Law, be presented to the President of the United States; If he approves he shall sign it, but if not he shall return it, with his Objections to that House in which it shall have originated, who shall enter the Objections at large on their Journal, and proceed to reconsider it. If after such Reconsideration two thirds of that House shall agree to pass the bill, it shall be sent, together with the Objections, to the other House, by which it shall likewise be reconsidered, and if approved by two thirds of that House, it shall become a Law. But in all such Cases the votes of both Houses shall be determined by Yeas and Nays, and the Names of the Persons voting for and against the Bill shall be entered on the Journal of each House respectively. If any Bill shall not be returned by the President within ten Days (Sundays excepted) after it shall have been presented to him, the Same shall be a Law, in like Manner as if he had signed it, unless the Congress by their Adjournment prevent its Return, in which Case it shall not be a Law.

Every Order, Resolution, or Vote to which the Concurrence of the Senate and House of Representatives may be necessary (except on a question of Adjournment) shall be presented to the President of the United States; and before the Same shall take Effect, shall be approved by him, or being disapproved by him, shall be repassed by two thirds of the Senate and House of Representatives, according to the Rules and Limitations prescribed in the Case of a Bill.

Section 8. The Congress shall have Power to lay and collect Taxes, Duties, Imposts and Excises, to pay the Debts and provide for the common Defence and general welfare of the United State; but all Duties, Imposts and Excises shall be uniform throughout the United States

To borrow money on the credit of the United States;

To regulate Commerce with foreign Nations, and among the several States, and with the Indian Tribes;

To establish a uniform rule of Naturalization, and uniform Laws on the subject of Bankruptcies throughout the United States;

To coin Money, regulate the Value thereof, and of foreign Coin, and fix the Standard of Weights and Measures;

To provide for the Punishment of counterfeiting the Securities and current Coin of the United States;

To establish Post Offices and post Roads;

To promote the Progress of Science and useful Arts, by securing for limited Times to Authors and Inventors the exclusive Right to their respective Writing and Discoveries;

To constitute Tribunals inferior to the Superior Court;

To define and punish Piracies and Felonies committed on the high Seas, and Offenses against the Law of Nations;

To declare War, grant Letters of Marque and Reprisal, and make Rules concerning Captures on Land and Water;

To raise and support Armies, but no Appropriation of Money to that Use shall be for a longer Term than two years;

To provide and maintain a Navy;

To make Rules for the Government and Regulation of the land and naval Forces;

To provide for calling forth the Militia to execute the Laws of the Union, suppress Insurrections and repel Invasions;

To provide for organizing, arming, and disciplining the Militia, and for governing such Part of them as may be employed in the Service of the United States, reserving to the States respectively, the Appointment of the Officers, and the Authority of training the Militia according to the discipline prescribed by Congress;

To Exercise the exclusive Legislation in all Cases whatsoever, over such District (not exceeding ten Miles square) as may, by Cession of particular States, and the acceptance of Congress, become the Seat of the Government of the United States, and to exercise like Authority over all Places purchased by the Consent of the Legislature of the State in which the Same shall be, for the Erection of Forts, Magazines, Arsenals, dock-Yards, and other needful Buildings;-And

To make all Laws which shall be necessary and proper for carrying into Execution the foregoing Powers, and all other Powers vested by this Constitution in the Government of the United States, or in any Department or Officer thereof.

Section 9. The Migration or Importation of such Persons as any of the States now existing shall think proper to admit, shall not be prohibited by the Congress prior to the year one thousand eight hundred and eight, but a tax or duty may be imposed on such Importation, not exceeding ten dollars for each Person.

The privilege of the Write of Habeas Corpus shall not be suspended unless when in Cases of Rebellion or Invasion the public Safety may require it.

No Bill of Attainder or ex post facto Law shall be passed.

No capitation, or other direct, Tax shall be laid, unless in Proportion to the Census of Enumeration herein before directed to be taken.

No Tax or Duty shall be laid on Articles exported from any State.

No Preference shall be given by any Regulation of Commerce or Revenue to the Ports of one State over those of another; nor shall Vessels bound to, or from, one State, be obliged to enter, clear, or pay Duties in another.

No Money shall be drawn from the Treasury, but in Consequence of Appropriations made by Law; and a regular Statement and Account of the Receipts and Expenditures of all public Money shall be published from time to time.

No Title of Nobility shall be granted by the United States: And no Person holding any Office of Profit or Trust under them,, shall, without the Consent of the Congress, accept of any present, Emolument, Office, or Title, of any kind whatever, from any King, Prince, or foreign State.

Section 10. No State shall enter into any Treaty, Alliance, or Confederation; grant Letters of Marque and Reprisal; coin Money; emit Bills of Credit; make any Thing but gold and silver Coin a Tender in Payment of Debts; pass any Bill of Attainder, ex post facto Law, or Law impairing the Obligation of Contracts or grant any Title of Nobility.

No State shall, without the Consent of the Congress, lay any Imposts or Duties on Imports or Exports, except what may be absolutely necessary for executing its inspection Laws: and the net Produce of all Duties and Imposts, laid by any State on Imports or Exports, shall be for the Use of the Treasury of the United States; and all such Laws shall be subject to the Revision and Control of the Congress.

No State shall, without the Consent of Congress, lay any duty of Tonnage, keep Troops, or Ships of War in time of Peace, enter into any Agreement or Compact with another State, or with a foreign Power, or engage in War, unless actually invaded, or in such imminent Danger as will not admit of delay.

ARTICLE II: EXECUTIVE DEPARTMENT

Section 1. The executive Power shall be vested in a President of the United States of America. He shall hold his Office during the Term of four Years, and, together with the Vice President, chosen for the same Term, be elected, as follows.

Each State shall appoint, in such Manner as the Legislature thereof may direct, a Number of Electors, equal to the whole Number of Senators and Representatives to which the State may be entitled in the Congress: but no Senator or Representative, or Person holding an office of Trust or Profit under the United States, shall be appointed an Elector.

The Electors shall meet in their respective States, and vote by Ballot for two persons, of whom one at least shall not be an Inhabitant of the same State with themselves. And they shall make a List of all the Persons voted for, and of the Number of Votes for each; which List they shall sign and certify, and transmit sealed to the Seat of the Government of the United States, directed to the President of the Senate. The President of the Senate shall, in the Presence of the Senate and House of Representatives, open all the Certificates, and the Votes shall then be counted. The person having the greatest Number of Votes shall be the President, if such Number be a Majority of the whole Number of Electors appointed; and if there be more than one who have such Majority, and have an equal number of Votes, then the House of Representatives shall immediately choose by Ballot one of them for President; and if no Person have a Majority, then from the five highest on the List the said House shall in like Manner choose the President. But in choosing the President, the Votes shall be taken by States, the Representation from each State having one Vote; a quorum for this Purpose shall consist of a Member or Members from two thirds of the States, and a Majority of all the States shall be necessary to a Choice. In every Case, after the Choice of the President, the Person having the Greatest Number of Votes of the Electors shall be the Vice President. But if there should remain two or more who have equal Votes, the Senate shall choose from them by Ballot the Vice President.

The Congress may determine the Time of choosing the Electors, and the Day on which they shall give their Votes; which Day shall be the same throughout the United States.

No person except a natural born Citizen, or a Citizen of the United States, at the time of the adoption of this Constitution, shall be eligible to the Office of President; neither shall any Person be eligible to that Office who shall not have attained to the Age of Thirty-five Years, and been fourteen Years a Resident within the United States.

In a Case of the Removal of the President from Office, or of his Death, Resignation, or Inability to discharge the Powers and Duties of the said Office, the same shall devolve on the Vice-President, and the Congress may by Law provide for the Case of Removal, Death, Resignation or Inability, both of the President and the

Vice President, declaring what Officer shall then act as President, and such Officer shall act accordingly, until the Disability be removed, or a President shall be elected.

The President shall, at stated Times, receive for his Services, a Compensation, which shall neither be encreased nor diminished during the Period for which he shall have been elected, and he shall not receive within that Period any other Emolument from the United States, or any of them.

Before he enter on the Execution of his Office, he shall take the following Oath or Affirmation:—"I do solemnly swear (or affirm) that I will faithfully execute the Office of the President of the United States, and will to the best of my Ability, preserve, protect and defend the constitution of the United States."

Section 2. The President shall be Commander in Chief of the Army and Navy of the United States, and of the Militia of the several States, when called into the actual Service of the United States; he may require the Opinion in writing, of the principal Officer in each of the executive Departments, upon any subject relating to the Duties of their respective Offices, and he shall have Power to Grant Reprieves and Pardons for Offenses against the United States, except in Cases of Impeachment.

He shall have Power, by and with the Advice and Consent of the Senate, to make Treaties, provided two thirds of the Senators present concur; and he shall nominate, and by and with the Advice and Consent of the Senate, shall appoint Ambassadors, other public Ministers and Consuls, Judges of the supreme Court, and all other Officers of the United States, whose Appointments are not herein otherwise provided for, and which shall be established by Law: but the Congress may by Law vest the Appointment of such inferior Officers, as they think proper, in the President alone, in the Courts of Law, of in the Heads of Departments.

The President shall have Power to fill up all Vacancies that may happen during the Recess of the Senate, by granting commissions which shall expire at the End of their next Session.

Section 3. He shall from time to time give to the Congress Information of the State of the Union, and recommend to their Consideration such Measures as he shall judge necessary and expedient; he may, on extraordinary Occasions, convene both Houses, or either of them, and in Case of Disagreement between them, with Respect to the Time of Adjournment, he may adjourn them to such Time as he shall think proper; he shall receive Ambassadors and other public Ministers; he shall take Care that the Laws be faithfully executed, and shall Commission all the Officers of the United States.

Section 4. The President, Vice President and all other civil Officers of the United States, shall be removed from Office on Impeachment for, and Conviction of, Treason, Bribery, or other high Crimes and Misdemeanors.

ARTICLE III: JUDICIAL DEPARTMENT

Section 1. The judicial Power of the United States, shall be vested in one supreme Court, and in such inferior Courts as the Congress may from time to time ordain and establish. The Judges, both of the supreme and inferior Courts, shall hold their offices during good Behavior, and shall, at stated Times, receive for their services, a Compensation, which shall not be diminished during their Continuance in Office.

Section 2. The judicial Power shall extend to all Cases, in Law and Equity, arising under this Constitution, the Laws of the United States, and Treaties made, or which shall be made, under their Authority:-to all Cases affecting Ambassadors, other public Ministers and Consuls;-to all cases of admiralty and maritime Jurisdiction:-to Controversies to which the United States shall be a Party;-to Controversies between two or more States;-between a State and Citizens of another state;-between Citizens of different states;-between Citizens of the same State claiming Lands under Grants of different States, and between a State, or the Citizens thereof, and foreign States, Citizens or Subjects.

In all Cases affecting Ambassadors, other public Ministers and Consuls, and those in which a State shall be Party, the supreme Court shall have original Jurisdiction. In all the other Cases before mentioned, the supreme Court shall have appellate Jurisdiction, both as to Law and Fact, with such Exceptions, and under such Regulations as the Congress shall make.

The trial of all Crimes, except in cases of Impeachment, shall be by Jury; and such Trial shall be held in the State where the said Crimes shall have been committed; but when not committed within any State, the Trial shall be at such Place or Places as the Congress may by Law have directed.

Section 3. Treason against the United States, shall consist only in levying War against them, or in adhering to their Enemies, giving them Aid and Comfort. No Person shall be convicted of Treason unless on the Testimony of two Witnesses to the same overt Act, or on Confession in open Court.

The Congress shall have Power to declare the Punishment of Treason, but no Attainder of Treason shall work Corruption of Blood, or Forfeiture except during the Life of the Person attainted.

ARTICLE IV: RELATIONS AMONG THE STATES

Section 1. Full Faith and Credit shall be given in each State to the public Acts, Records, and judicial Proceedings of every other State. And the Congress may by general Laws prescribe the Manner in which such Acts, Records and Proceedings shall be proved, and Effect thereof.

Section 2. The Citizens of each State shall be entitled to all Privileges and Immunities of Citizens in several States.

A Person charged in any State with Treason, Felony or other Crime, who shall flee from Justice, and be found in another State, shall on demand of the executive Authority of the State from which he fled, be delivered up, to be removed to the State having Jurisdiction of the Crime.

No Person held in Service or Labour in one State, under the laws thereof, escaping into another, shall, in Consequence of any Law or Regulation therein, be discharged from such Service or Labour, but shall be delivered up on Claim of the Party to whom such Service or Labour may be due.

Section 3. New States may be admitted by the Congress into this Union; but no new State shall be formed or erected within the Jurisdiction of any other State; nor any State be formed by the Junction of two or more States, or parts of States, without the Consent of Legislatures of the States concerned as well as of the Congress.

The Congress shall have Power to dispose of and make all needful Rules and Regulations respecting the Territory or other Property belonging to the United States; and nothing in this Constitution shall be so construed as to Prejudice any Claims of the United States, or of any particular State.

Section 4. The United States shall guarantee to every State in this Union a Republican Form of Government, and shall protect each of them against Invasion; and on Application of the Legislature, or of the Executive (when the Legislature cannot be convened) against domestic Violence.

ARTICLE V: AMENDING THE CONSTITUTION

The Congress, whenever two thirds of both Houses shall deem it necessary, shall propose Amendments to this Constitution, or, on the Application of the Legislatures of two thirds of the several States, shall call a Convention for proposing Amendments, which, in either Case, shall be valid to all Intents and Purposes, as part of this Constitution, when ratified by the Legislatures of three fourths of the several States, or by Conventions in three fourths thereof, as the one or the other Mode of Ratification may be proposed by the Congress: Provided that no Amendment which may be made prior to the Year One thousand eight hundred and eight shall in any Manner affect the first and fourth Clauses in the Ninth Section of the first Article; and that no State, without its consent, shall be deprived of its equal Suffrage in the Senate.

ARTICLE VI: GENERAL PROVISIONS

All Debts contracted and Engagements entered into, before the Adoption of this Constitution, shall be as valid against the United States under this Constitution, as under the Confederation

This Constitution, and the Laws of the United States which shall be made in Pursuance thereof; and all Treaties made, or which shall be made, under the Authority of the United States, shall be the supreme law of the Land; and the Judges in every State shall be bound thereby, any Thing in the Constitution or Laws of any State to the Contrary notwithstanding.

The Senators and Representatives before mentioned, and the Members of the several State Legislatures, and all executive and judicial Officers, both of the United States and of the several States, shall be bound by Oath or Affirmation, to support this Constitution; but no religious Test shall ever be required as a Qualification to any Office or public Trust under the United States.

ARTICLE VII: RATIFICATION

The Ratification of the Conventions of nine States shall be sufficient for the Establishment of this Constitution between the States so ratifying the Same.

DONE in Convention by Unanimous Consent of the States present the Seventeenth Day of September in the Year of our Lord one thousand seven hundred and eighty-seven and of the Independence of the United States of America the Twelfth. In Witness whereof We have hereunto subscribed our Names.

AMENDMENTS

The first ten amendments to the Constitution, ratified by the states in 1791, are called the Bill of Rights.

AMENDMENT I (1791) Congress shall make no law respecting an establishment of religion, or prohibiting the free exercise thereof: or abridging the freedom of speech, or of the press; or the right of the people peaceably to assemble, and to petition the Government for a redress of grievances.

AMENDMENT II (1791) A well regulated Militia, being necessary to the security of a free State, the right of the people to keep and bear Arms, shall not be infringed.

AMENDMENT III (1791) No soldier shall, in time of peace, be quartered in any house, without the consent of the Owner, nor in time of war, but in a manner to be prescribed by law.

AMENDMENT IV (1791) The right of the people to be secure in their persons, houses, papers, and effects, against unreasonable searches and seizures, shall not be violated, and no Warrants shall issue, but upon probable cause, supported by Oath or affirmation, and particularly describing the place to be searched, and the persons or things to be seized.

AMENDMENT V (1791) No person shall be held to answer for a capital, or otherwise infamous crime, unless on a presentment or indictment of a Grand Jury, except in cases arising in the land or naval forces, or in the Militia, when in actual service in time of War or public danger; nor shall any person be subject for the same offence to be twice put in jeopardy of life or limb; nor shall be compelled in any criminal case to be a witness against himself, nor be deprived of life, liberty, or property, without due process of law; nor shall private property be taken for public use, without just compensation.

AMENDMENT VI (1791) In all criminal prosecutions, the accused shall enjoy the right to a speedy and public trial, by an impartial jury of the State and district wherein the crime shall have been committed, which district shall have been previously ascertained by law, and to be informed of the nature and cause of the accusation; to be confronted with the witnesses against him; to have compulsory process for obtaining witnesses in his favor, and to have the Assistance of Counsel for his defense.

AMENDMENT VII (1791) In suits at common law, where the value in controversy shall exceed twenty dollars, the right of trial by jury shall be preserved, and no fact tried by a jury, shall be otherwise reexamined in any court of the United States, than according to rules of the common law.

AMENDMENT VIII (1791) Excessive bail shall not be required, nor excessive fines imposed, nor cruel and unusual punishments inflicted.

AMENDMENT IX (1791) The enumeration in the Constitution, of certain rights, shall not be construed to deny or disparage others retained by the people.

AMENDMENT X (1791) The powers not delegated to the United States by the Constitution, nor prohibited by it to the States, are reserved to the States respectively, or to the people.

AMENDMENT XI (1798) The Judicial power of the United States shall not be construed to extend to any suit in law or equity, commenced or prosecuted against one of the United States by Citizens of another State, or by Citizens or Subjects of any Foreign State.

AMENDMENT XII (1804)

The Electors shall meet in their respective states and vote by ballot for President and Vice-President, one of whom, at least, shall not be an inhabitant of the same state with themselves; they shall name in their ballots the person voted for as President, and in distinct ballots the person voted for as Vice-President, and they shall make distinct lists of all persons voted for as President, and of all persons voted for as Vice-President, and of the number of votes for each, which lists they shall sign and certify, and transmit sealed to the seat of the government of the United States, directed to the President of the Senate;-The President of the Senate shall, in the presence of the Senate and House of Representative, open all the certificates and the votes shall then be counted;-The person having the greatest number of votes for President, shall be the President, if such number be a majority of the whole number of Electors appointed; and if no person have such majority, then from the persons having the highest numbers not exceeding three on the list of those voted for a President, the House of Representatives shall choose immediately, by ballot, the President. But in choosing the President, the votes shall be taken by states, the representation from each state having one vote; a quorum for this purpose shall consist of a member or members form two-thirds of the states, and a majority of all the states shall be necessary to a choice. And if the House of Representatives shall not choose a President whenever the right of choice shall devolve upon them, before the fourth day of March next following, then the Vice-President shall act as President, as in the case of the death or other constitutional disability of the President:-The person having the greatest number of votes as Vice-President, shall be the Vice-President, if such number be a majority of the whole number of Electors appointed, and if no person have a majority, then from the two highest number on the list, the Senate shall choose the Vice-President; a quorum for the purpose shall consist of two-thirds of the whole number of Senators, and a majority of the whole number shall be necessary to a choice. But no person constitutionally ineligible to the office of President shall be eligible to that of Vice-President of the United States.

AMENDMENT XIII (1865)

Section 1. Neither slavery nor involuntary servitude, except as a punishment for crime whereof the party shall have been duly convicted, shall exist within the United States, or any place subject to their jurisdiction.

Section 2. Congress shall have power to enforce this article by appropriate legislation.

AMENDMENT XIV (1868)

Section 1. All persons born or naturalized in the United States, and subject to the jurisdiction thereof, are citizens of the United States and of the State wherein they reside. No state shall make or enforce any law which shall abridge the privileges or immunities of citizens of the United States; nor shall any State deprive any person of life, liberty, or property, without due process of law; nor deny any person within its jurisdiction the equal protection of the laws.

Section 2. Representatives shall be apportioned among the several States according to their respective numbers, counting the whole number of persons in each State, excluding Indians not taxed. But when the right to vote at any election for the choice of electors for President and Vice-President of the United States, Representatives in Congress, the Executive and Judicial officers of a State, or the members of the Legislature thereof, is denied to any of the male inhabitants of such State, being twenty-one years of age, and citizens of the United States, or in any way abridged, except for participation in rebellion, or other crime, the basis of representation therein shall be reduced in the proportion which the number of such male citizens shall bear to the whole number of male citizens twenty-one years of age in such state.

Section 3. No person shall be a Senator or Representative in Congress, or elector of President and Vice-President, or hold any office, civil or military, under the United States, or under any State, who having previously taken an oath, as a member of Congress, or as an officer of the United States, or as a member of any State legislature, or as an executive or judicial officer of any State, to support the Constitution of the United States, shall have engaged in insurrection or rebellion against the same, or given aid or comfort to the enemies thereof. But Congress may by a vote of two-thirds of each House, remove such a disability.

Section 4. The validity of the public debt of the United States, authorized by law, including debts incurred for payment of pensions and bounties for services in suppressing insurrection or rebellion, shall not be questioned. But neither the United States nor any State shall assume or pay any debt or obligation incurred in aid of insurrection or rebellion against the United States, or any claim for the loss or emancipation of any slave; but all such debts, obligations and claims shall be held illegal and void.

Section 5. The Congress shall have power to enforce, by appropriate legislation, the provisions of this article.

AMENDMENT XV (1870)

Section 1. The right of citizens of the United States to vote shall not be denied or abridged by the United States or by any State on account of race, color, or previous condition of servitude.

Section 2. The Congress shall have power to enforce this article by appropriate legislation.

AMENDMENT XVI (1913)

The Congress shall have power to lay and collect taxes on incomes, from whatever source derived, without apportionment among the several States, and without regard to any census or enumeration.

AMENDMENT XVII (1913)

The Senate of the United States shall be composed of two Senators from each State, elected by the people thereof, for six years; and each Senator shall have one vote. The electors in each State shall have the qualifications requisite for electors of the most numerous brand of the State legislature.

When vacancies happen in the representation of any State in the Senate, the Executive authority of such State shall issue writs of election to fill such vacancies: *Provided,* That the legislature of any State may empower the executive thereof to make temporary appointments until the people fill the vacancies by election as the legislature may direct.

This amendment shall not be so construed as to affect the election or term of any Senator chosen before it comes valid as part of the Constitution.

AMENDMENT XVIII (1919)

Section 1. After one year from the ratification of this article, the manufacture, sale, or transportation of intoxicating liquors within, the importation thereof into, or the exportation thereof from the United States and all territory subject to the jurisdiction thereof for beverage purposes is hereby prohibited.

Section 2. The Congress and the several States shall have concurrent power to enforce this article by appropriate legislation.

Section 3. This article shall be inoperative unless it shall have been ratified as an amendment to the Constitution by the legislatures of several States, as provided in the Constitution, within seven years from the date of the submission hereof to the States by the Congress.

AMENDMENT XIX (1920)

The right of citizens of the United States to vote shall not be denied or abridged by the United States or by any State on account of sex.

Congress shall have power to enforce this article by appropriate legislation.

AMENDMENT XX (1933)

Section 1. The terms of President and Vice-President shall end at noon on the 20th day of January, and the terms of Senators and Representatives at noon on the 3rd day of January, of the years in which such terms would have ended; if this article had not been ratified; and the terms of their successors shall then begin.

Section 2. The Congress shall assemble at least once in every year, and such meeting shall begin at noon on the 3rd day of January, unless they shall by law appoint a different day.

Section 3. If, at the time fixed for the beginning of the term of the President, the President elect shall have died, the Vice-President elect shall become President. If a President shall not have been chosen before the time fixed for the beginning of his term, or if the President elect shall have failed to qualify, then the Vice-President elect shall act as President until a President shall have qualified; and the Congress may by law provide for the case wherein neither a President elect nor a Vice-President elect shall have qualified, declaring who shall then act as President, or the manner in which one who is to act shall be selected, and such person shall act accordingly until a President or Vice-President shall have qualified.

Section 4. The Congress may by law provide for the case of the death of any of the persons from whom the House of Representatives may choose a President whenever the right of choice shall have devolved upon them, and for the case of the death of any of the person from whom the Senate may choose a Vice-President whenever the right of choice shall have devolved upon them.

Section 5. Sections 1 and 2 shall take effect on the 15th day of October following the ratification of this article.

Section 6. This article shall be inoperative unless it shall have been ratified as an amendment to the Constitution by the legislatures of three-fourths of the several States within seven years from the date of its submission.

AMENDMENT XXI (1933)

Section 1. The eighteenth article of amendment to the Constitution of the United States is hereby repealed.

Section 2. The transportation or importation into any State, Territory, or possession of the United States for delivery or use therein of intoxicating liquors, in violation of the laws thereof, is hereby prohibited.

Section 3. This article shall be inoperative unless it shall have been ratified as an amendment to the Constitution by conventions in the several States, as provided in the Constitution, within seven years from the date of the submission hereof to the States by the Congress.

AMENDMENT XXII (1951)

Section 1. No person shall be elected to the office of the President more than twice, and no person who has held the office of President, or acted as President, for more than two years of a term to which some other person was elected President shall be elected to the office of the President more than once. But this Article shall not apply to any person holding the office of President when this Article was proposed by the Congress, and shall not prevent any person who may be holding the office of President, or acting as President, during the term within which this Article becomes operative from holding the office of President or acting as President during the remainder of such term.

Section 2. This article shall be inoperative unless it shall have been ratified as an amendment to the Constitution by the legislatures of three-fourths of the several States within seven years from the date of its submission to the States by the Congress.

AMENDMENT XXIII (1961

Section 1. The District constituting the seat of Government of the United States shall appoint in such manner as the Congress may direct:

A number of electors of President and Vice-President equal to the whole number of Senators and Representatives i Congress to which the District would be entitled if it were a State, but in no event more than the least populous State; they shall be in addition to those appointed by the States, but they shall be considered, for the purposes of the election of President and Vice-President, to be electors appointed by a State; and they shall meet in the District and perform such duties as provided by the twelfth article of amendment.

Section 2. The Congress shall have power to enforce this article by appropriate legislation.

AMENDMENT XXIV (1964

Section 1. The rights of citizens of the United States to vote in any primary or other election for President or Vice President, for electors for President or Vice president, or for senator or representative in Congress, shall not be denied or abridged by the United States or any state by reason of failure to pay any poll tax or other tax

Section 2. The Congress shall have power to enforce this article by appropriate legislation.

AMENDMENT XXV (1967)

Section 1. In case of the removal of the President from office or of his death or resignation, the Vice President shall become President.

Section 2. Whenever there is a vacancy in the office of Vice President, the President shall nominate a Vice President who shall take office upon confirmation by a majority vote of both Houses of Congress.

Section 3. Whenever the President transmits to the President pro tempore of the Senate and the Speaker of the House of Representatives his written declaration that he is unable to discharge the powers and duties of his office, and until he transmits to them a written declaration to the contrary, such powers and duties shall be discharged by the Vice President as Acting President.

Section 4. Whenever the Vice President and a majority of either the principal officers of the executive departments or of such other body as Congress may by law provide, transmit to the President pro tempore of the Senate and the Speaker of the House of Representatives their written declaration that the President is unable to discharge the powers and duties of his office, the Vice President shall immediately assume the powers and duties of the office as Acting President.

Thereafter, when the President transmits to the President pro tempore of the Senate and the Speaker of the House of Representatives his written declaration that no inability exists, he shall resume the powers and duties of his office unless the Vice President and a majority of either the principal officers of the executive department or of such other body as Congress may by law provide, transmit within four days to the President pro tempore of the Senate and Spreaker of the House of Representatives their written declration that the president is unable to discharge the powers and duties of his office. Thereupon, Congress shall decide the issue, assembling within forty-eight hours for that purpose, if not in session. If the Congress, within twenty-one days after receipt of the latter written declaration, or, if Congress is not in session, within twenty-one days after Congress is required to assemble, determines by two-thirds vote of both Houses that the President is unable to discharge the powers and duties of his office, the Vice President shall continue to discharge the same as Acting President; otherwise, the President shall resume the powers and duties of his office.

AMENDMENT XXVI (1971)

Section 1. The right of citizens of the United States who are eighteen years of age or older to vote shall not be denied or abridged by the United States or by any state on account of age.

Section 2 The Congress shall have power to enforce this article by appropriate legislation.

INDEX

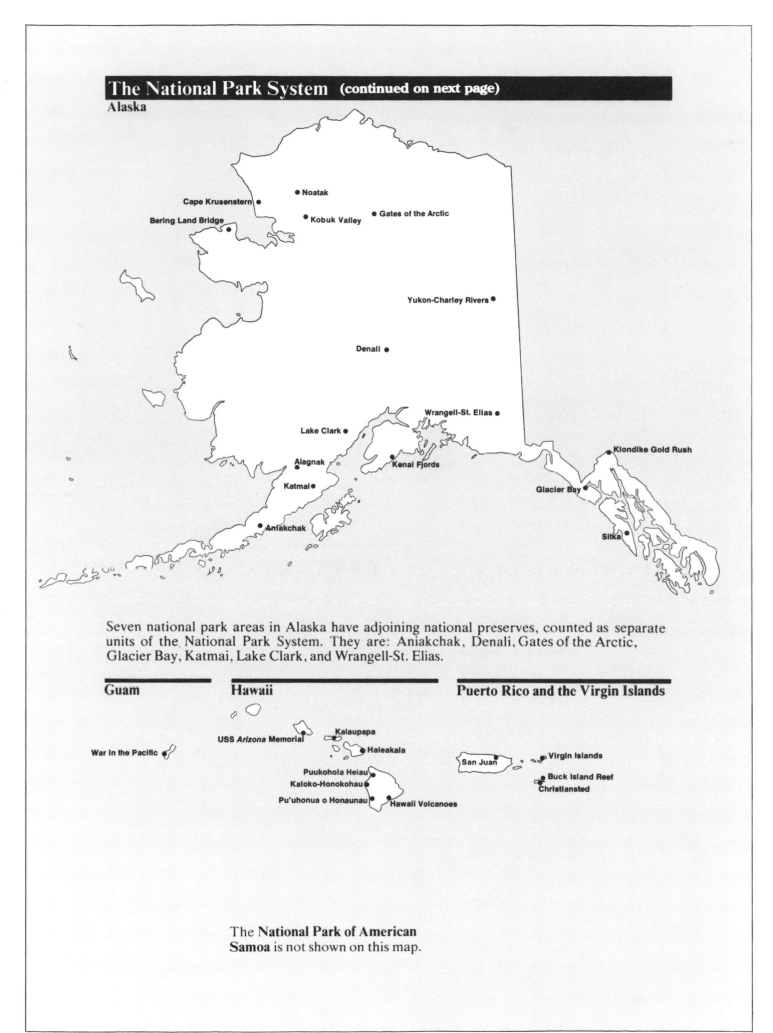

Alaska

Noatak

Cape Krusenstern

Kobuk Valley

Gates of the Arctic

Bering Land Bridge

Yukon-Charley Rivers

Denali

Wrangell-St. Elias

Lake Clark

Klondike Gold Rush

Alagnak

Kenai Fjords

Katmai

Glacier Bay

Aniakchak

Sitka

Seven national park areas in Alaska have adjoining national preserves, counted as separate units of the National Park System. They are: Aniakchak, Denali, Gates of the Arctic, Glacier Bay, Katmai, Lake Clark, and Wrangell-St. Elias.

Guam

War in the Pacific

Hawaii

Kalaupapa

USS *Arizona* Memorial

Haleakala

Puukohola Heiau

Kaloko-Honokohau

Pu'uhonua o Honaunau

Hawaii Volcanoes

Puerto Rico and the Virgin Islands

San Juan

Virgin Islands

Buck Island Reef

Christiansted

The **National Park of American Samoa** is not shown on this map.

The National Park System

- North Cascades
- San Juan Island
- Ross Lake
- Lake Chelan
- Olympic
- Klondike Gold Rush
- Coulee Dam
- Glacier
- WASHINGTON
- Mount Rainier
- Fort Clatsop
- Fort Vancouver
- Whitman Mission
- Nez Perce
- MONTANA
- Grant-Kohrs Ranch
- Big Hole
- Fort Union Trading Post
- Theodore Roosevelt
- Knife River Indian Villages
- NORTH DAKOTA
- John Day Fossil Beds
- OREGON
- Custer Battlefield
- Bighorn Canyon
- Crater Lake
- IDAHO
- Yellowstone
- Devils Tower
- SOUTH DAKOTA
- Oregon Caves
- Craters of the Moon
- John D. Rockefeller, Jr. Parkway
- Grand Teton
- Mount Rushmore
- Badlands
- Pipestone
- Redwood
- Hagerman Fossil Beds
- Jewel Cave
- Wind Cave
- Lava Beds
- WYOMING
- Whiskeytown-Shasta-Trinity
- City of Rocks
- Lassen Volcanic
- Golden Spike
- Agate Fossil Beds
- Missouri
- CALIF.
- Fossil Butte
- Fort Laramie
- Scotts Bluff
- NEBRASKA
- Timpanogos Cave
- Dinosaur
- Point Reyes
- NEVADA
- Muir Woods
- John Muir
- UTAH
- Rocky Mountain
- Homestead
- Eugene O'Neill
- Great Basin
- COLORADO
- Fort Point
- Yosemite
- Golden Gate
- Devils Postpile
- Colorado
- Florissant Fossil Beds
- San Francisco Maritime
- Capitol Reef
- Arches
- Black Canyon of the Gunnison
- KANSAS
- Pinnacles
- Kings Canyon
- Cedar Breaks
- Bryce Canyon
- Canyonlands
- Curecanti
- Fort Larned
- Sequoia
- Death Valley
- Zion
- Glen Canyon
- Natural Bridges
- Bent's Old Fort
- Fort S
- Hovenweep
- Yucca House
- Pipe Spring
- Rainbow Bridge
- Mesa Verde
- Great Sand Dunes
- Lake Mead
- Navajo
- Grand Canyon
- Aztec Ruins
- Canyon de Chelly
- Chaco Culture
- Capulin Volcano
- Santa Monica Mountains
- Sunset Crater
- Wupatki
- Hubbell Trading Post
- Fort Union
- Lake Meredith
- OKLAHOM
- Channel Islands
- Tuzigoot
- Walnut Canyon
- Bandelier
- Pecos
- Alibates Flint Quarries
- Joshua Tree
- Montezuma Castle
- Petrified Forest
- Zuni-Cibola
- Tonto
- El Morro
- El Malpais
- NEW MEXICO
- Chickasaw
- Cabrillo
- ARIZONA
- Salinas Pueblo Missions
- Hohokam Pima
- Casa Grande
- Gila Cliff Dwellings
- Saguaro
- White Sands
- Organ Pipe Cactus
- Fort Bowie
- Tumacacori
- Chiricahua
- Carlsbad Caverns
- Coronado
- Chamizal
- Guadalupe Mountains
- TEXAS
- Fort Davis
- Lyndon B. Johns
- Rio Grande
- Big Bend
- Amistad
- San Antonio Missions
- Padre Island
- Palo Alto Battlefield

Many of the places you have read about in *Adventure Tales of America* are areas of national significance administered by the National Park Service, under the United States Department of the Interior.

History will come alive for you as you visit these Federal areas designated as national parks, monuments, preserves, historic sites, battlefield sites, scenic trails, rivers, lakeshores, and seashores.

This map is reproduced through the courtesy of the National Park Service.